West Africa and the Global Financial Crisis

West Africa and the Global Financial Crisis

Edited by Diery Seck

AFRICA WORLD PRESS
TRENTON | LONDON | CAPE TOWN | NAIROBI | ADDIS ABABA | ASMARA | IBADAN | NEW DELHI

AFRICA WORLD PRESS
541 West Ingham Avenue | Suite B
Trenton, New Jersey 08638

First Printing 2013

Book and cover design: Saverance Publishing Services

Library of Congress Cataloging-in-Publication Data

West Africa and the global financial crisis / edited by Diery Seck.
p. cm.
Papers from a meeting of West African scholars with senior officials of West African Central Banks, the African Development Bank (AfDB), the West African Economic and Monetary Union (WAEMU) and the Economic Community of West African States (ECOWAS) held June 2010 in Accra, Ghana.
Contributions in English or French.
Includes bibliographical references and index.
ISBN 978-1-59221-888-2 (pbk.) -- ISBN 978-1-59221-887-5 (hardback)
1. Africa, West--Economic integration--Congresses. 2. Africa, West--Economic policy--Congresses. 3. Africa, West--Economic conditions--Congresses. 4. Union iconomique et monitaire ouest africaine--Congresses. 5. West African Monetary Zone--Congresses. 6. Global Financial Crisis, 2008-2009--Congresses. I. Seck, Diery.
HC1000.W45 2013
337.166--dc23

2012044996

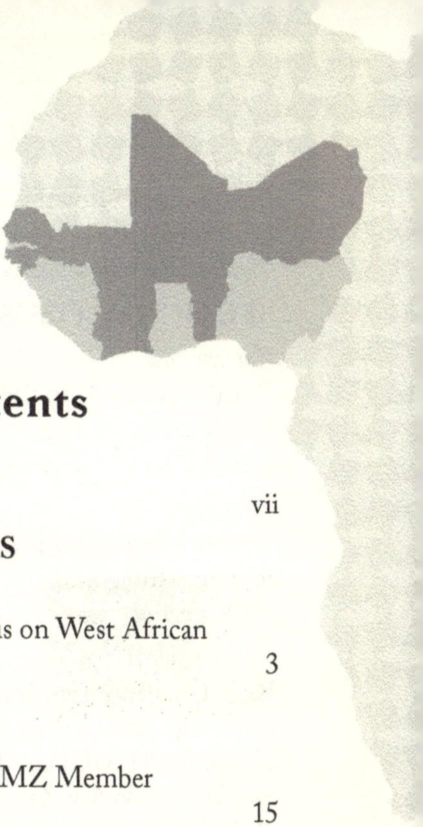

Table of Contents

Foreword

In June 2010, West African scholars based in Africa, Europe and North Africa met in Accra, Ghana, with senior officials of West African Central Banks, the African Development Bank (AfDB), the West African Economic and Monetary Union (WAEMU) and the Economic Community of West African States (ECOWAS) to debate for two days on issues pertaining to regional integration in their sub-region. A mix of policy-focused and academic manuscripts were presented and discussed with one single goal in mind: to expand and deepen current understanding of the challenges and opportunities that arise from West Africa's pursuit of economic and social progress through the strategy of regional integration. The deliberations of the Conference illustrated the extent to which African policymakers and researchers share a common understanding of the challenges faced by Africa in the present context and their eagerness to maintain a high level of policy debate.

This eagerness may perhaps have risen from the sense of urgency harbored by many actors and caused by the disappointingly insufficient volume of state-of-the-art research that currently supports the advanced level of progress in the sub-region's process of regional integration. Indeed, there is general consensus that research must quickly respond to, and sometimes even lead, policy-making to contribute to its success. The manuscripts that served as the basis for the discussions also helped revisit many commonly-held policy views through the scrutiny of rigorous scientific inquiry and therefore strengthened the factual foundations of regional policy undertakings. This no doubt enhances the reliance of policymaking on research and contributes to widespread consensus on what needs to be done. As a result, the combined contributions of all the authors provide a fair degree of achievement in the reconstruction of the jigsaw puzzle that is regional integration in West Africa and help formulate a comprehensive and coherent growth-inducing and socially acceptable integrative design.

The present book seeks to provide answers on many facets of the challenges related to region-wide policymaking. Through its 13 chapters it aims to cover a wide spectrum of policy issues of the day and to display a sense of vision that spans the entire planning horizon of most stakeholders. It opens with a chapter that reviews the impact of the recent global financial crisis on the economies of the sub-region, and a thorough examination of the economic shocks that are characteristic of the economies of West African Monetary Zone (WAMZ) countries – five non-CFA countries. In a second section that addresses the burning issue of the Common Currency, one study discusses the political economy of creating a West African Monetary Zone while a second one assesses the optimality underlying such a project. A third manuscript reports on the performance of the WAEMU after 15 years of operations and suggests strategies for its future institutional development. In section 3, two complementary studies examine the record and impact of inflation, one for the case of WAEMU countries and the other for WAMZ economies.

Section 4 hosts four studies on topics such as the implications of fiscal operations on regional economic integration, the challenges of financial and trade policies under regional integration, the relationship between bank concentration and monetary policy in WAEMU countries, and the volatility and convergence of stock markets in WAMZ countries. In a fifth and final section whose underlying stakes are paramount for the future of the West African sub-region, two studies deal with aspects of human development. One addresses the link between currency integration and human development and the other focuses on the relationship between education and development under regional integration.

It is true that 13 chapters cannot solve all the development challenges of West Africa. It is equally true that this is an ongoing process that has started and will most likely continue into the foreseeable future. Indeed, from now on science will drive the broader and deeper dialogue between research and policy in the sub-region, and, by all accounts, it is quite welcome. The book also aims to perpetuate the historic roles of leader and model played by West Africa in the integration process of the entire continent. Two final key considerations deserve mention and must be kept in mind by the reader. First, regional integration is unequivocally the strategy chosen by West African countries as their common quest for development. It is also a collective commitment to their shared fate and an expression of their strongest bond. Second, the way in which regional integration will be used by these countries to achieve social and economic progress will be designed by West African minds and implemented by the will of West African policymakers. One hopes that it is irreversible.

DIERY SECK, Editor

Dakar, June 2011.

Section I

Economic Shocks

Chapter 1

THE IMPACT OF THE GLOBAL FINANCIAL CRISIS ON WEST AFRICAN COUNTRIES

Diery Seck

INTRODUCTION

The current debate on regional integration and development prospects has sharply focused on the ongoing global financial crisis and its possible consequences on Africa. One of the prevailing arguments is that the region faces too many developmental challenges to support the adverse impact of the financial crisis. The discussion has also specifically targeted West Africa but the events have until recently been too fresh to have a proper assessment of their impact on the sub-region. The purpose of the present study is to document and evaluate the effect of the global financial crisis on West Africa using the most recent economic data available and drawing key lessons from the analysis. To that end, the first section of the paper will conduct a thorough assessment of the purported impact of the crisis on West Africa making use of five sets of economic variables through which the crisis could have been transmitted.

Six major countries of the sub-region with complete and reliable data sets are examined, three from the West African Economic and Monetary Union (WAEMU) zone – Benin, Côte d'Ivoire and Senegal – and three non WAEMU countries – Cape Verde, Ghana and Nigeria. In the second section, a number of lessons are drawn from the empirical evidence and several recommendations proposed to help West African countries stay on the course to economic and social development while avoiding the pitfalls of vulnerability to globally induced financial crises.

AN ASSESSMENT OF THE IMPACT OF THE FINANCIAL CRISIS ON WEST AFRICAN ECONOMIES

Considering the various transmission channels through which the impact of the international financial crisis could impact upon West African economies, the foregoing analysis aims at investigating the main target variables that are currently the object of public debate. The basic rationale is to identify a significant change in the medium-term trend of the variable and assess the extent to which such change is also observed in, or mirrors, what happens in industrial economies. The USA, UK and Euro Area serve as baseline comparators in the analysis. The assessment of the impact of the global financial crisis will be conducted through the following five sets of variables:

- Finance and the stock market
- Bank credit
- Money supply and reserves
- Foreign exchange and
- Current account.

The impact on real economic activity could not be assessed for lack of available indicators in this regard.

Finance and the stock market

One of the most spectacular consequences of the global financial crisis was the steep decline in stock exchange indices around the world. The loss of billions of US Dollars of equity wealth caused by stock price decreases was an unprecedented economic and social phenomenon that afflicted most countries. Table 1.1 below displays the annual returns on national stock market indices for three industrial countries – France, UK and USA – three West African exchange indices – Ghana, Nigeria and BRVM – and for each stock exchange the value at the end of 2009 of $100 invested at the end of 2007. The figures eloquently demonstrate that the financial crisis took effect in 2008 following a healthy episode of stock market growth in the six sampled exchanges. They also show that the impact of the crisis on the stock market was equally severe in 2009.

Table 1.1. Annual Rates of Return of National Stock Indices, in %, and Value of $100 invested in 2007

Country / Area	2005	2006	2007	2008	2009	$100 in '07 Value in '09
France	16.30	20.33	11.70	-25.24	-22.30	$58.09
United Kingdom	14.95	16.87	9.36	-17.51	-14.68	$70.38
United States	2.23	8.16	15.44	-14.56	-21.12	$67.40
Ghana	n.a	n.a	5.36	31.84	-15.57	$111.31
Nigeria	1.01	37.80	74.73	-45.77	-33.78	$35.91
BRVM	n.a	-0.03	77.05	-10.67	-25.89	$66.20

Source: France, UK, USA: International Financial Statistics, IMF, Online, March 2010; Nigeria: Central Bank of Nigeria, Financial Statistics, Table A.5.7.1., Nigeria Stock Exchange; BRVM: CGF Bourse, Senegal, Lettre mensuelle, Online; Ghana: Bloomberg.com, Regional Stock Indices.

The impact of the crisis on West African stock exchanges cannot be differentiated from what it was on the three industrial countries. Indeed, all the exchanges recorded large negative returns of a similar magnitude in the last two years and lost money over the period 2007- 2009, except for Ghana that had a cumulated two-year return of 11.31%. Overall, the three industrial countries had an equally-weighted aggregate two-year return of -34.71% while the three West African countries recorded a return of -28.9%.

Bank credit

One main characteristic of the recent crisis was the sharp decline in credit extended by the banking sector in industrial countries which translated into a system-wide liquidity crunch.

This credit crisis deprived firms of working capital and thwarted their planned investment outlays. The resulting reduced level of aggregate output and the harshly rationed credit availability at home may have translated into lower demand of imported primary commodity inputs from developing countries in general, and from West Africa in particular. West African firms facing a lower demand for their exports and increased volatility in global markets may have reacted by adjusting their production level downwards and required less working capital and therefore less credit. In the context of higher global volatility and lower world output, the local banking system could adapt its portfolio composition by lending less to export-dependent domestic firms or requiring more loan guarantees which, in both cases, would result in lower levels of domestic credit.

Table 1.2 displays the annual rates of change of the commercial banking sector's credit to the private sector in WAEMU, the Euro Area and selected West African economies for the period 2005 – 2008.

Table 1.2. Change in Deposit Money Banks' Claims on Private Sector, in %

Country / Area	2005	2006	2007	2008
WAEMU	11,3	8,5	15,5	14,7
Benin	20,2	10,9	25,0	20,1
Côte d'Ivoire	1,1	8,5	19,2	11,3
Senegal	21,3	7,1	10,7	17,1
Cape Verde	7,5	24,9	10,6	26,8
Ghana	43,9	37,4	62,0	43,1
Nigeria	27,2	26,5	108,8	61,3
Euro Area	9,7	11,3	13,5	7,7

Source: International Financial Statistics, IMF, Online, March 2010.

While the Euro Area experienced a sharp decline in the annual rate of change of claims on the private sector in 2008 compared to 2007 (13.5% vs 7.7%), the WAEMU Zone maintained about the same rate of annual growth (15.5% vs 14.7% and seems to have been considerably less affected by the global credit crunch. Furthermore, in 2008 the rate of change for the Euro Area is almost half that of the WAEMU and several times smaller than for the individual countries except for Côte d'Ivoire whose economy still lingers in a situation of political uncertainty. Finally, over the period 2005-2008 no West African country's economy has evolved in a manner that is consistent with a decline in credit to the private sector as a result of the global financial crisis.

By contrast, Table 1.3 shows that in 2008, West African Governments saw a significant decline in their level of borrowing from domestic banks - Côte d'Ivoire, Senegal, Cape Verde and Nigeria - and a modest increase in the case of Ghana and WAEMU as a whole. Benin is an exception with a two-fold increase in 2008 compared to 2007. There was no decrease in overall domestic credit in 2008 for any of the six West African countries. Therefore, if in 2008, the banking sector of West Africa responded to the global financial crisis by adjusting the composition of domestic credit, it was more at the expense of Government borrowing than of private sector debt which remained generally unaffected.

TABLE 1.3. CHANGE IN DEPOSIT MONEY BANKS' CLAIMS ON CENTRAL GOVERNMENT, IN %

COUNTRY / AREA	2005	2006	2007	2008
WAEMU	3.7	20.1	34.1	5.1
Benin	47.7	-15.9	100.3	194.3
Côte d'Ivoire	2.1	8.9	37.4	-22.3
Senegal	-1.8	107.3	60.7	-8.6
Cape Verde	10.2	-2.4	13.8	-7.8
Ghana	-7.2	36.3	24.9	16.3
Nigeria	3.6	81.6	94.5	-22.8
Euro Area	7.5	-6.1	4.3	6.0

Source: International Financial Statistics, IMF, Online, March 2010.

MONEY SUPPLY AND RESERVES

A contraction of domestic credit can, as in the case of the Euro Area during the financial crisis, induce lower money supply and a shortage of liquidity in the economy. As shown in Tables 1.2 and 1.3, in 2008, bank lending to the private sector increased for all West African countries but Government borrowing from banks decreased for most of them. However, aggregate domestic credit did not decrease for WAEMU or for individual countries.

Table 1.4 shows that the slower pace of economic activity induced a smaller increase in broad money in 2008 for WAEMU and five of the six countries, Benin being the exception.

Table 1.4. Change in Money and Quasi- money; in %

Country / Area	2005	2006	2007	2008
WAEMU	8.3	10.7	19.0	8.7
Benin	26.3	14.5	19.6	26.6
Côte d'Ivoire	7.7	10.3	23.6	5.7
Senegal	8.2	12.5	13.1	1.8
Cape Verde	15.6	18.7	9.7	7.9
Ghana	20.3	39.6	44.1	37.8
Nigeria	7.7	50.7	58.1	53.6
Euro Area	9.4	9.3	10.3	9.0

Source: International Financial Statistics, IMF, Online, March 2010.

Table 1.5 reports a significant reduction in reserves (minus gold) for WAEMU, Côte d'Ivoire, Senegal and Cape Verde. All countries and regions record drastic declines in their rate of change of reserves in 2008 relative to the two previous years.

Table 1.5. Change in Reserves Minus Gold, in %

Country / Area	2005	2006	2007	2008
WAEMU	-14.8	19.5	30.6	-3.2
Benin	2.6	38.9	32.6	4.5
Côte d'Ivoire	-22.0	36.0	40.1	-10.6
Senegal	-14.1	12.0	24.4	-3.5
Cape Verde	24.7	46.3	10.5	-8.1
Ghana	7.8	19.2	n.a	n.a
Nigeria	66.8	49.6	21.4	3.2
Euro Area	-12.9	6.6	9.3	1.5

Source: International Financial Statistics, IMF, Online, March 2010.

In conclusion, one of the impacts of the global financial crisis may have been slower growth of money supply and a significant reduction in non-gold reserves for many West African countries. These two factors may in turn affect the degree of liquidity of these economies in the short term and the expansion of their level of monetization in the medium to long term.

Foreign exchange

Table 1.6 indicates a faster erosion of the nominal exchange rates of the Ghanaian Cedi and the Nigerian Naira in the last two years, 2008 and 2009, than in the previous two, 2006 and 2007. Indeed, at the end of 2009, the Cedi had lost 28.6% of its value compared to the end of 2007 and the Naira's loss over the same period was 20.1%. But the Cape Verdian Escudo remained within the same range of 75 to 80 per US Dollar in the last three years. With a fixed peg to the Euro the CFA Franc of WAEMU countries cannot be ascribed any specific impact with respect to its nominal exchange rate. In short, while Ghana and Nigeria experienced significant declines in the nominal values of their respective currencies, the Escudo was more stable, which precludes a uniform impact of the global financial crisis on West African currencies. The degree of openness, structure of aggregate output, composition of exports and imports and the capacity and willingness of the Central Bank to defend the national currency may be among specific factors that helped determine the evolution of each national currency during the financial crisis.

Table 1.6. Nominal Exchange Rate: National Currency Per US DOLLAR

Country / Area	2005	2006	2007	2008	2009
WAEMU	556.0	498.1	445.6	471.3	455.3
Cape Verde	93.5	83.7	74.9	79.2	76.5
Ghana	0.9	0.9	1.0	1.2	1.4
Nigeria	129.0	128.3	118.0	132.6	147.6
Euro Area	0.848	0.759	0.679	0.719	0.694

Source: International Financial Statistics, IMF, Online, March 2010.

The Current Account

No specific pattern emerges from Table 1.7 regarding the evolution of the Current Accounts of the Balance of Payments of West African countries. Except for Côte d'Ivoire that displays a high degree of volatility, each country has steadily followed its own positive – Nigeria – or negative trend – Cape Verde and Ghana – without any significant break in its pattern. In other words, the evidence available does not allow to conclude that the Current Account served as an adjustment variable of the impact of the global financial crisis on West African economies.

Table 1.7. Current Account in Millions US Dollars

Country / Area	2005	2006	2007	2008
Benin	-270.321	-327.321	-653.208	n.a.
Côte d'Ivoire	39.674	478.965	-139.040	488.072
Senegal	-675.870	-861.189	-1310.780	n.a.
Cape Verde	-40.673	-82.730	-198.265	-205.479
Ghana	-1104.610	-1042.610	-2151.470	-3543.120
Nigeria	37263.600	38227.500	30927.500	39357.100

Source: International Financial Statistics, IMF, Online, March 2010.

WEST AFRICAN LESSONS FROM THE GLOBAL FINANCIAL CRISIS

For West Africa, the current global financial crisis has brought to the fore a number of developmental issues related to economic growth, international financial flows, volatility of global markets, aid, trade and investment. Considering that these issues are interconnected with respect to their relevance to West African economies, it is warranted to address the following three key questions: 1) What is the degree of integration of West African countries into the global economy?, 2) Is West Africa ready for the next global financial crisis, and 3) How to shield West Africa from the adverse consequences of future crises?

WEST AFRICAN INTEGRATION IN THE GLOBAL ECONOMY

The past decade has shown that Africa in general and West Africa in particular have not enhanced their degree of integration into the world economy when compared to other developing regions. Being one of the poorest regions in the world, West Africa has seen its share of world trade erode gradually despite several initiatives to support its exports e.g. AGOA, the European

Union's "Everything but Arms" Initiative and the Economic Partnership Agreements, not to mention China's vigorous attempts to increase its imports of primary commodities from Africa. The evidence also indicates that West Africa is not a prime destination for foreign direct investment except in the extractive industry, namely oil in Nigeria, gold in Ghana, Senegal and Mali, gems in Sierra Leone and Liberia, uranium in Niger, iron ore and phosphates in Senegal, etc. These enclave sectors have little spillover effect on the rest of local economies and therefore little impact on the overall integration of West African countries.

Despite some countries' efforts to diversify their export base, no significant new export sector has emerged from West Africa, which exposes their economies to the vagaries of single commodity export receipts and declining international competitiveness with adverse consequences on global integration. Although the West African economies are tuned to the movements of global financial markets as illustrated by the co-movement of their stock exchanges with those of industrial countries and their flexible exchange rate regimes, foreign portfolio investment and external borrowing by the private sector are very limited, and set West Africa far behind other developing regions. This low degree of integration into the global economy weakens channels of transmission of economic performance from the world to West Africa and shields it against adverse shocks. But it also deprives it of growth opportunities when there is a boom in the global economy.

Considering that over the last half century countries that recorded rapid economic growth were high exporters and fully integrated into the world economy, it is important for West Africa to formulate policies that will help it achieve further global integration.

WEST AFRICA'S READINESS FOR THE NEXT FINANCIAL CRISIS

West Africa's lack of financial development may limit its exposure to the adverse effect of global financial crises. But financial development is a necessity on the path to economic and social development. Therefore, as governments and the private sector succeed in attracting foreign capital, West Africa may increasingly be the adjustment destination of international investors who, in order to respond to global conditions, invest in the region last during booms, and divest from it first during busts, with untold variability in cross border capital flows and painful economic consequences for the domestic economies. It is noteworthy that West African countries lack the capacity to benefit from rapid and sizeable temporary balance of payments relief measures to alleviate the consequences of massive capital flight. Indeed, neither their private sector nor their governments have ready access to sizeable foreign borrowing from international private lenders.

In the absence of a strong export base and given its low savings rate, West Africa has the choice between remaining financially under-developed and, thanks to its low level of global integration, enjoy some degree of protection from future financial crises, or developing its financial sector and integrating it further into the world market, but also exposing it and being more vulnerable to global financial shocks. Naturally, some of the risks inherent in financial development could be curbed but the sub-region would need to design and implement its financial development strategy before the adequate hedging mechanisms can be identified and implemented. Current discussions on creation of a single monetary zone and dual listing of stocks at home and abroad constitute promising initial steps but much still needs to be accomplished on that score.

SHIELDING WEST AFRICAN COUNTRIES FROM FUTURE FINANCIAL CRISES

In light of the foregoing discussion it is legitimate to inquire about ways in which West African economies can be protected from future financial crises. Some of the implications of the description of these economies may provide sound starting points for the design of protective policies. First, West African countries could coordinate their efforts to achieve significant diversification of their exports thereby reducing the risk of commodity price fluctuations or lower demand of their exports caused by the onset of financial downturns, e.g. oil exports. Second, one of the desirable effects of a single currency arrangement is the pooling of foreign reserves which, in itself, is a mechanism of cross-insurance among member countries especially in cases of financial crises with differentiated impacts on members. Such reserves would also serve as an adequate instrument to mitigate the consequences of capital flight. Third, further regional integration of trade and financial markets would reduce reliance on and exposure to, international economic conditions and secure lower variability economic growth for the sub-region.

Finally, the sub-region could undertake counter-cyclical policies with respect to its external sector in three areas. The first one is related to foreign reserve management. In periods of export booms, countries could use the windfall increase in foreign assets to pay down their external debt rather than engage in expansionary spending that could not be sustained after the boom but would require external borrowing to complete spending programs started during the boom. If reserves are not used to pay back external debt, they could be accumulated and drawn down and used to supplement lower revenues during economic downturns.

Servicing of external debt provides a second area of counter-cyclical policies. West African countries could agree with their creditors to make service of their external debt contingent on the performance of their external sector. Accordingly, scheduled debt service payments would be reduced or postponed altogether if the borrower country's export earnings fall below an agreed-upon level. This facility could be coupled with capitalization or forgiveness of accrued interest or indefinite postponement of payments until conditions improve on the basis of full transparency and accountability. Scheduled debt service payments would resume when the borrower country's external performance improves.

A third countercyclical measure would make foreign aid a substitute for West African countries' foreign reserves if reserves are depleted in the advent of a global financial crisis to procure essential imports or to service external debt. The size of aid flows would be commensurate with the magnitude of the reserve drawdown and would ensure a smoother economic growth trajectory for recipient countries.

CONCLUSION

The advent of the global financial crisis is too recent and, in fact still ongoing in various parts of the world, to conduct a proper assessment of its impact on West African countries. However, the empirical evidence that is available has shown a rather strong impact with respect to stock markets but to varying degrees across countries. There was no significant adverse effect of the crisis on bank credit to the private sector or on money supply. However the levels of reserves and of nominal exchange rates of West African countries have changed noticeably during the crisis but more research is needed to attribute these variations to the global financial crisis. Trade and the current account do not seem to have been negatively impacted upon by the crisis.

West African countries' poor integration into the world economy have created a weak economic transmission mechanism that protects them in case of crisis but limits their capacity to benefit from global booms. Arguably, there is need for enhanced financial development in the sub-region to secure economic and social development even if it temporarily exposes countries more to future economic and financial crises. Ways to increase the level of protection of West African countries from future adverse financial shocks include further region-wide export diversification, more regional integration of trade and financial markets, pooling of foreign reserves and adoption of a number of counter-cyclical policies to stem the severity of capital outflows during episodes of financial adversity.

Chapter 2

PATTERNS OF ECONOMIC SHOCKS IN WEST AFRICAN MONETARY ZONE (WAMZ) MEMBER COUNTRIES

Douglason G. Omotor

INTRODUCTION

Other than the global financial crisis of 2008, the most remarkable and recent economic event since the twentieth century was the formation of the European Monetary Union (EMU). The success of the EMU partly as an economic union with a single currency (Euro) launched in January, 1999, has thus aroused more interest in regional monetary integration.

The rationale for monetary integration dates back to the 16th century when Copernicus (1526) observed that simultaneous circulation of various sort of coins has both exchange and price instability effects. And to avoid such problems, money should be coined in one single place and used in a greater currency area. Mundell (1961) provided an articulated thought on the general framework that rationalizes the theory of optimum currency area (OCA) in any monetary integration. According to Gandolfo (1995) as enunciated by Cavoli and Rajan (2006), OCA comprises a group of countries which have a common currency (implying existence of full monetary integration) or which, though maintaining different national currencies, have permanently and rigidly fixed exchange rates among themselves and full convertibility of their respective currencies into one another; while the exchange rates in respect to non-partner countries are flexible. The benefits in forming a common currency area are well outlined in the seminal works of Mundell (1961) and McKinnon (1963). First, is the elimination of exchange rate variability within the area, and second, the monetary efficiency gain from lower transaction costs. The opposite strand to the benefits of forming a common currency area is the major cost associated with the inability of the area to pursue independent monetary policies, particularly using exchange rate as an instrument of adjustment (Hsu, 2009). The beneficial aspects of OCA can be rationalized as one reason that may have influenced the establishment of the ECOWAS in 1975 as an economic union.

Many countries belong to a multiple of customs unions, development associations or cross-country institutions whose objectives and perception of economic and monetary cooperation vary in degrees. Examples include, Common Market for Eastern and Southern Africa (COMESA), Southern African Development Community (SADC), Central African Economic and Monetary Community (CAEMCS), European Union (EU), Economic Community of West African States (ECOWAS), Gulf Corporation Council (GCC), West African Economic and Monetary Community (UEMOA), and West African Monetary Zone (WAMZ) among others.

In the year 2000, as part of a process to actualize the ECOWAS integration agenda a second monetary zone (WAMZ) was established in the region for non-UEMOA members of the ECOWAS community. Five of the non-UEMOA members (The Gambia, Ghana, Guinea, Nigeria and Sierra Leone) under a declaration agreed to form a common currency union in 2003 with the eventual set-up of West African Monetary Institute (WAMI) to facilitate the proposal. Notwithstanding, the launch date was pushed to 2005 then December 1, 2009. The December 1, 2009 was not achieved and this led to a rescheduling of a new launch date on or before 2015.

At the June 2001 forum for the Central Banks of the West African Monetary Zone, the Committee of Governors requested that a seminar by the Bank of England be held to provide assistance to WAMI towards realization of the objective of common currency. The seminar identified three challenges that confront the monetary union. First, the ability to keep fiscal operations of government in consonance with monetary programme of achieving price stability and reasonable economic growth of the Common Central Bank. Second, the challenge of maintaining macroeconomic convergence and asymmetric shocks in the group of the countries that is unable to satisfy the preconditions for an optimum currency area. Finally, producing consistent, adequate, timely and accurate statistics for purpose of multilateral surveillance; necessary for a robust monetary policy design and implementation. This journey that started in 2000 following the Accra Declaration of WAMZ, still grapples with less trade linkages among member states and the perceived asymmetric patterns of shocks. Limited trade among member countries, coupled with real and artificial barriers inhibit mobility of labour and capital. This reinforces the difficulty in achieving monetary union as the zone may not be considered a feasible and possible candidate for an optimum currency area. Despite these constraints, there is strong expectation as indicated in the outcome of the WAMZ Convergence Council Meeting (May, 2009) in Abuja, Nigeria that in the long term, WAMZ is plausible, the programme is working and its convergence criteria are at least restrictive relatively.

The glib to foster closer economic integration by the WAMZ members other than the perceived benefits as mentioned above are connected to the following facts; first, the non-attainment of WAMZ will inhibit the process of "fast-tracking" the integration agenda of ECOWAS; second, if first holds, the WAMZ and by extension, the ECOWAS may probably be further marginalized in the face of growing regional integration in other parts of the world and third, accomplishment of monetary cooperation with its attendant advantage of ensuring a stable financial environment and reduced uncertainty in regional exchange rates will preclude the zone particularly and the ***Community*** in general. However, Maskay (2003) has observed that movement toward greater monetary cooperation need not occur immediately. Rather, what is crucial is information which highlights the processes for achieving the cooperation and how to minimize the risks of derailing regional economic integration.

This paper in assessing the desirability of achieving greater monetary cooperation of WAMZ member countries follows the lead of Bayoumi and Eichengreen (1994); and Maskay (2003) by analyzing the pattern and symmetry of economic shocks affecting the members of the zone. We consider this an important study because of the likely implications of its results on policy-making in the zone. For instance, if economic disturbances among member economies are similar or relatively more influential shocks that are also positively correlated, then the idea of a currency union and greater monetary cooperation is feasible. This information are not only necessary in designing the processes required to achieve higher levels of monetary cooperation in the zone; it also implies that it would be less costly to pursue a region-wide monetary policy to stabilize output fluctuations (Hsu, 2009). The paper also examines the suitability of WAMZ forming a currency union from a descriptive perspective in accordance with some OCA criteria.

The remaining part of this paper is organized as follows. Section 2 presents a review of the literature on OCA including the theory and empirical studies that have been applied among others, the structural vector autoregression (SVAR) and some other simplified techniques. Section 3 presents some stylized facts on the economies of the WAMZ. Section 4 examines the methodology; Section 5 reports the empirical results; while Section 6 concludes.

LITERATURE REVIEW

The literature on the rationale for monetary union is provided by the general framework of the theory of optimum currency areas pioneered by Mundell (1961) and subsequently by McKinnon (1963) and Kenen (1969). Mundell (1961), in his well articulated article on optimal currency areas, cited the following quote from John Stuart Mill (1894: 176):

> Almost all independent nations choose to assert their nationality by having, to their own inconvenience and that of their neighbours, a currency of their own.

This may perhaps be the political reason that influenced the official dollarization of some Latin American countries like Panama since 1909, Ecuador since 2000 and El Salvador since 2001. In the case of Africa; although the continent has a chequered experience of monetary integration, attempts date back to the pre-and post-colonial eras. In East Africa for instance, a common currency area was established in 1919 for Kenya, Uganda and Tanganyika (now Tanzania) with the creation of the East African Currency Board. The West African Economic and Monetary Union (UEMOA), is a customs union and monetary union of eight states (Benin, Burkina Faso, Cote d'Ivoire, Mali, Niger, Senegal, Togo and Guinea Bissau) of West Africa that share a common currency, the CFA Franc.

The optimum currency areas according to Gandolfo (1995) comprises a group of countries which have a common currency, or which, though maintaining different national currencies, have permanently and rigidly fixed exchange rates among themselves and full convertibility of the respective currencies into one another; while maintaining flexible exchange rates with non-partner countries. An OCA as a union according to Batiz and Batiz (1994), represents a group of countries that fix their exchange rates vis-à-vis each other and abdicate the active use of domestic monetary policy, with a common Central Bank or Fund that coordinates the monetary actions of the union's members. These definitions suggest the complementary of an optimum currency area and a monetary union.

In addition, the formation of an OCA may imply that member countries will lose their independent monetary policy (a key to macroeconomic stabilization) and be unable to use exchange rate as an instrument of adjustment. There exist three strands of argument in the facilitation of exchange rate adjustment in attainment of both internal and external balance simultaneously. According to Mundell (1961), exchange rates regime (fixed or flexible) is optimal in the adjustment process provided it can maintain external balances without causing unemployment. He also emphasized the importance of high factor mobility of labour and capital particularly between nations within a region. He proposed that countries featuring high factor mobility should join together in a single currency area or a multi-currency area with fixed exchange rates (optimum currency area), while countries whose factors are relatively immobile should adopt flexible exchange rates with each other (i.e. monetary union is undesirable). To illustrate this, Mundell used an illustration of two countries with an implication that the more mobile resources or factors are (say labour and capital), the less need there is for exchange rate to equilibrate differences in relative productivity levels (Bustaman, 2007).

In deference to Mundell (1961), McKinnon (1963)'s suggested a criterion for determining the optimality of a monetary union as a function of the country's openness to intra-regional trade. The degree of openness measured as the ratio of traded to non-traded goods of both exportable and importable, will determine whether a change in nominal exchange rate will be sufficient to change the real exchange rate in order to eliminate excess supply or demand (Bustaman, 2007 and Hsu, 2009).

Kenen (1969) similar to McKinnon (1963) faulted Mundell (1961) approach of factor mobility as inadequate and proposed product diversification in a country as a more relevant factor in the determination of optimum currency areas. Kenen stressed that diversified economies sharing the same industries are less likely to face asymmetric industry-specific shocks while economies specializing in sectors and using primary products may experience asymmetric industry-specific shocks. Consequently, he concluded in the diversification bid that fixed exchange rate regime is most appropriate to well diversified national economies. This is because a country with high product diversification will have a lesser need for exchange rate changes and so will be able to tolerate fixed exchange rates, whilst the contrary holds for a country having low product diversification (Caroli and Rajan, 2006).

The preceding criteria of Mundell (1961), McKinnon (1963) and Kenen (1969) in the operation of an optimal currency area were incorporated by Bayoumi (1994) in a formal equilibrium model of optimum currency area. Since then, the OCA theory has been modified along developments in economic theory with several empirical studies investigating the feasibility and viability of forming a common currency area. Other considerations proposed in various studies of OCA include the degree of financial integration; inter regional price and wage flexibility, similarity in rates of inflation, and degree of policy integration. These characteristics and the earlier three factors have been used empirically in various combinations in determining whether countries would benefit from joining a monetary union, OCA or not.

Some of the first empirical papers to specifically deal with the issue of macroeconomic disturbances is by Bayoumi and Eichengreen (1993, 1994). Bayoumi and Eichengreen (1993) in their seminal paper apply a variant of the bivarate vector autoregression (VAR) methodology proposed by Blanchard and Quah (1989) to uncover the structural shocks for a number of countries in Western Europe, the Americas and East Asia regions. The rationale for their study is that countries which experience similar disturbances are likely to respond with similar policies, thus making them better candidates for a monetary union (Yuen, 2000). The results of the study which analyzed the importance of asymmetric demand and supply shocks indicate that first, in the European Community (EC), a "core" group of countries, made up of Germany, France, Netherlands, Belgium and Denmark as neighbours have stronger "structural" correlations than the "peripheral" ones, and second, the supply and demand shocks of the core EC countries were on average smaller and more correlated with each other (Yuen, 2000). Also in a related study, Bayoumi and Eichengreen (1994) constructed series of supply and demand disturbances to analyze whether these disturbances were symmetrically distributed across the different countries in each of the regions of Europe, Asia and the Americas. Their results indicate that correlations of both output and inflation disturbances were low in the Americas. The authors concluded that there is no evidence supporting the formation of a currency union involving Latin American countries – either among themselves, or with the U.S or Canada (Edwards, 2006).

Since the works of Bayoumi and Eichengreen (1993, 1994), a large literature that applied the VAR methodology or related approaches to different compositions of country groups globally have emerged. Some recent studies that have applied the VAR approach or structural vector autoregression (SVAR) and other methodologies are Faust and Leeper (1997), Eichengreen (1998), Ferrando (2000), Lavagna and Giambiagi (2000), Yuen (2000),

Larrain and Tavares (2003), Maskay (2003), Buigut and Valer (2005), Ramayanid (2006), Edwards (2006), Louis, Balli and Osman (2008), Zhang, Sato and McAleer (2004) and Hsu (2009). A few of these shall be summarized below.

In their paper, Faust and Leeper (1997) estimated two sets of structural shocks using the income-unemployment model according to Blanchard and Quah and the income-prices model according to Bayoumi and Eichengreen for the U.S. data set. They found that the identified supply shock estimated from the income-unemployment model involves substantial commingling with the demand shock, while this is not the case for the estimated structural shocks from the income-prices model (Ramayandi, 2006).

Bayoumi and Ostry (1997) review existing exchange rate arrangements in Sub-Saharan Africa. The study also discussed a number of Sub-Saharan African countries' structural characteristics, including those relating to export diversification. Preliminary information which underlies disturbances was reported using some summary data on the mean and variability of inflation and growth and also on the correlation of growth and inflation. This method as the authors equally noted is an imperfect measure of underlying shocks since observed inflation performance conflates the effects disturbances and responses. To overcome this problem, Bayoumi and Ostry (1997) estimated a simple time series model of growth and the residuals from the model were analyzed to determine how correlated shocks are across countries. Their results suggest that shocks of Sub-Saharan African economies other than being large and economically significant, they are on the average not highly correlated across countries groupings. Consequently, there was little evidence that Sub-Saharan African countries would benefit in the near future from larger currency unions.

Yuen (2000) applied the Bayoumi and Eichengreen (1994) vector autoregression (VAR) approach to empirically assess the suitability of East Asian economies for potential monetary integration, on the basis of their symmetry in macroeconomic disturbance. The preliminary findings suggest that there exists a scope for deeper monetary integration among selected groups of Asian economies. The implication of the findings is that sub-groupings could result in a single currency area subject to the fulfillment of the necessary preconditions and harmonization requirements. Zhang, *et. al.* (2004) also examined the viability of regional monetary integration in East Asia by focusing on the symmetry of structural shocks as one precondition for forming an OCA. They extended the conventional structural VAR approach by employing a 3-variable and a 5-variable VAR model to identify the corresponding supply, demand, and exchange rate shocks. Also included are the foreign shocks and country specific shocks. They also applied the impulse response function analysis to examine the size of these underlying shocks and speed of adjustment to disturbances. Using quarterly data expressed in natural logarithms and seasonal adjusted variables except for exchange rates, the results show that OCA is less suitable for the whole of East Asian region.

Maskay (2003) sets to determine the possibility of the South Asian Association for Regional Cooperation to achieve an economic union by 2020. The data from South Asia suggest that member states have minor trade linkages and face asymmetric patterns of shocks. The estimated technique in order to allow for comparison across the region, given that applying the VAR technique was not feasible due to data constraint, applied a simpler time series model of growth, where growth of real output was regressed upon its own lags. Taking the residuals to represent the underlying disturbances, the results of both the one-and two-period lags suggests that the member states were not suitable candidates for a currency union and that the SAARC group was prone to asymmetrical economic disturbances with large adjustment costs and exhibited low economic integration. The results suggest that the sequence of monetary cooperation in SA should be structural and harmonized with the level of regional economic integration.

Buigut and Valev (2005) used the VAR techniques to investigate the potential for forming monetary unions in Eastern and Southern Africa. The paper also sets to sort out which countries in the region are suitable candidates for a monetary union based on the synchronicity of demand and supply disturbances. The annual data for 21 Eastern and Southern African countries focused on shocks to aggregate output growth and inflation from 1970 to 2001. The time series of the variables were investigated using the Augmented Dickey-Fuller test. Both variables were found to be

I(1). Tests for stability show that the eigenvalues of the VAR all lie inside the unit root circle except for one of the countries. The covariance stationary two-variable VAR with optimal lags set to two indicates that the results do not provide evidence in favour of broad monetary union encompassing all countries in the region. Equally, a support linkage of Southern Africa (SADC) currency to any of the hard currencies considered was not established.

Edwards (2006) analyzed the desirability of a monetary union from a Latin American perspective. The data set used covered 187 countries, for the period 1970-2001. The unbalanced panel data was applied on a probit model specification. The covariates used are the ratio of the current account deficit to GDP lagged one period; a sudden stop dummy that takes the value of one if the country in question experienced a sudden stop in the previous year; an index that measures the relative occurrence of sudden stop in the country's region (excluding the country itself) during the particular year, thus capturing the effect of "regional contagion"; one-year lagged rate of domestic credit growth; the lagged ratio of the country's fiscal deficit relative to GDP; the country's initial GDP per capita (in logs); and a dummy variable that takes the value of one if the country in question belongs to a currency union (CU). The coefficient of CU is of interest because it captures the effect of currency unions on the probability of a country experiencing a reversal or a sudden stop. The result from the variance-component probit model supports the contagion hypothesis, since the variable that measures the incidence of sudden stops in the country's region is significantly positive. The results obtained suggest that belonging to a currency union does not lower the probability of experiencing either a sudden stop or a current account reversal. The results also indicate that negative effects of external crises on GDP growth tend to be more severe in currency union countries than in countries with a currency of their own and flexible exchange rates.

Ramayandi (2006) study attempts to assess the reliability of the estimated structural shocks produced by applying long-run identifying restrictions to a simple bivariate VAR model. The study used both annual and quarterly shocks specifically on Hong Kong, Malaysia, Singapore, Indonesia and Thailand. The bivariate SVAR applied data on real GDP (as a measure of real output), and the GDP deflector (as a measure of aggregate prices). The period from 1960-2002 is covered. For demand-specific policy variables also considers growth of reserve money, changes in the level of short-run discount rate as proxies of monetary policy, growth of government expenditure as proxy for fiscal policy and change in the level of domestic currency exchange rate to the US dollar as a proxy for internationally induced demand effects. Though the data were collected for different length of observation according to availability, the finding suggests that the commingling shocks problems identified in underlying structural shocks exist.

Louis, Balli and Osman (2009) employ a bivariate structural vector autoregression of output growth and inflation identified with long-run restriction to extract shocks as postulated by Blanchard and Quah (1989). The paper sets out to determine first, whether aggregate demand and non-oil supply shocks are symmetrical across the Arab Gulf Cooperation Council (AGCC) countries; and second, whether there is any commonality of shocks with the United States and the three major European countries (France, Germany and Italy). The results reveal among others that aggregate demand shocks are unequivocally symmetrical but non-oil supply shocks are weakly symmetrical across AGCC countries (Bahrain, Kuwait, Oman, Qatar, Saudi Arabia, and United Arab Emirates).

Hsu (2009) apply a three-variable model with global, regional and domestic outputs similar to Chow and Kim (2003) to determine whether or not in nine East Asian economies if they are affected by a common symmetric shock and whether or not it is possible to pursue region-wide monetary policies if a common currency area is formed. The period of analysis is from the 1980s to 2006. The empirical results though do not provide strong support for forming a common currency area; it found that since the 1990s the importance of asymmetric domestic shocks has declined while that of symmetric global and regional shocks has increased. The findings suggest that most East Asian economies have become symmetric in terms of economic shocks; implying that a common currency area may become viable through deepening regional integration.

Consequent upon the studies summarized above, it is unequivocal that the feasible formation and viability of a common currency area across various regions is still a mix. In addition, particular researches on the possibility of forming a currency union for the Africa Monetary Zone (WAMZ) are scanty especially using recent data. Further investigation is thus required to assess the desirability of achieving greater monetary cooperation of WAMZ member countries. This paper follows the lead of Bayoumi and Eichengreen (1994) and Maskay (2002, 2003) by analyzing the patterns and symmetry of economic shocks affecting the members of the zone.

SOME STYLIZED FACTS ON THE ECONOMIES OF WAMZ MEMBER COUNTRIES

Basic Characterization

The West African Monetary Zone (WAMZ) is a group of five countries (at formation in 2000- The Gambia, Ghana, Guinea, Nigeria and Sierra Leone, until recently when Liberia joined as the sixth member) in ECOWAS that plan to introduce a common currency, the ***Eco*** programmed for 2020. The total area of four of the countries is only 61.53 per cent of Nigeria (the fifth country). The WAMZ is dominated by Nigeria, Africa's largest oil producer and most populous country, with an estimated 149.1 million people. All members of the group are English-speaking countries, apart from Guinea, which is Francophone. The member countries of WAMZ share some similar social values and culture. Table 2.1 shows the divergence of country size and population, GDP and human development index (HDI). Although, Nigeria is the largest country both in terms of population density and income per capita U.S. dollar of $2,300 in 2008, the WAMZ countries have similar levels of human development (HDI). Nigeria accounts for 86.1 percent of WAMZ GDP with 78.2 percent of WAMZ 190 million (2007 estimate) inhabitants residing in Nigeria.

GDP Growth (Annual %)

The GDP growth patterns are different among the WAMZ countries particuarly in the early 2000s. Figure 2.1 illustrates the economic growth path in the last 9 years. Precisely, Gambia has an average GDP growth of 6.02 percent, Ghana and Guinea average growth was 5.44 percent and 2.83 percent and respectively. Nigeria and Guinea recorded the highest growth in the zone having recorded respectively, 6.21 percent and 11.00 percent during the period. These growth when viewed critically may seem less similar, however in recent years, particularly 2006, the growth rates except for Guinea, have been converging at a growth rate of 6 percent.

Inflation

The summary statistics of inflation for WAMZ member countries is presented in Table 2.4. The figures show both positive and negative correlations between individual member countries. Using the 5 percent significance level, statistical significance requires a 71 percent coefficient of correlation; given the initial number of observations (2001 – 2008). The significant coefficients are highlighted in Table 2.4. The correlation are fairly dispersed which may not necessarily reflect suitability of forming a monetary cooperation. However, as recent data indicate there is evidence of a remarkable progress in the WAMZ countries on the possibility of attaining single digit inflation if not for the recent global economic crisis, thus making the WAMZ countries candidates for OCA. For instance, inflation in Ghana dropped from an average of 22.9 per cent to 13.5 per cent (2004-2008).

Trade Openness

Trade openness relates the degree to which an economy is open to the whole world. This is commonly calculated as the ratio of sum of export and import to gross domestic product (GDP). According to Mckinnon (1963), the higher the openness levels of potential members of a monetary union, the lower the demand for the formation of the union. As can be observed from Table 2.5 and Figure 2.3, the openess ratios are similar hovering around 50 percent for the WAMZ countries (1970-2008) except Guinea (whose avreage was for 1980 to 2008 due to lack of data) with an average above 100 percent. These percentage ratios though are competitive to some other monetary unions, they are relatively closed. As Figure 2.6 shows, Ghana particularly tend to be more open in the late 2000 as against other countries that seem to closing up.

Exchange Rate

The OCA choice of an exchange rate regime is that the currency union exchange rates are fixed among member countries, but flexible or float in relation to other countries outside the group. As Jikang and Yin (2005) further noted, high volatility of exchange rate will more likely favour floating exchange regime, while low harmony in the movement of exchange rate will inhibit cooperation of potential OCA members. Tables 7, 8 and 9 show the correlation coefficients of the exchange rate (LUC per US), nominal effective exchange rate (NEER) and real effective exchange rate (REER) respectively of member countries.

The correlation coefficients of all types of exchange rates (NEER and REER) including the bilateral (NER) of the member states studied are all positively signed and statistically significant at 5 percent level as the cut-off. Statistical significance requires 33.5 percent coefficient of correlation for nominal exchange rate; while NEER and REER requires 34.9 percent and 38.1 percent respectively. Tables 7, 8 and 9 explicate the nominal rate, nominal effective exchange rate and real effective exchange rate. Table 2.7 shows a remarkable divergence in the nominal exchange rate, while Tables 8 and 9 show a convincingly converging trend in NEER and REER of WAMZ member countries except Guinea due to availability of data constraint. Reminiscent of Jikang and Yin (2005) for China, Japan and Korea, this may be due to the fact that both NEER and REER are set to 2003 = 100. The effective exchange rates (nominal and real) however fluctuate differently during the period analyzed.

The volatility of the exchange rates was also examined in the second panels of Tables 7, 8 and 9. All forms of the exchange rates show that the Ghanaian cedi with standard deviations of 33.09, 71.28 and 53.44 points for NER, NEER and REER respectively may hinder monetary cooperation but not totally. However, the generally decreasing trend and convergences of these exchange rates (NEER and REER) over the time period as confirmed by the statistical significance of high correlation coefficients, with all being positive may reflect similarly in trading patterns of WAMZ members.

Common Market and Budget Deficit/GDP Ratio

Trade integration remains a veritable concern in the OCA. Although notable progress has been made, significant challenges are still copious. As Figure 2.4 exhibits, WAMZ countries are yet to be sufficiently open to WAMZ and compares poorly with ASEAN and Euro areas. There is still the continued existence of trade barriers, ineffective compensation schemes etc.

The budget deficit to GDP ratio as presented in Table 2.6 reflects a declining trend from the 2000 reference year. However, much improvement is still expected as most of the WAMZ countries ratios fall into a bracket of 3 per cent to 9 per cent.

Productive Structure

Certainly, there exist some differences in the development stage of the WAMZ countries. However, they all belong to the class of developing countries. Nigeria's productive structure is quite different from that of Gambia, Ghana, Guinea and Sierra Leone. Figure 2.5 shows that agriculture accounts for 59.7 percent of Sierra Leone's total output in 2008, whereas the corresponding contributions of this sector are 31.6 percent for Gambia, 36 percent for Ghana 20.85 percent for Guinea and 32.9 percent in Nigeria.

The sectoral contribution of agriculture dominated the economies of both Sierra Leone and Ghana, and ranked second in the economies of the Gambia and Nigeria. Services sector dominates the economies of the Gambia, Ghana and Guinea, while it is the second largest in Sierra Leone. In Nigeria, the service sector lags behind industrial and agricultural sector. The largest share of Nigeria's output comes from the industrial production. This may be due to the high activities in the oil sub-sector, the major driver of the Nigerian economy.

Financial Integration

One of the prerequisite for joining a currency union, is the integration of financial markets across markets. This criterion is well articulated in the Banjul Action Plan. Activities highlighted under this programme are the enacment of legal instruments to ensure; (i) full capital account liberalization (ii) cross listing of stocks; (iii) regional currency convertibility; and (iv) harmonization of banking supervision. So far as Figure 2.7 depicts, there is evidence of significant reduction in cross sectional dispersion in lending rates of WAMZ countries. Volatality of interest rate differentials have narrowed. This is expected to gradually *crystallize* into the law of one price. Quoting in WAMZ currencies has been formalized and cross-listing of stocks, though low, it is progressing as Nigeria and Ghana are ahead of Gambia, Guinea and Sierra Leone.

Political Commitment

Since the launching of the WAMZ in December 2000, many efforts have been made towards the establihment of a single currency for the zone. So far all the WAMZ countries have adopted the ECOWAS External Tariff (CET) and the ECOWAS Trade Libralization Scheme (ETLS). The Supplementary Act for common investment framework has equally been adopted by the WAMZ. Quoting in WAMZ member states currencies has been formalized, while the West African Central Bank (WACB), the West African Monetary Zone Secretariat Statutes have been signed by the Authority of Heads of States and Governments of the WAMZ. Supervisory frameworks for the West African Financial Services Authority (WAFSA) and the non-bank regulations have been prepared. Although only The Gambia complied with all four primary convergence criteria with Nigeria satisfying three in 2008 as Table 2.11 indicates, there is the strong convincsion that the political support for the OCA project regained the needed momentum towards satisfying the quantitative and structural criteria.

METHOD OF STUDY

As observed in the section on review of the literature, different criteria have been proposed in the determination of candidacy for a common currency area and particularly, the choice of optimal exchange rate. According to Masson and Taylor (1993:17) comment cited in Maskay (2003: 8) on how best to eliminate the problems of applying individual OCA criteria in putting forward conflicting policy prescriptions about a country's optimal exchange rate policy, the "shock-absorption (approach) which combines the net influence of several traditional criteria" is recommended. Consequently, this paper like most recent empirical papers on OCA determination (Maskay, 2003; Buight and Valer, 2005; Louis et al 2008; Hsu, 2009 among others), uses one particular aspect of the criteria for determining OCA – the pattern of economic shocks facing a set of countries in order to determine if they are candidates for a currency union. Countries that face similar shocks would likely encounter lower costs of losing the tools of monetary and exchange rates for adjustment than would other sets of countries facing economic shocks.

Series of estimating techniques exist in the measure of the pattern of shocks facing a set of countries. The most popular is the vector autoregression (VAR) techniques. A VAR model is a simultaneous equation system, and is often used to examine the dynamic impacts of exogenous shocks on endogenous variables. The VAR technique decomposes shocks from responses and allows analyzing the size of disturbance and speed of adjustment. However, due to time constraint in data gathering, the use of the VAR technique in this study is not feasible.[1]

Moreover, the use of VAR techniques as Bayoumi and Ostry (1997:428) noted is not well designed for us in the African context. This is because, VAR techniques in their various forms assume aggragate demand shocks have temporary impact on output, while aggregate supply shocks have a permanent impact. However, in Africa including the WAMZ, many of the shocks which affect the economies are temporary supply disturbances such as climate shocks to agriculture or terms of trade disturbances (being producers and exporters of primary goods).

Consequent upon this and to allow for comparison across member countries, a simpler time series model of growth which focuses on the behaviour of real output is applied. This method regresses the annual growth of real output per capita (measured as the change in the logarithm of real GDP per capita) on its own lags, with the residuals extracted to represent the underlying real output disturbances. The correlation coefficients of the extracted residuals are then estimated. The sizes of the underlying disturbaces were calculated using the standard deviations of the residu-

1 A follow-up paper which extends this study shall apply the VAR technique.

als. This approach has been applied in some other studies notably Bayoumi and Ostry (1997) and Maskay (2002, 2003) with satisfying results, which compare favourably with the VAR technique.

SYMMETRY OF UNDERLYING REAL OUTPUT SHOCK

As earlier noted, should members of a currency union face symmetric shocks, then the costs of adjusting to one single currency is reduced. For this reason, a simple model of growth of real output was regressed upon its own lags. One and two-periods were used given that the data is annual and the periods not long enough. The residuals from both regressions were made to represent the underlying disturbances for each of the five member countries. Tables 10 and 11 display the correlation coefficients of the disturbances with one and two-period lags respectively. The results of the disturbances with a single and double lags are similar in both terms of signs and statistical significance. In terms of signs, there seem to be some consistencies in the pattern of shocks. In the single-lag case, there were six positively signed coefficients out of the ten, while in the double lag case, it increased to seven and were all very low in sizes. All the coefficients in both cases are not statistically significant at 5 percent level ($\alpha_{0.05} = .349$). This suggests that the member states tend to face similar but asymmetric patterns of output shocks during the period under review. This is similar to the findings for Africa (Bayoumi and Ostry, 1997) and Maskay, (2000) for South Asia who applied similar methodology, but at variance with the findings of Bayoumi and Mauro (2000) for East Asia and Western Europe.

The volatility of the real shocks[2] (same as the size of the underlying disturbances), estimated as the standard deviations of the

---

2 Cortinhas (2007: 9) holds the view that countries are better candidates for a currency union if their disturbances are correlated and small, and adjustment to them are rapid. According to Cortinhas, the speed and size of adjustment can be inferred by analyzing the associated impulse response functions (in the case of a VAR analysis), where the size of the supply shock is measured as the long-run effect (say 12-year horizon) of a unit shock on changes in real GDP. The speed of adjustment to shocks on the other hand is the proportion of the long-run adjustment in the first two years after the occurrence of a structural break.

residuals were also examined as well as their mean values. These descriptive statistics of the errors are reported in Panel B of Tables 10 and 11 for lags 1 and 2 respectively. The standard deviations of the errors for both lags are similar lying approximately within the neigbourhood of 4 and 6 percents in most cases except for Guinea. These values by way of comparison are far larger than 2 - 2.5 per cent produced by Bayoumi and Ostry (1997) for Germany, Japan, and the United States using the same calculations (methodology). One reason for these larger sizes of disturbances across the WAMZ, as Bayoumi and Ostry (1997) point out; is undoubtedly that countries in Africa are highly specialized in production of a limited number of primary goods. Thus, their economic progress tends to follow the vagaries of markets for the particular products which they produce with limited ability to absorb uncertainties. The implications of this though with some caution are first, that the WAMZ may not be a suitable candidate for a currency union, and second, that the WAMZ countries may be better-off retaining their ability to conduct monetary and exchange rate policies.

SUMMARY AND CONCLUSION

In this paper, we modestly examined the patterns of economic shocks of WAMZ member states in order to assess their economic suitability for an optimum currency area. Some of the economic indicators stressed by the OCA theories were analyzed for various periods. A good number of the indicators especially in recent times suggest mix fillings of the WAMZ being favourably dispose to satisfying the OCA criteria. The WAMZ generally exhibit less coherence in their output fluctuations relatively, thus making it difficult to suggest that the similarity of output shocks could be a driving force to lead member countries as candidates for a currency union. Also underscoring this observation is the low compliance level of WAMZ member states to the primary convergence criteria.

Although there is a decreasing trend and convergence of NEER and REER of the WAMZ, what seems to give some live breath of WAMZ becoming an OCA candidate may be the satisfactory political solidarity which national leaders expressed in their commitment. To rein enforce this, this paper canvasses for greater and deepened economic integration among member states for the realization of the OCA. This may be achieved if members are sufficiently open to WAMZ intra-trade through removal of trade barriers, effective compensation among others.

References

Bayuoumi, T and B. Eichengreen, (1993); Shocking Aspects of European Monetary Unification, in F. Torres and F. Giavazzi (eds.), *Adjustment and Growth in the European Monetary Union*, Cambridge, Cambridge University Press.

Bayuoumi, T and B. Eichengreen, (1994); One Money or Many? Analyzing the Prospects for Monetary Unification in Various Parts of the World. Princeton Studies in International Finance, 76, Princeton University.

Bayoumi, T. and Ostry, J. D. (1997). "Macroeconomic shocks and trade flows within Sub-Saharan Africa: implications for Optimum Currency Arrangements." *Journal of African Economies*, 6(3): 412-444.

Bayoumi, Tamim, and Paolo Mauro, 2001, "The Suitability of ASEAN for a RegionalCurrency Arrangement," *World Economy*, 24:. 933–45.

Blanchard, O. and Quah, D. (1989); The Dynamic Effects of Aggregate Demand and supply disturbances. *American Economic Review*, 79: 655-673.

Buigut, S.K. and N.T. Valer (2005); "Eastern and Southern African Integration". A Structural Vector Autoregreesion Analysis.

Bustaman, A. (2007); "Optimum Currency Area: A Conceptual and Practical Consideration". Paper presented and the LP3E Monetary Discussion.

Cavoli, T. and R.S. Rajan (2006); "Exploring the Case for Monetary Integration between Mainland China and Hong Kong".

Chow, H.K. and Y. Kim, (2003); A Common Currency Peg in East Asia? Perspectives from Western Europe, *Journal of Macroeconomics*, 25: 331 – 350.

Copernicus, N. (1526) "Montae Cudendae Ratio"

Cortinhas, C (2007), 'Asymmetry of Shocks and Convergence in Selected Asean Countries: A Dynamic Analysis, in Koveos', P.E. (ed.), *Critical Issues for the 21st Century Global Economy: Economics, Finance, Management & Entrepreneurship*, Athens: Athens Institute for Education and Research (ATINER), pp. 25-42.

ECOWAS Commission (2008); Annual Report: Forging Regional Response to Global Economic and Financial Crises; Abuja, Nigeria.

Edwards, S. (2006); "Monetary Uions, External Shocks and Economic Performance". A Latin American Perspective. *IEEP* 3:225 – 247.

Faust, J. and E.M. Leeper (1997). When Do Long-Run Identifying Restrictions Give Reliable Results? *Journal of Business and Economic Statistics.* 15(3): 345-353.

Ferrando G.F. (2000) iUn Area Monetavia para el Mercusor? In Carrera J, Sturzzenegger, F. (ed.) Coordinacion de Politicas Macroeconomicas en al MERCOSUR, fondo de caltura Economica, Mexico, DF.

Gandolfo, G. (1995). *International Economics II.* 2nd Edition, Berlin: Springer – Verlag.

Hsu, H. (2009); "Is A Common Currency Area Feasible for East Asia? A Multivariate Structural VAR Approach". *Osaka School of International Public Policy (OSIPP)* Discuss Paper: DP–2009-E-006.

Jikang, Z. and L. Yin (2005) Is East Asia Suitable for a Monetary Union? "Experience from EU and Evidence from China, Japan and South Korea. www.ieem.org.mo/nesca/documents/papers/Zhang-Jikang.doc [downloaded 10-03-10]

Kenen, P.B. (1969); The Theory of Optimum currency Areas: An Eclectic view. In: Mundell RA, Swoboda AK (Eds), *Monetary Problems of the International Economy.* University of Chicago Press, Chicago and London; pp. 41-60.

Larrain,F. and J. Tavares (20030.Regional Currencies versus Dollarization Option for Asia and the Americas. *Policy Reforms* 6(1): 35-49.

Lavagna R, Giambiagi F (2000) Hacia la Creación de una Moneda Común: Una Propuesta de Convergencia Coordinada de Políticas Macroeconómica en el MERCOSUR. In: Carrera J, Sturzenegger F (eds) *Coordinación de Políticas Macroeconómicas en el MERCOSUR,* Fondo de Cultura Económica México, D.F.

Jin, N.K, (2002). "Financial and monetary cooperation in East Asia: Issues and Options", Institute of Southeast Asian Studies

Kiess, H.O. (1989). *Statistical Concepts for the Behavioural Sciences.* Boston: Allyn and Bacon

Louis, R.N.; F. Balli and M. Osman (2008); Monetary Union Amongst Arab Gulf Cooperation Council (AGCC) Countries: Does the Symmetry of Shocks Extend to the Non-oil Sector? University Library of Munich, Germany. *MPRA Paper* with number 11611.

Maskay, N.M. (2000), "A Cautionary Note in Using Patterns of Shocks to Determine Optimal Exchange Rate Policy; An Exploration of Nepalese and Indian Exchange Rate relations of 1964–1994," *Applied Economics,* Vol. 32, No. 4, pp. 491–98.

Maskay, N.M. (2003); "Patterns of Shocks and Regional Monetary Cooperation in South Asia". *International Monetary Fund (IMF) Working Paper.* WP/03/240.

Masson, Paul R., and Mark P. Taylor, eds., 1993, *Policy Issues in the Operation of Currency Unions.* Cambridge: Cambridge University Press)

McKinnon, R.I. (1963); Optimum Currency Areas *American Economic Review,* 51: 717-724.

Mundell, R. (1961); A Theory of Optimum Currency Areas. *American Economic Review,* 51: 657-665.

Oshikoya, T. (2009); State of Preparedness of the WAMZ Countries for Monetary Union on December 1, 2009. Presented at the WAMZ Convergence Council Meeting, Abuja, Nigeria.

Ramayandi, A. (2006); "Reliability of Structural Shocks Estimates from Bivariate SVAR Model: The Case of Southeast Asian Countries". *Pacific Economic Papers* No. 357, Australia-Japan Research Centre.

Ravira-Batiz, F.L. and L. Ravira-Batiz (1994). *International Finance and Open Economy Macroeconomics*, 2nd ed. Macmillan.

West African Monetary Institute (2009); West African Monetary Zone (WAMZ) Macroeconomic Development and Convergence Report, End – June, 2009, WAMI- IMAO/CC.B/2009/02, Accra, Ghana.

West African Monetary Institute (2002), Proceedings of the West African Monetary Institute/Bank of England Seminar on Monetary Union, Accra, Ghana.

World Bank (2010): *World Development Indicators*. Monetary Integration in Africa ( ). www.uneca.org/aria3/Chap6.pdf[12-03-10]

Yuen, H. (2000); Is Asia an Optimum Currency Area? "Shocking" Aspects of Output Fluctuations in East Asia. *National University of Singapore Working Paper*

Zhaoyong Zhang & Kiyotaka Sato & Michael McAleer, 2004. "Is a monetary union feasible for East Asia?," *Applied Economics*, 36(10): 1031-1043.

Table 2.1: Basic Characterization of WAMZ Member States

Country	Population (million) 2008	Land Area (1000 km²)	Pop. density (pop/km²)	HDI 2007	GDP US & bil (Ppp) 2008	Per Capita US & 2008
The Gambia	1.8 (0.94)	11.3 (0.76)	159.29	0.456	2.3	1,300
Ghana	23.9 (12.49)	239.5 (16.05)	99.79	0.526	34.0	1500
Guinea	10.1 (5.28)	245.9 (16.48)	41.07	0.435	10.4	1100
Nigeria	149.1 (77.94)	923.8 (61.91)	161.40	0.511	338.1	2300
Sierra Leone	6.4 (3.35)	71.7 (4.80)	89.26	0.365	4.3	700

Sources: Oshikoya (2009); Wikipedia, the free encyclopedia.

TABLE 2.2: MACROECONOMIC INDICATORS OF WAMZ MEMBER STATES

COUNTRY	INFLATION		EXCHANGE RATE (LCU/USD)		TRADE BALANCE (USD MILLION)		CURRENT ACCT (USD MILLION)	
	2007	2008	2007	2008	2007	2008	2007	2008
Gambia	5.4	6.4	24.9	20.6	-172	-187	-80	-112
Ghana	10.7	14.1	9355.0	10524.3	-3879	-3974	-1885	-1686
Guinea	43.43	19.3	4485.0	4639.3	-14	-86	-456	-658
Nigeria	5.4	11.0	125.8	117.8	26973	31517	5873	6917
Sierra Leone	11.51	13.21	2,987.51	2981.1	-100	-174	-64	-141

TABLE 2.3. CORRELATIONS OF GDP GROWTH (ANNUAL %) 2001-2008

COUNTRY	GAMBIA	GHANA	GUINEA	NIGERIA	SIERRA LEONE
Gambia	1.00				
Ghana	0.43	1.00			
Guinea	-0.53	0.22	1.00		
Nigeria	0.59	0.27	-0.63	1.00	
Sierra Leone	-0.34	-0.39	0.03	0.23	1.00

$\alpha_{0.05} = 0.707$

Mean	6.02	5.44	2.83	6.20	11.00
Std. Deviation	1.91	1.14	1.22	1.46	6.64

Source: ECOWAS Commission Annual Report (2008)

TABLE 2.4. CORRELATIONS OF INFLATION (2001-2008)

COUNTRY	GAMBIA	GHANA	GUINEA	NIGERIA	SIERRA LEONE
Gambia	1.00				
Ghana	0.69	1.00			
Guinea	-0.61	-0.65	1.00		
Nigeria	0.72	0.94	-0.41	1.00	
Sierra Leone	-0.30	-0.16	0.51	-0.07	1.00

$\alpha_{0.05} = 0.707$

Mean	7.71	15.95	18.1	13.05	9.10
Std. Deviation	5.58	4.62	12.86	5.41	6.05

Source: ECOWAS Commission Annual Report (2008)

TABLE 2.5. DESCRIPTIVE OF WAMZ MEMBER COUNTRIES DEGREE OF OPENNESS

COUNTRY	GAMBIA	GHANA	GUINEA	NIGERIA	SIERRA LEONE
Mean	1.012	0.553	0.566	0.573	0.481
Std. Deviation	0.177	0.336	0.087	0.216	0.104

Source: World Bank World Development Indicators (2010)

Table 2.6. Budget Deficit/GDP Ratio

Country	2000	2005	2006	2007	2008
Gambia	3.6	8.4	2.7	0.5	3.9
Ghana	10.1	6.9	12.6	14.7	8.9
Guinea	5.2	1.5	2.0	0.9	3.7
Nigeria	2.7	1.3	0.6	1.2	1.2
Sierra Leone	17.6	9.5	8.5	5.6	9.0

Source: ECOWAS Commission Annual Report (2008)

Table 2.7. Exchange Rate Correlations of WAMZ Member states (LUC per US$) 1970-2008

Country	Gambia	Ghana	Guinea	Nigeria	Sierra Leone
Gambia	1.00				
Ghana	0.90	1.00			
Guinea	0.92	0.78	1.00		
Nigeria	0.93	0.90	0.90	1.00	
Sierra Leone	0.94	0.87	0.94	0.97	1.00

α= 0.05=0.325

Std. Deviation	0.087 E+2	33.09 E+2	13.68 E+2	0.51 E+2	10.81 E+2

Source: World Bank, World Development Indicators (2008 CD-ROM) and WAMI

Table 2.8. Nominal Effective Exchange Rate Correlations of WAMZ Member states (2003=100) 1975-2008

Country	Gambia	Ghana	Nigeria	Sierra Leone
Gambia	1.00			
Ghana	0.65	1.00		
Nigeria	0.89	0.71	1.00	
Sierra Leone	0.85	0.89	0.92	1.00

α= 0.05=0.349

Std. Deviation	0.124 E+02	71.28 E+02	4.64 E+02	43.04 E+02

Source: World Bank, World Development Indicators (2008 CD-ROM) and WAMI

Table 2.9. Real Effective Exchange Rate Correlations of WAMZ Member states (2003=100) 1980-2008

Country	Gambia	Ghana	Nigeria	Sierra Leone
Gambia	1.00			
Ghana	0.59	1.00		
Nigeria	0.64	0.65	1.00	
Sierra Leone	0.70	0.60	0.96	1.00

α= 0.05=0.381

Std. Deviation	5.75 E+02	53.44 E+02	18.95 E+02	8.07 E+02

Source: World Bank, World Development Indicators (2005 CD-ROM) and WAMI

Table 2.10. Correlations and Standard Deviations of Output Disturbances (single lag) 1972-2008

Country	Gambia	Ghana	Guinea	Nigeria	Sierra Leone
Gambia	1.00				
Ghana	-0.27	1.00			
Guinea	0.06	0.17	1.00		
Nigeria	-0.11	0.28	0.21	1.00	
Sierra Leone	-0.07	0.19	-0.03	0.09	1.00

α= 0.05=0.325

Std. Deviation	5.56	4.26	2.05	6.32	6.47

Source: www.unctad.org

Table 2.11. Correlations and Standard Deviations of Output Disturbances (double lag) 1972-2008

Country	Gambia	Ghana	Guinea	Nigeria	Sierra Leone
Gambia	1.00				
Ghana	-0.27	1.00			
Guinea	0.03	0.04	1.00		
Nigeria	-0.14	0.31	0.15	1.00	
Sierra Leone	0.05	0.22	-0.02	0.07	1.00

α= 0.05=0.349

Std. Deviation	4.93	4.18	1.90	6.36	6.42

Source: www.unctad.org

Table 2.12. Number of Primary Convergence Criteria Met by Countries (2001-2008)

Country	2001	2002	2003	2004	2005	2006	2007	2008
The Gambia	2	1	1	3	3	4	4	4
Ghana	1	0	2	2	2	2	2	0
Guinea	3	2	0	0	2	1	2	2
Nigeria	3	3	2	3	3	4	4	3
Sierra Leona	3	3	0	2	2	2	2	2

Source: Oshikoya (2009)

Figure 2.1. Real GDP Growth Rate 2000-2006

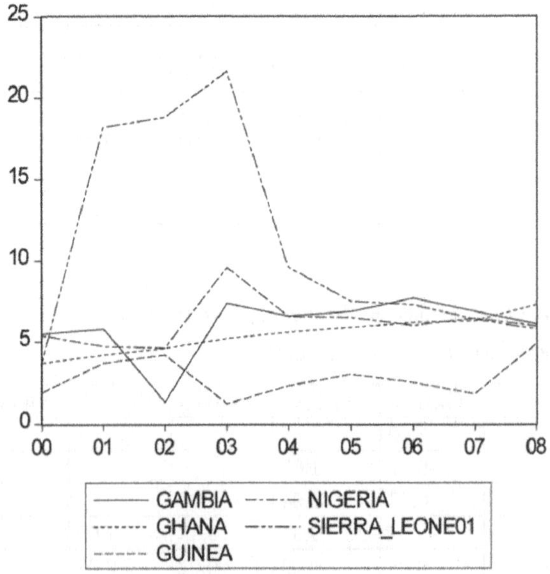

Figure 2.2. Per Capita GDP at Constant Prices of 2001 (in US dollars)

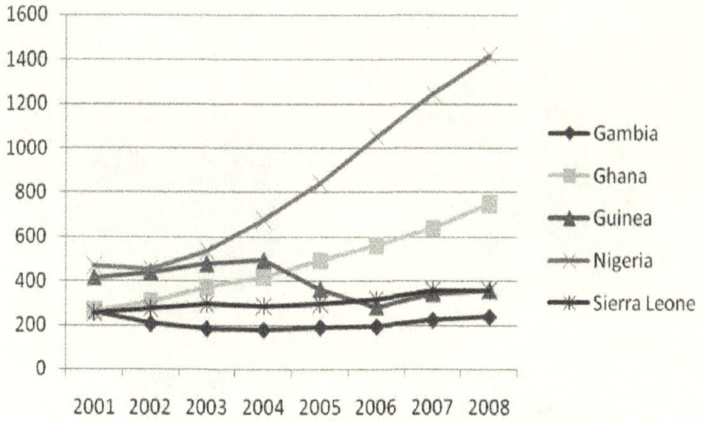

Figure 2.3. Degrees of Openness

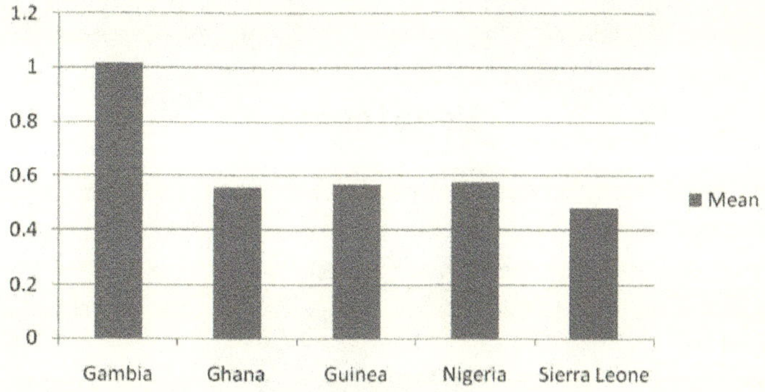

Figure 2.4. Common Market

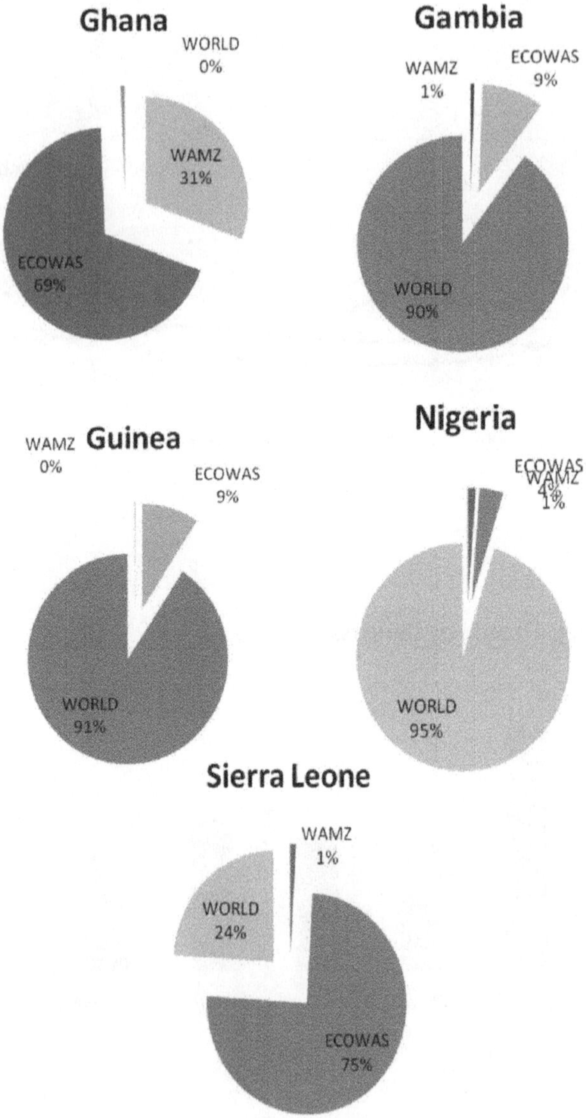

Figure 2.5. Structure of Output in 2008.

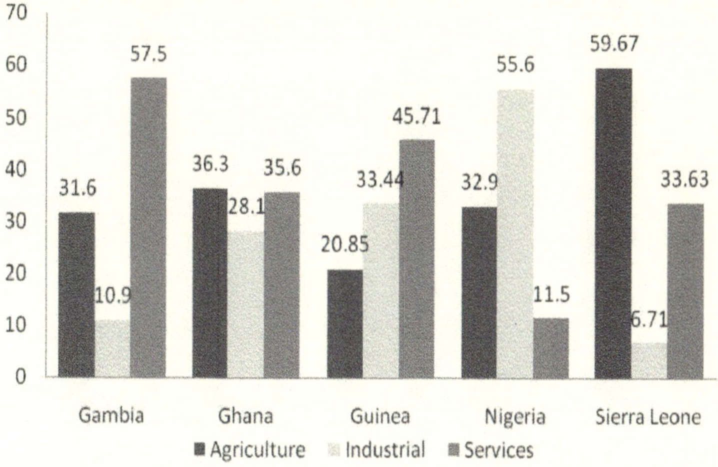

Figure 2.6. Degree of Openness.

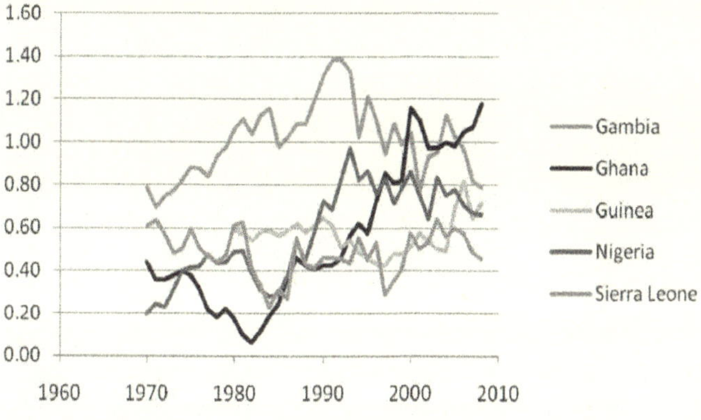

Figure 2.7. Cross-Sectional Dispersion of Interest Rates in the WAMZ

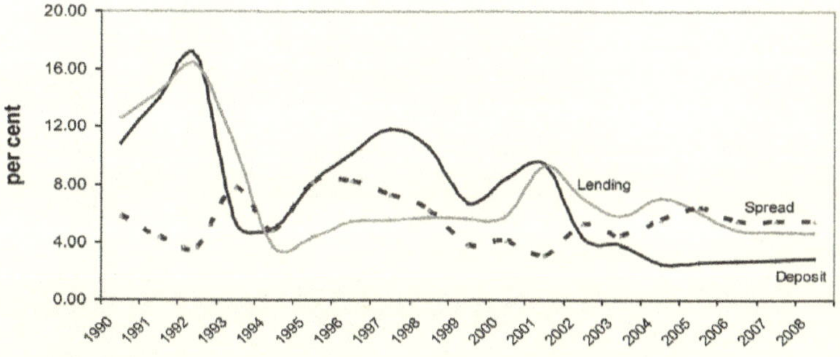

Section II

Common Currency

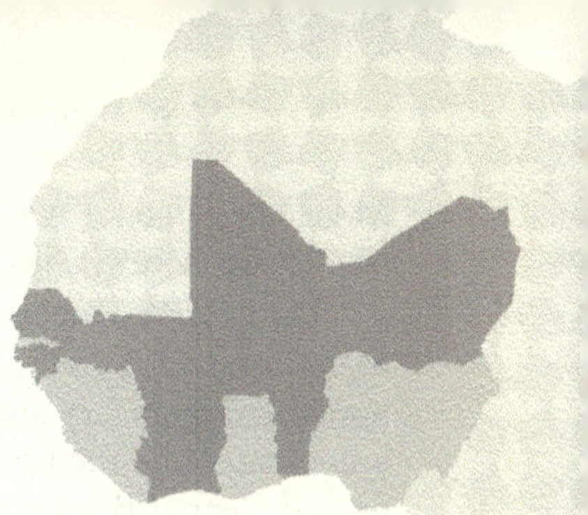

Chapter 3

WEST AFRICAN MONETARY ZONE AS AN OPTIMUM CURRENCY AREA

Edward E. Ghartey

INTRODUCTION

The Economic Community of West African States (ECOWAS) has made it an urgent goal to introduce a single currency among its members to deepen their economic and trade integrations. The adoption of a common currency will assist the ECOWAS to adopt policies to ensure free mobility of capital, labor, goods and services within its members to improve the low intra members' trade which hovers below 10 percent as it advances its aspirations to become a viable single market economy. This necessitated the need to set up the West African Monetary Zone (WAMZ) in 2000 with the task of expediting the convergence process in the region by following the establishment of the European Union (EU) in 1999. The West African Monetary Institute (WAMI) was also set up as a formal institution of the ECOWAS to establish a well-coordinated economic and financial monitoring system to drive the English speaking West African countries comprising of The Gambia, Ghana, Nigeria, Sierra Leone and Guinea, a former independent French colony which was not a member of the CFA zone (or West Africa

Monetary Union (WAMU)) to achieve an ECOWAS Single Market Economy (ESME).[1]

The ECOWAS' position was to independently assist members of both the CFA zone and WAMZ to achieve the status of economic and monetary union, with the intention of joining the two unions later into the ESME. Unfortunately, the task of forming a unified Central Bank with a common currency known as the eco has become illusive, with the goal post of deadlines for achieving its objective consistently moved with no end in sight.

In light of the above, the object of this study is to attempt to find out whether the optimum currency area (OCA) criteria pertaining to symmetry of shocks across regional economies proposed by Mundell (1961) to determine the adoption of a single currency for a group of countries can be met by members of the WAMZ. We have therefore measured the degree of correlation in macroeconomic variables such as real GDP and prices across member countries of the WAMZ as was done by Kwan (1998) for East Asian countries (EAC).

We have examined the convergence of the WAMZ economies which have certain common characteristics such as being closed economies as measured by their degree of openness and are primary producers of agricultural, mineral and petroleum and its related products. We have also estimated the structural shocks of the WAMZ economies by using a structural vector error correction model (VECM)[2] which consists of economic growth, inflation rates and growth in exchange rates to study the effect of underlying supply, demand and monetary shocks in the WAMZ economies.[3] According to Bayoumi and Eichengreen (1994)

1. Liberia has expressed interest to join the WAMZ.
2 Bayoumi and Eichengreen (1992), and Zhang et al. (2004) used the vector autoregressive (VAR) model, and employed Blanchard and Quah's (1989) method to identify the VAR model. We have employed the VECM as suggested by Blanchard and Quah (1993) in response to Lippi and Reichlin (1993). See Ghartey (2008) for application.
3 Mundell (1961, p.664) argues that for central banks to achieve internal stability, they need to change exchange rates but not interest rates to produce the desired stabilizing effects. Hence our emphasis on exchange rates instead of interest rates.

and Zhang et al. (2004), to name a few, fluctuations in supply are unlikely to be affected by policy effects. Thus, supply shocks contain more information to enable effective evaluation of symmetry of shocks to determine the feasibility of economies of the WAMZ becoming a successful OCA (Mundell, 1961; McKinnon, 1963; Bayoumi and Eichengreen, 1992; Ghartey, 2008).

We have also employed impulse response functions to measure the relative sizes of the underlying shocks and their speed of adjustment to disturbances. Note that asymmetric shocks cannot adversely affect economies if the sizes of those shocks are smaller and the responsiveness to such shocks by respective economies are fast. Additionally, an economy which meets the OCA criteria will be expected to have a high correlation of underlying supply shocks because the literature of endogenous OCA suggests that an increase in trade produces more highly correlated business cycle which intensifies trade integration. See Frankel (1999) and Frankel and Rose (1998). Macroeconomic variables such as real GDP and prices from the United States of America (USA) are also included in the VECM and decomposed into supply and demand shocks, respectively, to test the robustness of our results and to compare them with the effect of global (or USA) shocks in the region (Bayoumi and Eichengreen, 1992; Zhang et al., 2004; Ghartey, 2008).

The rest of the study is organized as follows: the case for a single market for the WAMZ members is made in Section 2. The methodology and data are discussed in Section 3. The empirical analysis is presented and discussed in Section 4, and the paper is summarized and concluded with policy recommendations in Section 5.

THE CASE FOR A COMMON CURRENCY OR MONETARY UNION

Genesis of the WAMZ

The ECOWAS was founded on June 10, 1975 but it became functionally operational in January 1977. It consisted of 16 member countries of different economic and political interests, a combined population of 150 million in 1985 in the West African sub-region with a principal objective of achieving economic integration. In the ECOWAS Treaty of 1993, the idea of creating a WAMZ was born, and it was to be established as an economic and monetary union as stipulated in the ECOWAS Treaty of 1993 starting from 20 April 2000. The initial members include The Gambia, Ghana, Guinea, Liberia, Nigeria and Sierra Leone, and they were required to lay the foundation for the establishment of a second single monetary zone after the WAMU, within the framework of the ECOWAS single monetary zone objective by 2004. All the countries except Liberia which was then faced with social and political unrest signed on to be members of the WAMZ.

Members of the WAMZ agreed to adjust their macroeconomic policy to meet convergence criteria which were stipulated as follows:

(a) single digit inflation rate by the year 2000 and 5% by 2003
(b) gross international reserves were to be accumulated to finance at least three months of imports by 2000, and six months of imports by the close of 2003
(c) central banks were to finance at most 10% of the previous year's tax revenue equivalent of budget deficits, and finally
(d) the ratio of budget deficits (net of grants) to GDP must be at most 5% by 2000 and 4% by 2002.

The WAMI with its Headquarters in Accra was also created as an interim institute in January 2001 to lay the foundation for the creation of the West African Central Bank (WACB), and The Stabilization and Cooperation Fund of the WAMZ was set at $100 million.

The WAMZ failed to take off by adopting a single currency, eco, in 2009 after failing to meet the previous deadlines on July 1, 2005 and January 1, 2003 as members failed to meet the convergence criteria. According to reports of the WAMI members' macroeconomic conditions to meet the convergence criteria deteriorated from their achievements in 2002. In 2003, eco was named as the currency for the WAMZ, and the WACB head office was located at Accra, where operations were to begin on July 1, 2005.

It was however, established that the principal reason for the failure of the WAMZ members to meet the convergence criteria in 2003 was due to fiscal dominance, which was caused by the continuous financing of budget deficits by central banks through money printing. But Dornbusch (1997) concludes: "... that the concern with fiscal criteria lacks a basis once an independent central bank with a precise stability mandate and no-bailout provision are in place." The question is, shoud members of the WAMZ adopt the monetarist approach which recommends that members of a regional bloc should first adopt a single currency, and use it as a vehicle to advance trade and economic integration required for a viable single market economy? This is important considering that the EU took 41 years from the commencement of the European common market, and 10 years after the Delor's Report on convergence criteria to adopt the euro. Recent global developments make it incumbent upon the WAMZ members to seriously consider the monetarist approach alternative to adopt the eco (Ghartey, 2005).

The WAMZ market economies

The OCA literature presents a list of criteria for the use of a single currency. These are (1) openness to mutual trade, (2) diversification of economies within the union, (3) mobility of factors of production across the union, (4) correlation of underlying shocks or convergence of business cycles among members, (5) similarities in characteristics, (6) flexibility in setting wages and prices to allow members to respond effectively to external shocks without depending on changes in interest rates and exchange rates, and (7) finally, versatile fiscal institutions to allow net transfers to replace immobile factors of production by ensuring a system of risk-sharing among members.[4] See Mundell (1961), McKinnon (1963), and Kenen (1969). But if indeed the OCA criteria are jointly endogenous, then simply meeting them on the basis of historical data cannot be the only justification for becoming a member of a currency union as was done by the EU. See Frankel (1999) and Frankel and Rose (1998).

The WAMZ members are different from the EU members. They are relatively closed, and their degrees of openness (imports/GDP or exports/GDP) ratios are less than 35 percent in 1995,

4 For a discussion on "New" Theory of Optimum Currency Area, see George S. Tavlas (1993).

and even in 2005. See Table 3.1a. They are very specialized as their degree of trade specialization measured by the Herfindhal index which is defined as the sum of squared of shares of specific export products of each member country is near unity.[5] Thus they have an extremely low level of diversification, with Nigeria reporting about 95 percent of export earnings from petroleum and related products. The rest of the countries' exports earnings are from minerals and agricultural primary products. As a result, the WAMZ members are more likely to be adversely affected by asymmetric shocks, unless of course such shocks are small in size and they can adjust to them rather quickly.

The WAMZ members do not meet the labor mobility criterion of the OCA. Most of the Anglophone economies of ECOWAS are not contiguous as they are separated by the Francophone countries. Additionally, unlike their European counterparts, they do not have any well laid infrastructure like roads to connect them. Unfortunately, we could not estimate gravity models to determine whether distance between any two capitals of a pair of economies within the WAMZ enhance or adversely affects their international trade because of absence of recorded intra trade time series data among members. The only positive effect among the WAMZ members is that with the exception of Guinea they all share a common language which is English.[6]

Prices are not well integrated although a casual view of the degrees of correlation between prices range from 88 percent to 99 percent. The amplitude of inflation over the sample period is 104 percent in Sierra Leone with standard deviations ranging from 8 percent in The Gambia to 26.4 percent in Sierra Leone. The degree of correlation of inflation indicates a high divergence as

---

5 $$H_{it} = \sum_{j=1}^{j=J} (x_{ijt}/X_{it})^2,$$

where x_{ijt} denotes export of SITC subgroup product j in year t for country i, Xit denotes total export products of country i at year t, and it is summed over the entire SITC subgroups. H ranges from zero to unity. A high value of H implies that the country is specialized in few goods, whereas a low value of H implies that the country is well diversified.

6 Guinea is not included in most of the empirical study because of inadequate price data.

most members record either negative or extremely low correlation. It must be noted though that the significance of inflation as an OCA criterion is contentious. Fleming (1971) for instance considers it to be a very useful criterion because of the policy implications of Philips curve, whereas Parkin (1972) does not attribute any usefulness to it.

Mundell (1961) has argued that economies with highly synchronized business cycles as measured by correlation between real GDP are more likely to succeed at adopting a common currency. This criterion appears to be met as the correlation between real GDP of the WAMZ economies ranges from 88 percent for Ghana and The Gambia to 99 percent for Nigeria and Ghana. Thus their real GDP are highly and systematically correlated. Again, one can argue that this is not a very strong OCA criterion as even the nine initial signatories of the EU treaty in Maastricht did not meet such a real growth rates convergence criterion.

Additionally, symmetric correlations of real GDP have conflated information which can be attributed to either an increase in productivity or upsurge in demand due to world-wide boom or both. It is for this reason that Bayoumi and Eichengreen (1992) employed the VAR method in the tradition of Blanchard and Quah (1989) to decompose real GDP into supply shocks. On the other hand, Frankel and Rose (2000) also argue that the formation of a common currency area fosters the degree of economic integration among economies. According to Rose (2000) the international business cycles correlations increase for economies that belong to a common currency area by 10 percent.

Thus we have employed the VECM to estimate correlation between underlying structural shocks of supply, demand and monetary disturbances to determine the viability of forming the WAMZ. We have also employed impulse response functions to measure the size of the underlying shocks and the speed by which these economies adjust to them.

THE MODEL

Convergence test

The unit root test of relative regional real income is done by using the augmented Dickey-Fuller (ADF) test and Philip-Perron test. The augmentation in the ADF test is set to unity because our data set is under sized sample. The ADF test is specified as follows:

$$\Delta yt = \alpha + \beta t + \rho yt\text{-}1 + + \xi t \qquad (1)$$

The PP which is a first order autoregressive process is specified as

$$\Delta yt = \alpha + \beta' t + \rho' yt\text{-}1 + \xi' t \qquad (2)$$

The ADF test corrects for higher order serial correlation by adding lagged differenced terms as explanatory variables. The PP test employs Newey and West dynamic estimates with truncation lags to correct the t-statistic of the coefficient of the lagged endogenous variables in the first order autoregressive process for serial correlation in the error term. The correction is non parametric, and robust to heteroscedasticity and autocorrelation of unknown forms.

The vector error correction model

Bayoumi and Eichengreen (1992) who are the first to employ correlation of shocks to determine the feasibility of OCA criteria for the European countries (EC) employed a vector autoregressive (VAR) model by following Blanchard and Quah (1989) method. They identified the VAR model by imposing restrictions to identify the Choleski decomposition from the following economic theory: (i) demand shocks have positive effect on prices over the long run; (ii) positive effect on both prices and output over the short run; (iii) supply shocks have negative effect on prices; and (iv) a positive effect on output over both short run and long run. They employed the VAR methodology to decompose real GDP and prices into supply and demand shocks.

In this study, we have employed the VECM to decompose real GDP, exchange rates and price levels into underlying supply, demand and monetary shocks, respectively. This approach uses cointegration to identify restrictions in the VAR model. It also allows us to include many variables in the VECM without being hamstrung by limitations associated with finding economic theory to identify restrictions for the corresponding Choleski decomposition.

The basic vector autoregressive model is expressed as

$$D^*(B)X_t = u_t \tag{3}$$

where $D^*(B) = I - D_1B - D_2B^2 - D_3B^3 - \ldots$, $E(u_t) = 0$, $E(u_tu_s') = \Omega \ \forall \ t = s$, $E(u_tu_s') = 0 \ \forall \ t \neq s$, $E(X_tu_s') = 0 \ \forall \ t < s$, and $X = [\Delta y \ \Delta p \ \Delta x]'$ is a 3x1 column vector of observable endogenous variables. The lower case letters in X denote the logarithmic form of the variables and subscript t denotes time period.

The reduced form of equation 1 is

$$X_t = D(B)X_{t-1} + u_t \tag{4}$$

where $D(B) = (I - D^*(B))B^{-1} = D_1 + D_2B + D_3B^2 + \ldots$. The VAR representation of the stochastic vector of variables exists only if the process is invertible, meaning that the elements of the coefficient matrices Di $\rightarrow$ 0 as i $\rightarrow \infty$. The reduced form equation 4 can be consistently estimated by using the Johansen and Juselius (1990) full information maximum likelihood method. The Choleski decomposition of the contemporaneous covariance positive definite matrix Ω is

$$\Omega = P^{-1}P^{-1'} \text{ or } P\Omega P' = I$$

where P and P^{-1} are lower triangular matrix, such that $E(Putut'P') = P\Omega P' = I$. The corresponding dynamic vector moving average (VMA) representation of the reduced form of X_t in equation 4 is written in the form of Wold (1938) decomposition as follows:

$$PX_t = PD(B)X_{t-1} + Pu_t, \tag{5}$$
$$\Rightarrow P(I - D(B)B)Xt = Pu_t$$

Thus $Xt = (I - D(B)B)\text{-}1P\text{-}1et$, where et = Put, and the Wold VMA becomes as follows:

$$X_t = F(B)e_t \tag{6}$$

where $F(B) = (I - D(B)B)^{-1}P^{-1}; F(B) = P^{1} + F_1B + F_2B^2 + \ldots; B^je_t = e_{t-j}, E(e_t) = E(e_te_s') = 0, \forall t \neq s$, and $E(etes') = I, \forall t = s; e_t = [e_{yt}\ e_{pt}\ e_{xt}]'$ is a column vector of unobservable exogenous orthogonal structural innovations which are serially and mutually uncorrelated at leads and lags with a dimension of 3x1, and F(B) is a 3x3 matrix of polynomials in the backshift operator B.

The coefficient matrix of F(B) represents the response of the system to a one standard error innovation in et. A representative element of F(B) is $f_{ij}(B)$, and it shows the response of all future values of xi to a one standard error's one-time current innovations in xj. Thus, $f_{ij}(B)$ is the impulse response function of xi with respect to a shock in xj. From equation 4, the ith element of X at time t+h is $x_{it+h} = \sum_{j=1}\sum_{s=0} f_{ij,s} e_{j,t+h-s}$. Thus, the percentage of the expected h-period-ahead squared prediction error of x_{it} produced by an innovation in x_j is zero if x_i is exogenous. This is the necessary and sufficient condition for x_i to be exogenous with respect to the remaining variables in the system.

The reduced form structural VAR model of equation 4 is recovered in the form of VECM in the tradition of Johansen (1991) and Beveridge-Nelson (1981) decomposition as follows:

$$R(B)X_t = \Delta R^*(B)X_t + R(1)BX_t = R^*(B)\Delta X_t + R(1)X_{t-1} = e_t \quad (7)$$

where, $R(B) = F^{-1}(B)$ and $\Delta R^*(B) = R(B) - R(1)$ which means $R(1) = F^{-1}(1)$.

Thus, equation 7 is the simultaneous-equations system. It captures the VMA representation of the structural equation 6, and its corresponding reduced-form system is

$$Q\alpha' xt\text{-}1 + \varphi(B)\,\Delta x_t = e_t^* \quad (8)$$

The reduced rank (0< q < 3) implies that R(1) can be factorized as $R(1) = Q\alpha'$. Thus, R(1) is a singular matrix and is expressed as a product of two rectangular matrices with full column rank, where Q measures the adjustment speed to close deviations of the errors from equilibrium and α captures the matrix of cointegrating vectors. The common trend's representation of equation 5 was transformed by Johansen's (1991) VECM into equation 6, and its long-run cointegration of the variables were used to restrict and identify the non fundamental representations of the VAR model in the study to give a reasonable or economically acceptable impulse-response functions and vector decomposition (Blanchard and Quah, 1993; Lippi and Reichlin, 1993; Crowder, 1995; Ghartey, 2008).

The resulting level forms of the ordered variables included in the VECM are estimated, and the long-run estimates from the VECM were then used to identify and obtain a more robust impulse response functions and innovation accounts.

The global effect of shocks on the WAMZ members is estimated by including similar macroeconomic variables of the USA in the VECM to test the robustness of the results. The a priori expectation is that a positive correlation in underlying shocks between countries implies that shocks are symmetric, and if the correlations are either negative or insignificant, then the shocks are asymmetric. We have also employed impulse response functions to measure the size of shocks and the speed of adjustment to disturbances because asymmetric shocks are manageable if their sizes are small and countries can adjust to them speedily. Additionally, a highly correlated business cycle will have a positive and highly significant correlation between underlying shocks; and such economies are likely to increase their trade after becoming members of a common currency.

Data

Consumer price index (CPI) for The Gambia and USA ranges from 1961-2008; 1965-2008 for Ghana with 1995 as the base year; 1960-2008 for Nigeria and 1961-2007 for Sierra Leone ranges. The base year of CPI for all the countries is 2005. The CPI of Sierra Leone is collected from Freetown. Gross domestic product (GDP) spans 1964-2007 for the Gambia; 1963-2004 for Ghana; 1960-2006 for Nigeria; 1963-2005 for Sierra Leone; and 1960-2008 for the USA. The WAMZ economies include The Gambia, Ghana, Nigeria and Sierra Leone. We have not included Guinea and Liberia because of paucity of their data. Exchange rates of The Gambia, Guinea, Nigeria, Sierra Leone and the USA span 1960-

2008; and 1970-2007 for Ghana. All exchange rates are defined as national currencies per dollar and are defined as the period's average. The US dollar is defined as dollars per Special Drawing Rights (SDR). The main sources of data are the IMF's *International Financial Statistical (IFS) Yearbook*, various years; 2010 and 2001 IFS Data Browser, and the website of the CIA World Factbook.

DISCUSSION OF ESTIMATED RESULTS

Convergence of economies of WAMZ

The international trade theory posits that convergence is driven by international trade, as factor-price-equalization (FPE) theorem indicates that prices of factors of production such as wages, rents and interests are made equal across countries by free trade. Convergence of economies is defined here as a reduction in the dispersion of real income among countries. We have therefore tested conditional convergence which is defined as convergence that occurs once the determinants of steady-state real income are controlled for economies of the WAMZ, as a first approximation to determine how feasible the WAMZ members meet the OCA criteria.

The correlation coefficients of real income between members are calculated to determine the extent by which they move together. We have also calculated degrees of correlations of their consumer price indices. The assumption here is that economies with high correlations in real incomes and prices can form a monetary union and forego their monetary autonomy as external shocks can then be dealt with by implementing the same monetary and exchange rate policy for those economies. On the other hand, if correlations are either negative and/or small, then economies in regional bloc cannot form a monetary union as a uniform monetary and exchange rate policy will aggravate any external shocks that will affect them. The results in Table 3.1b show a high correlation in prices between members, although their real incomes show low correlations and asymmetric relationship with Sierra Leone.

However, the literature on economic growth and endogenous growth concentrate on real income because exchange rates and prices tend to have conflated information. This is because a small variability of prices and exchange rates between two economies may be due to the fact that either both economies experience similar shocks to their market fundamentals or their factors of production are highly mobile that they swiftly flow from the economy experiencing a fall in prices to the economy where prices are increasing to either equalize or minimize variations in prices and exchange rates between members. For this reason, the behavior of prices does not contain any definite information to assist us to determine symmetry of shocks and speed of adjustment.

Results of convergence in Table 3.1b indicate that correlations of prices between members are very high ranging from 88 to 99 percent (see Cohen and Wyplosz, 1989; Bayoumi and Eichengreen, 1994). However, the results of their growth rates show low and often negative correlation between the WAMZ economies as depicted in Table 3.4. In this case, convergence is defined as a situation where economies with certain common characteristics have their growth rates converging or reverting to a steady state level over time. This means economies converge when shocks to their real incomes are temporary judging by time series analysis.

Results of unit root tests reported in Tables 2 using ADF and PP tests indicate that shocks to real income are temporary for The Gambia, Ghana, Nigeria and Sierra Leone at 0.01 significant levels. The critical values are computed from MacKinnon (1996). Thus it can be concluded that real income results of members of the WAMZ converge, so members will benefit from adopting a common currency and foregoing their monetary autonomy over the long run.

Johansen and Juselius (1991) cointegration results in Tables 3a-b show real incomes and growth in exchange rates of all four members to be cointegrated as judged by both trace and λ_{Max} statistics for both cases with deterministic and deterministic including stochastic trends. Thus confirming that economic growth converge to long run equilibrium levels for all four members. The results for inflation rates show only one cointegrated equations for both cases with deterministic and deterministic including stochastic trends for all four members at 0.05 significant levels.

Additionally, estimates of the long-run restrictions and error-correction terms in Table 3.5 show that with Nigeria as anchor for both inflation and economic growth, and Ghana as anchor for the exchange rates, deviations from equilibrium will be corrected in the long run, although the speed of adjustment is faster for growth in exchange rates and slower for inflation rates.[7] Thus, the results indicate that the four members including the USA share a common trend to the extent that short run departures from equilibrium will be brought back to the long run equilibrium by internal dynamic forces to correct any misalignment just as Darrat and Al-Shamsi (2005) observed for the Gulf region.

Correlation of underlying structural shocks

Bayoumi and Eichengreen (1992) note that if an investigator who is interested in determining symmetry of shocks relies on correlation of real income, he is likely to encounter conflated information similar to what is experienced by relying on prices.[8] This is because an increase in real income can result from either an increase in supply shock (or productivity shock as it is termed in real business cycle theory) or from responses to demand shocks stemming from a world-wide boom or both. Thus a shock to real income is affected by both effects of shocks and responses. They therefore adopted a VAR technique by following Blanchard and Quah's approach to decompose real income and prices into supply shocks, and demand shocks, respectively.

We have followed suit by using a VECM which uses cointegration or long-run equilibrium relationship shown in Table 3.5 as an identifying restriction to decompose real income, exchange rates and prices into supply shocks, demand shocks and monetary shocks. Note that supply shocks are the ideal mechanism for investigating the feasibility of forming a monetary union by a group of economies, as it is less likely to include the effect of macroeconomic policy, unlike demand and monetary shocks which normally include the impact of such implemented macroeconomic policies (Bayoumi and Eichengreen, 1994; Demertzis et al.2000). The general observation is that the minimal the variability of output and prices across a

---

7 A country is chosen as anchor if it yields significant error-correction term that has correct sign and magnitude as predicted from statistics and economics theory.

8 Note that unit root tests which allow the separation of temporary shocks from permanent shocks are one possible method for circumventing the problem of conflated information from real income disturbances (see also Nelson and Plosser, 1982).

region, the better the chances of the regional members succeeding in adopting a common currency and exchange rate regime.

The incidence of shocks on members is examined as a chief determinant of forming a monetary union in the WAMZ. A symmetrically distributed shock in a region will mean that a positive shock can be addressed by monetary contraction for members of the monetary union. However, if shocks are distributed asymmetrically across a region, then the ideal response to such shocks is asymmetric, and members in such a region are best served by maintaining independent monetary autonomy.

Results of standard deviation of shocks affecting the WAMZ in Table 3.4 indicate that the variability in supply and demand shocks are higher than the US, a country that stands as the best example of a monetary union. This suggests that a monetary union may not be best for the WAMZ.

A much detailed analysis from correlations of underlying structural shocks in Table 3.6 indicates asymmetric supply shock correlations between The Gambia and Ghana, and Ghana and Nigeria, and very low and insignificant correlation supply shocks among the rest of the members. Only Ghana and Nigeria reveal a significant demand shock correlation, whereas the correlation of demand shocks between The Gambia and Sierra Leone is low and insignificant. The remaining members exhibit asymmetric demand shock correlations.

The results are extended to include the US to capture global influences in Tables 7-9. This global effect causes deterioration in the supply shock correlations among the WAMZ members. The Gambia and Nigeria show asymmetric supply shock correlations with all the members including the US. Ghana has asymmetric supply shock with The Gambia and Nigeria, while Sierra Leone has asymmetric shock with all the countries except Ghana. In all the cases the supply shock correlation results are low and insignificant.

Only Ghana's demand shock correlations with Nigeria and the US are positive, with the former being significant. The remaining members and the US exhibit asymmetric demand shock correlations among themselves. This suggests clearly that the WAMZ economies are not yet suited to adopt a monetary union.

Monetary shocks which capture monetary disturbances in the region with global effect show a much improved results than the demand shocks. The results of Table 3.8 reveal correlations of monetary shocks among The Gambia, Ghana and Guinea and Sierra Leone to be significant. Nigeria had very low and insignificant monetary shock correlations with all the countries including the US. Guinea and Sierra Leone show a significant correlation with the US. In fact the correlations of monetary shock results are better than results obtained for the East Asian countries (EAC) by Zhang et al. (2004, p.1037).

Relative sizes and speed of adjustment to shocks

The size and speed of estimated structural shocks are calculated from impulse response functions considering that estimated structural shocks have unit variances in the structural VAR. Results of relative sizes of underlying structural shocks of supply and demand of members are measured by five-year responsiveness from a unit innovations on changes in real GDP, and two-year responsiveness from a unit innovations on changes in prices, respectively. The speed of supply shock adjustment is measured by the response after five-year as a share of the long-run effect which is measured by response after a 20-year horizon, and the speed of demand shock adjustment is measured by the response after two-year horizon as a share of the long-run.[9]

The results of sizes and speed of adjustment to shocks including global effects are reported in Table 3.9. We have also included results of the EAC and EC reported in Zhang et al. (2004, p.1040) for comparison. The results show that with respect to the speed and sizes of supply shocks which is the chief determinant for forming a monetary union, apart from Ghana, the rest of the WAMZ economies have larger relative sizes than their corresponding speed of adjustment to supply shocks across members.

Our supply shock result of the US yields the same size as Zhang et al. (2004) for the US. However, our speed of adjustment is faster than Zhang et al. (2004) for the US. Generally, the speed

9 Bayoumi and Eichengreen (1992, p.33) cite the simple measure of the speed of adjustment to shocks as the ratio of the impulse response function in the third-year to its long-run level. A higher ratio indicates a faster speed of adjustment to shocks and a lower ratio shows a slower speed of adjustment to shocks.

of adjustment of supply shocks across members of the WAMZ is comparable with the EAC and EC averages. The only problem is that the sizes of supply shocks of the WAMZ members are relatively larger, with an average supply shock of 9.8 percent compared with the EAC average of 2.1 percent and EC average of 1.1 percent.

The average sizes of demand shocks of the WAMZ members are also slightly larger than the EC average but comparable with the EAC average. The average size of their demand shock is 5.7 percent with average speed of adjustment of 0.898 compared with the average size of 1.8 percent and an average speed of 0.968 for EC, while the EAC average size is 4.6 percent with an average speed of 0.969. The size of demand shock of the US is 1.8 percent with a speed of 1.300. Note that although Ghana's size of demand shock is 1.5 percent which is slightly smaller than the US, its speed of adjustment of 0.189 is extremely slow. Nigeria's size of demand shock is 11.7 percent with a speed of 1.264 which is close to the US speed. Thus, with the US as a yardstick, the efficacy of forming of a common currency and exchange rate system in the WAMZ is doubtful but achievable over the long run. In the short term, the relatively larger sizes of shocks indicate that the WAMZ members will have difficulty in maintaining a fixed exchange rate regime or monetary union.

CONCLUSION

The empirical evidence indicate that the WAMZ members are small but close with degrees of openness below 35 percent; and highly specialized as judged by their Herfindhal indices of near unity, as most of their exports earnings are from agricultural, mineral and petroleum and its related products. Their economies converge as the first differenced forms of their real incomes are stationary which show that shocks to their economies are temporary.

The variability of supply shocks, demand shocks and monetary shocks are relatively high as compared to the US, which suggest that they are not suitable to adopt a common currency and exchange rate system. Correlations of supply shocks among members are either asymmetric or insignificant; correlation of demand shocks between Ghana and Nigeria is significant whereas the rest of members exhibit either low or insignificant or asymmetric shocks.

When the US is included in the study for global effect, the results virtually remain the same, with the exception of the correlation of demand shocks between Ghana and Nigeria which improves significantly. The correlations of monetary shocks among all four members except Nigeria are highly significant. The relative sizes of supply and demand shocks are greater than the respective average in the EAC and EC, but their speed of adjustments to shocks are comparable. In the short term when compared to the US, the WAMZ members do not meet the OCA criteria to qualify them to use a common currency and exchange rate system. But the long run prospect of convergence bode well for some WAMZ members to improve the coordination of their monetary policies, and to deepen their joint financial markets to meet the OCA criteria goal, in their quest for integration.

TABLE 3.1A: SOME IMPORTANT INDICATORS IN 2005

	GAMBIA	GHANA	GUINEA	NIGERIA	S. LEONE
X	201.04 (D, m)	2.642 (C, b)	3.237 (F, m)	4.664 (N, b)	49(02) (L, m)
M	636.12 (D, m)	3.24 (C, b)	3.655 (F, m)	2.813 (N, b)	264(02)(L, m)
GDP	17.327 (D, b)	44.440 (C, b)	11.987 (F, m)	14.735 (N, b)	3057 (L, m)
DOP1(%)	1.16	5.94	27.00	31.66	1.60
DOP2(%)	3.67	7.29	30.49	19.09	8.63
DOP3(%)	4.83	13.24	57.49	50.75	10.24
Δp (%)	14	26.7	12.9	13.8	1
Δy (%)	3	4.7	3	7.1	6.5
BD($m)	-4.01	-249.0	-297.8	-3070.0	-255.0
CAB ($b)	-42	110	-0.252	1.439	-
FRS ($m)	118	1469	191	7128	-
ED ($m)	476 (01)	7398	3250 (01)	31070	1500 (02)
Pop. (m)	1.78	23.89	10.06	149.23	5.13
Area (km^2)	11300	239400	245857	923768	71740

Notes: Data sources are: (i) International Monetary Funds' (IMF) January 2010 and September 2001 CD Database and Browser (ii) The IMF's International Financial Statistics Yearbook, various issues, (iii) The CIA World Fact book which contains estimates and projections from the countries own Finance and Planning Ministry's budget projections and estimates. Figures in parentheses are the dates of the data in question. X denotes exports of goods and services, M is imports of goods and services, GDP is gross domestic output, DOP1 is X/GDP ratio, DOP2 is M/GDP ratio, DPO3 is (X+M)/GDP ratio, p is inflation rates, y is real GDP or economic growth rates, BD is budget deficits, CAB is current account balance, FRS is foreign exchange reserves including gold, ED is external balance, Pop is population, m is millions, b is billions. D is Dalasis, C is Cedis, F is Francs, N is Naira, L is Leone, and $ is US Dollars. (iv) Ghartey (2005).

Table 3.1b: Correlation of Prices and Real GDP

	Gambia	Ghana	Nigeria	Sierra Leone
Gambia	1.000	0.407*	0.652*	-0.214
Ghana	0.882*	1.000	0.499*	-.225
Nigeria	0.916*	0.988*	1.000	-0.035
Sierra Leone	0.923*	0.961*	0.985*	1.000

Note: Upper triangular matrix contains real GDP and lower triangular matrix contains prices. Fisher⊠s variance-stabilizing transformation of estimated correlation coefficient (r) reported in Rodriguez (2006) is used to test the significance levels of correlation coefficients. Z = 0.5ln[(1 + r)/(1 – r)], where z ~ N(0, s^) and s^ ~ (n – 3)-1/2. Thus if n = 28, then s^ = 0.204. The critical value at the 5 percent significant level is absolute value of 0.24. *, ** and *** denotes 0.01, 0.05 and 0.10 significant levels, respectively.

Table 3.2: Unit Roots Tests

		Without Intercept and Trend			
Variables		Level Form		First Difference Form	
Prices	k	ADF	PP	ADF	PP
pga	1	1.694[0.98]	3.244[0.99]	-2.254**[0.02]	-2.114**[0.03]
pgh	1	0.666[0.85]	0.390[0.79]	-1.249[0.19]	-2.972*[0.00]
pni	1	0.148[0.72]	0.837[0.89]	-2.014**[0.04]	-1.896***[0.06]
psl	1	-0.639[0.43]	-0.572[0.46]	-1.610***[0.10]	-2.566*[0.01]
pus	1	1.510[0.96]	4.644[1.00]	-1.326[0.17]	-0.836[0.35]
pgh§	1			-14.65*[0.00]	-17.385*[0.00]
pus§	1			-6.942*[0.00]	-5.418*[0.00]
Real Incomes					
yga	0	1.906[0.98]	2.267[0.99]	-6.702*[0.00]	-6.701*[0.00]
ygh	0	0.505[0.82]	0.505[0.82]	-3.241*[0.00]	-7.776*[0.00]
yni	0	1.816[0.98]	1.775[0.98]	-5.318*[0.00]	-5.267*[0.00]
ysl	0	0.349[0.78]	0.353[0.78]	-6.402*[0.00]	-6.402*[0.00]
yus	0	3.038[0.99]	7.343[1.00]	-3.013*[0.00]	-2.822*[0.00]
Exchange Rates					
xga	1	1.238[0.94]	1.805[0.98]	-4.143*[0.00]	-4.230*[0.00]
xgh	1	0.972[0.91]	1.843[0.98]	-2.577*[0.01]	-2.442**[0.02]
xni	0	1.948[0.99]	1.358[0.95]	-4.804*[0.00]	-4.883*[0.00]
xsl	1	0.615[0.84]	1.366[0.95]	-2.607*[0.01]	-2.389**[0.02]
xus	1	-0.036[0.66]	0.404[0.80]	-4.407*[0.00]	-3.998*[0.00]

		With Intercept			
Variables		Level Form		First Difference Form	
Prices	k	ADF	PP	ADF	PP
pga	1	-0.412[0.90]	-0.041[0.95]	-3.381**[0.02]	-3.318**[0.02]
pgh	1	-0.636[0.85]	-0.586[0.86]	-2.884**[0.05]	-5.543*[0.00]
pni	1	0.222[0.97]	0.999[0.97]	-3.357**[0.02]	-3.209**[0.02]
psl	1	-0.022[0.95]	0.201[0.97]	-3.460**[0.01]	-3.304**[0.02]
pus	1	-1.498[0.53]	-1.02[0.74]	-3.165**[0.03]	-2.279[0.18]
pus§					-5.212*[0.00]
Real Incomes					
yga	0	-0.352[0.91]	-0.232[0.93]	-7.569*[0.00]	-7.261*[0.00]
ygh	0	-0.946[0.76]	-0.930[0.77]	-8.235*[0.00]	-7.892*[0.00]
yni	0	-0.864[0.79]	-0.897[0.78]	-5.658*[0.00]	-5.597*[0.00]
ysl	0	-1.729[0.41]	-1.761[0.39]	-6.333*[0.00]	-6.333*[0.00]
yus	0	-2.393[0.15]	-2.394[0.15]	-4.653*[0.00]	-4.292*[0.00]
Exchange Rates					
xga	1	-0.266[0.92]	0.020[0.95]	-4.569*[0.00]	-4.604*[0.00]
xgh	1	-0.794[0.81]	-0.429[0.89]	-3.480*[0.01]	-3.356**[0.02]
xgu	1	0.214[0.97]	0.189[0.97]	-6.444*[0.00]	-6.444*[0.00]
xni	1	0.636[0.91]	0.362[0.98]	-5.341*[0.00]	-5.350*[0.00]
xsl	1	-0.341[0.91]	0.133[0.96]	-3.154**[0.03]	-3.046**[0.04]
xus	1	-1.372[0.59]	-0.944[0.76]	-4.972*[0.00]	-4.652*[0.00]

Table 3.3a: Johansen and Juselius' Maximum Likelihood Estimation of Cointegration Tests

Hypothesized No. of CE(s)	Eigenvalues	Trace Statistics	MHM p-values	λ_{Max} Statistics	MHM p-values
Cointegration equation of Δyni Δyga Δygh Δysl without deterministic trend					
None	0.504	64.880*	0.00	25.974*	0.03
At most 1	0.415	38.905*	0.00	19.868*	0.02
At most 2	0.236	19.038*	0.00	9.955***	0.08
At most 3	0.218	9.063*	0.00	9.083*	0.00
Cointegration equation of Δpni Δpga Δpgh Δpsl without deterministic trend					
None	0.472	42.677**	0.03	25.585**	0.03
At most 1	0.243	17.092	0.30	11.118	0.37
At most 2	0.119	5.974	0.44	5.090	0.46
At most 3	0.022	0.883	0.40	0.883	0.40
Cointegration equation of Δxni Δxga Δxgh Δxgu Δxsl without deterministic trend					
None	0.744	109.038*	0.00	47.722*	0.00
At most 1	0.571	61.317*	0.00	29.634*	0.01
At most 2	0.461	31.682*	0.00	21.625*	0.01
At most 3	0.198	10.057	0.12	7.710	0.19
At most 4	0.065	2.347	0.15	2.347	0.14

Note: MHM denotes MacKinnon, Haug and Michelis (1999). *, ** and *** denote significant at 0.01, 0.05 and 0.10 levels, respectively.

Table 3.3b: Johansen and Juselius' Maximum Likelihood Estimation of Cointegration Tests With Global Effect

Hypothesized No. of CE(s)	Eigenvalues	Trace Statistics	MHM p-values	λ_{Max} Statistics	MHM p-values
Cointegration equation of Δyni Δyga Δygh Δysl Δyus without deterministic trend					
None	0.569	83.423*	0.00	31.162*	0.04
At most 1	0.453	52.261*	0.00	22.312***	0.09
At most 2	0.409	29.949*	0.01	19.453**	0.03
At most 3	0.226	10.496***	0.10	9.488***	0.09
At most 4	0.027	1.008	0.37	1.008	0.36
Cointegration equation of Δpni Δpga Δpgh Δpsl Δpus without deterministic trend					
None	0.550	71.694*	0.00	31.910**	0.03
At most 1	0.418	39.784**	0.05	21.649	0.10
At most 2	0.272	18.135	0.24	12.719	0.25
At most 3	0.111	5.416	0.51	4.691	0.52
At most 4	0.018	0.725	0.45	0.725	0.45
Cointegration equation of Δxni Δxga Δxgh Δxgu Δxsl Δxus without deterministic trend					
None	0.759	142.709*	0.00	49.833*	0.00
At most 1	0.625	92.876*	0.00	34.345*	0.01
At most 2	0.534	58.531*	0.00	26.701**	0.02
At most 3	0.438	31.829*	0.00	20.167**	0.02
At most 4	0.231	11.662***	0.06	9.213	0.11
At most 5	0.067	2.449	0.14	2.449	0.14

Table 3.4: Standard Deviation and Correlation of Inflation, Economic Growth and Depreciation

	Economic Growth		Inflation		Depreciation	
Country	Std. Dev.*	Corr.**	Std. Dev.	Corr.	Std. Dev.	Corr.
Gambia	0.18	-0.01(**0.15**)	0.08	0.01(**1.00**)	0.13	-0.05(**1.00**)
Ghana	0.15	-0.16(**0.12**)	0.22	0.32(**0.14**)	0.32	-0.07(**0.33**)
Nigeria	0.16	-0.30(**1.00**)	0.13	-0.04(**-0.01**)	0.27	0.17(**0.27**)
Sierra Leone	0.17	-0.02(**0.00**)	0.26	-0.13(**0.47**)	0.28	0.24(**0.46**)
USA	0.02	1.00(**-0.30**)	0.03	1.00(**0.01**)	0.04	1.00(**-0.05**)

Notes: Bold face figures represent correlation calculations. Economic growth is measured by the real GDP. *Std. Dev. = Standard Deviation. **Corr. = Correlation. See Notes in Table 3.1b.

Table 3.5: Estimates of Long-run Restrictions

	Economic Growth (Δyt), (1968-2004)	Inflation (Δpt), (1968-2007)	Depreciation (Δxt), (1973-2007)
Gambia	2.217**[2.855]	0.505[1.400]	0.168[0.407]
Ghana	0.782[1.265]	-0.661*[4.765]	1.000
Nigeria	1.000	1.000	0.095[0.459]
Sierra Leone	-1.360*[3.193]	-0.253**[2.242]	-0.164[0.852]
Guinea		-0.978*[5.808]	
USA	-11.917*[4.126]	4.582*[4.968]	2.908**[2.966]
C	0.189	-0.194	-0.130
Error-correction Terms(t-1)	-0.317*[3.565]	-0.282**[2.117]	-0.340*[2.222]

Notes: T-ratios are reported in square brackets. See the Note in Table 3.1b.

Table 3.6: Correlation of Structural Shocks between WAMZ Members

Supply Shocks				
	Gambia	Ghana	Nigeria	Sierra Leone
Gambia	1.000			
Ghana	-0.087	1.000		
Nigeria	0.198	-0.006	1.000	
Sierra Leone	0.079	0.063	0.156	1.000
Demand Shocks				
	Gambia	Ghana	Nigeria	Sierra Leone
Gambia	1.000			
Ghana	-0.018	1.000		
Nigeria	-0.169	0.321*	1.000	
Sierra Leone	0.159	-0.171	-0.122	1.000

Note: See Notes in Table 3.1b.

Table 3.7: Correlation of Structural Shocks between WAMZ Members and Global Effects

Supply Shocks, 1968-2004					
	Gambia	Ghana	Nigeria	Sierra Leone	USA
Gambia	1.000				
Ghana	-0.245	1.000			
Nigeria	-0.066	-0.187	1.000		
Sierra Leone	-0.002	0.116	-0.140	1.000	
USA	0.102	-0.155	-0.027	0.067	1.000

DEMAND SHOCKS, 1968-2007					
	Gambia	Ghana	Nigeria	Sierra Leone	USA
Gambia	1.000				
Ghana	-0.093	1.000			
Nigeria	-0.097	0.371*	1.000		
Sierra Leone	0.115	-0.354	-0.199	1.000	
USA	-0.253	0.217***	-0.181	-0.012	1.000

Note: See the Note in Table 3.1b.

TABLE 3.8: CORRELATION OF MONETARY SHOCKS BETWEEN WAMZ MEMBERS AND GLOBAL EFFECTS, 1973-2007

	GAMBIA	GHANA	GUINEA	NIGERIA	SIERRA LEONE	USA
Gambia	1.000					
Ghana	0.548*	1.000				
Guinea	0.526*	0.535*	1.000			
Nigeria	0.019	0.009	0.095	1.000		
Sierra Leone	0.252**	0.444*	0.323*	-0.058	1.000	
USA	-0.047	0.122	0.482*	0.060	0.307*	1.000

Note: See the Note in Table 3.1b.

TABLE 3.9: SIZES AND SPEED OF ADJUSTMENT TO SHOCKS ACROSS WAMZ MEMBERS AND GLOBAL EFFECTS

	SUPPLY SHOCK		DEMAND SHOCK	
	SIZE	SPEED	SIZE	SPEED
Gambia	0.114	0.982	0.057	0.961
Ghana	0.078	0.995	0.015	0.189
Nigeria	0.107	0.998	0.119	1.264
Sierra Leone	0.155	1.032	0.077	0.775
USA	0.010	1.094	0.018	1.300
Average	0.093	1.020	0.057	0.898
EC Average	**0.011**	**0.931**	**0.018**	**0.968**
Germany	**0.015**	**1.002**	**0.016**	**0.992**
EAC Average	**0.021**	**0.977**	**0.046**	**0.969**
Japan	**0.011**	**0.871**	**0.056**	**0.980**
USA	**0.009**	**0.972**	**0.029**	**0.994**

Note: Speed of supply shock is measured as impulse response at a five-year shock as a ratio of long-run (20-year) effect, and demand shock is measured as impulse response at a two-year shock as a ratio of long-run (20-year) effect. Bold figures are reported from Zhang et al. (2004, p. 1040) Table 3.7 for comparison. EAC denotes East Asian countries and EC denotes European countries.

References

Bayoumi, T. and B. Eichengreen (1992), "Shocking Aspects of European Monetary Unification," *NBER*, Working Paper No. 3949: 1-39.

_____ and _____ (1994), "One Money or Many? Analyzing the Prospects for Monetary Unification in Various Parts of the World," *Princeton Studies in International Finance*, 76.

Beveridge, S. and Nelson, C.R. (1981), "A New Approach to Decomposition of Economic Time Series into Permanent and Transitory Components with Particular Attention to Measurement of the "Business Cycle'," *Journal of Monetary Economics*, March, 7, 151-174.

Blanchard, O.J. and D. Quah (1989), "The Dynamic Effects of Aggergate Supply and Demand Disturbances," *American Economics Review*, 79: 655-673.

Blanchard, O.J. and Quah, D. (1993), "The Dynamic Effects of Aggregate Demand and Supply Disturbances: Reply," *American Economic Review*, 83(3), 653-658

Cohen, D. and C. Wyplosz (1989), "The European Monetary Union: An Agnostic Evaluation," *CEPR*, Discussion Paper No. 306.

Crowder, W.J. (1995), "Effects of Aggregate Demand and Supply Disturbances: Another Look," *Economic Letters*, 49: 231-237.

Darrat, A.F. and Al-Shamsi, F.S. (2005), "On the Path of Integration in the Gulf Region," *Applied Economics*, 37: 1055-1062.

Demertzis, M., A.H. Hallet and O. Rummel (2000), "Is the European Union a National Currency Area, or is it held together by Policy Makers?" *Weltwirtschaftliches Archiv*, 135: 657-679.

Dickey, R.A. and W.A. Fuller, (1979), "Distribution of the Estimators for Autoregressive Time Series with a Unit Root," *Journal of the American Statistical Association*, 74: 312-336.

Dornbusch, R. (1997), "Fiscal Aspects of Monetary Integration," *American Economic Review*, 87 (2): 221-223.

Fleming, J.A. (1971), "On Exchange Rate Unification," *Economic Journal*, 81: 467-488.

Frankel, J.A. (1999), "No Single Currency Regime is Right for all Countries or at all Times," *NBER*, Working Paper 7338, September.

_____ and A.K. Rose, (2000), "Estimating the Effect of Currency Unions on Trade and Output," *NBER*, Working Paper 7857, August.

_____ and _____ (1998), "The Endogeneity of Optimum Currency Area Criteria," *Economic Journal*, 108: 1009-1025.

Ghartey, E.E. (2008), "Is the Caribbean Community an Optimum Currency Area?" *Economic Studies of International Development*, 8-1: 5-36.

_____. (2005), *A Common Currency and Exchange Rate System for the West African Monetary Zone: Is the Coronation Approach Feasible?* IEA Monograph 7.

Johansen, S. (1991), "Statistical Analysis of Cointegration Vectors," *Long-run Economic Relationships*, R.F. Engle and C.W.J. Granger, (editors), (Oxford: Oxford University Press), 133-152.

______ and Juselius, K. (1990), "The Full Information Maximum Likelihood Procedure for Inference on Cointegration – with Applications to the Demand for Money," *Oxford Bulletin of Economics and Statistics*, 52, 169-210.

Kenen, P.B. (1969), "The Theory of Optimum Currency Areas: An Eclectic View," in *Monetary Problems of the International Economy*, R.A. Mundell and A.K. Swoboda (editors) (Chicago: University of Chicago Press): 41-60.

Kwan, C.H. (1998), "The Theory of Optimum Currency Areas and the Possibility of Forming a Yen Bloc in Asia," *Journal of Asian Economics*, 9: 555-580.

Lippi, M. and L. Reichlin (1993), "The Dynamic Effects of Aggregate Demand and Supply Disturbances: Comment," *American Economic Review*, 83 (3): 644-652.

MacKinnon, J.G. (1996), "Numerical Distribution Functions for Unit Root and Cointegration Tests," *Journal of Applied Econometrics*, 11: 601-618.

MacKinnon, J.G. (1999), "Numerical Distribution Functions of Likelihood Ratio Tests for Cointegration," *Journal of Applied Econometrics*, 14 (5): 563-577.

McKinnon, R.I. (1963), "Optimum Currency Areas," American Economic Review, 53: 717-725.

Mundell, R.A. (1961), "Theory of Optimum Currency Areas," *American Economic Review*, 51: 657-665. Nelson, C.R. and Plosser, C.I. (1982), "Trends and Random Walks in Macroeconomic Time Series: Some Evidence and Implications," *Journal of Monetary Economics*, 10: 139-162.

Parkin, M. (1972), "An overwhelming Case for European Monetary Union," *Banker*, 122: 1139-1142.

Phillips, P.C.B. and P. Perron (1988), "Testing for a Unit Root in Time Series Regression," *Biometrika*, 75: 335-346.

Rodriguez, R.N. (2006), "Correlation," *Encyclopedia of Statistical Sciences*, Wiley-Inter-Science, 2: 1375-1385.

Rose, A.K. (2000), "One Money One Market," *Economic Policy*, 15-30: 7-46.

______ and C. Engel (2000), "Currency Union and International Integration," *NBER*, Working Paper 7872, September.

Tavlas, G.S. (1993), "The "New' Theory of Optimum Currency Areas," *World Economy*, 16: 663-685.

_____ (1997), "The International use of the Dollar: An Optimum Currency Area Perspective," *The World Economy*, 20: 709-747.

Zhang, Z., K. Sato and M. McAleer (2004), "Is a Monetary Union Feasible for East Asia?" *Applied Economics*, 36: 1031-1043.

Wold, H. (1938), *A Study in the Analysis of Stationary Time Series*, (Uppsala, Sweden: Almqvist and Wiksell).

Chapter 4

L'UEMOA À 15 ANS: BILAN ET STRATÉGIES FUTURES

Diery Seck

INTRODUCTION

L'Union économique et monétaire ouest-africaine (UEMOA) a été créée en janvier 1994 pour suppléer à l'Union monétaire ouest-africaine (UMOA) et servir de cadre de formulation et de mise en œuvre des politiques de développement dans la zone franc de l'Afrique de l'Ouest, à la suite de la dévaluation du Franc CFA. Les conditions économiques et sociales qui ont mené à sa création peuvent succinctement se résumer comme suit. Bien que la zone UMOA ait enregistré un taux moyen de croissance du PIB supérieur à celui des pays africains au sud du Sahara de 1970 à 1985, sa situation s'est graduellement détériorée entre 1985 et 1993 du fait de la détérioration des termes de l'échange qui ont baissé de 40% durant cette période. La baisse du Dollar par rapport au Franc Français auquel le Franc CFA était arrimé par une parité fixe avait sensiblement réduit la compétitivité des exportations de la Zone. En outre, les cours du café et du cacao avaient continué de s'effondrer, creusant les déficits des balances commerciales des pays membres et affectant leurs réserves de change.

La masse salariale du secteur public se révéla particulièrement élevée face au déficit budgétaire croissant et eut des répercussions négatives sur la performance du secteur privé confronté à une forte imposition, des arriérés considérables de l'Etat et un alignement onéreux de ses grilles salariales sur celles, assez élevées, de l'Administration publique. Il s'en suivit que, malgré un taux d'inflation modéré, la situation monétaire empira rapidement du fait de la fuite des capitaux et de la monétisation des déficits budgétaires des Etats qui contournaient les plafonds statutaires de préfinancement de la Banque Centrale des Etats de l'Afrique de l'Ouest (BCEAO), par le recours au crédit des banques commerciales que refinancait l'Autorité monétaire. En conséquence, la discipline budgétaire se relâchât pour amoindrir les tensions sociales et aggrava l'éviction des entreprises privées du marché du crédit affectant ainsi l'investissement et la production. Le cercle vicieux s'était donc installé et appelait des mesures radicales.

Compte tenu de la faible capacité des Etats à mobiliser davantage de recettes budgétaires, de l'érosion du taux de change effectif réel de la zone, de l'inefficacité des programmes d'assistance des Institutions de Bretton Woods et de la rigidité des salaires sur le marché formel du travail, le changement de parité du Franc CFA s'imposa comme une mesure inévitable qu'il fallait accompagner de reformes audacieuses pour prévenir les grands déséquilibres intérieurs et extérieurs de la décennie précédente.

L'UEMOA fut créée comme cadre adéquat pour la conception et l'exécution des réformes et initiatives propres à restaurer les équilibres macro-économiques des pays de la Zone, asseoir la crédibilité de la monnaie, relancer la croissance économique par l'investissement privé, l'intensification du commerce intra-zone et le retour à la discipline budgétaire. La plus grande intégration de la Zone que visait le nouveau train de mesures avait pour but ultime l'amélioration des conditions de vie de ses résidents. Beaucoup de ces mesures on été mises en œuvre tant au niveau communautaire que national avec des résultats variés et l'objet de la présente étude est d'en faire le bilan, tirer les leçons les plus importantes et dégager les perspectives d'avenir qui doivent gouverner à l'action future de l'UEMOA.

CONDITIONS NÉCESSAIRES AU SUCCÈS DE L'UNION

ARRANGEMENTS MONÉTAIRES ET ÉCONOMIQUES NÉCESSAIRES

Au vu des textes qui régissent l'UEMOA, notamment les critères de convergence de premier rang, le caractère monétaire du projet semble dominant, les aspects économiques venant renforcer ce dernier. Aussi, il convient d'étudier, à la lumière des expériences passées, les facteurs qui contribuent à la réussite des unions monétaires. Quatre grandes leçons se dégagent.[1] Premièrement, le succès d'une union monétaire dépend avant tout de la volonté de ses membres de renoncer de manière irrévocable à la souveraineté monétaire et à tout usage des instruments de politique monétaire et de change, et de la création d'une institution disposant du pouvoir exclusif de concevoir et d'appliquer la politique monétaire et de change. En outre, l'union doit avoir une seule monnaie et, s'il y'en a une autre, celle-ci doit avoir un taux de change nominal fixe et immuable vis-à-vis de la monnaie principale et une convertibilité libre et sans limite de telle sorte que les deux monnaies soient des substituts parfaits.

Deuxièmement, l'Autorité monétaire doit pouvoir prévenir, sans pression et sans possibilité de contournement de la part de ses membres, toute monétisation de leurs déficits budgétaires, ce qui est facilité si elle dispose d'un droit de regard sur le niveau d'expansion budgétaire et donc d'une certaine capacité à dialoguer avec ses membres. En effet, il est indispensable que, dans sa politique de défense de la monnaie, elle puisse juguler les tendances inflationnistes qui résulteraient d'un recours excessif à la création monétaire par un emprunt direct auprès de l'Autorité monétaire ou indirect auprès des banques commerciales refinancé par celle-ci. En troisième lieu, la réussite d'une union monétaire peut dépendre de son organisation autour d'une économie forte et stable ou simplement de la monnaie de celle-ci, qu'il s'agisse d'une parité fixée officiellement ou d'une parité à laquelle ses membres adhèrent librement mais respectent scrupuleusement.[2] Cet arrangement permet

---

1 Voir Masson et Patillo, 2001.

2 La parité fixe officielle est choisie par l'UEMOA, la Communauté économique et monétaire de l'Afrique centrale (CEMAC) et la Zone Euro. L'UEMOA et la CEMAC ont le Franc CFA qui était arrimé au Franc Français et maintenant à l'Euro alors que l'Euro s'est organisé autour de la Bundesbank et du Mark allemand.

aux membres de l'union de bénéficier d'une discipline qui leur est imposée de l'extérieur car la stabilité monétaire s'appuie sur la discipline budgétaire d'une économie avancée peu susceptible d'absence de discipline budgétaire, donc maîtrisant l'inflation. Finalement, une union monétaire peut réussir sans produire ou être facilitée par une plus grande intégration commerciale ou institutionnelle de ses membres. Pour atteindre des objectifs communs autres que monétaires, l'union peut avoir besoin d'initier des réformes complémentaires en harmonie avec les instruments de politique monétaire et ayant leur propre ambition et programme de mise en œuvre.

La réussite d'une union économique et monétaire repose sur un cadre institutionnel adéquat dont les règles de fonctionnement renforcent l'efficacité de son action. Cependant, elle dépend également de la maîtrise des mécanismes à travers lesquels l'impact positif de l'effort d'intégration doit être canalisé. Six étalons permettent de mesurer les gains potentiels qui pourraient résulter de l'union.

Augmentation du commerce intra-zone

L'intensification des échanges commerciaux au sein de la zone intégrée bénéficie à ses agents économiques et peut stimuler l'investissement privé, créer des économies d'échelle et parfois désenclaver des régions qui se trouvent sur les principaux axes de commerce intérieur. Le gain résultant d'un commerce intra-zone accru dépend de la complémentarité des productions nationales, de la fluidité du transport des biens et des personnes à travers le territoire de l'union et de l'existence de moyens de paiement rapides et fiables ainsi que d'un cadre juridique harmonisé.

Faible corrélation des effets des chocs sur les économies des membres

Qu'il s'agisse de chocs externes tels que les changements des prix mondiaux de certains produits, ou la variation des taux d'intérêt, des taux de change nominaux ou du niveau de l'activité économique mondiale ou alors de chocs internes, les membres de l'union disposent d'une meilleure protection si la structure de leurs économies respectives sauvegarde certains quand d'autres sont affectés de telle sorte que l'effet agrégé est amoindri.

Mobilité de la main d'œuvre au sein de l'union

Le processus de convergence des taux de rentabilité des investissements privés, des taux de chômage et de croissance économique entre les membres de l'union est d'autant plus facilité que la main d'œuvre circule librement sur le territoire. L'absence de barrières aux frontières intérieures de l'union, la liberté de résidence et d'acquisition de biens mobiliers et immobiliers, l'égalité de traitement fiscal et la reconnaissance des diplômes et certifications professionnelles constituent des facteurs favorables à la mobilité de la main d'œuvre.

Compétence budgétaire de l'union et solidarité des membres

Une union qui dispose de la capacité budgétaire d'aider ses membres à accélérer la convergence économique et à faire face aux chocs est d'un grand apport à ceux-ci. Cela suppose un accord total sur les formules de calcul des interventions d'assistance, l'absence de comportement de hasard moral des membres et d'un membre dont la satisfaction des besoins éventuels ruinerait le fonds de solidarité. Enfin cela requiert aussi une solidarité constante entre les membres, même en cas de chocs simultanés. L'octroi d'une compétence budgétaire à l'union constitue un transfert de souveraineté budgétaire qui, même limité et circonscrit à des cas bien identifiés, revêt un caractère symbolique important dans l'expression de l'engagement des membres à avoir un avenir commun.

Irréversibilité unilatérale des arrangements communautaires

La possibilité qu'aurait un membre de l'union d'influer sur la conduite de la politique monétaire ou celle de l'Autorité monétaire d'accommoder unilatéralement l'expansion budgétaire de ses membres réduirait sensiblement l'efficacité de l'arrangement communautaire et menacerait la viabilité à long terme de celui-ci. Tant au plan de la perception que de la réalité, les membres de l'union ainsi que le secteur privé doivent avoir la conviction que l'autorité monétaire a les mains liées et que l'arrangement communautaire ne peut souffrir d'aucune exception afin que la politique monétaire de la Banque centrale ne puisse être tributaire de la politique budgétaire des Etats, notamment par le biais de la monétisation non statutaire des déficits de ceux-ci.

Adhésion des membres aux critères de convergence nominale

L'utilisation consacrée de critères de convergence strictement observés par les membres de l'union constitue une condition majeure à l'existence d'une institution unique chargée de la politique monétaire et de change ainsi qu'à l'avènement d'une monnaie commune viable sur le territoire communautaire. L'enjeu sous-jacent est d'amener des économies différentes quant à leurs structures, tailles, performances, atouts, défis et histoires à observer ces critères et à s'y tenir durablement et en dépit des chocs qui ne manquent pas de les affecter de manière différenciée. La tache est encore plus difficile en l'absence de mécanismes communautaires d'assistance qui sont activés quand un choc important touche une partie des membres.

Le dispositif institutionnel de l'UEMOA et son fonctionnement

Cadre institutionnel de l'UEMOA

Par traité signé le 10 janvier 1994, et entré en vigueur le 1er août 1994, le Bénin, le Burkina Faso, la Côte d'Ivoire, le Mali, le Niger, le Sénégal et le Togo ont créé l'UEMOA pour compléter l'UMOA qui la précédait. Les objectifs de l'UEMOA ont été formulés comme suit:[3]

a) renforcer la compétitivité des activités économiques et financières des Etats membres dans le cadre d'un marché ouvert et concurrentiel et d'un environnement juridique rationalisé et harmonisé;

b) assurer la convergence des performances et des politiques économiques des Etats membres par l'institution d'une procédure de surveillance multilatérale;

c) créer entre les Etats membres un marché commun basé sur la libre circulation des personnes, des biens, des services, des capitaux et le droit d'établissement des personnes exerçant une activité indépendante ou salariée, ainsi que sur un tarif extérieur commun et une politique commerciale commune;

d) instituer une coordination des politiques sectorielles nationales, par la mise en œuvre d'actions communes et

3 La Guinée Bissau est devenue membre de l'Union le 2 mai 1997.

éventuellement de politiques communes notamment dans les domaines suivants : ressources humaines, aménagement du territoire, transport et télécommunications, environnement, agriculture, énergie, industrie et mines;

e) harmoniser, dans la mesure nécessaire au bon fonctionnement du marché, les législations des Etats membres et particulièrement le régime de la fiscalité.

Pour son fonctionnement l'Union s'est dotée des organes suivants:

- La Conférences des Chefs d'Etat et de gouvernement
- Le Conseil de Ministres
- La Commission
- La Cour de justice
- La Cour des comptes.

En outre la Banque Centrale des Etats d'Afrique de l'Ouest (BCEAO) et la Banque Ouest-Africaine de Développement (BOAD) constituent des institutions spécialisées de l'UEMOA, la première remplissant les fonctions de banque centrale et la seconde de banque sous-régionale de développement. Le Comité Interparlementaire et la Chambre consulaire régionale complètent le dispositif institutionnel de l'UEMOA. Tous les organes de l'Union fonctionnent depuis 1998.

CRITÈRES DE CONVERGENCE

En 1999, les membres de l'UEMOA adoptèrent le Pacte de convergence, de stabilité, de croissance et de solidarité qui fut amendé en 2003 et en 2009. En vertu de la version actuelle du Pacte, l'Union établit des critères de convergence qui doivent être observés par tous ses membres.

Critères de premier rang:

- Ratio du solde budgétaire de base rapporté au Produit intérieur brut (PIB) nominal supérieur ou égal à 0%.
- Taux d'inflation annuel moyen de 3% par an au maximum.

- Ratio de l'encours de la dette intérieure et extérieure rapporté au PIB nominal n'excédant pas 70%.
- Pour les arriérés de paiement intérieurs et extérieurs, aucune accumulation n'est permise sur la gestion de la période courante.

Critères de second rang:

- Ratio de la masse salariale rapporté aux recettes fiscales n'excède pas 35%.
- Ratio des investissements sur ressources intérieures rapporté aux recettes fiscales d'au moins 20%.
- Ratio du solde extérieur courant hors dons rapporté au PIB nominal d'au moins -5%
- Ratio des recettes fiscales rapporté au PIB d'au moins 17%.

Dispositions complémentaires de l'Union

La BCEAO et la BOAD agissent au sein de l'UEMOA, en tant qu'institutions spécialisées autonomes, respectivement comme Autorité monétaire et banque d'investissement. Dans le but d'atteindre ses objectifs, l'Union a entrepris des actions et adopté des mesures qui peuvent être succinctement résumées comme suit. Au plan de l'harmonisation des législations nationales elle a mis en œuvre le Système Comptable Ouest-africain (SYSCOA), la nomenclature budgétaire de l'Etat ainsi que le Plan comptable de l'Etat. Elle a aussi harmonisé la législation en matière de Taxe à la Valeur Ajoutée (TVA) et créé la Bourse Régionale des Valeurs Mobilières (BRVM). L'institution des Comités nationaux de politique économique et l'adoption de l'Indice harmonisé des prix à la consommation (IHPC) sont les principales actions relatives à la surveillance multilatérale des politiques macroéconomiques.

Dans le cadre de ses efforts visant à créer le marché commun, l'Union a procédé à la levée des barrières non tarifaires et mis en place la libre circulation, en toute franchise de droits et taxes, des produits du cru et de l'artisanat. En outre, elle a réduit progressivement les tarifs douaniers des produits industriels originaires non agréés et accompli le désarmement tarifaire intégral de 100% des produits industriels originaires agréés. Elle a aussi adopté une législation communautaire de la concurrence. Le Tarif extérieur commun (TEC) a été mis en place et assorti d'un droit de douane maximum de 20% auquel s'ajoutent une Redevance statistique de 1% et un Prélèvement communautaire de solidarité de 1%. Des politiques sectorielles ont été adoptées dans les domaines suivants : énergie, industrie, mines, agriculture, environnement, mer, télécommunications, transport routier, transport aérien, enseignement et recherche scientifique, santé, femme et emploi. Au titre du financement du développement, l'UEMOA a mis en place le Fonds d'aide à l'intégration régionale (FAIR) et le Programme d'intervention d'assistance aux pays membres.

Analyse du dispositif institutionnel de l'UEMOA

A sa naissance, l'UEMOA a amplement bénéficié de l'expérience de l'UMOA qui l'avait précédée notamment en matière de rôle et de prérogatives de la Banque centrale, de coopération entre les Etats membres, de la politique monétaire sous-régionale et de la supervision bancaire. Ces acquis ont été réactualisés à l'avènement de l'UEMOA sans aucune remise en cause significative et ont été complétés par les nouveaux arrangements économiques qui venaient renforcer l'Union. A la lumière de ses 15 années d'expérience, l'Union peut être considérée comme un succès dans trois de ses quatre volets institutionnels. En effet, elle a su s'assurer de l'engagement de ses membres à déléguer leur souveraineté monétaire pleine et entière au profit d'une banque centrale, la BCEAO, dont les prérogatives, bien que supervisées par l'autorité politique des Etats, sont exercées en toute autonomie et sans pression particulière par celle-ci, rehaussant de ce fait sa crédibilité, donc celle de la monnaie. La politique monétaire et la politique de change sont pratiquées sans partage par la BCEAO et seul le Franc CFA a cours légal sur le territoire de l'Union et n'est concurrencé par aucune autre monnaie.

L'Autorité monétaire a, en outre, été dotée de la capacité de prévenir les pressions inflationnistes qui pourraient résulter d'une expansion budgétaire des Etats incontrôlée et monétisée par le truchement de l'accommodement monétaire. La tendance grandissante des Etats membres à chercher à financer leur déficit budgétaire sur le marché financier de la BRVM par voie d'emprunt obligataire constitue un mécanisme de marché qui amplifie la crédibilité institutionnelle de la BCEAO. Enfin l'arrimage du Franc CFA à l'Euro et la garantie de sa convertibilité assurée par le Trésor français renforcent la solidité de l'Union car encourageant les agents économiques à transiger dans leur monnaie et à la détenir sans crainte de perte de sa valeur.

Cependant, le succès de l'Union a été moins retentissant dans ses aspects économiques plutôt que monétaires du fait du caractère plus récent de cette dimension dans l'arrangement communautaire et de la prépondérance nationale dans la politique budgétaire, outil de prédilection de la politique économique. Bien qu'un nombre important d'instruments juridiques et d'outils d'harmonisation aient été édictés en vue de faciliter la pratique des affaires ou l'uniformisation des normes, l'absence de compétence budgétaire de l'Union a fait de la politique économique le parent pauvre de l'UEMOA au regard de l'envergure de sa dimension monétaire. Cette situation institutionnelle n'est pas sans conséquence sur les perspectives à long terme du projet communautaire et donc de sa réussite finale.

A présent, l'analyse va porter sur le degré d'adéquation des canaux par lesquels les gains communautaires potentiels peuvent se concrétiser. Il s'agit de l'augmentation du commerce intra-zone, de la corrélation des effets des chocs sur les économies des membres, de la mobilité de la main-d'œuvre, de l'étendue des ressources fiscales de l'Union qui appuient la solidarité de ses membres, de l'irréversibilité unilatérale des arrangements communautaires et de l'adhésion des membres aux critères de convergence.

Comme l'indique le Tableau 4.1, les exportation intra-zone des grands pays de l'Union – Côte d'Ivoire, Sénégal et Bénin- ont fortement augmenté pendant la période 1996 – 2006. A l'opposé, les pays enclavés que sont le Burkina Faso, le Mali et le Niger ont connu des exportations intra-communautaires dont la croissance a été plus modeste et plus volatile. Dans l'ensemble, l'UEMOA a augmenté son commerce transfrontalier, renforçant le rôle des états côtiers en tant que fournisseurs des membres privés d'accès à la mer et donc intégrant davantage l'ensemble de l'Union à un monde plus globalisé.

TABLEAU 4.1. EXPORTATIONS INTRA-COMMUNAUTAIRES DES PAYS DE L'UEMOA, EN MILLIONS DE FRANCS CFA

	1996	1997	1998	1999	2000	2001
Bénin	4,140	3,782	4,580	5,626	7,542	7,259
Burkina Faso	13,665	16,695	22,382	39,686	21,214	23,928
Côte d'Ivoire	249,742	311,584	344,837	391,308	422,590	406,341
Mali	49,426	37,592	45,192	26,817	38,769	15,630
Niger	9,127	7,108	8,932	8,045	7,975	3,783
Sénégal	53,212	60,047	64,865	70,676	61,304	81,501
Togo	3,766	4,016	5,723	10,585	12,677	42,598
	2002	**2003**	**2004**	**2005**	**2006**	
Bénin	6,036	8,722	25,291	21,136	27,648	
Burkina Faso	20,462	112,204	128,731	99,028	5,168	
Côte d'Ivoire	390,079	320,789	349,930	416,961	455,530	
Mali	37,910	18,620	42,376	52,357	39,294	
Niger	7,374	3,519	15,527	8,344	6,371	
Sénégal	121,416	132,640	162,360	179,463	198,093	
Togo	57,356	105,749	90,907	78,377	96,689	

Source: Commission de l'UEMOA

Les instruments d'intégration communautaire tels que l'Organisation pour l'Harmonisation du Droit des Affaires en Afrique (OHADA), le Système Comptable Ouest Africain (SYSCOA), le Tarif Extérieur Commun (TEC), le programme commun du transport routier et le programme commun du transport aérien jouent un rôle important dans l'expansion du commerce intra-zone. Cependant l'Union continue de subir les effets néfastes des barrages routiers intempestifs qui retardent l'acheminent des marchandises et impose un cout économique supplémentaire.

Il est généralement admis qu'une croissance économique saine des pays en voie de développement est basée sur les exportations. Donc, tout choc qui compromet les exportations peut entraver la croissance économique. Un des intérêts particuliers d'une union économique réside dans l'assurance implicite qui résulte d'une faible corrélation des impacts des chocs sur les exportations des membres. La matrice de corrélation des taux de croissance des exportations des Etats membres de l'UEMOA qui figure au Tableau 4.2 offre une image contrastée. Les deux plus fortes économies – Côte d'Ivoire et Sénégal – ont la plus forte corrélation, soit 0.599. Les économies les plus faibles ont des coefficients de corrélation faibles ou négatifs, ce qui semble indiquer leur plus grande insensibilité aux chocs externes ainsi qu'une meilleure propension à s'assurer mutuellement.

Dans son ensemble la matrice de corrélation souligne le gain significatif qui peut résulter de l'Union du fait de la mutualisation des risques liés à l'impact des chocs sur les économies des membres. Il faut tout de même noter que l'UEMOA ne s'est pas encore dotée d'un fonds de garantie des exportations de ses membres ou d'un instrument quelconque de compensation de baisse significative de leurs recettes d'exportation. En outre, le Prélèvement communautaire de solidarité qui s'élève à 1% des importations non communautaires peut amplifier le revers économique d'un Etat membre si celui-ci augmente ses importations non communautaires pour combler un déficit de production passager.

Tableau 4.2. Matrice de corrélation des taux de croissance des exportations FOB des pays de l'UEMOA 1990 — 2008

	Burkina	Togo	Sénégal	Niger	Mali	Côte d'Ivoire	Bénin
Burkina	1.000						
Togo	0.270	1.000					
Sénégal	0.457	0.238	1.000				
Niger	0.327	-0.109	0.485	1.000			
Mali	0.209	-0.608	-0.023	-0.015	1.000		
Côte d'Ivoire	0.548	0.310	0.599	0.447	0.154	1.000	
Bénin	-0.297	-0.001	-0.149	0.046	-0.006	0.035	1.000

Source: Statistiques Financières Internationales, FMI; Calculs de l'auteur.

L'UEMOA bénéficie de deux facteurs qui devraient rendre plus facile son ajustement à des chocs. La taille relativement élevée du secteur informel dans le marché du travail et sa forte capacité à s'ajuster rapidement aux chocs constituent un avantage non négligeable dont les effets d'entraînement concernent aussi le secteur formel. Le deuxième facteur a trait à l'effort soutenu de l'Union visant à faciliter la libre circulation des personnes à travers le développement croissant de l'infrastructure routière, la suppression des visas pour les résidents de l'Union et leur droit de s'établir, de travailler et d'acquérir des biens mobiliers et immobiliers dans tous les pays de la communauté. L'UEMOA se distingue par ses forts courants migratoires tels qu'illustrés par la communauté Burkinabé en Côte d'Ivoire dont un tiers de la population est considéré d'origine étrangère.

La solidarité constitue une des forces majeures d'une union économique et monétaire et s'appuie sur la capacité de celle-ci à assister les membres qui font face à des difficultés passagères ou à hisser ses membres les plus faibles au niveau des autres, préservant ainsi la cohésion et facilitant la convergence. A l'examen, l'UEMOA ne semble pas s'être dotée de ressources adéquates pour remplir cette fonction malgré l'existence du Fonds d'Assistance à l'Intégration Régionale (FAIR) et du Programme d'intervention. L'insuffisance de ressources financières visant à renforcer la solidarité peut amoindrir la volonté politique d'approfondir le processus d'intégration et donc limiter le développement de l'Union. De ce point de vue, compte tenu de l'insuffisance et de l'incertitude relatives à l'Aide publique au développement, le Prélèvement communautaire et de solidarité qui s'élève à 1% des importations non communautaires gagnerait à être revu à la hausse afin de donner à l'Union plus de souveraineté et de présence dans l'avenir de ses membres. A titre de comparaison, l'Union Européenne (UE) tire ses ressources budgétaires de quatre sources : les droits de douane sur les importations extra-communautaires, des droit de douane sur certains produits alimentaires importés de l'extérieur de l'Union, un pourcentage de la taxe à la valeur ajoutée prélevée par ses membres et une contribution directe des Etats membres représentant un certain pourcentage de leur Produit national brut. Les ressources budgétaires de l'UE représentent environ 1,24% du Revenu national brut de l'Union.

Depuis sa création, l'UEMOA s'est caractérisée par une stricte adhésion à ses principes de gouvernance et à une absence de modifications unilatérale des règles qui sous-tendent la conduite de la politique monétaire et de change, qu'elle vienne de l'Autorité monétaire ou des Etats membres. Cette stabilité dans les rapports de gouvernance renforce la crédibilité de la Banque centrale et prévient toute expansion budgétaire incontrôlée qui miserait sur la monétisation du déficit d'un Etat membre. En revanche, elle impose à celle-ci de se confiner à la stricte gestion de la monnaie et donc peut exclure la poursuite d'autres objectifs qui pourraient entrer en conflit avec la défense de la valeur du Franc CFA. En d'autres termes, l'Union peut avoir besoin de concevoir et mettre en œuvre des instruments de politique non-monétaires dans la poursuite de ses objectifs économiques.

Il est communément admis que la clé de voûte d'une union monétaire réside dans la capacité de ses membres à définir ensemble des critères de convergence et de les respecter aussi régulièrement que possible. Les huit critères retenus par l'UEMOA sont compatibles avec le développement de l'Union et s'imposent à tous ses membres bien que les délais pour s'y conformer aient été repoussés à 2013. Le Tableau 4.3 détaille l'expérience des Etats membres dans ce domaine.

Trois grands enseignements ressortent de l'expérience des années 2004 à 2006, soit dix ans après la création de l'UEMOA. Le premier est qu'aucun critère n'a été respecté par tous les Etats pour une année donnée et aucun Etat n'a respecté un critère quelconque à chaque année. Il convient donc de s'interroger sur le réalisme des niveaux fixés pour les critères retenus ou de l'Union à imposer à ses membres de se conformer aux engagements pris volontairement. Une approche alternative consisterait à explorer un transfert de compétences dans certains domaines, notamment budgétaires, qui pourrait faciliter le respect de certains critères. Le deuxième enseignement est qu'en moyenne les Etats membres se sont conformés à 3,88 critères en 2004, 2,88 critères en 2005 et 3,25 critères en 2006, soit moins de la moitié des huit critères, ce qui n'indique pas une tendance à l'amélioration dans le temps. Le respect d'aucun critère n'a été amélioré dans le temps. On peut en conclure que l'UEMOA ne maîtrise pas encore l'évolution du respect des critères de convergence.

Le troisième enseignement réside dans la différenciation entre les critères les plus respectés et les moins respectés. Le contrôle de l'inflation, critère de premier rang, est le plus observé mais a la caractéristique d'être le plus influencé par l'Autorité monétaire par le biais du contrôle de l'expansion monétaire. Les critères les plus violés concernent la politique budgétaire – Solde budgétaire de base et Taux de pression fiscale – ainsi que le Solde extérieur courant. Ces trois variables relèvent de la politique nationale et semblent indiquer les domaines qui nécessitent le plus d'efforts dans la consolidation de l'Union.

TABLEAU 4.3. ETAT DE RÉALISATION DES CRITÈRES DE CONVERGENCE DES PAYS DE L'UEMOA

CRITERES DE CONVERGENCE (sur la base des indicateurs complémentaires de convergence)		ETAT DE REALISATION DES CRITERES EN 2006[1] PAR ETAT ET RAPPEL DES PERFORMANCES EN 2004 ET 2005 en UEMOA								Nombre de pays ayant respecté le critère		
		Bénin	Burkina Faso	Côte d'Ivoire	Guinée Bissau	Mali	Niger	Sénégal	Togo	2006	2005	2004
1	Solde budgétaire de base [2] sur PIB nominal (norme >=0)	0,8	-1,4	-1,9	-2,2	2,9	-0,5	-1,1	-0,1	2	4	4
2	Taux d'inflation sous-jacente (norme <=3%)	3,9	2,5	2,5	2,2	3,6	0,7	1,6	1,8	6	1	8
3	Encours de la dette publique totale rapporté au PIB nominal (norme <=70%)	14,8	17,1	80,5	323,8	23,9	25,6	40,5	95,9	5	5	4
4	Non-accumulation d'arriérés de paiement (en milliards)	0	0	426,2	nd	0	nd	0	nd	4	4	5
4.1	Arriérés de paiement intérieurs	0	0	23,7	nd	0	nd	0	nd	7	5	5
4.2	Arriérés de paiement extérieurs	0	0	402,5	21,8	0	0	0	26,8	5	5	4
5	Masse salariale [3] sur recettes fiscales (norme <= 35%)	35,2	36,3	43,1	86,2	24,9	31,0	30,3	34,6	4	3	4
6	Invest .financés sur ressources intérieures [4] sur recettes fiscales (norme >=20%)	17,6	30,6	11,8	2,1	17,4	21,2	27,8	5,5	3	4	4
7	Solde extérieur courant hors dons sur PIB nominal (norme >= -5%)	-7,0	-11,3	1,8	-12,2	-8,4	-9,9	-10,4	-20,1	1	1	1
8	Taux de pression fiscale (norme >=17%)	15,3	12,0	15,1	10,9	14,7	11,4	19,1	14,2	1	1	1
Nombre de critères respectés par pays	2006	3	4	2	1	4	4	6	2			
	2005	3	3	1	0	5	3	7	1			
	2004	4	6	2	1	6	2	7	3			

[1] Dans les zones ombragées, les normes des critères sont respectées.
[2] Corrigé des dons budgétaires et des ressources PPTE.
[3] Corrigé des dons budgétaires et des ressources PPTE.
[4] Corrigé des dons budgétaires et des ressources PPTE.
Source : Commission de l'UEMOA, Avril 2007

A titre de conclusion de la section qui précède, le Tableau 4.4 résume les efforts consentis par l'UEMOA et propose une mesure de leur degré d'adéquation au regard du projet d'intégration des Etats membres. Les dispositions qui relèvent de l'Autorité monétaire ont été observées et assez bien exécutées. Il s'agit de l'abandon de la souveraineté monétaire des Etats membres, de la conception et la mise en œuvre de la politique monétaire et de change, de l'arrimage à une monnaie forte du Franc CFA et de la garantie de convertibilité, et de l'irréversibilité unilatérale des arrangements monétaires communautaires. Des progrès ont été faits, bien qu'insuffisants, dans la diversification des économies nationales, notamment en ce qui concerne les exportations et la mobilité de la main d'œuvre. Une plus grande attention doit être portée sur quatre grands domaines à savoir 1) le renforcement de la capacité de l'UEMOA à mener des politiques économiques régionales en complément des politiques économiques nationales, 2) l'expansion du commerce intra-communautaire, 3) l'augmentation des ressources financières et de la compétence budgétaire de l'Union et 4) le renforcement de la capacité de l'Union à faire respecter les critères de convergence ou à trouver des solutions alternatives propres à promouvoir leur respect.

Tableau 4.4. Evaluation du dispositif institutionnel et opérationnel de l'UEMOA

Critère de réussite	Mise en œuvre	Degré d'effort accompli
Critères institutionnels		
Souveraineté et monnaie unique régionale	Banque centrale unique et autonome Abandon total de souveraineté monétaire nationale Monnaie unique et convertible dans toute la zone	+ + +

Contrôle de l'expansion budgétaire et de l'inflation	BCEAO contrôle expansion monétaire, prévient monétisation déficits budgétaires des membres Concertations entre BCEAO et Etats sur leur budget Déficits budgétaires des Etats financé par emprunts obligataires	+ + +
Arrimage à une économie ou une monnaie forte et stable	Arrimage institutionnel à l'Euro Garantie de convertibilité illimitée du Franc CFA par le Trésor français	+ + +
Mesures complémentaires pour l'intégration économique	Normes et réglementations édictées Absence de capacité interne d'exécution Insuffisance du budget de la Commission pour mise en œuvre de programmes Influence limitée de la Commission sur la politique économique des Etats	+
CRITÈRES OPÉRATIONNELS		
Augmentation du commerce intra-zone	Augmentation du commerce intra-zone total Amélioration sensible des exportations des pays côtiers Faible augmentation et grande variabilité des exportations des pays enclavés	+
Faible corrélation des effets des chocs sur les économies des membres	Corrélation modérée des exportations des deux grandes économies Exportations des petits pays peu ou pas corrélées	+ +
Compétence budgétaire de l'Union	Financement de l'Union insuffisant pour politique économique régionale Faible capacité d'absorption des Etats (FAIR)	+
Mobilité de la main d'œuvre	Législations nationales favorables à la mobilité et l'établissement des résidents de l'Union Infrastructure régionale de transport insuffisante	+ +
Irréversibilité unilatérale des arrangements communautaires	- Bon dispositif bénéficiant d'une grande crédibilité	+ + +
Adhésion des membres aux critères de convergence	- Adhésion insuffisante dans le temps, pour chaque critère et pour chaque pays	+

LE BILAN DE L'UEMOA

L'examen du bilan de l'UEMOA au terme de ses 15 années d'existence se fera sous trois angles principaux à savoir le bilan économique et social, le bilan monétaire et financier et la convergence entre les économies nationales de l'Union.

Bilan économique et social

Le Tableau 4.5 ci-dessous donne un portrait du développement humain des Etats membres de l'Union tel que mesuré par l'Indice de développement humain du Programme des Nations Unies pour le Développement (PNUD). Il suscite trois remarques. Premièrement, le classement moyen des pays de la zone UEMOA a régressé continuellement de 1990 à 2007. En d'autres termes le niveau de développement humain d'avant la création de l'UEMOA est supérieur à celui que connaît la Zone après 15 ans de fonctionnement. En second lieu, entre 1990 et 2007, à l'exception du Bénin qui a régressé de 12 rangs, chaque Etat pris individuellement a vu son classement reculer de 20 places ou plus, la Côte d'Ivoire ayant connu un recul de 40 places. Enfin, les faibles classements des pays et la détérioration continue de ceux-ci font de l'UEMOA l'un des espaces communautaires les plus défavorisés du monde et risquent de la maintenir dans cette situation dans un avenir prévisible si des actions vigoureuses ne sont pas entreprises pour y remédier.

L'évolution du produit intérieur brut (PIB) per capita des membres de l'Union est présentée dans le Tableau 4.6. Elle indique que les pays les plus riches en 1990, Côte d'Ivoire, Sénégal et Bénin, le sont restés et ont vu leurs revenus respectifs progresser. A l'inverse, des pays économiquement faibles tels que la Guinée Bissau, le Niger et le Togo ont stagné ou même reculé. Il convient également de noter la forte variabilité des revenus de ces derniers, ce qui constitue un facteur aggravant dans leur effort de développement et de redistribution intérieure. Le défi majeur de l'UEMOA dans ce domaine réside dans la disparité significative et grandissante entre les revenus de ses membres. A titre d'exemple, en 1990, le revenu moyen de ses trois membres les plus riches était de $1205 alors que le revenu moyen de ses trois membres les plus faibles était de $611 soit un écart de $594. En 2007, le revenu moyen des premiers est passé à $1556 alors celui des seconds n'était que de $630

TABLEAU 4.5. CLASSEMENT DES PAYS DE L'UEMOA PAR RAPPORT À L'INDICE DE DÉVELOPPEMENT HUMAIN (PNUD), 1990 - 2007

	1990	1995	2000	2005	2007
Bénin	149	145	158	163	161
Burkina Faso	157	172	169	176	177
Côte d'Ivoire	123	148	156	166	163
Guinée Bissau	152	164	167	175	173
Mali	155	171	164	173	178
Niger	156	173	172	174	182
Sénégal	137	158	154	156	166
Togo	132	144	141	152	159
Classement moyen des pays	145.1	159.4	160.1	166.9	169.9
Nombre total de pays classés	160	174	173	177	182
Classement 1) moyen standardisé / 100	90.7	91.6	92.6	94.3	93.3

Source: Rapport du Programme des Nations Unies pour le Développement, 1992, 1998, 2002, 2007/08, 2009

Note: Le classement moyen standardisé est le classement moyen rapporté au nombre total de pays classés dans l'année multiplié par 100.

TABLEAU 4.6. PRODUIT INTÉRIEUR BRUT PER CAPITA DES PAYS DE L'UEMOA EN DOLLARS COURANTS, 1990 — 2007, (MÉTHODE PPP, EN $US)

	1990	1995	2000	2005	2007
Bénin	1043	1800	990	1141	1312
Burkina Faso	618	784	976	1213	1124
Côte d'Ivoire	1324	1731	1630	1648	1690
Guinée Bissau	841	811	755	827	477
Mali	572	565	797	1033	1083
Niger	645	765	746	781	627
Sénégal	1248	1815	1510	1792	1666
Togo	734	1167	1442	1506	788

Source: PNUD, Rapport sur le développement humain ; Parutions de 1993, 1998, 2002, 2007/2008, 2009.

créant une différence de $926. Donc, l'écart entre les deux groupes a augmenté de 56%. Dans leur ensemble, ces résultats soulignent le besoin urgent et impérieux pour l'UEMOA de se pencher sur la situation de ses membres les plus faibles afin de les hisser au niveau des autres, de les aider à faire face à leurs défis sociaux qui, faute de solution, peuvent engendrer des désordres sociaux-politiques. Il faut aussi noter les gains de revenu importants enregistrés par le Burkina Faso et le Mali, deux pays enclavés qui ont progressé régulièrement sans trop de variabilité.

Bilan monétaire et financier

L'examen du bilan monétaire de l'UEMOA se fait sous l'angle de l'inflation et du financement de l'économie. Les taux d'inflation historiques des pays membres et de l'Union dans son ensemble sont présentés au Tableau 4.7. Ils révèlent qu'hormis la période inflationniste qui a suivi le changement de parité du Franc CFA en janvier 1994, l'inflation a été bien maîtrisée dans tous les pays, exception faite de la Guinée Bissau en proie à une guerre civile et faisant ses premiers pas en tant que membre de l'Union. L'Union a donc maintenu sa tradition de faible inflation qui datait d'avant la dévaluation du France CFA – voir les taux en 1990 – et su créer une grande uniformité dans ce domaine et respecter son critère de convergence de premier rang relatif à l'inflation qui prescrit un taux qui ne dépasse pas 3% annuellement. Il faut souligner le rôle prépondérant de l'Autorité monétaire dans ces réalisations et peut être s'en inspirer pour la conception et la mise en œuvre de politiques dans les domaines non monétaires compte tenu des résultats plutôt modestes des politiques de développement nationales.

Le rôle de financement de l'économie est primordial dans une zone en développement telle que l'UEMOA et participe à sa libéralisation financière. Le ratio de la masse monétaire (M2) rapporté au PIB en donne une indication fiable et est présenté au Tableau 4.8. Des progrès notables ont été enregistrés dans ce domaine depuis la création de l'UEMOA sauf pour le Niger dont la situation appelle une attention particulière au regard de son faible niveau de monétisation et du grand écart qui le sépare des autres membres de l'Union. Il faut noter que des pays comme la Guinée Bissau et le Togo dont les PIB per capita sont relativement

TABLEAU 4.7. TAUX D'INFLATION DES 5 ANNÉES ANTÉRIEURES DES PAYS DE L'UEMOA

	1990	1995	2000	2005	2007
Bénin	n.d	17,8	3,7	2,8	2,6
Burkina Faso	-0,4	6,7	2,4	3,0	2,0
Côte d'Ivoire	4,8	9,7	2,9	3,2	2,6
Guinée Bissau	58,0	47,2	22,9	1,5	1,5
Mali	0,3	6,4	1,7	2,4	1,0
Niger	-3,0	6,6	2,7	2,6	1,3
Sénégal	0,2	7,5	1,4	1,5	2,0
Togo	0,8	11,3	3,1	2,6	1,9
UEMOA	n.d	11,0	2,4	2,8	2,3

Source : Statistiques financières internationales, FMI.

TABLEAU 4.8. RATIO DE LA MASSE MONÉTAIRE (M2) RAPPORTÉ AU PIB DES PAYS DE L'UEMOA

	1990	1995	2000	2005	2007
Bénin	25.1	22.9	28.6	25.8	30.7
Burkina Faso	18.1	21.4	20.9	18.8	22.5
Côte d'Ivoire	28.8	28.7	21.8	22.7	28.2
Guinée Bissau	8.0	9.4	42.7	31.5	36.5
Mali	20.1	18.7	21.4	26.3	28.4
Niger	19.8	14.1	8.8	6.5	9.1
Sénégal	22.6	20.6	23.7	32.3	35.0
Togo	36.1	26.0	26.0	27.5	35.9

Source : Statistiques financières internationales, FMI.

faibles comme le montre le Tableau 4.6 ont bénéficié d'un niveau relatif de masse monétaire qui pourrait contribuer à leur rattrapage des autres membres, sans pression inflationniste particulière, si l'hypothèse du rôle positif de la monnaie dans le développement économique se vérifie dans l'espace UEMOA.

L'analyse va maintenant porter sur le bilan financier de l'Union. D'une situation de resserrement du crédit à l'économie au lendemain de la dévaluation du Franc CFA, le système bancaire est progressivement retourné à des taux comparables à ceux de 1990, évolution qui a été facilitée par le recours croissant des Etats à l'emprunt obligataire pour financer leurs déficits budgétaires et réduisant ainsi l'éviction du secteur privé sur le marché du crédit. L'évolution est à mettre en rapport avec la croissance économique des membres de l'Union qu'elle accompagne. En dehors de la Côte d'Ivoire qui subit une situation de quasi partition socio-politique qui a tendance à réduire l'activité bancaire dans certaines régions, une plus grande attention doit être portée sur la Guinée Bissau et le Niger dont le secteur privé souffre depuis longtemps d'un niveau d'accès au crédit trop bas pour être compatible avec une croissance économique durable. Pour l'Union en général et pour ces deux pays en particulier, une analyse plus poussée devrait porter sur les liens de causalité entre l'expansion du crédit à l'économie et la croissance économique, dans le respect des critères de convergence nominale de l'UEMOA pour, peut être, soutenir l'effort de développement.

Tableau 4.9. Ratio du crédit au secteur privé rapporté au PIB des pays de l'UEMOA

	1990	1995	2000	2005	2007
Bénin	19.1	7.4	11.6	15.3	18.4
Burkina Faso	16.8	6.1	11.7	16.0	16.0
Côte d'Ivoire	36.5	20.4	15.2	13.4	15.2
Guinée Bissau	2.6	4.9	7.9	2.0	5.6
Mali	12.5	9.7	15.1	16.1	17.4
Niger	12.3	4.4	5.2	6.5	9.1
Sénégal	26.4	14.7	18.7	21.6	21.9
Togo	22.6	17.1	15.6	17.1	20.4

Source : Statistiques financières internationales, FMI,

La Bourse Régionale des Valeurs Mobilières (BRVM) a, depuis son démarrage en septembre 1998, activement participé au financement de la sous-région. Selon la Banque Mondiale, la capitalisation boursière des sociétés qui y sont listées représentait 11.4% du PIB de la Côte d'Ivoire, son pays hôte, en 2000, 14.2% en 2005 et 42.2% en 2007. Le caractère intégrateur de la BRVM et sa capacité à mobiliser l'épargne communautaire et étrangère constituent une des grandes réalisations de l'UEMOA au plan financier même si une concentration encore trop prononcée profite plutôt au Sénégal et à la Côte d'Ivoire, accentuant le déséquilibre déjà observé sur le marché du crédit au secteur privé.

CONVERGENCE COMMUNAUTAIRE RÉELLE

Une des mesures principales du succès de l'UEMOA réside dans la convergence des économies de ses Etats membres vers une croissance soutenue marquée par un rattrapage des plus faibles sur les plus avancées. Deux types de mesure de convergence seront utilisés pour évaluer la performance de l'Union : la convergence absolue – ou convergence β- et la convergence σ qui montre par le biais de la baisse dans le temps du coefficient de dispersion des valeurs respectives d'une variable entre les pays qu'ils ont une similitude grandissante. La convergence σ a été testée par Wane (2004), Boogaerde et Tsangarides (2005), Masson et Patillo (2005) et Ndiaye (2007) sur le PIB per capita des pays de l'UEMOA. La plupart de ces travaux concluent à une absence de convergence σ, ce qui indique, dans le cas de l'UEMOA, que les pays les plus riches le demeurent à travers le temps et les plus pauvres restent les plus pauvres, résultat qui est en accord avec le Tableau 4.6 présenté plus haut.

Des tests de convergence σ ont également été conduits sur d'autres indicateurs économiques des pays de l'UEMOA. Ainsi N'Diaye (2007) a mis en évidence une absence de convergence dans le cas de l'investissement rapporté au PIB alors que Boogaerde et Tsangarides (2005) trouvent une faible convergence. Dans le cas du taux d'épargne mesuré par le ratio de l'épargne brute rapportée au PIB, les résultats de Boogaerde et Tsangarides (2005) indiquent une divergence σ. Sy (2006) a trouvé une divergence croissante des secteurs bancaires des Etats membres en mesurant l'évolution dans le temps de la dispersion entre les écarts des taux d'intérêt prêteurs par rapport aux taux emprunteurs.

Les rares tests de convergence absolue sur l'économie des pays de l'UEMOA ont donné les résultats suivants. Pour Wane (2004) la vitesse de convergence mesurée par le coefficient β de sa régression du PIB per capita sur la valeur décalée de celui-ci est lente et s'élève à 6% par an. A l'inverse, Masson et Patillo (2005), utilisant les chaînes de Markov, trouvent plutôt un processus de divergence des PIB per capita des pays de la Zone. Enfin Sy (2006) suggère qu'il n'y a pas de convergence β dans le cas des écarts entre taux prêteurs et taux emprunteurs des pays de l'UEMOA, ce qui indique une absence d'intégration du secteur bancaire de l'Union.

En conclusion, l'examen relatif à la convergence des secteurs réels des économies des Etats membres montre un bilan pas très satisfaisant tant du point de vue de la réduction de la disparité entre celles-ci que de la vitesse à laquelle les pays retardataires rattrapent les leaders. Les défis les plus importants sont à mettre au compte des Etats membres dans le domaine de la politique budgétaire et économique plutôt que dans la politique monétaire, l'Autorité monétaire faisant montre d'une grande maîtrise de l'inflation. Il convient donc de s'interroger sur le niveau de ressources mises à la disposition de la Commission pour assister les pays les plus faibles afin de les aider à mieux s'intégrer à l'Union pour faciliter sa progression.

RECOMMANDATIONS DE STRATÉGIES FUTURES

Au terme de cette brève analyse du dispositif institutionnel de l'UEMOA et du bilan de ses opérations et de ses performances, quelles priorités stratégiques se dégagent pour insuffler à l'Union un regain de dynamisme? Les résultats qui sont présentés et qui motiveraient des actions spécifiques peuvent être organisés en quatre grandes lignes directrices à savoir i) le renforcement des compétences de politique régionale de la Commission, ii) la mise en place d'une politique plus vigoureuse des pays faibles de l'Union, iii) la création d'un Pacte social et iv) l'accroissement de la mobilité des biens, des personnes et du capital. Auparavant, il est impérieux de rappeler la force principale de l'Union qui réside dans sa longue expérience et la qualité de son arrangement monétaire. Cet acquis constitue son fondement et peut être le modèle dont elle devra s'inspirer dans l'architecture institutionnelle qui lui assurera le succès à l'avenir.

Renforcement des compétences de politique de l'Union

La réussite de la BCEAO et de la BRVM et les difficultés auxquelles font face les Etats dans leurs politiques intérieures respectives offrent un contraste saisissant et soulèvent la question de la nécessité de conférer plus de compétences à la Commission afin que, profitant des économies d'échelle et s'inspirant des expériences de ses institutions spécialisées, elle rehausse la qualité des politiques. Par ailleurs, la délégation de souveraineté monétaire doit, pour bénéficier amplement à l'Union, s'accompagner d'une délégation comparable quoique inégale de compétences en matière de politique budgétaire. Un tel changement profiterait sensiblement aux pays les plus faibles dont les capacités financières et humaines ne peuvent assurer, du moins pour le moment, la conduite de politiques susceptibles de produire le développement.

Au stade actuel, la Commission s'est attelée à édicter des normes et réglementations qui créent un environnement favorable au développement de l'Union. Mais elle n'a pas encore entrepris le vaste programme de développement économique régional dont la Zone a besoin faute de ressources. Et pourtant, ce travail constitue un aspect important de sa mission. Il est symptomatique qu'un grand nombre des projets contenus dans le document de stratégie de développement 2006-2010 de l'UEMOA ne sont pas entrepris car n'ayant pas de financement. L'UEMOA pourrait envisager la possibilité de transférer à son profit un certain nombre de compétences nationales et recevoir en compensation un niveau de recettes fiscales plus élevées par le biais d'un Prélèvement communautaire plus élevé ou un financement provenant des profits de ses institutions spécialisées.

POLITIQUE DE RELÈVEMENT DES PAYS LES PLUS FAIBLES

La divergence économique et l'absence de rattrapage des pays les plus faibles de l'Union constituent un des résultats les plus marquants de la présente étude. Tant du point de vue de leur niveau de développement humain que de leurs performances économiques le Niger et la Guinée Bissau en premier lieu et le Burkina Faso et le Mali dans une moindre mesure méritent une attention particulière pour les aider à se hisser au niveau des autres Etats membres. Trois domaines d'intervention pourraient être retenus à cet effet. Premièrement, un programme de transfert accru de compétences techniques et d'appui direct aux administrations nationales pourrait être conçu pour améliorer le processus de formulation et de mise en œuvre des politiques nationales. Les difficultés des Etats à se conformer aux critères de convergence nominale ou à opérer le rattrapage qu'implique la convergence réelle peuvent être largement attribuées aux déficiences des politiques nationales budgétaires et commerciales.

Le deuxième domaine d'intervention possible est le financement accru de l'économie et du secteur privé des pays les plus faibles. Les taux de monétisation de leurs économies (M2/PIB) et le niveau de financement bancaire de leur secteur privé ne peuvent raisonnablement être considérés comme compatibles avec un développement économique durable. Il faut également admettre que la faible capacité d'absorption financière des Etats faibles et le faible niveau du secteur privé constituent des contraintes non négligeables pour l'expansion du développement financier de leurs économies. Aussi, convient-il de réfléchir sur les moyens propres à réaliser cet objectif si crucial pour la réussite à long terme de l'Union. La lutte contre la grande variabilité des indicateurs économiques des pays les plus faibles constitue le troisième domaine d'intervention possible. Plusieurs mesures combinées pourraient être d'un grand apport dans la poursuite de cet objectif. Parmi les plus importantes il faut compter la diversification des exportations par la création de nouveaux secteurs d'avantages comparatifs, la maitrise de l'eau et la modernisation des techniques culturales, le rehaussement du niveau de l'encadrement agricole et la mise en place de programmes d'assurances liés au niveau des exportations ou du PIB nominal.

Création du Pacte social

La Zone UEMOA est l'une des plus défavorisées du monde parce que son niveau de développement social est l'un des plus modestes. La plupart des défis sociaux de la région sont communément partagés par tous les Etats membres et donc justifient une action collective porteuse de synergies, les pays les plus faibles rencontrant beaucoup de difficultés à accomplir seuls les progrès sociaux nécessaires à leur développement. A l'instar du Pacte de convergence, de stabilité, de croissance et de solidarité, les membres de l'UEMOA pourraient faire front commun à travers un Pacte social dont le but serait de formuler une politique sociale commune assortie de transferts de compétences des Etats au profit de la Commission dans le même esprit qu'initialement conçu pour le Nouveau Partenariat pour le Développement de l'Afrique (NEPAD). Une telle entreprise s'inspirerait du fonctionnement et de la gouvernance des institutions spécialisées de l'UEMOA telles que la BCEAO, la

BOAD et la BRVM. L'autonomie d'opération et de financement et le caractère régional de la mission conféreraient au Pacte social une efficacité difficile à atteindre dans un seul pays.

A titre indicatif, les programmes du Pacte social pourraient inclure la santé (grandes endémies, campagnes de vaccination et de prévention, hôpitaux universitaires), l'habitat social, l'eau et l'enseignement supérieur. L'UEMOA pourrait également avoir ses programmes d'intervention dans les zones d'urgence telles que les conflits, les épidémies et les désastres naturels, appuyée en cela par le dispositif humanitaire international classique.

ACCROISSEMENT DE LA MOBILITÉ

La mobilité du capital, des biens et des personnes est un des fondements de l'intégration régionale. Les politiques qui visent à encourager le secteur privé à faire des investissements transfrontaliers doivent être activement poursuivies afin de favoriser le transfert de technologie et de savoir faire, mais aussi de promouvoir le crédit bancaire à l'économie, surtout pour les pays où celui-ci est faible. Les efforts entrepris par l'UEMOA pour lever les barrières non tarifaires et les barrages routiers gagneraient également à persévérer afin de rendre les échanges économiques intra-communautaires plus fluides. Une mobilité accrue des marchandises pourrait favoriser la transformation dans l'espace de l'UEMOA des produits agricoles grâce leur transfert rapide et économique des zones rurales vers les régions industrielles créant ainsi une plus grande complémentarité géographique au sein de l'Union. L'édification de nouvelles infrastructures devrait être une des priorités dans l'effort d'accroissement de la mobilité au sein de l'Union.

CONCLUSION

Au terme de 15 ans d'existence, l'UEMOA a enregistré des succès indéniables, particulièrement dans la gestion de sa monnaie, de sa politique de change et l'organisation de son marché de valeurs mobilières. Elle a également su préserver la solidité et la fiabilité de ses institutions ainsi que l'adhésion de ses membres au projet communautaire. Sa neutralité, son autonomie et son autorité continuent d'être respectées malgré les évènements tels que la crise ivoirienne et les désordres en Guinée Bissau qui ont secoué son espace. Cependant, il faut noter que l'Union a atteint ses limites, du moins dans sa configuration actuelle, quant à la poursuite de certains de ses objectifs. Autant ses succès se sont confirmés dans le temps autant elle peine à s'améliorer dans les domaines, certes nouveaux dans ses champs de compétence, où elle rencontre des difficultés.

En effet, après 15 ans d'efforts, l'UEMOA constitue encore, du point de vue du développement humain, l'un des espaces communautaires les plus défavorisés du monde et son classement moyen dans l'Indice du développement humain du PNUD a constamment régressé et est en-deca de ce qu'il était avant l'avènement de l'Union. Il est donc urgent d'améliorer les conditions de vie de ses citoyens. Par ailleurs, la divergence économique grandissante entre les pays les plus riches et les pays les plus faibles met en exergue l'insuccès des politiques nationales prises individuellement et l'incapacité de l'Union à les assister de manière significative dans le cadre du dispositif actuel. Une telle situation n'est pas sans risque pour la cohésion de l'Union et peut émousser la volonté politique de ses membres au moment précis où celle-ci doit se renforcer et sous-tendre un projet communautaire plus ambitieux.

Les améliorations significatives qu'on peut attendre de l'Union ne sont pas dans le domaine monétaire où elle a su préserver et renforcer les acquis de l'UMOA, son prédécesseur, mais plutôt dans ceux qui relèvent encore des compétences nationales. A ce titre, le modèle de ses institutions spécialisées auquel l'Union doit ses plus francs succès gagnerait à être étendu à d'autres secteurs. Il s'agirait de transférer certaines compétences jusqu'ici nationales et dont les Etats, particulièrement les plus faibles, ont eu du mal à s'acquitter, au profit de la Commission en contrepartie d'une augmentation des ressources budgétaires dont elle dispose. Plusieurs formes de financement additionnel de la Commission pourraient être envisagées dont le relèvement du Prélèvement communautaire, le transfert à son profit d'une partie des bénéfices des institutions spécialisées ou le recours au marché des valeurs mobilières assorti de contributions extérieures sous forme de garantie ou de co-remboursement.

Les priorités d'action stratégiques qui ressortent de l'analyse du bilan institutionnel et programmatique de l'UEMOA sont de quatre ordres. Premièrement, les compétences de politique économique et sociale donc budgétaires de l'UEMOA devraient s'étendre au delà de la question monétaire et les Etats devraient envisager de céder une partie de leur souveraineté, ce qui favoriserait une exploitation pleine et entière du potentiel de l'Union. L'augmentation des recettes de la Commission rendrait plus aisée la mise en œuvre des projets communautaires qui ont été suspendus ou abandonnés, faute de financement. Une telle décision serait d'un grand apport pour les pays les plus faibles car elle seconderait leurs capacités nationales limitées de manière non négligeable et mutualiserait une partie des ressources budgétaires transférées des membres les plus forts.

Deuxièmement, l'Union devrait s'atteler à relever les pays plus faibles autant pour améliorer la situation sociale de leurs résidents que pour faciliter le processus de rattrapage qui est au cœur de tout projet communautaire. A cette fin, la Commission pourrait initier un programme de transfert de compétences techniques et d'appui aux administrations nationales afin d'améliorer le processus de formulation des politiques nationales. Elle pourrait aussi promouvoir un financement plus élevé de l'économie de ces Etats notamment en stimulant le crédit au secteur privé et en encourageant une expansion monétaire contrôlée qui réduirait le degré de répression financière, tel que mesuré par un ratio M2/PIB trop faible pour être compatible avec un développement économique durable. Enfin, la grande variabilité des principaux indicateurs économiques de ces pays devrait être combattue par un ensemble de mesures appropriées et durables.

En troisième lieu, l'Union devrait édicter un Pacte social dont le but principal est de rehausser les conditions de vie de tous ses résidents. La mise en œuvre du Pacte social s'exécuterait au niveau communautaire avec de grandes prérogatives de la Commission et un financement adéquat. Les synergies et la mise à niveau de tous les pays qui en découleraient ne manqueraient pas de renforcer l'adhésion de tous ses membres. L'opérationnalisation du Pacte social pourrait s'inspirer de l'architecture des institutions spécialisées de l'Union. La quatrième priorité stratégique de l'UEMOA concerne l'accroissement de la mobilité. Il s'agit de lever les barrières non tarifaires et les barrages routiers intempestifs, d'encourager le développement de chaines de valeurs transnationales dans l'espace de l'Union et de renforcer la création d'infrastructures qui favorisent la mobilité.

Il est possible de poursuivre toutes ces priorités stratégiques de front car l'engagement politique des Etats membres est présent et intact. En outre, des facteurs extérieurs tels que la globalisation et ses défis qui nécessitent une réponse collective ainsi que le regain d'attachement des pays aux unions économiques tel qu'illustré récemment en Europe en réaction à la crise économique qui secoue le monde plaident pour un renforcement de l'Union et à une plus forte adhésion au projet communautaire. Il est donc temps d'agir vigoureusement et les conditions sont propices.

Références

Agbodji, A. E., 2007, « Intégration et Echanges Intra Sous-régionaux : Le Cas de l'UEMOA », Revue africaine de l'intégration, Vol. 1 No. 1, Janvier 2007, pp. 161-188.

Bamba, L. N., 2004, « Analyse du Processus de Convergence dans la Zone UEMOA », Research Paper No. 2004/18, February, World Institute for Development Economics Research (WIDER), United Nations University, Helsinki.

Bamba, L.N., and Diomande, K., 1998, "Convergence Nominale vs Convergence Réelle et/ou Conver gence des Politiques Economiques vs Convergence des Structures Economiques dans les Pays de l'UEMOA », Symposium International sur « L'Avenir de la Zone Franc avec l'Avènement de l'Euro », CODESRIA, Dakar, 4-6 novembre.

Bayoumi, T., and J. D. Ostry, 1995, "Macroeconomic Shocks and Trade Flows within Sub-Saharan Africa: Implications for Optimum Currency Arrangements", IMF Working Paper No. 95/142, Washington D.C. International Monetary Fund.

Berthelemy J. C. and Vadourkakis A., 1996, "Economic Growth, Convergence Clubs and the Role of Financial Development" Oxford Economic Papers, Vol. 48 No. 2, pp. 300-328.

Bleaney, M., and Nishiyama, A., 2004, "Economic Growth, Income Distribution and Poverty: Time-series and Cross-country Evidence from the CFA-zone Countries of sub-Saharan Africa", Research Paper No. 2004/03, January, World Institute for Development Economics Research (WIDER), United Nations University, Helsinki.

Clément, J., Mueller, J., Cossé, S., and LeDem J., 1996, « Aftermath of CFA Franc Devaluation », Occasional Paper Paper No. 138, Washington D.C., International Monetary Fund.

Coulibaly, S., 2007, "Evaluating the Trade Effect of Developing Regional Trade Agreements: A Semi-Parametric Approach", World Bank, Policy Research Working Paper No. WPS 4220, May.

Doré, O. and P.R. Masson, 2002, "Experience with Budgetary Convergence in the WAEMU", IMF Working Paper No. 02/108, Washington D.C. International Monetary Fund.

Faroutan, F., and L. Pritchett, 1993, "Intra-Sub-Saharan African Trade: Is There Too Little? Journal of African Economies, Vol. 2, pp. 74-105.

Fielding, D., 2005, "Macroeconomic Policy in The Franc Zone", Editor, Palgrave Macmillan, Houndmills Basingstoke, U.K.

Fielding D., 2004, "How Does Monetary Policy Affect the Poor? Evidence from the West African Economic and Monetary Union", Research Paper No. 2004/02, January, World Institute for Development Economics Research (WIDER), United Nations University, Helsinki

Fielding, D., Lee, K., and Shields, K., 2004, "The Characteristics of Macroeconomic Shocks in the CFA Franc Zone", Research Paper No. 2004/21, March, World Institute for Development Economics Research (WIDER), United Nations University, Helsinki.

Goretti, M., and H. Weisfeld, 2008, "Trade in the WAEMU: Development and Reform Opportunities", IMF Working Paper No. 08/68, Washington D.C., International Monetary Fund.

Goreux, L. M. 1995, « La Dévaluation du Franc CFA: Un Premier Bilan en Décembre 1995 », Rapport de consultation, 28 décembre 1995, Banque Mondiale, 152 pages.

Hernadez-Cata, E., Francois, C.A., Masson, P., Bouvier, P., Peroz, P., Desruelle, D., and Vamvakidis, A., 1998, "The West African Economic and Monetary Union, Recent Developments and Policy Issues", Occasional Paper Paper No. 170, Washington D.C., International Monetary Fund.

Hinkle, L., and P. J. Montiel, 1999, "Exchange Rate Misalignment: Concepts and Measurement for Developing Countries", Washington D. C., World Bank.

Kenen, P. B., 1969, "The Theory of Optimum Currency Areas: An Eclectic View", in Monetary Problems of the International Economy, edited by Mundell, R., and A. Swoboda, University of Chicago Press, Chicago.

Konseiga, A., 2005, "Regionalism in West Africa: Do Polar Countries Reap the Benefits? A Role for Migration", Institute for the Study of Labor (IZA), IZA Discussion Paper No. 1516, Bonn, Germany.

Leonard, D., 2005, "Guide to the European Union", Profile Books, London.

Linjouom, M., 2004, "The Costs and Benefits Analysis of CFA Membership: The Choice of an Exchange Rate Regime for the CFA Countries Zone ",Research Paper No. 2004/14, February, World Institute for Development Economics Research (WIDER), United Nations University, Helsinki.

Masson, P., and C. Patillo, 2001, "Monetary Union in West Africa: An Agency of Restraint for Fiscal Policy?", IMF Working Paper No. 01/34, Washington D.C., International Monetary Fund.

Masson, P., and C. Patillo, 2001, "Monetary Union in West Africa (ECOWAS): Is It Desirable and How Could It Be Achieved?", IMF Occasional Paper No. 204, Washington D.C., International Monetary Fund.

Masson, P., and C. Patillo, 2005, "The Monetary Geography of Africa", Washington D.C., Brookings Institution.

Mundell, R., 1961, "A Theory of Optimum Currency Areas", American Economic Review, Vol. 51, (November), pp. 657-665.

Nashashibi, K., and S. Bazzoni, 1994, "Exchange Rate Strategies and Fiscal Performance in Sub-Saharan Africa", IMF Staff Papers, International Monetary Fund, Vol. 41, pp. 76-122.

Ndiaye, M. B. O., 2007, « Respect des critères de convergence vs harmonisation des critères de convergence : étude comparative des performances des indicateurs de convergence économique dans la zone Franc en Afrique (UEMOA et CEMAC) », Revue africaine de l'intégration, Vol. 1 No. 2, Juillet 2007, pp. 31-69.

Rogoff, K., and C. Reinhart, 2003, "FDI to Africa: The Role of Price Stability and Currency Instability", IMF Working Paper No. 03/10, Washington D.C. International Monetary Fund.

Rosenberg, C., 1995, "Fiscal Policy Coordination in the WAEMU After the Devaluation", IMF Working Paper No. 95/25, Washington D.C. International Monetary Fund.

Rother, P. C., 1998, "Money Demand and Regional Monetary Policy in the West African Economic and Monetary Union", IMF Working Paper No. 98/57, Washington D.C. International Monetary Fund.

Roudet, S., M. Saxegaard, and C. G. Tsangarides, 2007, " Estimation of Equilibrium Exchange Rates in the WAEMU: A Robustness Analysis", IMF Working Paper No. 07/194, Washington D.C. International Monetary Fund.

Sy, Amadou, 2006, "Financial Integration in the West African Economic and Monetary Union", IMF Working Paper No. 06/214, Washington D.C. International Monetary Fund.

UEMOA, 2006, « Le Programme économique et régional 2006 – 2010 », Juillet. Le Programme Economique Régional de l'UEOMA (PER): 2006-2010

Van Den Boogaerde, P., and C. G. Tsangarides, 2005, "Ten Years After the CFA Franc Devaluation: Progress Toward Regional Integration in the WAEMU", IMF Working Paper No. 05/145, Washington D.C. International Monetary Fund.

Wane, A. A., 2004, "Growth and Convergence in WAEMU Countries", IMF Working Paper No. 04/198, Washington D.C. International Monetary Fund.

Yehoue, E., 2006, "On the Pattern of Currency Blocs in Africa", Journal of African Development, Spring 2006, Vol. 1, No. 1, pp. 39-86.

Chapter 5

TOWARDS A WEST AFRICAN MONETARY UNION: BEYOND STYLIZED CONVERGENCE CRITERIA

Oladele Omosegbon

INTRODUCTION

By the establishment of a second monetary zone for the West Africa region, WAMZ, in 2000, it was envisaged that a merger of the new monetary zone with the erstwhile Economic and Monetary Union of West Africa, UEMOA, would take place within five years. Ten years on, we are yet to witness that merger. Ostensibly, the inability of member countries to meet the set of primary and secondary criteria (see Box 5.1) stipulated for that purpose has been given as the cause of delay. Convergence criteria, including the fairly reasonable ones specified in the WAMZ pact could lead to a full functioning monetary union as envisaged, but we argue in this paper that they are by no means sufficient or even necessary for a monetary union to exist. It is a questionable expectation that member states meet certain macro benchmarks before pooling human and natural resources for the benefit of a people who share common history, culture and destiny. Neither the Anglo-Scottish Union of 1707, nor the German reunification of

1990 met any set of macroeconomic and policy conditions.[1] What is more, if European countries were to wait for member states to achieve comparable economic performances, the European Union would still have been in the works as we speak.[2]

While any set of criteria that prescribes economic improvement is always beneficial, none of them has been shown to be either necessary or sufficient for monetary or economic integration to take place. In the same vein, none of them has been shown to be deterministic for the benefits of agglomeration and scale economies flowing into constituent states. The paper argues that what may be more important in the WAMZ case is the historical lesson of the need to pool resources and bring about full flexibility and adaptability of the region's labor market. For this to occur, more than the set primary and secondary criteria (Box 5.1) are needed.[3] It would require historical will and an awareness of the common destiny of survival or decay that awaits the more than 210 million Africans that live in WAMZ nations.

The remainder of the paper is organized in the next section to look, briefly, at the convergence literature and use that idea to review more recent investigations of convergence within WAMZ. The main contribution of the paper is then presented in the discussion of the importance of instituting labor and geographic mobility in the monetary zone area. The discussion is next linked to the wider issue of the unfinished work of the transformation of West African traditional societies before the negative effects of external contacts with the West and the Orient disrupted that momentum. An example of non stylized convergence in the monetary union, school integration, is suggested in the section that follows. After this, the paper is summarized and concluded.

---

1 See OECD (1999, pp22-26)

2 Stunning was the fact that one of the countries that met all the set criteria for Euro convergence, the United Kingdom, opted out of the monetary union.

3 It is interesting to observe that the set of primary and secondary criteria stipulated by the West African Monetary Institute was inspired by the 1992 Maastricht criteria designed by the European Community. Europeans required these criteria for convergence and had to be satisfied by member countries wishing to join the euro.

BOX 5.1. CRITERIA FOR CONVERGENCE IN THE WAMZ

The four primary criteria are:

1. Inflation <10%; ≤ 5%;
2. GDP/Deficit ratio ≤ 5%, ≤ 4%;
3. central bank financing of government ≤ 10% of previous year's tax revenue;
4. import/reserves cover > 3 months.

The six secondary criteria relate to

1. prohibition of accumulation of domestic arrears;
2. tax revenue/GDP ratio – ≥ 20%;
3. wage bill/total tax ratio ≤ 35%,
4. public investment/tax revenue >20%;
5. positive real interest rate;
6. and stable real exchange rates.

Note: Inspired by the four criteria set forth in the 1992 Maastricht Criteria document of the European Community.

A CURSORY LOOK AT THE CONVERGENCE LITERATURE

A Monetary Union of the type being pursued by the Economic Community of West African States, represents the most advanced form of economic integration; the weakest being a preferential trade agreement, PTA, which involves only the reduction of tariffs on some traded goods among participating countries. A monetary union like WAMZ seeks to establish a common currency among member nations. The establishment of a common currency presupposes the existence of free trade in goods and services and the free movement of labor and capital, among others, across the unifying states. Countries planning any form of economic integration usually set a number of criteria necessary for the realization of the proposed economic coordination and cooperation. The idea being that for the benefits of economic integration to accrue to participating members, any existing disparities in economic, financial and labor markets would have to be narrowed. An exercise to evaluate the readiness of willing members to cooperate and coordinate their economic activities is an exercise in convergence testing. It is assumed that only when countries pass this battery of tests would there be a need to enter economic integration of any kind. It is hoped that the coordination that comes with the integration would bring benefits that each of the member countries would not have received before joining the new union.

Economists are fascinated whenever there is an opportunity to utilize mathematics to illuminate their discussions and propositions. One central question economists wish to answer is whether nations tend to close the income gap that exists among them overtime or whether the gap tends to diverge. β-convergence is used to measure whether the growth of income in a country is approaching a predetermined level of, usually, long run balanced growth. Economists are also interested in whether the distribution of income across countries is growing more equal, that is converging, overtime. In this case, σ-convergence is used as the measure. It is a recurring problem in the empirical literature obtaining σ-convergence. Young, Higgins and Levy (2007) show that β-convergence is a necessary but not sufficient condition for σ-convergence. In fact, it is not unusual to find σ-divergence in economies that are in a union.[4]

With a sleuth of distortions already in place and persistent in Africa, it is doubtful if any of these measures of convergence is useful. In fact, some of the assumptions behind the model, including flexible prices and the policy of redistribution, are not borne by countries in WAMZ. In addition, governments do not embark on meaningful programs of income equalization when the market system does not appear to deliver optimal results. Given the appropriate institutional framework, it would seem β-convergence may be more meaningful in Africa. But then, being in an economic union, acquiring requisite economies of scale and operational efficiencies may even create a more conducive environment for the income of nations to grow toward a steady state; which makes the convergence criteria not a necessary condition for economic integration.

The idea behind both σ and β convergences is generalized to test many economic series for this property. For this purpose,

4 See Young, Higgins and Levy (2007 pp2-4 and Tables 1-3) for evidence with a U.S. County data

Macro variables and models are often subjected to high level mathematical evaluation for desirable properties of convergence, cointegration and stability. Relationships are tested on income, prices, exchange rates, interest rates, imports, exports and their derivatives. The most widely used convergence criterion is on income, particularly per capita income. In a recent study of the EU, using seasonally adjusted per capita income to perform many panel unit root tests, Dogan and Saracoglu (2007) found no income convergence among member countries. The test failed even more when the convergence was benchmarked on the average GDP of the first 15 EU countries.

RECENT CONVERGENCE ISSUES IN THE WEST AFRICAN MONETARY ZONE

Akande, Adewuyi and Adeoye (2007) studied the performance of Nigeria on the set of primary and secondary criteria of convergence set forth for the West African Monetary Institute, WAMI, as shown in Box 5.1. The authors found that Nigeria was not meeting three of the primary factors. Success rate in achieving stability on the secondary criteria was also mixed. Similar findings were noted for the other WAMZ member states of Ghana, Sierra Leone, Guinea and The Gambia. In the charts below, we have also confirmed the absence of consistency in achieving these criteria across the countries in the monetary union. In Figure 5.1, we see that inflation rate behaves differently when the six countries are compared[5]. There is no particular pattern of behavior we can isolate except that they tend to have an uptick in the most recent positions, after an erratic trend from 2001 to 2007. Only in the Gambia do we see a downward trend at the end of the period in 2008.

In Figure 5.2, performance is a little bit discernible: tending toward a common growth rate of real GDP of better than 5%. Even the wild swings noticed for Liberia in previous years have begun to settle to a common WAMZ rate by late 2005.

---

5 Liberia is included in discussions in this paper because she was one of the original signatories of the 2000 statutes of WAMI. It is anticipated she would return into membership in due course.

Figure 5.1. Inflation in WAMZ

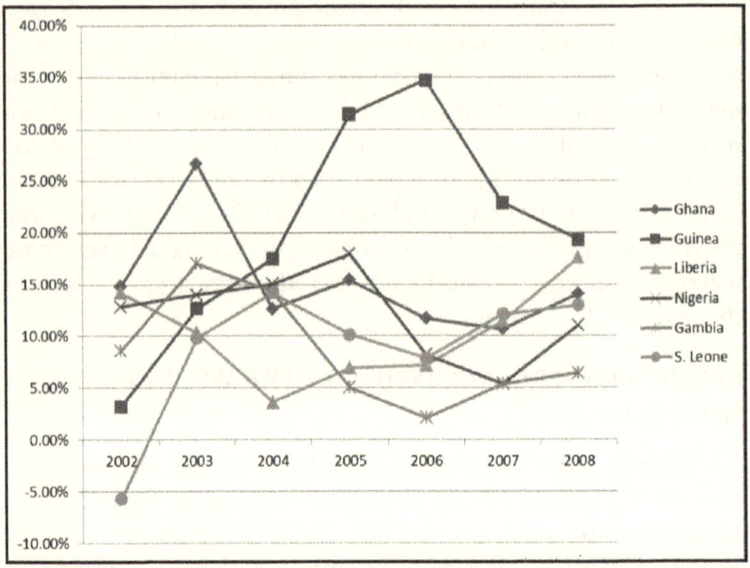

Source: *African Statistical Yearbook 2009*: Table 2-6 (2000=100)

Figure 5.2. Real GDP Growth Rate in WAMZ

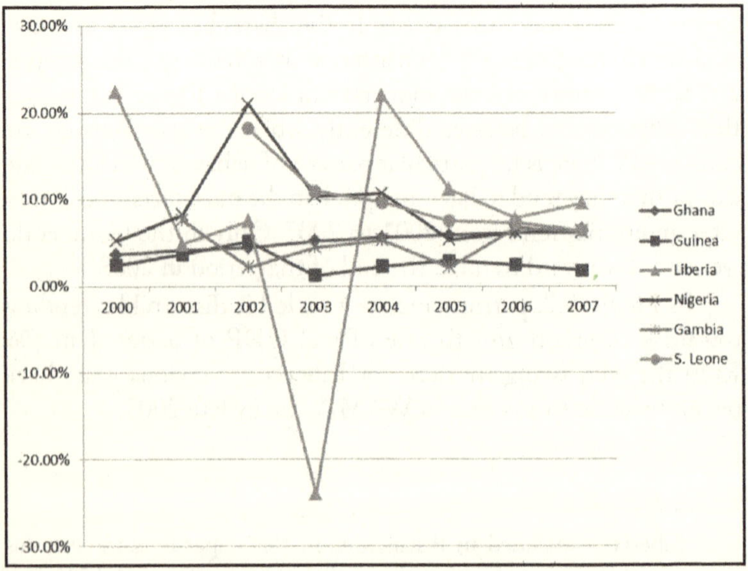

Source: *African Statistical Yearbook 2009*. Table 2-2

Current IMF data, reflecting economic activities for late 2009, show that only Nigeria can maintain an import cover of more than three months; the rest five countries record a current account balance as a percent of GDP in the range of about -41.8% for Liberia, to a volatile -1.7% in Guinea. In addition, the countries carry an average inflation of more than 5%, well above the best practice of ≤ 5% set forth in Box 1 by WAMI itself, and only in The Gambia is inflation currently at 6.49% meeting the < 10% ceiling stipulated in the primary convergence criteria.

In general, there are various ways in which time series variables are studied. Recently, Silvia and Iqbal (2010) suggest three properties critical in identifying and characterizing the behavior of most macroeconomic series. These are mean reversion, volatility and trend. For this purpose, we may ask if key macro variables in the integrating countries tend to exhibit mean reversal over time. Secondly, what is the relationship between the mean values of the criteria for convergence and their standard deviations? Finally, given recent pervasiveness of business cycles, one may investigate macro series in WAMZ countries and observe if these series grow differently from their long term trends; that is, if they exhibit β-convergence.

LABOR MOBILITY AND LABOR MARKET INTEGRATION

The Euro area is touted as the most successful regional monetary union experiment in recent memory. Even then, with the real threat of sovereign meltdown in Greece, Portugal and Ireland, many countries in the European Union are asking if monetary union is all that it's cut to be. In addition to common currency constraint, the most serious problem appears to be with the integration of the labor market. Even though full movement of labor prevails in the European Union, less than 1.5% of the 370 million Europeans actually live in other countries[6]. OECD (2007) lists problems of limited cross border portability of social protection, lack of comparability and reciprocal recognition of professional qualifications as some of the limiting factors. Fortunately, these limitations are not pronounced in the West African case as social security and public assistance of the sort in Europe are absent in

6 OECD (2007, pp17-18)

WAMZ countries. In addition, many of the West African professionals are already sharing common experiences across the region in certification and licensing, and there are common standardized public examinations like the General Certificate of Education, GCE and the West African Examinations Council.

It is a yawning lacuna in our thinking that we all take labor mobility as either sticky or of less priority in handling monetary or economic unions of nations. At best, flexible labor policy comes very late in policy considerations and the signing of the pacts for integration, and at worst, many traditional economists assume labor is immobile and focus instead on fiscal and monetary convergences. It would seem to me, at least in the West African case, that considering the initial endowments of these countries – their common experiences with Oriental and Western socio cultural clashes, tied with the unfinished ongoing integration of the region prior to external contacts, the unification of the people should precede the unification of capital and other mundane market and economic characteristics.

Although ECOWAS, at inception, had free movement of all citizens in the region as a high priority, thirty five years later, we have only an ECOWAS passport and a ninety day stay without visa to show for it. The more recent info regarding free movement of people in ECOWAS is reported in *AllAfrica.com*:

> Lagos — On May 17, President Olusegun Obasanjo launched the Economic Community of West African States (ECOWAS) passport to be carried by citizens of member countries. While launching the new passport in Abuja, Obasanjo said the need for a common passport for ECOWAS countries was initiated six years ago by members of the organisation (immigration) to pave way for easy transit and movement of people and goods across borders.[7]

Notice that there is no push to liberalize labor markets in the community. The passport is only for visitors for now. Yet, the issues of labor market flexibility and movement of persons are central to

7 May 22, 2007. http://allafrica.com/stories/200705230159.html. Last accessed 04/22/2010

any successful attempt at economic integration, especially of the most advanced form being contemplated in the monetary union of WAMZ countries. Economists generally think of integration as proceeding in succeeding stages of

Preferential Trade Agreement → Free Trade Area → Customs Union → Common Market → Economic Union → Monetary Union.

In the chart above, the success of a monetary union really begins at the stage of the common market, wherein member states allow citizens to hold a common passport and seek employment anywhere in the union. The difference among the last three stages is that in economic union, a common fiscal or commercial policy emanating from a supranational agency is pursued. The stage of monetary union is seen as the culmination of integration and at that point, member states lose control of monetary policy, in addition to some form of loss of control in fiscal policy characteristic of the preceding stage of economic union.

It is enough to note that the Treaty of Rome in 1957 established the European Common Market, even though it took some time before labor market union was realized, Suranovic (2010). Nevertheless, the Europeans did not begin the monetary union phase until the movement of labor and capital had been liberalized. Similarly, the crucial test of the feasibility of the working of a supra national authority should have been put in place by WAMZ countries at the stage of economic union. As an example, similar to the European Union, ECOWAS could have started with a common agricultural policy; especially when we know that in agriculture; most West Africans live and work. ECOWAS did nothing of that but instead has been trying to combine key elements of common market, economic union and monetary union at the last stage of monetary union. This kind of convenient choice was followed by its sister organization, the CFA Zone countries and it is no surprise that that zone is riddled with monetary and financial instability today.

It appears ECOWAS has skipped an indispensable criterion of free labor movement in its march toward regional integration. The success or failure of ECOWAS has direct implications for the overall effort of the African Union at bringing about an African Economic Community. ECOWAS is the major pillar in AU's regional economic community objective and planning. Deregulating labor market participation is also consistent with the goal of employment expansion and poverty eradication in these countries, and will greatly facilitate the success of monetary and exchange rate policies. In addition, economic integration is not an arcane and esoteric topic reserved only for the niceties of economic theorizing and analysis; it is about bringing a better life to the people living in these lands through a deliberate coordination and harmonization of policies of member nations, of which the most important is perhaps, employment.

HISTORY'S UNFINISHED BUSINESS

Despite an early oriental intrusion especially through the Sahara desert, there is no evidence that material and social progress in Black Africa lagged any other region's progress up until the 17th century and beyond, Amin (1972), Diop (1974, 1991) and Inikori (2002). But it was the push first begun in the slavery-mercantilist era and perfected during colonial expansionism that reversed the evolutionary universals and momentum of African states and empires. Today's political and socio economic map and configuration of the continent, arising from the infamous Scramble for Africa, remains an uncomfortable patchwork of misalignment and forced unions. A newly organized and systematic but voluntary in-migration agenda has the potential to more naturally align cognate interests of the various groups and individual choices, even in the face of over three centuries of demographic and political transformations at national and provincial levels.

What is being suggested is not an out of the box or avant garde invention of the mind. Complete labor mobility is already a part of the laundry list of prerequisites for any successful monetary union. The European Monetary Union, for instance, keenly aware of the risks posed currently by the remaining legal and institutional barriers to labor mobility and geographic relocation has warned member states that such risks may undermine the union's ability to adapt and reduce its susceptibility to shocks OECD (1999, pp 9-20). It just works well, when same policy instrument can also be used to achieve a wider social cultural objective as being contemplated in the ongoing discussion.

In this sense, regional economic communities of the type planned by the African Union, of which ECOWAS is but a shining example, has the potential to achieve multiple objectives, including direct material betterment, as envisaged, as well as an innocuous but needed realignment of populations and labor settlements all over Africa. Thus, resuming the broken path engendered by the intrusions from the Orient and the West some five hundred years ago. This is in the interest of everyone both in the short and long runs. ECOWAS officials and policy leaders do not seem to be broad minded enough or there does not seem to be any new idea on the table which is anchored on the lessons of history of the immediate past. When one takes a look at the objectives of ECOWAS in its statutes, one wonders if such objectives, and as revised, are really in tune with the contemporary pressing socio cultural and politico economic conditions of its populations.

> ECOWAS integration policies and programmes are influenced by the prevailing economic conditions in its member countries, the need to take the principal provisions of the AEC Treaty into account, and relevant developments on the international scene[8].

This statement inserted into its official objectives, gives the impression that the 16 governments anticipated and are collectively disinterested in the slow pace of progress at integration since the founding of ECOWAS. However, one would think "prevailing economic conditions" call for an accelerated integration into ECOWAS objectives of, "a common market and a single currency."

One economic condition worth discussing is the recent, bold and sophisticated attempt by Deaton (2010), to estimate world poverty and inequality. Regional comparison is shown in Figure 5.3. Clearly, Sub-Saharan Africa is worst: it is the only region where poverty has refused to fall for the past twenty five years and remains stubbornly high at over fifty percent. The poverty line itself is constant $1.25 purchasing power parity, per person

---

8 Profile (2010, p.2)

per day.[9] Save Sub-Saharan Africa, poverty in every region of the world declined. In fact, for East Asia and the Pacific, poverty fell by more than 78% during the 25 year period covered in the study, even though the region's poverty rate was much higher than that of Africa in 1980, the beginning of the period covered by the study. Comparative results like these do show that the prevailing economic conditions in Black Africa are challenging enough to warrant immediate change and action. Yet, the promise of economic integration is bright if the political will to remove constraints in the labor markets and on the free movement of persons is exercised.

Figure 5.3. World Poverty by Region

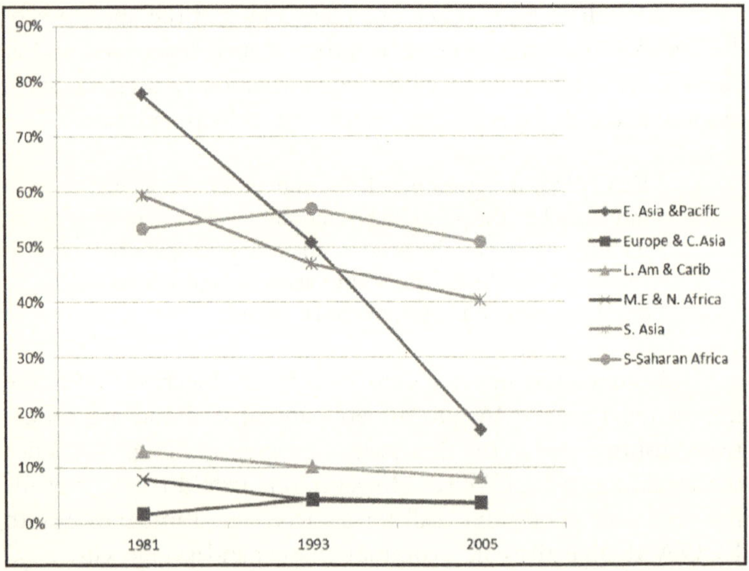

Source: Deaton (2010). Data extracted from Table 1

THE POSITIVE AND THE NORMATIVE

There is no illusion that the heavy analytical part of the work needed to bring the ECO to fruition and for the complete union

9 This is the popular $1 a day world poverty line which was $1.25 per person a day in 2005 international dollars. See Deaton (2010 pp7-8) for narratives and detailed methodology.

of Africa and its peoples is going to be driven by the training and basic scholarship established in Europe and European inspired cultures. A recent academic ranking of world universities and research institutions shows the first African university to appear on that list ranks in the lower part of the 201-302 position.[10] Despite this rather demoralizing development, it is inconceivable that the normative task, the crafting of the values binding, the idea of what Africa should become and the way Africa wants to present itself to the rest of humanity, is left exclusively in the hands of overseas exporters of knowledge and intellectual property. Still, this normative task has to be the prerogative and guarded domain of the truly African. Experience elsewhere in history does not show anything different.

So, we have a problem: the analytical mind is Western trained and the value mind is expected to be African born and raised. The problem now is how to disembody the two. The answer lies in the creating of a somewhat invisible new African leader who is engaged to the teeth in the latest scholarship but uncompromisingly immersed in indigenous African values and needs. It is necessary that these cadres of scholar activists love Africa in the sense of a philosophical clear mindedness that solutions to African problems are indeed outcomes and outflows from African institutions and African minds. The foregoing discussion does not have anything to do with, and indeed it excludes, identifying who is the scholar activist by some sort of ideological or political acid test of yore.[11] No Cold War type mentality or mustard seed test is implied in any way. There is a legion of sources by which an individual's commitment or engagement can be ascertained these days. But in addition to these, Africa should also more actively seek to perpetu-

---

10 The University of Cape Town, South Africa is ranked # 1 in Africa but ranked lower than the 250th in the world. http://www.arwu.org/ARWU2009_3.jsp.

11 I realize that in yesteryears, such scholars were called Africanists. Today, we still have this word in the literature and popular parlance. The Africanist, as the term has evolved, is rather too amorphous and ideological for our needs here. In fact, in one vein, it is either everyone is an Africanist or no one is! What we have in mind by an African scholar activist is close to the concept of an Afrocentric scholar – one who truly believes that the best way to study Africa and its people is by placing African ideals at the center of such analyses.

ate itself by breeding institutions devoted to the teaching, research and scholarship of its finest traditions and beliefs.

OUT OF STYLIZED CIRCLES: THE INTEGRATION OF SCHOOLING

If serious thought is given to preparing the populations for integration, there would be less opposition and mutual distrust in matters of economic and political integration and cooperation. Suppose, as a thought experiment, the countries in WAMZ exchange 2,000 secondary school students yearly, on a bilateral or multilateral basis. This would mean each country receives 10,000 students (assuming there are six countries in WAMZ) and sends out 10,000 students each year. The number could also be based on existing formula for allocating resources in ECOWAS, such as the weight of the GDP or the population of each country, with a minimum of 2,000 students for the smallest country. Supposed this has been carried out twenty out of the thirty five years ECOWAS has been in existence? This would have been a new day begun regarding integration in West Africa or in any part of Africa for that matter. Can we begin to think of the linguistic, cultural and diffusion effects of such programs? This would be in addition to the direct gains in making the labor market flexible by enhancing additional sectoral and geographical mobility and adaptability. We know that free movement of labor itself is crucial to the success of the objective of price stability, the most important single monetary policy goal in a monetary union.

Between 1976-1970, Nigeria fought an unfortunate civil war, which, from all angles, had the promise of tearing the country into the smithereens of religion and ethnic divisions. Somehow, the war ended and the leaders of the new Nigeria, under military leader, Yakubu Gowon, began what it called reconciliation, reconstruction and rehabilitation. One of the reconciliation programs was the establishment of a National Youth Service Corps, NYSC, for university graduates in 1975. In it, those finishing bachelor's degree or equivalent were required to work, *serve* was the word used, in states other than their own. So, young Nigerian men and women were posted all over the country to work and live with other Nigerians who they never imagined they would meet in their lifetime.

In addition, the program brought the children of Civil War friends and foes together; it united, in one fell swoop, the victorious and the vanquished populations. But it also led to measurable improvement in the workforce and the agglomeration of a national identity and traditions never seen before. Nigerian indigenous cultures began to mesh, meld and merge; and for a while all the divisions carried over from colonial times which deepened during the inter-ethnic war of 1967-1970, dissipated. Not only did higher education become national, secondary education was now feeding on the new Nigerian zeal for uniting. Parents did not hesitate to send their children to boarding secondary schools anywhere in the nation. Other effects included the cultivation of tolerance by various ethnic and religious groups. One indication of this was the sharp increase in inter ethnic, interregional and interdenominational romance and consummate marriages. It is generally believed by Nigerians that the period of 1970-1979 was one of the most progressive and meaningful in its modern history.[12]

The ensuing discussion can be accommodated in measurable ways in the role of quality of labor in economic growth. The literature is well developed that human capital is vital to economic growth. Of particular importance for this paper is the quality of human capital as may be embodied in quality measures, transmitted from productivity to growth. In fact, Hanushek and Kimko (2000) show in an endogenous growth model, a specification that human capital quality differences provide a large effect of international differences in economic growth of nations. The key is: what constitutes the quality of human capital? Hanushek and Kimko suggest variables which may capture sets of school and family resources and characteristics. In the latter may inhere qualities acquired from cross country educational and cultural experiences and skills arising from the exchange program suggested in this paper. Let us now consider the principles of the model as laid out by Hanushek and Kimko.

12 Nigerians refer to the decade of 1980-1990 as the lost years and those who reached leadership age (25-50) during the decade are sentimentally called wasted generation.

The growth of a nation g is given by its labor force quality, QL, and a set of other factors **X** in equation (1)

$$g = \mathbf{X}\beta + \gamma QL + \varepsilon \quad (1)$$
$$R = \mathbf{W}\delta + \eta g + \nu \quad (2)$$
$$QL = \mathbf{Z}\alpha + \pi R + \mu \quad (3)$$

In equation (2), growth now contributes along with other factors **W**, a vector, to determine the amount of resources set aside for human capital growth and for schools development, R. But equation (3) appears to be the most important in the sequence of this system of relationships. We now propose that school resources and human capital production coupled with other inputs **Z** determine the labor force quality for each economy (Hanushek and Kimko, 2000, p.1191). Under these conditions, it is clear that a direct estimation of (3) is able to detect the impact of quality on growth and related labor quality to aggregate resources in the school system as well as family and other population features in each country. This way also, the impact of a student exchange program, such as suggested above, implemented over very many years on latent and real genuine features of civic and public convergence within the region of monetary union is captured in the equation. The system in (1) to (3) is capable of showing us how family and school resources relate to the productivity of generation of students, and hence how those resources relate to the economic growth of nations. If we are able to construct appropriate variables, including instrumental variables, then, this kind of thinking will enable us to look at the traditional box in a new way. Hanushek and Kimko found large variations between countries when a production function of this type that relates human capital to aggregate resources for schools and family factors are estimated.[13]

SUMMARY AND CONCLUSION

The paper was inspired by the repeated conventional housekeeping practices in the corridors of economic theorizing and policy formulation. Even though, the paper does not call for reinventing

13 See their Table 3 p. 1192 for results.

the wheel, it is suggested that solutions that are simple but relevant can work, especially when it comes to the perennial question of how to make the benefits of economic growth available to the majority of Africans. Among the WAMZ countries, the paper shows that pursuing economic integration in the pattern of the experience of the past thirty five years of the founding of ECOWAS gives little promise of quick and assured beneficial results. We are of the opinion that while the stated criteria are important, it serves no good purpose to continue to wait until all of the temporal conditions are met. Meeting those criteria in their letters is rarely practical, even within the experience of societies that are more advanced in the rules of the game and in material living than African countries.

We suggest the crux of the labor market as an all encompassing element in the tool kit of WAMI. We are not sure that even if a monetary union is declared today and the ECO currency begins to circulate, monetary control and the goal of price stability would be achieved. This is because, at the heart of the needed social, political and economic transformation of West Africa lays the need to liberalize and deregulate the labor market. Besides, allowing West Africans the freedom to live and work in any part of the region of their choosing will likely resume the dormant motions of stability prevailing in the entire region before the external contacts from the West and the Orient. It is our position that history's unfinished business of state formation is at the heart of ongoing structural and institutional disarticulation in West African nations. The functioning of a mobile labor market has the potential to confer on West African institutions and demographic characteristics, an enduring adaptability and continuing flexibility to shock absorption for years to come.

References

Academic Ranking of World Universities. http://www.arwu.org/ARWU2009_3.jsp last accessed 06/05/2010.

Akande, Tunji, Adeolu O. Adewuyi and Babatunde W. Adeoye. 2007. *Meeting the Challenges of Macroeconomic Convergence Criteria in the Second West Africa Monetary Zone (WAMZ): The Case ofNigeria.* Ibadan, Nigerian Institute of Social and Economic Research.

Akonor, Kwame. 2010. *Global Institutions: African Economic Institutions.* New York: NY, Routledge.

African Statistical Yearbook 2009.

Amin, Samir. 1972. "Underdevelopment and Dependence in Black Africa: Historical Origin". *Journal of Peace Research* 9(2):105-120.

Bearce, H. David.2007. *Monetary Divergence: Domestic Policy Autonomy in the Post-Bretton Woods Era.* Ann Arbor: MI, The University of Michigan Press.

Deaton, Angus. (2010). "Price Indexes, Inequality, and the Measurement of World Poverty",*American Economic Review* 100(1):5-34.

Diop, Cheikh Anta (1991). *Civilization or Barbarism: An authentic Anthropolo.gy.* Chicago: IL Lawrence Hill Books.

Diop, Cheikh Anta (1974). *The African Origin of Civilization: Myth or Reality?* Chicago: IL, Lawrence Hill Books.

Fielding, David, ed.2005. *Macroeconomic Policy in the Franc Zone.* New York:NY, Palgrave Macmillan.

Gogan, Nukhet and Bedriye Saracoglu. 2007. "Income Convergence of European Union and Candidate Countries: Are they all the Same?" *International Research Journal of Finance and Economics,* 12 (160-164).

Hanushek, Eric A. and Dennis D. Kimko. 2000. "Schooling, Labor-Force Quality, and the Growth of Nations", American Economic Review 90(5): 1184-1208.

Horn, Henrik, Giovanni Maggi, and Robert W. Staiger. 2010. "Trade Agreements as Endogenously Incomplete Contracts." *American Economic Review,* 100(1): 394-419.

Inikori, Joseph E.2002. *African and the Industrial Revolution in England: A Study in International Trade and Economic Development,* Cambridge, Cambridge University Press.

Kamar, Bassem and Bakardzhieva, Damyana. 2006. "The Appropriate Monetary Policy Coordination for the GCC Monetary Union", Twenty-six Annual Meeting of the Middle East Economic Association (MEEA), Allied Social Science Associations, Boston, Massachusetts, January 6-8, 2006.

OECD. 1999. *EMU: Facts, Challenges and Policies.* Paris: France, OECD.

Profile: Economic Community of West African States (ECOWAS). Last accessed 04/22/2010.

Quintyn, Marc and Genevieve Verdier, ed. 2010. *African Finance in the 21st Century.* New York: NY, Palgrave Macmillan.

Silvia, John and Azhar Iqbal. 2010. "Three Simple Techniques to Analyze a Complex Economic Phenomenon: The Case of Profits", *Business Economics: The Journal of the National Association for Business Economics,* 45(2):116-125.

Suranovic, Stephen. 1997-2009. *International Trade, Theory and Policy.* http://internationalecon.com/Trade/T-toc.php. Last accessed 04/22/2010.

Young, Andrew, Matthew Higgins and Daniel Levy.2007. "Sigma Convergence versus Beta Convergence: Evidence from U.S. County-Level Data". *Working Papers 03_16,* Department of Economics, Emory University.

Section III

Inflation

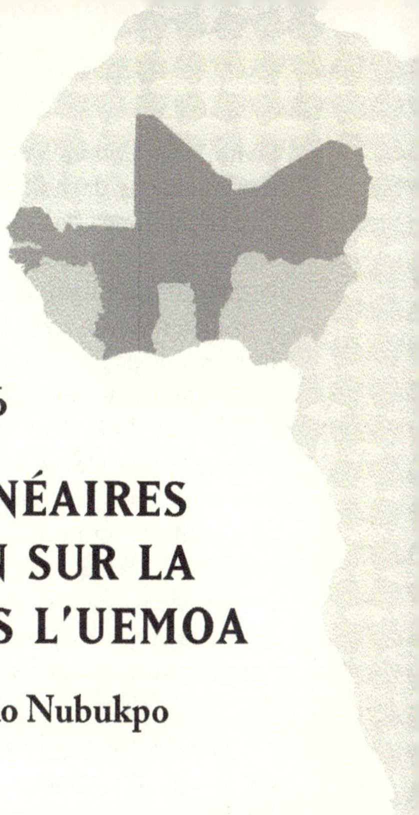

Chapter 6

EFFETS NON LINÉAIRES DE L'INFLATION SUR LA CROISSANCE DANS L'UEMOA

Adama Combey & Kako Nubukpo

INTRODUCTION

L'inflation et la croissance économique entretiennent des rapports complexes, à l'origine de nombreuses controverses au sein de la science économique, dont la plus célèbre est celle relative à la pertinence de la courbe de Phillips[1]. Dans le cas spécifique de

---

1 La courbe de Phillips rend compte de l'arbitrage existant entre inflation et chômage : en effet, elle suggère qu'il est possible d'obtenir un supplément de croissance économique devant se traduire par une baisse du chômage, par le biais d'une politique monétaire expansionniste. La hausse du taux d'inflation, conséquence de la politique monétaire expansionniste, serait le prix à payer pour obtenir la croissance. Un tel enchaînement des mécanismes a été remis en cause par Phelps et Friedman, puis Sargent et Wallace, qui montrèrent grâce à l'introduction des anticipations dites adaptatives, puis rationnelles dans les modèles keynésiens, l'absence d'arbitrage entre inflation et chômage. La réponse des nouveaux keynésiens fut de réhabiliter la courbe de Phillips en passant par l'hypothèse d'imparfaite flexibilité des prix.

l'Union Économique et Monétaire Ouest Africaine (UEMOA)[2], regroupement de huit (8) États ayant notamment en commun l'usage du franc CFA et la politique monétaire sous la conduite de la Banque Centrale des États de l'Afrique de l'Ouest (BCEAO), la question des liaisons existant entre inflation et croissance économique revêt un intérêt particulier à plusieurs égards. En effet, le fort taux de pauvreté prévalant au sein de cette zone rend impérative l'atteinte des Objectifs du Millénaire pour le Développement (OMD) et donc d'un taux de croissance d'au moins 7% par an, nécessaire à la réduction de la pauvreté de 50% à l'horizon 2015. De même, dans la mesure où il constitue un véritable impôt sur les plus pauvres, un taux d'inflation élevé doit être combattu vigoureusement. Par ailleurs, le caractère fortement extraverti des économies de la zone UEMOA rend difficile l'appréhension exacte des déterminants respectifs de la croissance économique et de l'inflation au sein de cette zone et, surtout, les canaux de transmission de l'une à l'autre.

Ces défis se posent avec une singulière acuité pour la BCEAO, en charge du pilotage de la politique monétaire de la zone UEMOA. Chargée d'assurer la stabilité des prix, de préserver la valeur interne et externe de la monnaie commune le CFA, et le financement des économies des pays membres, la BCEAO dans l'administration de la politique monétaire de la zone a traditionnellement accordé beaucoup de poids à l'objectif de lutte contre l'inflation qui est intrinsèquement lié à celui de préservation de la valeur interne et externe de la monnaie. A cet effet, depuis 1989, la politique monétaire se fonde sur un recours accru aux mécanismes de marché, consacrant l'option d'une régulation indirecte de la liquidité bancaire. Un rôle primordial est ainsi accordé au taux d'intérêt qui devient l'instrument privilégié de la politique monétaire, en particulier depuis l'abandon de l'encadrement du crédit intervenu en janvier 1994. Ce dispositif a permis à la zone d'enregistrer de bonnes performances en termes de stabilisation de l'inflation mais semble-t-il, au prix d'une croissance économique plus faible (voir figure 6.1).

2 L'UEMOA est composé de huit (8) pays : Bénin, Burkina, Côte d'Ivoire, Guinée Bissau, Mali, Niger, Sénégal, Togo.

Ainsi, la BCEAO est en bûtte à des critiques récurrentes relatives à son obsession anti-inflationniste qui pourrait en partie, expliquer la faible croissance économique que la zone a enregistrée au cours des quinze dernières années. Jamais une union économique et monétaire n'aura connu un suivi aussi strict de politiques dites de désinflation compétitive, d'inspiration monétariste.

FIGURE 6.1 : INFLATION - CROISSANCE DANS LA ZONE UEMOA

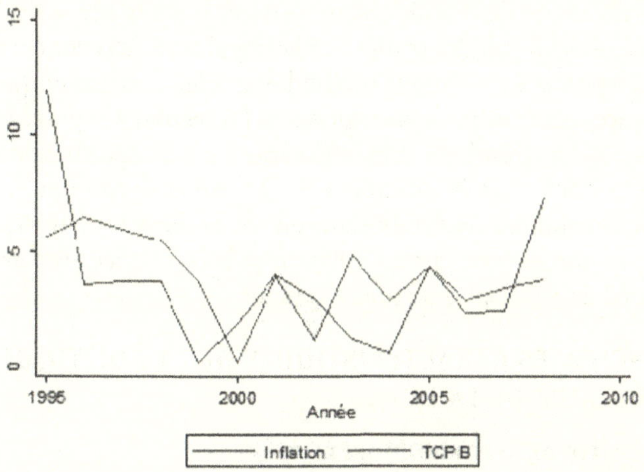

Source : Auteurs sur la base des données de la Commission de l'UEMOA

Or, il est de plus en plus admis qu'un niveau d'inflation structurellement faible est non seulement source de distorsions dans l'activité économique, mais peut également accentuer le risque de déflation. Ces différentes analyses fondent les débats sur l'existence d'une relation non linéaire entre l'inflation et la croissance et la question de la détermination du seuil d'inflation optimal.

Dans la littérature empirique récente, les travaux de Ghosh et Phillips, (1998) portant sur un vaste échantillon dont les pays de l'OCDE et quelques pays en développement, montrent que le seuil d'inflation optimal se situe entre 2% et 8% pour les pays de l'OCDE et de 5% à 10% pour les pays en développement. Ceux de Bruno et Easterly, (1998) 10% ; et de Faria et Carneiro, (2001) aboutissent à des résultats similaires. Sarel (1996) a par ailleurs, fait remarquer à partir d'un échantillon de pays développés et de pays en développement qu'en dessous du seuil de 8%, l'inflation a un impact positif sur la croissance économique et qu'au-delà du seuil, l'effet devient nuisible. De même, Khan et Senhadji (2001) ont par ailleurs trouvé que le niveau d'inflation acceptable est de l'ordre de 1% à 3% pour les pays développés et de 11 à 12% pour les pays en développement.

De fait, le présent article tente de mettre en évidence, sur la base de la procédure d'identification du seuil endogène à la Hansen (2000), les spécificités de la zone UEMOA en termes de seuil d'inflation. Il s'appuie pour ce faire sur la description des conditions d'exercice de la politique monétaire conduite par la BCEAO, dans le souci de rendre compte de la singularité de la zone (section 2). La section 3 présente la méthodologie, les données et quelques évidences descriptives sous régionales. La section 4 expose, analyse et discute les résultats. Les estimations de la spécification non linéaire d'un modèle de croissance en panel dynamique confirment l'hypothèse d'existence au sein de la zone UEMOA, d'une relation non linéaire entre l'inflation et la croissance avec un seuil optimal de 8,08%. La section 5 conclut.

PRINCIPALES CARACTÉRISTIQUES DE LA POLITIQUE MONÉTAIRE DE LA BCEAO

Dispositif de Gestion Monétaire

L'objectif principal de la politique monétaire conduite par la BCEAO est la préservation de la valeur interne et externe de la monnaie. Cette politique a connu de nombreuses transformations, en 1975, en octobre 1989, en octobre 1993 et en avril 2010, de sorte que le nouveau dispositif de gestion monétaire de l'UEMOA se fonde sur un recours accru aux mécanismes de marché, privilégiant ainsi les méthodes de régulation indirecte de la liquidité.

La politique monétaire de la BCEAO (2002, a) repose sur l'utilisation de taux d'intérêt directeurs propres à l'Institut d'émission, sur un marché monétaire rénové et sur la libéralisation des conditions de banque. En appui à ces instruments, un système de réserves obligatoires permet de modifier le comportement du système bancaire et d'agir sur le coût du crédit. A la suite des décisions prises au mois de juillet 1996, dans le cadre de l'approfondissement du marché monétaire, le dispositif de gestion monétaire de la BCEAO comprend trois volets essentiels : (i) le marché monétaire utilisant le guichet d'appel d'offres avec le système d'adjudications (injection ou reprise de liquidités) et le marché interbancaire ; (ii) les procédures permanentes de refinancement, notamment celles de la pension et du réescompte, mises en œuvre à l'initiative des établissements de crédit ; et (iii) le système des réserves obligatoires, comprenant trois champs d'intervention, à savoir, le champ d'application des réserves, l'assiette de calcul et le coefficient des réserves obligatoires.

Plus généralement, les innovations portent sur le remaniement de la grille des taux directeurs de la BCEAO, avec l'instauration d'un taux de prise en pension, dont l'évolution est adaptée à celle du taux du marché monétaire, qu'il influence et pour lequel il peut servir de signal. Le marché monétaire a également subi de profonds changements, dans le but de constituer un instrument privilégié de gestion des trésoreries bancaires et des interventions de l'Institut d'émission. La Banque Centrale y participe désormais comme intervenant.

Le volume et la nature de ses interventions sont déterminés en fonction des orientations qu'elle se propose d'impulser au marché et au comportement des banques, au regard de ses objectifs en matière de politique de la monnaie et du crédit et de la situation conjoncturelle de liquidité. La libéralisation des conditions de banque se traduit notamment par des taux débiteurs applicables aux crédits à la clientèle, libres et fixés d'accord parties, sous réserve qu'ils ne dépassent pas, tous frais, commissions et rémunérations de toute nature compris, le taux légal de l'usure, défini comme le double du taux d'escompte de la BCEAO.

L'expérience de l'intégration monétaire dans l'UMOA/UEMOA[3] est atypique, dans la mesure où l'instauration d'une

3 Le traité instituant l'Union Monétaire Ouest Africaine (UMOA) date de mai 1962, alors que celui instituant l'UEMOA ne date que de janvier 1994. Contrairement aux idées reçues, le traité de l'UEMOA n'a pas remplacé celui de l'UMOA. Les deux traités coexistent et celui de l'UMOA sert encore de base juridique aux aspects strictement monétaires. Cependant, dans le présent article nous avons choisi, sauf à de rares reprises, de ne mentionner que l'UEMOA pour faciliter la lecture, le recours au traité de l'UEMOA nous permettant d'évoquer à la fois les aspects réels et les aspects monétaires et financiers. De plus, il est prévu à terme une unification des deux traités, même si le traité de l'UMOA vient d'être révisé de manière unilatérale et est entré en vigueur le 1er avril 2010.

monnaie commune au mois de mai 1962 a précédé la mise en place des conditions économiques de sa pérennité, en particulier l'effectivité de règles édictées en matière de convergence et de bonne gestion macroéconomiques. La coopération monétaire existant avec la France est illustrée par l'existence du mécanisme dit du « compte d'opérations »[4], qui contribue à garantir une parité fixe entre le franc CFA et l'Euro. Dans ce cadre, la recherche de la stabilité des prix est présentée comme un objectif susceptible d'assurer la soutenabilité à long terme du taux de change et la compétitivité des économies de l'UEMOA. Par ailleurs, fortement dépendantes des chocs d'offre exogènes (aléas climatiques, variations erratiques des cours des matières premières), cette zone a dû faire face à diverses fluctuations asymétriques auxquelles la politique monétaire commune a eu à répondre. En particulier, Guillaumont (2002) a analysé les facteurs pouvant favoriser l'occurrence dans l'UEMOA de chocs asymétriques, notamment la forte spécialisation agricole déterminée par la géographie. En effet, les économies sahéliennes sont relativement proches les unes des autres, mais se distinguent des économies des pays « côtiers ». D'autre part, deux économies, le Sénégal et la Côte d'Ivoire, sont plus industrialisées que les autres.

Une étude[5] s'est attachée à décrire et à évaluer l'impact des mouvements des taux directeurs de la BCEAO sur la croissance et l'inflation entre 1989 et 1999 (Nubukpo, 2002).

A cet égard, un modèle a été spécifié, dont les principaux résultats sont au nombre de trois. En ce qui concerne l'inflation, l'impact d'une variation du taux du marché monétaire est significatif aussi bien à court qu'à long terme et présente le signe négatif attendu dans l'Union prise globalement. En revanche, l'impact est d'une très faible intensité, proche de zéro. En outre, le taux de prise en pension exerce un impact significatif contraire au signe attendu, aussi bien à court qu'à long terme, dans l'Union et dans les différents pays, sauf

4 Pour cerner les tenants et aboutissants du fonctionnement du compte d'opérations, se référer aux ouvrages de Hugon (1999, p. 19) et Claveranne (2005, p. 50)

5 Les résultats de cette étude ont été validés par les autorités monétaires de la zone et publiés dans le « rapport annuel » de la BCEAO, 2002, b, pp 20-21.

au Bénin et au Niger. L'estimation de l'équation de croissance révèle ensuite l'existence d'un impact significatif mais très faible, à court et long terme, des modifications des taux d'intérêt de la BCEAO. Les coefficients de correction d'erreur, qui illustrent le degré d'homogénéité des réponses des différentes économies de l'UEMOA suite à une même politique monétaire, sont enfin fortement différents d'un pays à l'autre. Ces différences traduisent une grande hétérogénéité entre les économies, du point de vue de leur capacité à retrouver leur niveau d'équilibre de long terme, en réponse à une décision de politique monétaire. L'étude plaide pour une amélioration de la connaissance des mécanismes de transmission de la politique monétaire au secteur réel dans le cadre de l'UEMOA et surtout pour une évaluation des implications du cadre institutionnel d'exercice de la politique monétaire de la BCEAO, ainsi que la mise en évidence des paradoxes induits par ce contexte.

MÉTHODOLOGIE, DONNÉES ET ÉVIDENCES DESCRIPTIVES

Dans cette section, nous commençons par la spécification du modèle de croissance, puis nous décrivons la procédure d'estimation du seuil d'inflation optimal ainsi que les différents tests en particulier le test de non linéarité. Et finalement, nous exposons les sources des données et les évidences empiriques.

Modèle et Procédure d'estimation

Le modèle de croissance retenu dans le cadre du présent exercice empirique est inspiré de celui utilisé par Drukker et al. (2005) pour analyser sur un échantillon de 138 pays couvrant la période 1950 - 2000, l'effet de seuil de la relation entre l'inflation et la croissance. Notre spécification diffère de celle utilisée par ces auteurs dans la mesure où elle intègre non seulement la possibilité d'existence d'effet de seuil dans la relation entre l'inflation et la croissance mais aussi la dynamique de court terme.

En effet, dans la littérature empirique existante, la relation de non linéarité entre l'inflation et la croissance est examinée sous l'angle de long terme et donc une élimination des effets de court terme. De ce fait, les auteurs spécifient généralement un modèle de croissance en panel non dynamique qu'ils régressent sur données de fenêtre de cinq ans (c'est à dire que toutes les variables du modèle représentent une moyenne arithmétique sur cinq ans) sur plusieurs pays et couvrant plusieurs périodes.

En désignant par πi,t, le semi-logarithme[6] du taux moyen annuel d'inflation d'un pays i à une date t et par γ, le seuil d'inflation candidat[7] qui est supposé commun à tous les pays de la zone UEMOA, nous formulons les équations (1) et (2) qui représentent les deux (2) régimes de la relation «inflation-croissance».

$$y_{i,t} = \mu_i + \vartheta_i + \alpha y_{i,t-1} + \theta_1 \pi_{i,t} + \beta' X_{i,t} + \varepsilon_{i,t} \quad si \ \pi_{i,t} \leq \gamma \qquad (1)$$

$$y_{i,t} = \mu_i + \vartheta_i + \alpha y_{i,t-1} + \theta_1 \pi_{i,t} + \beta' X_{i,t} + \varepsilon_{i,t} \quad si \ \pi_{i,t} > \gamma \qquad (2)$$

$y_{i,t}$ est le Produit Intérieur Bruit (PIB) par tête ; i, effet spécifique pays (supposé fixe dans le temps et permet de contrôler l'hétérogénéité inobservée des sources de croissance des pays de l'UEMOA) ; t désigne l'effet fixe temporel commun à tous les pays et permet de contrôler l'effet tendanciel zone du taux de croissance économique ; $\varepsilon_{i,t}$ est l'écart aléatoire idiosyncratique et est supposé identiquement et indépendamment distribué (iid) ; $X_{i,t}$ représente l'ensemble des variables de contrôle c'est à dire le vecteur des autres variables pertinentes identifiées dans la littérature empirique comme facteurs affectant le taux de croissance économique.

Nous retenons eu égard aux études empiriques passées portant sur les déterminants de la croissance économique de la zone, les variables de contrôle suivantes : le taux d'investissement TINVi,t (proportion des investissements total dans le PIB) ; le taux d'ouverture OUVi, t (proportion du commerce extérieur dans

---

6 En effet, la fonction semi-logarithmique est utilisée à la place de la fonction logarithme compte tenu de l'existence des taux d'inflation négatif et donc empêchant l'opérationnalité de la fonction logarithme. De ce fait, la fonction semi-logarithme est utilisée comme suit : log ($\pi_{i,t}$) lorsque $\pi_{i,t}$ > 1 et $\pi_{i,t}$-1 si $\pi_{i,t}$ < 1.

7 C'est l'ensemble des valeurs de i;t après avoir éliminé les valeurs extrêmes. Eu égard aux enseignements de la littérature existante et des particularités de la zone UEMOA, nous avons retenu toutes les valeurs candidates comprises entre une fourchette de 1% à 30%. C'est à dire que nous faisons l'hypothèse que la valeur seuil se situerait entre cette fourchette pour éliminer les valeurs aberrantes.

le PIB c'est à dire la somme des exportations et des importations rapporté au PIB) ; la consommation publique GOUVi,t (part des dépenses publiques totales dans le PIB) et le taux de croissance des termes de l'échange TCTEi,t.

Les deux (2) équations de départ (1) et (2) spécifiant respectivement l'effet positif qu'aurait le niveau d'inflation sur la croissance économique avant le seuil et l'effet négatif au delà du seuil peuvent être combinées en une seule équation avec une redéfinition de la variable d'intérêt $\pi_{i,t}$. Ainsi, en définissant $Inf\pi_{i,t}$ et $Sup\pi_{i,t}$ tel que :

$$Inf\pi_{i,t} = \begin{cases} \pi_{i,t} & si \ \ \pi_{i,t} \leq \gamma \\ 0 & ailleurs \end{cases} \tag{3}$$

$$Sup\pi_{i,t} = \begin{cases} \pi_{i,t} & si \ \ \pi_{i,t} > \gamma \\ 0 & ailleurs \end{cases} \tag{4}$$

Nous obtenons l'équation[8] (5) suivante :

$$y_{i,t} = \mu_i + \vartheta_i + \alpha y_{i,t-1} + \theta Inf\pi_{i,t} + \delta Sup\pi_{i,t} + \beta' X_{i,t} + \varepsilon_{i,t} \qquad si \ \ \pi_{i,t} \leq \gamma \tag{5}$$

Où θ et δ représentent les effets marginaux de l'inflation sur la croissance et peuvent être différents suivant le régime. Tout l'art de la technique réside dans l'identification ou non du seuil, du test de linéarité et du calcul d'une marge de sécurité de l'inflation seuil optimal c'est l'intervalle de confiance pour un risque de première espèce donné.

A cet effet, nous avons adopté une démarche méthodologique à trois (3) étapes. Premièrement, nous avons estimé la valeur seuil $\hat{\gamma}$ et les différents coefficients du modèle : $\hat{\alpha}$; $\hat{\theta}$; $\hat{\delta}$; $\widehat{\beta'}$ à l'aide de l'estimateur Within (qui nous a permis d'éliminer les effets spécifiques pays) et

8 Il convient de remarquer que sous le régime 1 (avant le seuil $\pi_{i,t} \leq \gamma$), les observations de $Sup\pi_{i,t}$ sont nulles et donc $Sup\pi_{i,t}$ disparaît et nous retrouvons l'équation (1) car $\theta = \theta 1$ vice versa.

d'une procédure séquentielle. Puis, nous avons testé l'hypothèse de linéarité contre son alternatif qu'est le modèle à effet de seuil. Et finalement, nous avons construit un intervalle de confiance pour la valeur seuil identifié pour une meilleure interprétation des résultats.

Pour déterminer la valeur seuil et estimer les paramètres de l'équation (5), nous avons utilisé l'algorithme de détermination de seuil endogène fourni dans Hansen (1998, 2000). Il s'agit d'une procédure de régression basée sur la technique des moindres carrées séquentiels sur toutes les valeurs seuils candidates jusqu'à ce que l'on obtienne $\hat{\gamma}$ c'est à dire le seuil optimal correspond à la valeur de γ qui minimise la somme des carrés des résidus.

Soit $\hat{\gamma}$ = ArgMin (S1(γ)) avec S1(γ) = $e(\gamma)'e(\gamma)$.

A l'issue de la détermination de la valeur seuil, les paramètres d'intérêt $\hat{\theta}$ et $\hat{\delta}$ sont également connus, par conséquent l'étape suivante a consisté à tester la linéarité du modèle c'est à dire l'égalité de ces paramètres. Il s'agit de tester l'hypothèse nulle de linéarité (H0 : $\theta = \delta$) contre son alternatif (H1 : $\theta \neq \delta$). Le problème qui se pose dans l'administration de ce test est que sous H0, le seuil n'est pas identifié, par conséquent les tests classiques comme celui de Wald[9] n'ont plus de distribution standard. De ce fait, les valeurs critiques des statistiques associées à ces tests ne peuvent plus être directement lues dans des tableaux de distribution standard. Pour résoudre ce problème, nous avons suivi les recommandations de Hansen relatives à l'utilisation du test de ratio de vraisemblance et de la procédure de bootstrap. L'administration de ce test est fondée sur le ratio LRF comme l'indique la formule ci-dessous et une procédure de bootstrap qui permet d'approximer la distribution asymptotique de sa loi[10]

$$LR_F = \frac{S_0 - S_1(\hat{\gamma})}{\hat{\sigma}^2} \text{ avec } \hat{\sigma}^2 = \frac{S_1(\hat{\gamma})}{N(T-1)}$$

9 Nous avons quand même effectué ce test et corrigé la statistique du test à l'aide d'une procédure de bootstrap pour comparer les résultats avec le test de ratio de vraisemblance à la Hansen ; cependant, nous ne reportons pas les résultats du test dans le tableau 2 pour des raisons de simplification.

10 Voir Hansen (1998) pour plus de détails sur l'utilisation de la technique de bootstrap et les démonstrations mathématiques.

S0 représente la somme des carrés des résidus issus de l'estimation de l'équation dans l'hypothèse de linéarité et $\hat{\sigma}^2$ désigne la variance résiduelle issue de l'estimation de l'équation (5) sous l'hypothèse de non linéarité c'est celle correspondante au seuil optimal. La valeur de signification (p-value) de la statistique du test est obtenue à l'aide de la procédure de bootstrap.

Une fois que le test de non linéarité est concluant et confirme l'existence d'un seuil d'inflation, on aborde la dernière étape qui est celle de l'estimation de l'intervalle de confiance du seuil optimal $\hat{\gamma}$. L'estimation de l'intervalle de confiance est basée sur le ratio de vraisemblance LR(γ) calculé pour tout γ tel que :

$$LR(\gamma) = \frac{S(\gamma) - S_1(\hat{\gamma})}{\hat{\sigma}^2}$$

Hansen a simulé la distribution de ce ratio et trouve qu'elle est asymptotiquement distribuée suivent une loi spécifique[11] de tel sorte qu'en considérant un risque critique C(γ)[12] (tabulée par Hansen, 1998) correspondant à une erreur de première espèce α, l'intervalle de confiance est donnée par : $\hat{\Gamma} = \{\gamma,\ LR(\gamma) \leq C(\alpha)\}$

Données et Évidences Descriptives

L'équation 5 est estimée sur données de panel qui s'étendent de 1980 à 2008, pour un total de sept (7) pays de l'UEMOA17. Ces données proviennent de diverses sources (voir table 3 en annexes) notamment le « World Economic Outlook » ; les annexes des Rapports semestriels de surveillance multilatéral de l'UEMOA; le « World Development Indicator » et le « Global Development Finance ».

Le tableau 1 montre l'évolution conjointe du taux moyen annuel d'inflation et du taux de croissance économique sur la période 1990-2004 (subdivisée en sous période de cinq ans), pour les économies de la zone CEDEAO. Elle suggère que les pays de la zone UEMOA ont un niveau d'inflation plus faible que les autres pays de la CEDEAO cependant la différence du niveau de croissance est mitigée.

---

11 Voir Hansen 1998 pour plus de détails sur la loi.

12 Sur la base de la distribution asymptotique simulée par Hansen, la statistique $C(\alpha)$ pour un risque α est $C(\alpha) = -2\ln(1-\sqrt{1-\alpha})$

Tableau 6.1 : Relation Inflation-Croissance dans la zone CEDEAO

TAUX MOYEN PAR SOUS PÉRIODE EN % 1990-2004						
	1990-94	1995-99	2000-04	1990-94	1995-99	2000-04
	Croissance du PIB par tête			Inflation		
UEMOA						
Benin	1,74	2,17	1,11	9,62	5,86	2,60
Burkina Faso	-0,21	4,42	2,02	5,01	4,13	1,70
Côte d'Ivoire	-2,55	2,37	-3,64	6,64	5,85	2,36
Guinée Bissau	1,11	-2,78	-1,58	44,69	30,22	2,49
Mali	2,85	2,50	1,97	4,19	4,06	1,01
Niger	-3,23	-0,85	0,30	5,75	4,27	1,63
Sénégal	-1,84	1,92	1,71	5,98	2,88	1,30
Togo	-2,50	0,25	-2,03	7,63	5,32	1,66
Hors UEMOA						
Cape Vert	1,07	6,19	3,44	8,26	6,35	0,48
Ghana	1,59	1,79	2,05	23,04	32,06	22,44
Guinée	-0,39	1,04	-0,32	13,46	4,03	8,72
Liberia	n/a	n/a	-7,61	n/a	n/a	9,09
Nigeria	0,30	-0,60	8,14	35,84	25,43	13,54
Sierra Léone	-4,77	-13,46	10,38	65,10	26,75	3,96

Source : Calcul des Auteurs à partir des données du WEO

En considérant par exemple les pays comme le Mali, le Benin et la Guinée Biseau, on remarque que leurs taux d'inflation ont suivi, sur toute la période, une tendance baissière en particulier pour des valeurs de fin de période qui sont en dessous de la norme zone (3%). Or leurs taux de croissance du PIB réel par tête s'est également dégradés sur la période. On peut par exemple se poser la question de l'effet d'un niveau structurellement faible de l'inflation sur la croissance. La raison n'est pas claire à la lecture de la performance du Sénégal. Ce dernier contrairement aux pays mentionnés ci-dessus a vu s'améliorer le niveau de vie de ses habitants avec une désinflation sur toute la période. La relation inflation-croissance des autres pays est mitigée. Ces constats nous ont amené à élargir l'échantillon sur les pays d'Afrique subsaharienne et d'examiner à l'aide d'une représentation graphique le lien entre l'inflation et la croissance.

La figure 2 suggère sans surprise l'existence d'une relation non linéaire entre l'inflation et la croissance des pays, non seulement au sein de la zone UEMOA mais en Afrique subsaharienne 18.

Le graphique suggère que les pays l'Afrique subsaharienne ayant le taux moyen de croissance économique (moyenne sur 1995-2005) ont un taux d'inflation moyen se situant dans la fourchette de 5 à 20%.

Figure 6.2 : Afrique Subsaharienne : Inflation-Croissance

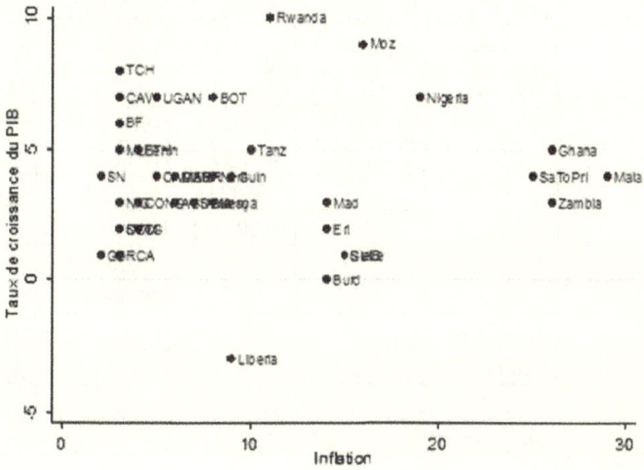

Note : Les données sont des moyennes arithmétiques sur 1995-2005

Les pays ayant un taux d'inflation annuel en dessous et au-delà de la fourchette ont un niveau de croissance moyenne faible. Quant aux pays de la zone UEMOA, la relation reste encore claire sur la figure. Étant donné que cette représentation graphique ne tient pas compte des facteurs autres que l'inflation qui pourraient avoir une incidence sur la croissance économique et donc porté préjudice à la marge de seuil identifiée graphiquement, il convient de mener une investigation empirique de manière à cerner plus spécifiquement cette relation et en particulier dans la zone UEMOA.

RÉSULTATS, ANALYSES ET DISCUSSIONS

Dans cette section, nous reportons dans le tableau 2, les résultats de l'identification du seuil optimal d'inflation. Nous avons estimé cinq (5) spécifications de modèle pour tester la robustesse de nos résultats en particulier la sensibilité du seuil par rapport aux effets des variables omises. Nous avons par ailleurs testé (voir tableau 3 en annexes) la robustesse du seuil par rapport aux perturbations de court terme en ré-estimant la version non dynamique.

Tableau 6.2 Identification du Seuil et Test de sensibilité

Variables	M1	M2	M3	M4	M5
Seuil	8,08%	8,08%	8,08%	8,08%	8,08%
IC	[6,9 10,4]	[6,4 9,35]	[6,4 8,68]	[6,4 9,07]	[6,4 9,07]
$y_{i,t-1}$	0,870***	0,893***	0,885***	0,891***	0,892***
	(0,0344)	(0,0346)	(0,0365)	(0,0339)	(0,0339)
TINV	0,00399***	0,00300***	0,00313***	0,00350***	0,00343***
	(0,000964)	(0,000882)	(0,000907)	(0,000965)	(0,000957)
GOUV	-0,000804		0,000943	0,000817	0,000837
	(0,00114)		(0,00111)	(0,0011)	(0,00111)
OUV	-0,000549			-0,000383	-0,000385
	(0,000595)			(0,000648)	(0,000645)
TCTE	2,20E-06				0,000109
	(0,000267)				(0,000273)
TCPOP	0,0279**				
	(0,0114)				
$Inf\pi_{i,t}$	0,00318**	0,00371***	0,00385***	0,00391***	0,00396***
	(0,00125)	(0,00123)	(0,00124)	(0,00127)	(0,00126)
$Sup\pi_{i,t}$	-0,00872**	-0,00988**	-0,0101**	-0,00948**	-0,00965**
	(0,00415)	(0,00403)	(0,00404)	(0,00417)	(0,00421)
Const	1,477***	1,265***	1,344***	1,285***	1,279***
	(0,406)	(0,421)	(0,438)	(0,407)	(0,408)
Observations	175	175	175	175	175
Nombre de pays	7	7	7	7	7
R^2	0,888	0,881	0,881	0,882	0,882
LR Hansen Test	15,95	15,28	15,89	14,37	14,57
Bootstrap p-value	0,00	0,00	0,00	0,00	0,00

Note : Robust standard errors in parentheses *** p<0,01, ** p<0,05, * p<0,1

Nos résultats suggèrent (colonne 1) que la valeur seuil qui minimise la somme des carrés des résidus issus des estimations des moindres carrés séquentiels est 8,08%. Le ratio de vraisemblance du test de non linéarité à la Hansen rejette l'existence de l'hypothèse nulle H0 d'absence d'effet de seuil, la statistique corrigée à l'aide de la procédure de bootstrap du test de Wald[13] confirme la non linéarité du modèle et l'existence de la valeur seuil. L'intervalle de confiance (voir la figure 6.3 en annexes) calculé sur la base de la distribution simulée par Hansen (1998) indique qu'à un risque de première espèce de 5%, le seuil d'inflation se situerait entre 6,09% et 10,4%.

Pour tester la sensibilité du seuil par rapport aux effets des variables omises[14], nous avons intégré l'une après l'autre (M2 à M5) toutes nos variables de contrôle et analysé les effets sur le seuil. Les résultats indiquent que le seuil de 8,08% est robuste par rapport aux effets des variables omises. De même la forme dynamique ou non dynamique de la spécification n'a pas d'impact sur le seuil identifié (voir résultats dans le tableau 4 en annexes pour les estimations en panel non dynamique).

Il ressort de ces résultats que l'effet marginal de l'inflation sur la croissance économique des pays de la zone UEMOA dépend du niveau initial du taux d'inflation. Si le taux d'inflation est en dessous de 6,09%, une augmentation du niveau d'inflation d'1% se traduit par une augmentation de 0, 003% de la croissance de court terme. L'effet devient plus important à long terme soit 0,024 (0,00318/(1-0,87))[15]. Cependant, une augmentation du niveau d'inflation à partir d'une valeur initial de 10,4% se traduit par un effet négatif tant sur la croissance de court terme que sur la croissance de long terme. L'effet est de -0,009 à court terme tandis qu'à

13 Les résultats de ce test ne sont pas reportés sur le tableau 2 pour des raisons de simplification.

14 Certaines variables telles que le taux de change effectif réel et la qualité des institutions qui sont identifiées dans la littérature n'ont pas été contrôlées eu égard aux données non disponibles.

15 L'effet de long terme est à relativiser dans la mesure où par construction du modèle dynamique, $y_{i,t-1}$ est endogène car cette variable est corrélée avec l'erreur idiosyncratique. De ce fait, il est possible que le coefficient de la variable retardée estimée par la technique Within soit biaisé.

long terme, il devient -0,06%. L'analyse des résultats permet de retrouver l'intuition d'un arbitrage entre le maintien de l'inflation à un niveau structurellement faible et la croissance économique de la zone.

CONCLUSION

La politique monétaire de la BCEAO souffre de deux principales faiblesses, nuisibles à son efficacité. D'une part, il existe incontestablement un déficit de réflexion endogène sur le rôle et les missions d'une banque centrale dans le contexte d'économies en développement parmi les plus pauvres du monde, faiblement monétarisées et bancarisées. L'objectif unique assigné à la politique monétaire, à savoir le maintien d'un taux d'inflation inférieur ou égal à 2%, semble exagérément restrictif, eu égard au seuil optimal d'inflation obtenu dans la présente étude (7,9%). Il apparaît souhaitable que la BCEAO, suite à la réforme de ses statuts en avril 2010, lui accordant désormais l'indépendance organique, tire exemple des débats en cours au sein des banques centrales des pays industrialisés, notamment dans le contexte de la crise économique internationale actuelle. En effet, de nombreuses voix autorisées plaident de façon croissante pour l'intégration explicite de l'objectif de croissance économique dans les missions d'une banque centrale. Tel est le cas par exemple de la banque centrale américaine, la FED.

En second lieu, les déterminants réels du principal objectif de la BCEAO, la stabilité des prix, ne semblent pas être en adéquation avec les moyens effectifs dont elle dispose pour l'atteindre. Ceci est d'autant plus vrai que l'on est dans un environnement caractérisé par de fortes contraintes et de puissantes incertitudes, internationales (flambée des prix des matières premières sur le marché mondial), physiques (aléas climatiques), organisationnelles (structure oligopolistique du marché du crédit) et institutionnelles (nature du régime de change avec la zone Euro et des accords de coopération avec la France).

La gestion monétaire de la BCEAO semble avoir un coût réel en termes de croissance économique pour la zone UEMOA. Cette situation devrait conduire les autorités monétaires à repenser les termes de l'arbitrage «inflation-croissance» et inciter les autorités politiques communautaires à repenser le *Policy-mix* de la zone UEMOA. Il convient d'explorer de nouvelles voies, par adaptation ou création d'instruments en adéquation avec l'environnement réel des économies de la zone UEMOA. Pour ce faire, une connaissance accrue des mécanismes de transmission des impulsions monétaires au secteur réel des économies de l'UEMOA semble plus que jamais impérative.

Références bibliographiques

ARAUJO C., BRUN J. L. et COMBES J. F., (2004), « Économétrie repères-cours- application », Amphi économie, pp 286-294.

BCEAO, (2002, a), « Évaluation de la mise en œuvre du dispositif de gestion monétaire de la Banque Centrale des États de l'Afrique de l'Ouest et réflexions pour un renforcement de son efficacité », mimeo, BCEAO, Direction du Crédit, Dakar, Février 2002.

BCEAO, (2002, b), « Rapport Annuel », Imprimerie de la BCEAO, Dakar, 137P.

BRUNO M., EASTERLY W., (1998), "Inflation Crises and Long-run Growth", Journal of Monetary Economics, February 1998, pp. 326

CAE (Conseil d'Analyse Économique), (2006), «Politique économique et croissance en Europe», Rapport n59, P. Aghion, E.

Cohen et J. Pisani-Ferry, (2003), « La Documentation Française », Paris, 2006, 305p.

CALVO G.A., CORICELLI F. (1993), "Output Collapse in Eastern Europe: The Role of Credit", IMF StaPapers, N1, Vol. 40, Mars 1993, PP.32-52.

CORICELLI F., (1998), "Macroeconomic Policies and the Development of Markets in Transition Economies", Budapest, Central European University Press, 1998

CLAVERANNE B., (2005), La Zone Franc : au-delà de la monnaie, Economica, Paris, 2005, 236p.

DOE L., DIALLO M.L., (1997), Déterminants empiriques de l'inflation dans les pays de l'UEMOA, Notes d'Information et Statistiques, BCEAO, n 476, décembre 1997.

DRUKKER D., GOMIS-PORQUERAS P., HERNANDEZ-VERME P., (2005), Threshold Effects in the Relationship between Inflation and Growth: A New Panel Data Approach , Paper Presented in the 11th International Conference on Panel Data, February 2005, 18P.

FARIA J. R., CARNEIRO G.F., (2001), "Does High Inflation Affect Growth in the Long and Short Run?" Journal of Applied Economics, N1 May, pp 89-105.

GHOSH A., PHILLIPS S., 1998), Inflation May Be Harmful to Your Growth, IMF StaPapers, December 1998, pp. 672710.

GUILLAUMONT -JEANNENEY S., (2002), Bilan de l'intégration monétaire dans l'UMOA, Communication au symposium du quarantième anniversaire de la BCEAO, Dakar, 13-14 mai 2002, 32p.

HANSEN B.E. (1999), Threshold Effects in non-dynamic panels: Estimation, testing, and inference, Journal of Econometrics, 93, 1999, pp.345-368.

HANSEN B.E. (1996), Inference when a nuisance parameter is not identified under the null hypothesis, Econometrica, 64, pp. 413-430.

HUGON P. (1999), La Zone Franc à l'heure de l'Euro, Karthala, Paris, 1999, 300p.

HURLIN C., MIGNON V., (2005), Une Synthèse des Tests de Racine Unitaire sur Données de Panel. LEO, Université d'Orléans, EconomiX et THEMA, Université Paris X Nanterre.

ISLAM N., (1995), "Growth Empirics: A Panel data Approach", Quarterly Journal of Economics, 110, 1995, pp. 1127-1170.

KHAN M., SENHADJI A., (2001), Threshold Eects in the Relationship between Inflation and Growth , IMF StaPapers, 48 : 1 pp.1-21.

NUBUKPO K., (2007), L'efficacité de la politique monétaire en situation d'incertitude et d'extraversion : le cas de l'Union Economique et Monétaire Ouest Africaine, The European Journal of Development Research, Vol. 19, N3, sept 2007, pp. 480-495.

NUBUKPO K., (2002), L'impact de la variation des taux d'intérêt directeurs de la BCEAO sur l'inflation et la croissance dans l'UMOA , Notes d'Information et Statistiques, Série Études et Recherches , n526, BCEAO, Dakar, juin 2002, 32p.

OULD-AHMED P., (1999), Politiques monétaires, comportements bancaires et crises de financement en Russie : les vicissitudes des années 90, Revue d'Études Comparatives Est-Ouest, n2-3, Vol. 30, pp. 89-121.

SAMBA MAMADOU O., (1998), Modèle Intégré de Projection Macroéconométrique et de Simulation pour les États Membres de l'UEMOA PROMES: estimation et application à la Côte d'Ivoire, Document d'Étude et de Recherche (D.E.R.) n98 / 06, Banque Centrale des États de l'Afrique de l'Ouest (BCEAO), Direction de la Recherche et de la Statistique, août 1998.

SAREL M., (1996), Nonlinear Effects of Inflation on Economic Growth, IMF StaPapers, March 1996, pp. 199215.

STIGLITZ J., WEISS A., (1981), Credit Rationing in Markets with Imperfect In- formation , American Economic Review, vol.71, 1981, pp. 393-410

TENOU K., (1999), Les déterminants de la croissance à long terme dans les pays de l'UEMOA, Notes d'Information et Statistiques, BCEAO, n493, juin 1999.

WIJNBERGEN S., (1983, a), Credit Policy, Inflation and Growth in a Financially Repressed Economy, Journal of Development Economics, vol.13, N1-2August, pp.45-

WIJNBERGEN S., (1983, b), Interest Rate Management in LDCs, Journal of Monetary Economics, Vol.12, N3, September, pp.433-452

ANNEXES

TABLEAU 6.3 : VARIABLES ET SOURCES DE DONNÉES

VARIABLES	DESCRIPTION	SOURCES
Y	Produit Intérieur Brut réel par tête d'habitant	World Economic Outlook
INFL	Taux moyen annuel d'inflation (variation de l'indice des prix à la consommation	UEMOA : Rapport de surveillance multiléral
INV	Investissement total rapporté au PIB	World Development Indicators (WDI)
OUV	Somme des exportations et importations rapporté au PIB	Global Development Finance (GDF)
GOUV	Part des dépenses publiques totales dans le PIB	
TCPOP	Taux de croissance de la population	
TCTE	Taux de croissance des termes de l'échange	

TABLEAU 6.4 : RELATION NON LINÉAIRE DE LONG TERME « INFLATION-CROISSANCE »

VARIABLES	M1	M2	M3	M4	M5
Seuil	8,08%	8,08%	8,08%	8,08%	8,08%
TINV	0.196*	0.210***	0.200***	0.184*	0.171*
	(0.104)	(0.0684)	(0.0766)	(0.0937)	(0.0973)
GOUV	-0.0201		-0.0871	-0.0859	-0.131
	(0.0598)		(0.0970)	(0.0978)	(0.102)
OUV	-0.225*			0.0147	-0.0108
	(0.115)			(0.0607)	(0.0613)
TCTE	0.00270				0.00787
	(0.0205)				(0.0216)
TCPOP	1.353				
	(1.035)				
$Inf\pi_{i,t}$	0.182	0.232*	0.216*	0.215	0.223*
	(0.132)	(0.134)	(0.130)	(0.130)	(0.132)
$Sup\pi_{i,t}$	-0.243	-0.673**	-0.662**	-0.678**	-0.292
	(0.421)	(0.267)	(0.261)	(0.278)	(0.425)
Constant	-3.824	-4.115***	-2.705	-3.241	-1.006
	(4.824)	(1.519)	(2.646)	(3.682)	(3.530)

Note : Robust standard errors in parentheses *** p<0,01, ** p<0,05, * p<0,1

Figure 6.3: Intervalle de confiance du seuil selon différents modèles

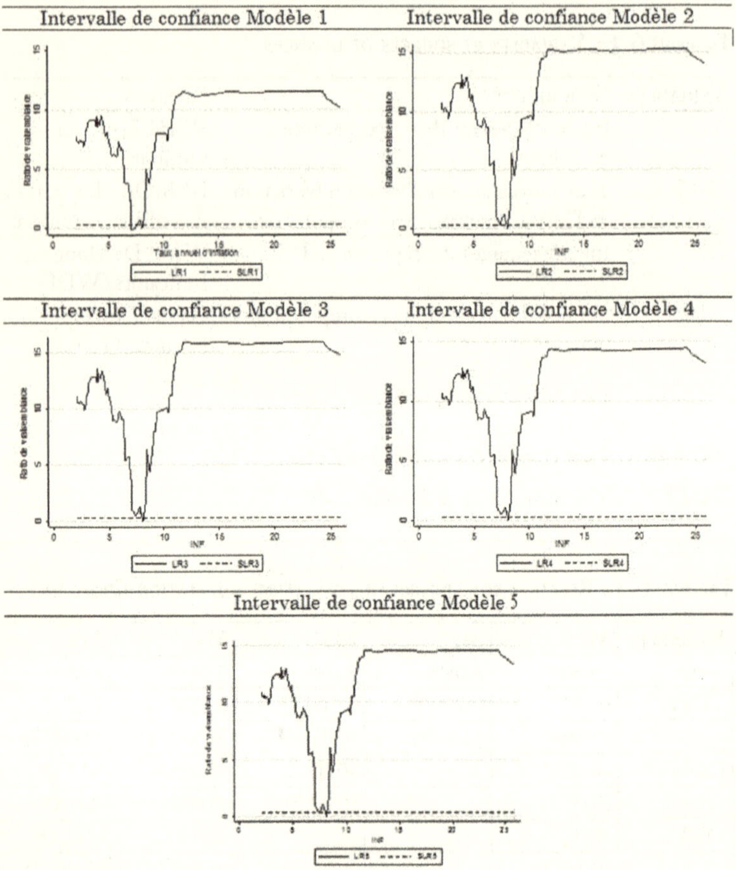

Chapter 7

INFLATION AND GROWTH: AN ESTIMATE OF THE OPTIMAL (THRESHOLD) LEVELS OF INFLATION IN THE WAMZ

Temitope Oshikoya and Abu Bakar Tarawalie

INTRODUCTION

The conventional view in macroeconomics holds that low inflation is a necessary condition for fostering economic growth. Over the years, the existence of a link between these two variables has become the subject of considerable interest and debate. It is widely believed that moderate and stable inflation rates promote the development process of a country, and hence economic growth. Low inflation levels promote economic growth by making prices and wages more flexible (Lucas, 1973). On the other hand, high price level may create uncertainty and hamper economic performance. Inflation may also reduce a country's international competitiveness, by making its exports relatively more expensive, thus negatively impacting on the balance of payments. Moreover, inflation can interact with the tax system to distort borrowing and lending decisions. High inflation hampers economic growth due to the adverse impact on efficient distribution of resources by changing relative prices (Fisher, 1993). If high inflation is detrimental to the economy and low inflation is beneficial, then it is natural to ask what the optimal level of inflation for an economy is. This debate raises an interesting policy issue of how much of inflation is too much; that is, how much inflation impedes economic growth. What level of inflation rate is required to propel growth in the WAMZ member countries?

Single digit inflation remains one of the primary convergence criteria required for the formation of a monetary union among member states of the West African Monetary Zone (WAMZ[1]). But over the years, this objective has become nearly elusive simply because apart from internal country specific economic difficulties that besiege individual countries, external shocks like hikes in oil prices, negative terms of trade, exchange rate depreciation, among others, have invariably worsen the inflation pressure in these countries. The question practitioners and policy makers seek to find answers to is whether should we have individual specific inflation targets based on specific economic structure of member states instead of single digit inflation for all member states? If so, what rate of inflation should the West African Monetary Institute (WAMI) advise member states to aim for? More generally, at what level of inflation does the relationship between inflation and economic growth become negative?

Although the relationship between inflation and economic growth remains controversial or somewhat inconclusive, several empirical studies confirm the existence of either a positive or negative relationship between these two major macroeconomic variables. Mundell (1965) and Tobin (1965) found a positive relationship between the rate of inflation and the rate of capital accumulation, which in turn, implies a positive relationship to the rate of economic growth. They argued that since money and capital are substitutable, an increase in the rate of inflation increases capital accumulation by shifting portfolio from money to capital, and thereby, stimulating

1 The member states of WAMZ include: The Gambia, Guinea, Ghana, Liberia, Nigeria and Sierra Leone.

a higher rate of economic growth (Gregorio, 1996). Conversely, Fischer and Modigliani (1978) suggest a negative and nonlinear relationship between the rate of inflation and economic growth through the new growth theory mechanisms (Malla, 1997).

There have been a number of formal empirical attempts to identify threshold level in the inflation-growth relationship. Khan and Senhadji (2001) found a 1% threshold level of inflation for industrialized countries, that is, an inflation rate beyond 1% would have negative effects on growth. Using the same countries, Burdekin (2000) found a threshold level of 8%. This result is consistent with the findings of Sarel (1996) which tested for structural break and found that inflation is negatively related to growth after 8% for industrialized countries. Furthermore, while, Ghosh and Phillips (1998) obtained a 2.2% threshold level of inflation for industrialized countries, the results of Judson and Orphanides (1996) showed a 10% threshold level.

While some researchers found a positive relationship between inflation and growth, e.g. Gillman et al (2002), Sweidan (2004), Thirlwall and Barton (1971), Mallik and Chowdhury (2001), others such as Motely (1994), Andres and Hernando (1997), De Gregoria (1991), found a negative relationship. Furthermore, differences exist in the threshold levels of inflation that is ideal for propelling economic growth. In view of these conflicting results, it is apparent that the impact of inflation on real output growth is an unresolved issue in the empirical literature.

The purpose of this study is to empirically estimate the threshold (optimal) level of inflation that is conducive for economic growth in the countries of the WAMZ. This paper is not only an attempt to contribute to the empirical debate vis-à-vis inflation and economic growth nexus, but also differs from previous studies in several respects. The study employed both time series and panel data techniques in estimating the desirable threshold inflation rate for countries of the WAMZ, which are characterised by inflationary pressures. The study also attempts to identify the determinants of growth in the WAMZ. In addition, the study employs a bivariate Granger Causality test to determine the direction of causality between inflation and economic growth. Furthermore, despite the existence of a plethora of empirical work on inflation and economic growth, there is a dearth of work in the case of the WAMZ economies. The researchers are not aware of any study on estimating the threshold level of inflation in the WAMZ.

Following the introduction, the rest of the paper is structured as follows. Section two discusses the development and trends in inflation and economic growth in the WAMZ countries. Section three provides the literature on inflation and economic growth including the theoretical and empirical literature. Section four addresses the analytical framework and methodology, including the model specification, while section five presents the empirical results. The conclusion and policy implications of the study are presented in section six.

INFLATION AND ECONOMIC GROWTH IN THE WAMZ

With the adoption of the convergence criterion aimed at ensuring macroeconomic stability to underpin the strength of the common currency, price development is being tackled with renewed vigor across the WAMZ countries. From a theoretical standpoint, price stability is seen as a recipe for fostering strong economic growth. The WAMZ countries are on the verge of forming a monetary union with a single currency and a common Central Bank, and the attainment of single digit inflation is considered as one of the convergence criteria for member countries to achieve. The WAMZ economies have experienced accelerated economic growth between 2001 and 2008, compared with the 1990s. In addition, inflationary pressures have also decelerated for most of the countries in the zone during this period. The sub-section provides trend analysis of inflation and real GDP growth for countries of the WAMZ.

The Gambia

In the early 1980s The Gambian economy was beset by series of adverse external and internal shocks that resulted in a decline in economic activities and rising inflation. The country experienced double digit inflation rate, which rose from an average of 11.3 percent during 1980-84 to 23.7 percent between 1985 and 1989, while real GDP growth declined from an average of 4.6 percent to 3.2 percent during the same period (see Tables 7.1 & 7.2).

Table 7.1: Inflation rates in the WAMZ

Country/Year	1980-84	1985-89	1990-94	1995-99	2000-04	2005-08
Gambia	11.3	23.7	7.7	3.7	9.0	3.8
Ghana	70.3	26.3	23.0	32.2	22.4	13.6
Guinea	32.2	35.2	1.3	4.4	11.8	22.8
Liberia*	3.3	4.0	3.3	0.7	8.1	3.3**
Nigeria	15.9	25.9	35.8	25.4	13.5	10.5
Sierra Leone	39.7	86.2	65.1	26.7	4.0	11.1

*GDP Deflator inflation
**2-year (2005-2006) average

Table 7.2: Real GDP Growth Rates in the WAMZ

Country/Year	1980-84	1985-89	1990-94	1995-99	2000-04	2005-08
Gambia	4.6	3.2	2.6	3.6	5.3	6.9
Ghana	-1.2	5.2	4.1	4.4	4.6	6.4
Guinea	1.5	4.3	3.8	4.8	2.7	3.1
Liberia	-2.5	-6.4	-31.0	15.1	0.7	-2.5**
Nigeria	-3.9	5.7	3.6	2.5	6.2	6.2
Sierra Leone	2.9	-0.6	-2.8	-5.9	14.3	6.8

** 2-year (2005-2006) average

Despite the introduction of the Structural Adjustment Programme (SAP) in 1986 which was aimed at reversing the economic down-turn of the early 1980s and setting the stage for a more stable macroeconomic environment, real GDP growth remained low in the early 1990s, averaging 2.6 percent during 1990-94. The decline was partly due to slower growth in agricultural output and tourism as well as the Military Coup in 1994, which led to disruption in economic activities in the tourism sector and suspension of cooperation from donor countries. However, inflation declined significantly during this period. Since 1995, the country has experienced accelerated economic growth, as real GDP growth increased from an average of 3.6 percent during 1995-99 to 6.9 percent between 2005 and 2008, arising from improved agricultural output, increased tourist activities and favourable external sector development, among others. In the same vein, price stability was also restored, attaining single digit inflation rate between 1995 and 2008. Critical investigation of Figure 7.1 revealed that for lower levels of inflation rate, there is some element of positive relationship between inflation and re al GDP growth, while at higher levels of inflation, an inverse relationship was evident.

Figure 7.1: Inflation and Real GDP Growth Rates in the Gambia, 1980-2008

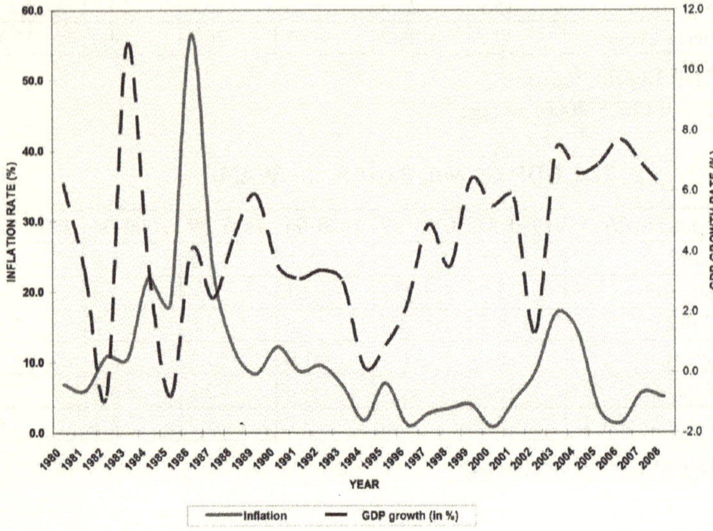

Sources: WAMZ data base and IFS year Book, 2008

Ghana

Ghana's macroeconomic performance in the early 1980s was sluggish, characterised by high inflationary pressure amidst declining growth. Inflation rate averaged 70.3 percent between 1980 and 1984, largely informed by increased money growth for government deficit financing. To curb the high inflationary pressure, the government instituted price control mechanisms, which subsequently distorted relative prices, caused economic stagnation and severe shortage of goods and consequently resulted in a decline in real GDP growth by -1.2 percent during the period.

However, the Economic Recovery Programme (ERP) adopted by Ghana in the mid 1980s sought to minimize both external and internal imbalances and placed the economy on a path of sustainable growth. Hence between the period 1985 and 1989, the Ghanaian economy grew by 5.2 percent, while inflation decelerated to 26.3 percent. Furthermore, between 1990 and 2008, real GDP growth remained positive, averaging above 4.0 percent. Increased government expenditure on infrastructure, as well as increased economic activities in the agriculture, services, and mining sectors, among others contributed to the positive growth rate during the period. During the period 1990 and 2004, inflation rate remained high averaging above 20.0 percent, largely explained by excessive demand pressure sustained by excessive fiscal expansion and accommodating monetary growth. The relationship between inflation and real GDP growth seems ambiguous as evident from Figure 7.2. However the figure showed some inverse relationship with higher levels of inflation rate.

FIGURE 7.2: INFLATION AND REAL GDP GROWTH RATES IN GHANA, 1980-2008

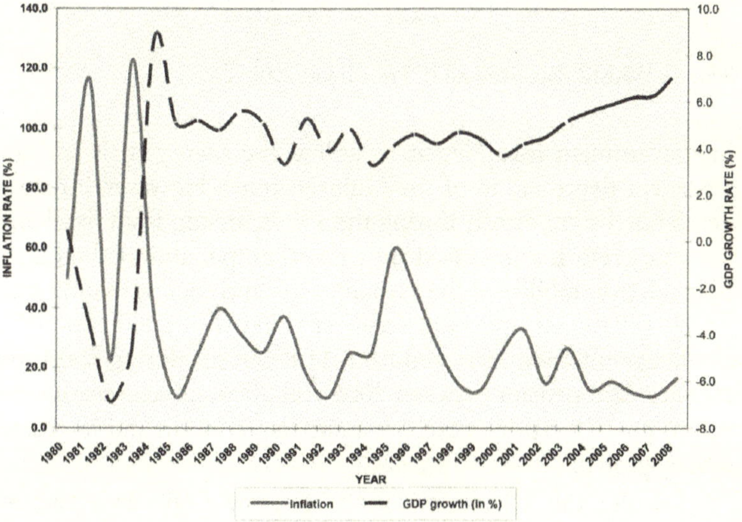

Sources: WAMZ data base and IFS year Book, 2008

GUINEA

Inflation in Guinea was relatively high in the 1980s, increasing from 32.2 percent between 1980 and 1984 to 35.2 percent during 1985 to 1989. The high inflation rate during this period was partly attributed to increased money growth for financ-

Figure 7.3: Inflation and Real GDP Growth Rate in Guinea, 1980-2008

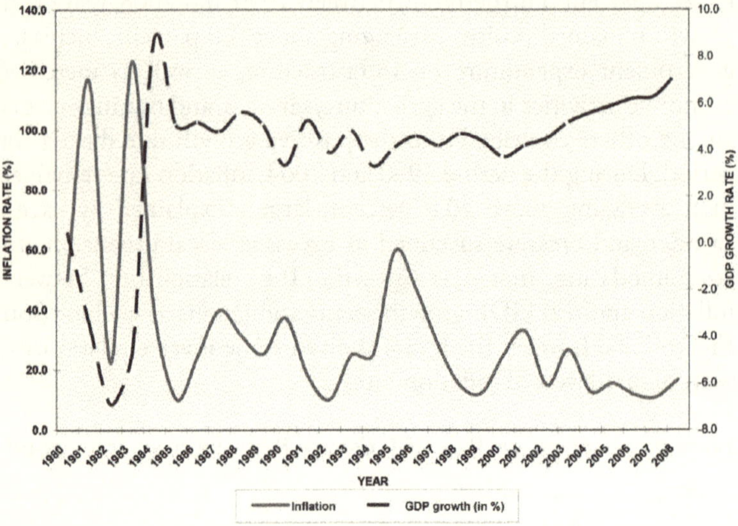

Sources: WAMZ data base and IFS year Book, 2008

ing government fiscal deficit, as well as the energy crisis and the persistent depreciation of the Guinean franc. However, inflation decelerated significantly during the 1990s, arising from fiscal and monetary reforms, increased agricultural output and food production, relative stability of the exchange rate and decline in imported prices. Inflationary pressure accelerated between 2000 and 2008, as average inflation increased from 11.8 percent during 2000 and 2004 to 22.8 percent between 2005 and 2008, driven mostly by a rise in non-food prices, exchange rate depreciation and increased money growth.

Despite the hike in inflation rate, the Guinean economy maintained positive growth during the review period, with real GDP growth accelerating from 1.5 percent between 1980 and 1984 to 4.8 percent during 1995 and 1999, arising from increased private sector investment as well as growth in the mining and agricultural sectors. Real GDP growth also increased from 2.7 percent between 2000 and 2004 to 3.1 percent during 2005 and 2008. The growth momentum during the 2000s was due to increased economic activities in the mining, agricultural and services sectors. A critical analysis of Figure 7.3, revealed some evidence of an inverse relationship between inflation and economic growth in Guinea.

Liberia

Generally, since 1980 the Liberian economy has witnessed low inflationary trend except in 1998 when inflation rate stood above 20.0 percent (see Figure 7.4). The real GDP growth rate had been in the negative since 1980. The deterioration in the economy was worsened by the first civil war as 5-year average real GDP growth rate declined from -2.5 percent in 1980-84 to -6.4 percent in 1985-89 (the onset of the first civil war) and further down to -31.0 percent during 1990-94. However, the country experienced positive growth between 1995 and 2004. The high growth rates recorded during this period were due to the economic resuscitation and relative peace experienced after the first civil war. Not long, the second civil war (1999-2003) eroded all the economic gains made after the first civil war, and thereby pushing the economy once again into a quagmire. As at end-2003, the economic decay was huge as real GDP growth rate stood at -31.3 percent. The growth rate assumed an upward trajectory (between 2 percent and 8 percent growth rates) after the second civil war but this was far lower than the growth trajectory after the first civil war (Figure 7.4).

For Liberia, the relationship between inflation and real GDP growth was not clear in the 1980s and early 1990s as can be seen in Figure 7.4. Of course, the war period, especially the first civil war, also distorted this relationship greatly. The relationship appeared to be more tilted towards a positive than a negative relationship. During the late 1980s and early 2000s, it appeared there was a negative relationship between inflation and real GDP growth as can be seen from Figure 7.4. While real GDP growth rate increased after the first civil war, inflation rate declined. During the second civil war, real GDP growth rate decreased, while inflation rate rose to double-digit level. The second post-war period witnessed a blurred relationship between inflation and economic growth.

Figure 7.4: Inflation and Real GDP Growth Rates in Liberia, 1980-2006*

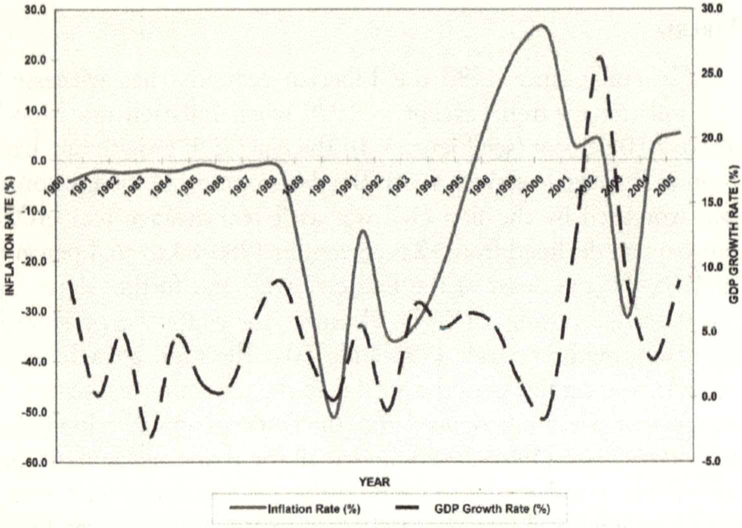

Sources: WAMZ data base and IFS year Book, 2008
*1997 and 1998 values were deleted because they were too large.

Nigeria

Since the 1980s, the Nigerian economy had experienced episodes of high inflation. From Table 7.1, inflation rate increased from an average of 15.9 percent between 1980 and 1984 to peak at an average rate of 35.8 percent during 1990 and 1994. The surge in inflation during the 1980s was partly due to collapse in the world oil market, import restrictions, foreign exchange constraints, among others, whilst excess money supply, severe shortage in commodity supply and continuous labour and political unrest following the annulment of the June 1993 election accounted for the rise in inflation rate in the 1990s.

Real GDP growth which remained negative in the early 1980s, increased to an average of 5.7 percent in the late 1980s, following the adoption of the Structural Adjustment Programme. Real GDP growth remained positive between 1985 and 2008, largely informed by growth in both the oil and non-oil sectors of the economy. An assessment of Figure 7.5 showed an inverse relationship between inflation and real GDP growth.

Figure 7.5: Inflation and Real GDP Growth Rates in Nigeria, 1980-2008

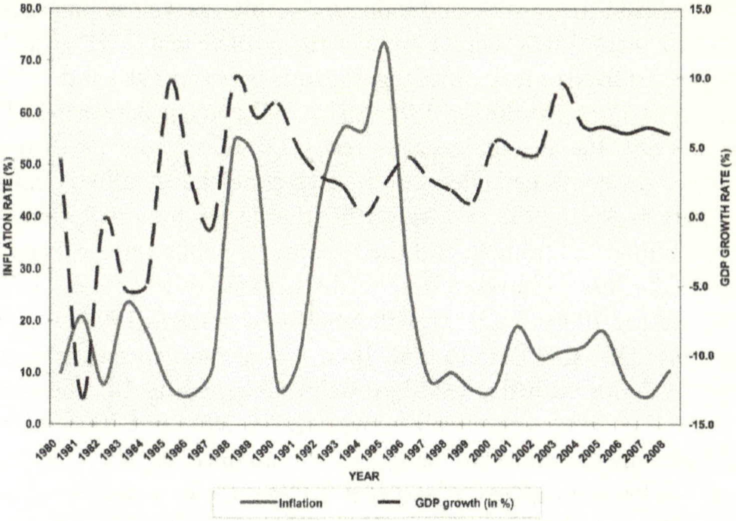

Sources: WAMZ data base and IFS year Book, 2008

Sierra Leone

Sierra Leone experienced series of inflationary episodes in the 1980s and 1990s. Inflation rate increased from an average of 39.7 percent between 1980 and 1984 to 86.2 percent during 1985 and 1989 (Table 7.1). Monetization of government fiscal deficit, removal of subsidy following the adoption of SAP as well as the persistent depreciation of the leone accounted for the surge in inflationary pressure in the 1980s. Despite being high, inflationary pressure eased in the 1990s, as average inflation rate decelerated from 65.1 percent between 1990 and 1994 to 26.7 percent between 1995 and 1999. The decline in inflation during the 1990s was partly due to a fall in local demand as factories and businesses scaled down, whilst most banks closed operations to the public. The civil war which officially ended in 2002 ushered in a climate of relative peace and stability. During the period 2000-2008, average inflation dropped significantly, due to increased business and consumer confidence following the restoration of peace and stability.

The country's growth trajectory remained robust in the early 1980s as real GDP growth rate increased by an average of 2.9

percent between 1980 and 1984, arising from increased economic activities in the mining and industrial sectors, as well as increased private sector investment. However, the positive real GDP growth was short lived as it declined significantly between 1985 and 1999, from -0.6 percent during 1985-89 to -5.9 percent between 1995 and 1999. The average negative real GDP during the 1990s was due to the combined effects of the civil conflict and military coup d'etats in April 1992 and May 1997 that led to the disruption of agriculture and mining, and the collapse of public service, health and education. However, despite the negative average real GDP during the 1990s, GDP growth rate was positive in 1992 (1.3%), 1993 (3.0%) and 1996 (5.0%). There was a resurgence of growth in the 2000s with real GDP growth rate averaging 14.3 percent and 6.8 percent, respectively between 2000-2004 and 2005-2008. Whilst an inverse relationship was maintained for most of the period between inflation and real GDP growth, a positive relationship remained prominent since 2004.

Figure 7.6: Inflation and Real GDP Growth Rates in Sierra Leone, 1980-2008

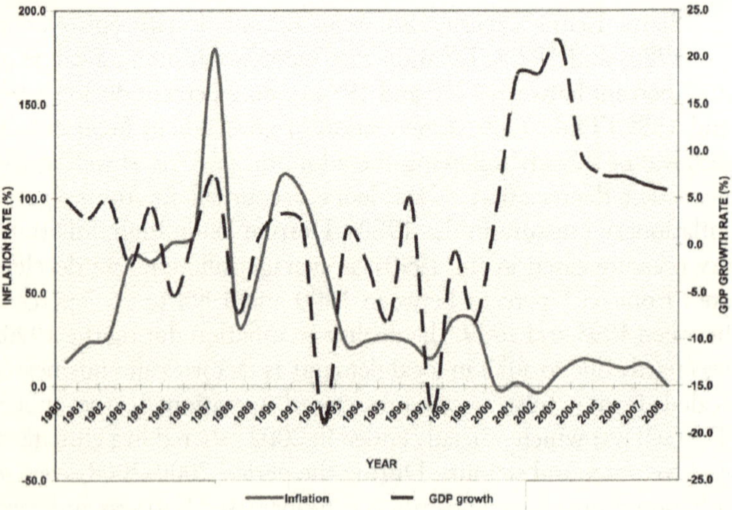

Sources: WAMZ data base and IFS year Book, 2008

INFLATION THRESHOLD AND ECONOMIC GROWTH: THEORY AND EVIDENCE

Theoretical Review

Theoretical literature on the relationship between inflation and economic growth reach a variety of conclusions about the responsiveness of output growth to inflation. This paper examines several different economic theories and empirical studies on the inflation-economic growth nexus. A review of the theoretical literature is pursued:

Classical Growth Theory

The Classicalists, championed by the works of Adam Smith, David Ricardo, and Karl Marx among others, presumed a supply-side driven growth model. Supply is specified as a function of land, labour, and capital. Consequently, output growth is driven by population growth, investment growth, and land growth[⊠], as well as the increase in the overall productivity. Smith assumed a self reinforcing growth (increasing return to scale) and that savings creates investment, hence growth. Further assumption in this postulate is that income distribution, fast or slow, determines the rate at which the economy grows. Profit declines, not necessarily because of decreasing marginal product of labour, but because competition for labour drives wages up. Implicit assumption here is the suggestion of a negative relationship between inflation and growth through higher wage cost.

Keynesian Theory

Keynesians' explanation of the long run economic growth path is implicitly captured in the business cycle concept (a short run phenomenon) developed within the aggregate demand (AD) and aggregate supply (AS) framework. According to this model, AS is assumed to be upward sloping in the short run and changes in the demand side of the economy affect both prices and output, arising from changes in expectations, labour force, fiscal and monetary policy, among others. They therefore advocated that there exist a positive relationship between inflation and output, such that even if there is an increase in prices of goods in the economy, output would not decline because producers have to satisfy the demand requirements of consumers.

Endogenous Growth Theory

According to this theory, economic growth depends on the rate of return on capital, which is inversely related to inflation. Inflation decreases the rate of return and this in turn reduces capital accumulation and hence reduces growth rate. Alternative models examine how inflation directly affects capital accumulation and hence output growth. High inflation drives down the return to deposits, resulting in slower rate of deposits accumulation. Given that capital is a fraction of deposits, decline in deposit rates will result in slow capital accumulation and hence lower output growth.

Neo-Classical Theory

The Neo-classical theory dates back to the works of Solow (1956), Swan (1956) and Mundell (1963). The theoretical review in the neoclassical model produces different results in the inflation-growth nexus. According to Mundell's model, an increase in inflation reduces people's wealth, arising from a fall in the rate of return on individual's real money balances. People save more by switching to financial assets in order to accumulate the desired wealth, thereby increasing asset prices, resulting in a decline in the real interest rate. Increased savings result to greater capital accumulation and hence faster output growth. The Tobin's (1965) framework also revealed a positive relationship between inflation and economic growth. It showed that higher inflation increases output growth although temporarily. Tobin's model suggests that individual's hold their asset in interest earning assets during inflationary period. This leads to greater capital intensity and hence promotes economic growth.

A variant of the neo-classical theory pioneered by Stockman (1981) found a negative relationship between inflation and economic growth. According to the Stockman model, increase in the inflation rate results in a lower steady state level of output. High inflation reduces the purchasing power of money, thereby forcing people to reduce their purchases of both cash goods and capital, resulting in a fall in the steady-state level of output.

Empirical Review

Inflation-Growth Relationships

While the controversies over inflation-economic growth linkage is yet unsettled, an appreciable consensus has been established. As Bruno and Easterly's (1996) summary review of inflation-growth suggest, theories on the subject can be classified into three segments across the decades of their emergence. First, is the traditional 1960s view of High Growth-Low Inflation Phillips Curve era, when inflation was believed to be positively correlated with economic growth in the short run, and to some degree, the long run. Second are the1970s and '80s inflationary experiential era, which focused mainly on the short run behaviour. During this period, the consensus as restated by Bruno-Easterly (1995) was that "stabilization of hyperinflation had little output costs, whereas sterilization of mere high inflation was indeed costly." The presumption of the 1980s was a positive short-run relationship between growth and inflation. The third wave was the 1990s and the new-Growth theorist postulating an inverse relationship in the inflation-growth nexus. This is especially so, because the new-Growth theorists are more concerned with long run relationship. Not only will persistent inflation reduces the level and/or growth rate of GDP in the long run [Barro (1991), Cozier and Selody (1992) and Fisher (1993)], in the face of a tax system not fully indexed, even a relatively low inflation imposes significant deadweight losses on the economy [Feldstein (1996)].

Barro (1997) used a panel data for 100 countries over the period 1960-1990 and estimated growth regression using Instrumental Variables (IV) technique. He found a negative relationship between inflation and economic growth. The result showed that a 10 percent inflation rate reduces real GDP per capita by 0.2% per year. Similarly, Bruno and Easterly (1995) studied inflation-growth relationship for 26 countries over the 1961- 1992 period. They found a negative relationship between inflation and growth when level of inflation exceeds some threshold. At the same time they showed that impact of low and moderate inflation on growth is quite ambiguous.

Fischer (1993) used cross-sectional data covering 93 countries to investigate the non-linear relationship between inflation and growth, using the growth accounting framework in order to detect the channels through which inflation impacts on growth. He found that inflation influences growth by decreasing productivity growth and investment. The result also showed that the effect of inflation is non-linear with breaks at 15 and 40 percent. In a related study, Sarrel (1995) used a panel data sample of 87 countries over 21 years (1970-1990) to investigate the relationship between inflation and growth with a fixed effect technique framework. He found evidence of structural break in interaction between inflation and growth. However, the main findings of his study was that the estimated threshold level was 8 percent, and an inflation rate exceeding this threshold would lead to negative, powerful and robust impact of inflation on growth.

Khan and Senhadji (2001) investigated the inflation-growth interaction using a panel data set on 140 countries (both industrial and developing) over the period 1960-1998. They employed the method of non-linear least squares to deal with non-linearity and non-differentiability of the inflation threshold level in growth regression. Their results showed an inverse relationship between inflation and growth, with estimates of the inflation threshold levels of 1-3 percent for developed and 11-12 percent for developing countries. Mallik and Chowdhury (2001) also examined the short-run and long-run dynamics of the relationship between inflation and economic growth for four South Asian economies: Bangladesh, India, Pakistan, and Sri Lanka, using co-integration and error correction techniques. Their results showed that the relationship between inflation and economic growth was positive and statistically significant for all four countries. They also found that the sensitivity of growth to changes in inflation rates is smaller than that of inflation to changes in growth rates.

Lee and Wong (2005) estimated the threshold levels of inflation for Taiwan and Japan using quarterly data set from the period 1965–2002 for Taiwan and 1970–2001 for Japan. Their estimation of the threshold models suggests that an inflation rate beyond 7.25

per cent is detrimental for the economic growth of Taiwan. On the other hand, they found two threshold levels for Japan, which are 2.52 per cent and 9.66 per cent. This suggests that inflation rate below the estimated level of 9.66 per cent is favorable to economic growth and beyond this threshold value it is harmful for the economic growth.

Mubarik (2005) estimated the threshold level of inflation for Pakistan using an annual data set from the period between 1973 and 2000. He employed the Granger Causality test as an application of the threshold model and the relevant sensitivity analysis of the model. His estimation of the threshold model suggests that an inflation rate beyond 9 percent is detrimental for the economic growth of Pakistan. This in turn, suggests that inflation rate below the estimated level of 9 percent is favorable for economic growth. In the same spirit, Ahmed and Mortaza (2005) explored Bangladesh annual data to investigate its experience regarding inflation-economic growth relationship. The paper employed Engle-Granger (1987) co-integration procedure and error correction model to evaluate the short-run and long-run features in inflation-growth relationship; subsequently, it adopts Khan and Senhadji (2001) model to estimate the threshold level for inflation rate. The finding is consistent with the consensus of a long-run (strong) negative relationship. The study posited a 6 percent threshold level of inflation, above which inflation adversely affects economic growth. Faria and Carneiro (2001) also investigated the relationship between inflation and economic growth in the context of Brazil, a country that had experienced persistent high inflation. Analyzing a bivariate time series model (i.e., vector auto regression) with annual data for the period between 1980 and 1995, they found a negative relationship between inflation and economic growth in the short-run. However, their result showed that inflation does not affect economic growth in the long-run. Their empirical results also support the *superneutrality* concept of money in the long run

The review of literature indicates a prevalence of significant differences among the results of empirical studies, as the effects of inflation on growth are quite different across countries. Such divergences of results were quite wide in cases of empirical studies which concentrated on estimation of threshold rate of inflation for individual countries. These studies generally found that for economies with initially low rates of inflation, modest increases in the rate of inflation do not affect long-run rates of real economic growth. But for economies with initially high rates of inflation, further increases in the inflation rate have adverse effects on real economic growth.

ANALYTICAL FRAMEWORK AND METHODOLOGY

This study adopts the Keynesian Aggregate Demand (*AD*) and Aggregate Supply (*AS*) framework to explain the inflation – growth relationship. The rationale for this framework is based on the fact that prices and output are significantly determined by AD and AS. The AD is derived from an open-economy IS-LM framework where the aggregate demand curve is a locus of points showing the price-output combinations that ensure internal and external equilibrium in the economy. The internal equilibrium is obtained when the goods and the money markets are in simultaneous equilibrium. The external equilibrium is derived from the Balance of Payments (BOP) equilibrium. Unlike the classical school of thought that holds that the economy is always in full equilibrium (implying vertical Aggregate Supply curve), this Keynesian framework postulates that the economy can be below full employment level, at least in the short run, implying upward sloping Aggregate Supply curve. The AS curve is derived from labour market conditions using the price-setting and Phillips' curve relationships together with the Okun's Law. Algebraically, the relationship between price (inflation) and output (growth) can be derived through the AD and AS formulations as outlined below.

Derivation of Price-Output Relationship in Aggregate Demand Framework

Suppose the open-economy flexible price IS-LM-BP framework is illustrated by the following relationships.

$$IS: \quad r = A + \alpha_1 (E/P) - \alpha_2 (Y/P), \qquad \alpha_1, \alpha_2 > 0$$

Equilibrium in the Goods Market (1)

$LM: \quad r = \beta_1(D/P) + \beta_2(R/P) + \beta_3(Y/P), \quad \beta_1, \beta_2, \beta_3 > 0$
Money Market Equilib. (2)
$BP: \quad R/P = B + \delta_1(E/P) - \delta_2(Y/P), \quad \delta_1 > 0; 0 < \delta_2 < 1$
External Sector Equilib. (3)

Where
$r \equiv$ Real interest rate
$E/P \equiv$ Real exchange rate
$Y/P \equiv$ Real output
$D/P \equiv$ Real domestic credit
$R/P \equiv$ Real foreign reserves
$P \equiv$ Price level
$A, B \equiv$ A set of autonomous or exogenous variables

It must be noted that the external sector equilibrium condition is derived on assumption that there is perfect capital mobility across countries; hence, the international interest rate equals the domestic interest rate. Thus, the balance of payments equilibrium is determined solely by the current account (trade) balance.

Substituting equation 3 into 2 gives

$$LM: \quad r = \beta_1(D/P) + \beta_2[B + \delta_1(E/P) - \delta_2(Y/P)] + \beta_3(Y/P) \qquad (4)$$

Re-arranging equation 4 produces

$$LM: \quad r = U + \gamma_1(D/P) + \gamma_2(E/P) + \gamma_3(Y/P) \qquad (5)$$

Where $U = \beta_2 B, \quad \gamma_1 = \beta_1, \quad \gamma_2 = \beta_2\delta_1, \quad \gamma_3 = \beta_3 - \beta_2\delta_2$

Solving equations 1 and 5 simultaneously gives

$$Y/P = V + \phi_1(E/P) - \phi_2(D/P) \qquad (6)$$

Where V is a set of autonomous or exogenous variables $(A-U)/(\gamma_3 + \alpha_2)$,

$\phi_1 = (\alpha_1 - \gamma_2)/(\gamma_3 + \alpha_2), \quad \phi_2 = -\gamma_1/(\gamma_3 + \alpha_2)$

Assuming that each term, apart from V, is time dependent, equation 6 can be written in growth terms (after taking the logarithmic form and differentiating each term with respect to time) as

$$y-\pi=\phi_1(e-\pi)-\phi_2(d-\pi) \tag{7}$$

Where $y=\frac{1}{Y}*\frac{\partial Y}{\partial t}$; $\pi=\frac{1}{P}*\frac{\partial P}{\partial t}$; $e=\frac{1}{E}*\frac{\partial E}{\partial t}$; $d=\frac{1}{D}*\frac{\partial D}{\partial t}$;

Re-arranging equation 7 gives

$$y=\phi_1 e-\phi_2 d+(1-\phi_1+\phi_2)\pi \tag{8}$$

If $\phi_1>1+\phi_2$, according to equation 8, the relationship between output growth and inflation rate in the aggregate demand framework will be negative. Otherwise, the relationship between output growth and inflation will be positive.

Derivation of Price-Output Relationship in Aggregate Supply Framework

The labour market developments give rise to wage and price settings. These in turn determine the short-run aggregate supply in the product market. The key assumption here is that in the long-run, the aggregate supply function is perfectly inelastic.

Labour Cost Function:

$$w=\pi^*-\alpha_1(u-u^*)+\alpha_2\eta, \qquad \alpha_1>0,\ 0\le\alpha_2\le 1 \tag{9}$$

Mark-up Price Function: $$\pi=w-\eta \tag{10}$$

From equations 9 and 10, the Phillips Curve can be derived by substituting equation 9 into equation 10 to obtain equation 11:

Phillips Curve: $$\pi=\pi^*-\alpha_1(u-u^*)-(1-\alpha_2)\eta \tag{11}$$

Okun's Law: $$u-u^*=-\beta(y-y^*), \qquad \beta>0 \tag{12}$$

Where $w \equiv$ wage rate, $\pi \equiv$ the rate of inflation, $\pi^* \equiv$ expected rate of inflation, $u \equiv$ actual rate of unemployment, $u^* \equiv$ natural rate of unemployment, $\eta \equiv$ growth rate of labour productivity, $y \equiv$ growth rate of output, and $y^* \equiv$ potential (optimal) growth rate of output.

By substituting equation 12 into equation 11, and assuming labour productivity growth is zero, we derive the short-run aggregate supply function which is given as:

Aggregate Supply Function: $\pi = \pi^* + \alpha_1 \beta \left(y - y^* \right)$ (13)

Making Y the subject of equation 13 gives

$$y = y^* + \left(1/\alpha_1 \beta \right) \left(\pi - \pi^* \right) \quad (14)$$

If expected inflation rate is assumed to be the optimal inflation rate, then equation 14 does not only establish a positive relationship between output growth and inflation but also highlights the fact that when realised inflation rate is below the optimal rate, there would be a negative relationship between output growth and optimal inflation differential, and vice versa. Thus, within the aggregate supply framework, it is clear that inflation rate has a positive relationship with output and, more importantly, there is a threshold within which inflation rate will have a positive impact on growth rate of output, and beyond which inflation rate will have a negative impact on output growth rate.

Re-stating the full employment output (potential output) as a function of factor inputs (since at full employment all factor inputs are assumed to be fully employed), equation 12 can be re-specified as

$$y = y(k^*, l^*) + \left(1/\alpha_1 \beta \right) \left(\pi - \pi^* \right) \quad (15)$$

Where k^* and l^* are full employment (steady state) growth rates of capital and labour respectively.

The model for the study is adopted from the model developed by Khan and Senhadji (2001) which is based on the AD-AS framework and has been widely used in the literature (E.g. Ahmed and Mortaza, 2005; Mubarik, 2005; Seleteng, 2005) to estimate optimal inflation for both developed and developing economies.

However, some modifications were made to the existing model taking into consideration the consistency in the theoretical framework as well as the structure of the WAMZ economies. These modifications relate essentially to the openness of the WAMZ economies as well as their political and economic developments. The general empirical threshold model is specified as follows:

$$GROWTH_t = \alpha_0 + \alpha_1 INF_{t-s} + \alpha_2 D_2(DINF_t) + X\beta + \varepsilon_t \qquad (16)$$

Where

$GROWTH = \Delta LN(RGDP) \equiv$ Real GDP growth rate
$INF = \Delta LN(CPI) \equiv$ Domestic inflation rate, current and lagged values
$DINF = \Delta LN(CPI) - K \equiv$ The differential between observed inflation rate $(\Delta LN(CPI))$ and the assumed optimal inflation rate (K)

$$D_2 = \begin{cases} 1 & \text{If } \Delta LN(CPI) > K \\ 0 & otherwise \end{cases}$$

$X = \{GROWTH_{t-p}, INV_{t-s}, APOPN_{t-s}, REX_{t-s}, TOT_{t-s}, OPEN_{t-s}, GEXP_{t-s}, OIL_{t-s}\} \equiv$ A row vector of other explanatory variables such as the lags of *GROWTH*,
$INV = \Delta N \ (INVESTMENT) \equiv$ Growth rate of real investment
$APOPN = \Delta LN(POPULATION) \equiv$ Active population growth rate
$REX = \Delta LN(EXCHANGERATE) \equiv$ Real rate of exchange rate appreciation/ depreciation,
$TOT = EXPORT\ VALUE\ INDEX / IMPORT\ VALUE\ INDEX \equiv$ Terms of trade
$OPEN = (EXPORT + IMPORT)/GDP \equiv$ Openness index
$GEXP = \Delta N \ (GOVEXPENDITURE) \equiv$ Growth rate of government expenditure
$OIL = \Delta N \ (OILREVENUE) \equiv$ Growth rate of oil revenue in real terms
$\beta \equiv$ A column vector of coefficients
$t \equiv$ Time indicator; $p = 1, 2, \ldots, n$; $s = 0, 1, 2, \ldots, n$; and $\varepsilon \equiv$ Error term

A Priori Expectations

Theoretically, the following relationships are expected to emerge:

- Inflation is expected to have a positive impact on real GDP growth at low levels. However, if inflation rate exceeds the optimal rate needed for growth, it will begin to have a negative impact on real GDP growth. Hence, the expected signs of the relevant coefficients are $\alpha_1 > 0$, $\alpha_2 < 0$.
- Lags of real GDP growth will have positive impact on current level of real GDP growth.
- Investment growth is expected to have a positive impact on real GDP growth, though some of its lags may have negative coefficients.
- Population growth is also expected have positive impact on real GDP growth, though some of its lags may have negative coefficients.
- Exchange rate depreciation is expected to improve real GDP growth. However, excessive depreciation may also be harmful to growth or the J-curve theory may apply. Hence, the sign of real exchange rate depreciation may be indeterminate.
- Terms of trade and openness index are expected to have positive impact on real GDP growth, though some of their lags may have negative coefficients.
- Government expenditure is expected to promote real GDP growth, though some of its lags may have negative coefficients.
- Oil revenue growth (applicable only in the case of Nigeria as at now) is expected improve real GDP growth, but the Dutch Disease problem may surface. Hence, the sign of the relevant coefficient is indeterminate *a priori.*

Data Description and Transformation

Data are mostly sourced from WDI CD-ROM (2007), IFS CD-ROM (2007), ADI CD-ROM (2009), World Economic Outlook Database, and Statistical Bulletin (2008) of Nigeria. Apart from variables which are ratios, all the variables undergo logarithmic transformation and definition. Nominal values are transformed in to real values. US producer price index is used to compute the bilateral real exchange rates for the various countries.

Estimation Techniques

To estimate the threshold level of inflation, we employ the conditional least square technique. The idea is to minimize the sum of squared residuals or maximize the coefficient of determination in the growth regression (equation 16), conditional on a particular threshold level, repeating the procedure for different threshold values from 1 percent to 20 percent. Stationarity tests are conducted on the model variables using Augmented Dickey-Fuller (ADF) unit root test techniques. The estimations are carried out using Eviews version 6.

PRESENTATION AND ANALYSIS OF RESULTS

In this section, empirical results of unit root tests, granger causality tests and the optimal inflation estimation are presented and analysed. The estimation was carried out for each of the six member countries of the WAMZ.

Unit Root Test Results

The unit root test results are presented in Appendix 1. For the Gambia, all the model variables were found to be stationary at levels. In the model for Ghana, all the variables were found to be stationary at levels except the terms of trade which was found to be integrated of order-one. Apart from active population growth, inflation rate and openness index which were integrated of order one, all the variables in the Guinean model were stationary at levels. The variables in the Liberian model have no unit roots except active population growth which was integrated of order-one. For Nigeria, all the variables were found to be stationary at levels, except terms of trade which was integrated of order-one. None of the variables in the Sierra–Leonean model has a unit root.

Optimal Inflation Estimation Results for the WAMZ countries

The Gambia

The explanatory variables in the estimated model for the Gambia includes inflation rate, active population growth, real investment growth, real exchange rate changes, terms of trade and openness index. Data were obtained for the period 1980 to 2006. Apart from real investment growth, all the variables had significant impact on real GDP growth in the Gambia over the period (Table 7.3). Inflation rate had positive impact on real GDP growth. However, optimal inflation differential had a negative impact on real GDP growth. The estimated model satisfied all the diagnostic tests except the residual normality test. The model had an explanatory power (coefficient of determination) of 85.2 percent at the least assumed optimal inflation rate of 1 percent. After varying the assumed optimal inflation rate, the explanatory power of the model increased until it reached a peak of 86.7 percent (while residual sum of squares attained its minimum of 0.002348) at the assumed optimal rate of 9 percent. Further increases in the assumed optimal rate led to a decline in the coefficient of determination and a rise in the residual sum of squares. This result is consistent with the findings of Mubarak (2005) for Pakistan. The estimation results therefore suggest that the optimal inflation rate for the Gambia based on the 1980-2006 data is 9 percent.

The results further indicate that the determinants of real GDP growth, in the Gambia over the period 1980-2006 were inflation, active population growth rate, real exchange rate, terms of trade and openness index. Current active population growth rate had a negative impact on real GDP growth, while in dynamic terms; active population had a positive impact on real GDP growth. However, the overall combined growth effect of active population growth on real GDP growth was negative. This implies that the active population growth rate was above what was required to propel growth in the Gambian economy.

Table 7.3: Optimal Inflation Results for the Gambia (Dependent Variable: RGDP)

Assumed Optimal Inflation	Explanatory Variables	Coefficients	Probability of Significance	Explanatory Power/ RSS
5%	C	0.139853	0.0130	R^2: 0.858542
	DCPI(-2)	0.123502	0.0440	RSS: 0.002495
	D5*(OPINF5-DCPI)	-0.060428	0.3014	
	DAPOPN	-44.25053	0.0069	
	DAPOPN(-1)	73.96820	0.0069	
	DAPOPN(-2)	-37.94490	0.0052	
	DREX	0.060005	0.0207	
	DREX(-1)	0.041808	0.1130	
	TOT	0.121154	0.0117	
	OPEN(-1)	0.142250	0.0001	
	OPEN(-2)	-0.095667	0.0045	
	DRINV	0.012542	0.6308	
8%	C	0.132697	0.0145	R^2: 0.865794
	DCPI(-2)	0.133155	0.0326	RSS: 0.002367
	D8*(OPINF8-DCPI)	-0.087916	0.1957	
	DAPOPN	-45.64580	0.0048	
	DAPOPN(-1)	74.81826	0.0054	
	DAPOPN(-2)	-37.40990	0.0046	
	DREX	0.057781	0.0196	
	DREX(-1)	0.041666	0.1029	
	TOT	0.123101	0.0094	
	OPEN(-1)	0.144752	0.0001	
	OPEN(-2)	-0.094485	0.0039	
	DRINV	0.016832	0.5528	
9%	C	0.131313	0.0154	R^2: 0.866854
	DCPI(-2)	0.136709	0.0295	RSS: 0.002348
	D9*(OPINF9-DCPI)	-0.093460	0.1839	
	DAPOPN	-45.48218	0.0046	
	DAPOPN(-1)	74.30529	0.0053	
	DAPOPN(-2)	-37.05276	0.0048	
	DREX	0.057905	0.0185	
	DREX(-1)	0.042854	0.0927	
	TOT	0.123470	0.0090	
	OPEN(-1)	0.145628	0.0000	
	OPEN(-2)	-0.094917	0.0037	
	DRINV	0.017319	0.5404	
10%	C	0.132102	0.0148	R^2: 0.866356
	DCPI(-2)	0.138790	0.0287	RSS: 0.002357
	D10*(OPINF10-DCPI)	-0.094799	0.1894	
	DAPOPN	-45.17413	0.0048	
	DAPOPN(-1)	73.88947	0.0055	
	DAPOPN(-2)	-36.96670	0.0049	
	DREX	0.058466	0.0172	
	DREX(-1)	0.043848	0.0865	
	TOT	0.123629	0.0091	
	OPEN(-1)	0.146095	0.0001	
	OPEN(-2)	-0.095457	0.0036	
	DRINV	0.017658	0.5340	

Source: WAMI Staff Computations

Real exchange rate depreciation had a positive impact on real GDP growth rate over the study period. Increasing (favourable) terms of trade also had a positive impact on real GDP growth in the Gambia. In static terms, openness index had a positive impact on real GDP, while in dynamic terms; it had a negative impact on real GDP growth. However, the overall combined effect of openness on real GDP was found to be positive. These results suggest that openness of the Gambian economy to the rest of the world is relevant for stimulating economic growth

Ghana

In the case of Ghana, the explanatory variables used in the optimal inflation model are inflation rate, active population growth, real investment growth, real exchange rate changes, terms of trade and a dummy variable that captures developments in the late 1980s and early 1990s. Data were available for the period 1970 to 2006. The results showed that apart from real investment growth, the coefficients of all other variables were statistically significant at the conventional level (Table 7.4). While the coefficient of inflation rate was found to be positive, optimal inflation differential had a negative impact on real GDP growth. The estimated model was consistent with economic theory and also satisfied all the diagnostic tests. The result also showed that 90.1 percent of the variations in real GDP growth in Ghana at the least assumed optimal inflation rate of 1 percent is accounted for by the explanatory variables. After varying the assumed optimal inflation rate, the explanatory power of the model rose, reaching a peak of 90.7 percent at the assumed optimal rate of 10 percent, while the residual sum of squares declined to its minimum of 0.006239. Further increases in the assumed optimal rate beyond 10 percent led to declines in the explanatory power and an increase in the residual sum of squares. A similar result was obtained by Seleteng (2005) for Lesotho. Thus, the optimal inflation rate for Ghana based on the 1970-2006 data is 10 percent.

In addition to inflation rate, the key determinants of real GDP growth rate in Ghana over the study period were active population growth rate, terms of trade, the real exchange rate and the dynamics of real GDP growth. Past level of real GDP growth had significant impact on current level of real GDP growth. This suggests that boosting economic growth in the current period; it will have ripple effect on economic growth in future. Active population growth had a negative impact on real GDP growth rate in static terms but a positive impact in dynamic terms. Overall economic growth impact of active population growth was positive.

The coefficient of terms of trade was positive as expected, but the lag of the real exchange rate had a negative impact on economic growth, implying that in dynamic terms real exchange rate depreciation was depressed economic growth in Ghana. The dummy variable had a significant positive impact on real GDP growth. This suggests that the reforms in the 1980s and 1990s had significant impact on economic growth in the Ghanaian economy. Overall, the Ghanaian economy could benefit greatly from improvement in the terms of trade but effort must be made to check the negative impact of trade openness and the pass-through effects of real exchange rate depreciation.

Guinea

The explanatory variables in the Guinean optimal inflation model were inflation rate, active population growth, real investment growth, real exchange rate changes, and terms of trade. Data on the model variables were available for the period 1980 to 2006. The results showed that the coefficients of the explanatory variables significantly explained variations in real GDP growth in Guinea (Table 7.5). Inflation rate had positive impact on real GDP growth. However, optimal inflation differential had a negative impact on real GDP growth. The estimated model passed all the diagnostic tests except the serial correlation test. Correlation-robust model was, therefore, estimated to take account of the serial correlation. The diagnostic test indicates that 84.0 percent of the variation in the dependent variable (with residual sum of squares of 0.000506) at the least assumed optimal inflation rate of 1 percent is accounted for by the explanatory variables. Increasing the assumed optimal inflation rate led to an increase in the explanatory power of the model until it reached a peak of 84.1 percent (with the residual sum squares reaching a minimum of 0.000503) at the assumed optimal rate of 5 percent. Further increases in the

Table 7.4: Optimal Inflation Results for Ghana: (Dependent Variable: RGDP)

Assumed Optimal Inflation	Explanatory Variables	Coefficients	Probability of Significance	Explanatory Power/ RSS
5%	C	-0.215927	0.0000	R^2: 0.901316
	DRGDP(-1)	0.512606	0.0000	RSS: 0.006632
	DCPI	3.978730	0.0000	
	D5*(DCPI-OPINF5)	-0.039671	0.0000	
	DAPOPN(-1)	11.11371	0.0000	
	DAPOPN	-10.05160	0.0000	
	DRINV(-3)	0.029343	0.1644	
	DTOT(-1)	0.067691	0.0016	
	DREX(-3)	-0.049632	0.0022	
	DUM2	0.014480	0.0240	
	AR(1)	-0.442080	0.0611	
	DRINV	0.012542	0.6308	
9%	C	-0.215927	0.0000	R^2: 0.901316
	DRGDP(-1)	0.512606	0.0000	RSS: 0.006632
	DCPI	2.215592	0.0000	
	D9*(DCPI-OPINF9)	-0.022039	0.0000	
	DAPOPN(-1)	11.11371	0.0000	
	DAPOPN	-10.05160	0.0000	
	DRINV(-3)	0.029343	0.1644	
	DTOT(-1)	0.067691	0.0016	
	DREX(-3)	-0.049632	0.0022	
	DUM2	0.014480	0.0240	
	AR(1)	-0.442079	0.0611	
	DRINV	0.016832	0.5528	
10%	C	-0.216431	0.0000	R^2: 0.907165
	DRGDP(-1)	0.512216	0.0000	RSS: 0.006239
	DCPI	2.005379	0.0000	
	D10*(DCPI-OPINF10)	-0.019961	0.0000	
	DAPOPN(-1)	11.18074	0.0000	
	DAPOPN	-10.11588	0.0000	
	DRINV(-3)	0.029593	0.1512	
	DTOT(-1)	0.067483	0.0014	
	DREX(-3)	-0.051531	0.0012	
	DUM2	0.016081	0.0107	
	AR(1)	-0.435518	0.0673	
	DRINV	0.017319	0.5404	
11%	C	-0.211652	0.0000	R^2: 0.906874
	DRGDP(-1)	0.524072	0.0000	RSS: 0.006258
	DCPI	1.775747	0.0000	
	D11*(DCPI-OPINF11)	-0.017719	0.0000	
	DAPOPN(-1)	11.35129	0.0000	
	DAPOPN	-10.23745	0.0000	
	DRINV(-3)	0.033163	0.1146	
	DTOT(-1)	0.064493	0.0017	
	DREX(-3)	-0.058770	0.0003	
	DUM2	0.019481	0.0033	
	AR(1)	-0.382448	0.1233	
	DRINV	0.017658	0.5340	

Source: WAMI Staff Computations

Table 7.5: Optimal Inflation Results for Guinea: (Dependent Variable: RGDP)

Assumed Optimal Inflation	Explanatory Variables	Coefficients	Probability of Significance	Explanatory Power/ RSS
3%	C	0.082121	0.0001	R^2: 0.840755
	D(DAPOPN(-1))	1.088955	0.0646	RSS: 0.000504
	D(DCPI(-1))	0.067091	0.0226	
	D2*(DCPI- OPINF2)	-0.065849	0.0012	
	DREX	0.016928	0.0005	
	DREX(-1)	-0.014205	0.0127	
	DRINV(-2)	0.052430	0.0001	
	TOT	-0.132035	0.0001	
	TOT(-2)	0.080633	0.0014	
	AR(1)	-0.627755	0.0185	
4%	C	0.081605	0.0001	R^2: 0.841220
	D(DAPOPN(-1))	1.095961	0.0639	RSS: 0.000503
	D(DCPI(-1))	0.068986	0.0206	
	D3*(DCPI- OPINF3)	-0.068314	0.0012	
	DREX	0.017239	0.0005	
	DREX(-1)	-0.014543	0.0115	
	DRINV(-2)	0.052970	0.0001	
	TOT	-0.133706	0.0001	
	TOT(-2)	0.082496	0.0013	
	AR(1)	-0.620525	0.0203	
5%	C	0.081386	0.0001	R^2: 0.841221
	D(DAPOPN(-1))	1.093525	0.0648	RSS: 0.000503
	D(DCPI(-1))	0.070228	0.0195	
	D4*(DCPI- OPINF4)	-0.070950	0.0012	
	DREX	0.017601	0.0005	
	DREX(-1)	-0.014771	0.0107	
	DRINV(-2)	0.053424	0.0001	
	TOT	-0.134836	0.0001	
	TOT(-2)	0.083541	0.0012	
	AR(1)	-0.616949	0.0212	
6%	C	0.081398	0.0001	R^2: 0.840775
	D(DAPOPN(-1))	1.085710	0.0665	RSS: 0.000504
	D(DCPI(-1))	0.071279	0.0189	
	D5*(DCPI- OPINF5)	-0.073758	0.0013	
	DREX	0.018030	0.0004	
	DREX(-1)	-0.014966	0.0101	
	DRINV(-2)	0.053945	0.0000	
	TOT	-0.135560	0.0001	
	TOT(-2)	0.083923	0.0012	
	AR(1)	-0.617508	0.0208	
	DAPOPN(-1)	11.35129	0.0000	
	DAPOPN	-10.23745	0.0000	
	DRINV(-3)	0.033163	0.1146	
	DTOT(-1)	0.064493	0.0017	
	DREX(-3)	-0.058770	0.0003	
	DUM2	0.019481	0.0033	
	AR(1)	-0.382448	0.1233	
	DRINV	0.017658	0.5340	

Source: WAMI Staff Computations

assumed optimal rate led to declines in the coefficient of determination, and an increase in the residual sum squares.. Hence, the empirical estimates point to an optimal inflation rate of 5 percent for Guinea.

The other determinants of real GDP growth rate in Guinea were active population growth rate, real investment growth rate, real exchange rate and terms of trade. Active population growth rate had a positive impact on real GDP growth in dynamic terms. Real investment growth rate also had a positive effect on real GDP growth rate in dynamic terms. While real exchange rate depreciation had an overall combined positive impact on real GDP growth, the terms of trade had both positive and negative influences in dynamic and static terms respectively. However, the overall effect of terms of trade on real GDP growth was found to be negative.

Liberia

The explanatory variables included in the empirical model for Liberia are inflation rate, active population growth, real exchange rate changes and a dummy variable that captures the war period. Variables such as real investment growth, openness index and terms of trade were excluded from the model due to unavailability of data. Data were available for the period 1980 to 2005. The results revealed that all the variables, except lag of inflation, had significant impact on real GDP growth in Liberia (Table 7.6). While the current level of inflation and the second lag of inflation had positive impact on growth, the first lag of inflation had a negative impact; with the Overall effect of inflation rate on real GDP growth being positive in dynamic terms. Optimal inflation differential was found to have a negative impact on real GDP growth. The diagnostic tests of the model were satisfactory, with the independent variables explaining 72.4 percent of the variations in real GDP growth at the least assumed optimal inflation rate of 1 percent. After varying the assumed optimal inflation rate, the explanatory power of the model increased until it reached a peak of 73.2 percent (with minimum residual sum of squares of 0.476691) at the assumed optimal rate of 7 percent. Further increases in the assumed optimal rate led to declines in the coefficient of determination and an increase in the residual sum square.

A similar result was obtained by Lee and Wong (2005 for Taiwan and Japan. The empirical results therefore suggest that the optimal inflation rate for Liberia is 7 percent.

The results further revealed that active population growth, real exchange rate and real GDP growth dynamics had significant impact on real GDP growth. The past level of real GDP growth impacted positively on the current level of real GDP growth, implying that increasing economic activities in the current period will positively propel growth in the future. Active population growth had a dynamic positive impact on real GDP growth. The first and second lags of real exchange rate had negative and positive impacts respectively on real GDP growth rate; however the combined effect of real exchange rate depreciation on economic growth was negative. Thus, to propel growth in the Liberian economy, there is the need to work on both supply- and demand-side variables.

Nigeria

The Nigeria's empirical model included explanatory variables such as inflation rate, active population growth, real investment growth, terms of trade and openness index, real growth of oil revenue, and a dummy variable that captures developments in the late 1990s and 2000s. Data were obtained for the period 1970 to 2006. Apart from openness index, all the variables had significant explanation for real GDP growth in Nigeria (Table 7.7). Inflation rate had an overall positive impact on real GDP growth in dynamic terms. However, optimal inflation differential had a negative impact on real GDP growth. The estimated model passed all the diagnostic tests and returned explanatory power of 88.0 percent at the least assumed optimal inflation rate of 1 percent. When the assumed optimal inflation rate was increased, the explanatory power of the model increased, reaching a peak of 88.2 percent (with minimum residual sum of squares of 0.010737) at the assumed optimal rate of 13 percent. Inflation rates beyond 13 percent reduced the explanatory power as the residual sum of squares increased. Thus, the empirical results point to an optimal inflation rate of 13 percent for Nigeria.

Table 7.6: Optimal Inflation Results for Liberia: (Dependent Variable: RGDP)

Assumed Optimal Inflation	Explanatory Variables	Coefficients	Probability of Significance	Explanatory Power/ RSS
5%	C	0.095330	0.0934	R^2: 0.730306
	DUM	-0.298497	0.0013	RSS: 0.479567
	DRGDP(-2)	0.569238	0.0003	
	DREX(-1)	-3.189415	0.0014	
	DREX(-2)	1.894427	0.0643	
	D(DAPOPN(-1))	14.23234	0.0001	
	DCPI(-1)	-2.278852	0.0062	
	DCPI(-2)	0.743432	0.2427	
	DUM*DCPI	2.925544	0.0041	
	D5*(OPINF5-DCPI)	-1.003297	0.2691	
6%	C	0.097854	0.0810	R^2: 0.730996
	DUM	-0.297563	0.0013	RSS: 0.478340
	DRGDP(-2)	0.566877	0.0003	
	DREX(-1)	-3.200631	0.0014	
	DREX(-2)	1.882614	0.0636	
	D(DAPOPN(-1))	14.21382	0.0001	
	DCPI(-1)	-2.290642	0.0060	
	DCPI(-2)	0.744975	0.2405	
	DUM*DCPI	2.932300	0.0038	
	D6*(OPINF6-DCPI)	-1.088852	0.2586	
7%	C	0.100562	0.0695	R^2: 0.731924
	DUM	-0.298306	0.0012	RSS: 0.476691
	DRGDP(-2)	0.565509	0.0003	
	DREX(-1)	-3.201762	0.0013	
	DREX(-2)	1.863325	0.0631	
	D(DAPOPN(-1))	14.11742	0.0001	
	DCPI(-1)	-2.291958	0.0057	
	DCPI(-2)	0.745862	0.2382	
	DUM*DCPI	2.931693	0.0037	
	D7*(OPINF7-DCPI)	-1.180628	0.2452	
8%	C	0.104805	0.0580	R^2: 0.729103
	DUM	-0.303250	0.0010	RSS: 0.481706
	DRGDP(-2)	0.565480	0.0003	
	DREX(-1)	-3.155313	0.0015	
	DREX(-2)	1.793614	0.0711	
	D(DAPOPN(-1))	13.89561	0.0001	
	DCPI(-1)	-2.236368	0.0065	
	DCPI(-2)	0.719771	0.2555	
	DUM*DCPI	2.971757	0.0034	
	D8*(OPINF8-DCPI)	-1.131760	0.2887	
	DAPOPN(-1)	11.35129	0.0000	
	DAPOPN	-10.23745	0.0000	
	DRINV(-3)	0.033163	0.1146	
	DTOT(-1)	0.064493	0.0017	
	DREX(-3)	-0.058770	0.0003	
	DUM2	0.019481	0.0033	
	AR(1)	-0.382448	0.1233	
	DRINV	0.017658	0.5340	

Source: WAMI Staff Computations

Economic growth determinants in Nigeria apart from domestic inflation rate over the period 1970-2006 were dynamics of real GDP growth, terms of trade, openness index, active population growth rate and the growth rate of oil revenue. The third and first lags of real GDP growth had positive and negative impacts on current real GDP growth rate. The combined impact was, however, positive, indicating that real GDP growth in Nigeria was driven partly by its own dynamics. While the terms of trade had significant dynamic positive impact on real GDP growth, the openness index had not. The oil revenue growth also had a significant positive impact on real GDP growth in Nigeria which is consistent with the related *a priori* expectation. Active population growth rate had static positive and dynamic negative impacts on real GDP growth rate but with an overall-combined negative growth impact. This may be explained by the high level of unemployment in Nigeria. A dummy variable capturing economic developments in the late 1990s and 2000s had a significant negative impact, suggesting that real GDP growth had slowed down due to economic developments (both internal and external) in recent years. Overall, working on the supply- and demand-side factors could improve economic growth in Nigeria.

Sierra Leone

The independent variables in the optimal inflation model for Sierra Leone were inflation rate, active population growth, real investment growth, real exchange rate changes, and a dummy variable that captures the war period. Data were obtained for the period 1970 to 2006. Dynamic modeling approach was adopted. All the remaining variables, except the dummy variable, had significant explanation for real GDP growth in Sierra Leone over the study period. Inflation rate had overall negative dynamic impact on real GDP growth. The optimal inflation differential also had a negative impact on real GDP growth. The estimated model passed all the diagnostic tests except for serial correlation. This was corrected and the model returned explanatory power of 88.1 percent at the least assumed optimal inflation rate of 1 percent. Increasing the assumed optimal inflation rate moved the explanatory power to a peak of 88.1 percent at the assumed optimal rate of 10%. This results is

Table 7.7: Optimal Inflation Results for Nigeria: (Dependent Variable: RGDP)

Assumed Optimal Inflation	Explanatory Variables	Coefficients	Probability of Significance	Explanatory Power/ RSS
5%	C	0.103688	0.2279	R^2: 0.880061
	DUM	-0.098200	0.0004	RSS: 0.010894
	DRGDP(-3)	0.811443	0.0000	
	DRGDP(-1)	-0.362084	0.0024	
	DCPI(-4)	-0.166125	0.0005	
	DUM*DCPI(-1)	0.258641	0.0009	
	D5*(DCPI-OPINF5)	-0.161564	0.0003	
	DTOT(-1)	0.115520	0.0000	
	DTOT(-2)	0.058806	0.0170	
	OPEN(-1)	0.015050	0.6568	
	DAPOPN	9.442859	0.0073	
	DAPOPN(-2)	-10.17496	0.0087	
	DOIL	0.016508	0.0331	
12%	C	0.112547	0.1931	R^2: 0.880702
	DUM	-0.102320	0.0003	RSS: 0.010836
	DRGDP(-3)	0.831059	0.0000	
	DRGDP(-1)	-0.368314	0.0021	
	DCPI(-4)	-0.157608	0.0008	
	DUM*DCPI(-1)	0.274106	0.0005	
	D12*(DCPI-OPINF12)	-0.183289	0.0003	
	DTOT(-1)	0.118721	0.0000	
	DTOT(-2)	0.063447	0.0110	
	OPEN(-1)	0.016849	0.6174	
	DAPOPN	9.389585	0.0074	
	DAPOPN(-2)	-10.79287	0.0059	
	DOIL	0.015248	0.0492	
13%	C	0.112423	0.1915	R^2: 0.881786
	DUM	-0.102154	0.0003	RSS: 0.010737
	DRGDP(-3)	0.837087	0.0000	
	DRGDP(-1)	-0.373734	0.0018	
	DCPI(-4)	-0.155851	0.0008	
	DUM*DCPI(-1)	0.275399	0.0005	
	D13*(DCPI-OPINF13)	-0.190409	0.0003	
	DTOT(-1)	0.119830	0.0000	
	DTOT(-2)	0.064818	0.0095	
	OPEN(-1)	0.016053	0.6327	
	DAPOPN	9.371945	0.0073	
	DAPOPN(-2)	-10.77650	0.0058	
	DOIL	0.014955	0.0529	
14%	C	0.112009	0.1933	R^2: 0.881603
	DUM	-0.101763	0.0003	RSS: 0.010754
	DRGDP(-3)	0.842909	0.0000	
	DRGDP(-1)	-0.380106	0.0016	
	DCPI(-4)	-0.154878	0.0009	
	DUM*DCPI(-1)	0.275400	0.0005	
	D14*(DCPI-OPINF14)	-0.197379	0.0003	
	DTOT(-1)	0.120622	0.0000	
	DTOT(-2)	0.066155	0.0085	
	OPEN(-1)	0.014815	0.6598	
	DAPOPN	9.334410	0.0075	
	DAPOPN(-2)	-10.70854	0.0060	
	DOIL	0.014787	0.0559	

Source: WAMI Staff Computations

Table 7.8: Optimal Inflation Results for Sierra Leone: (Dependent Variable: RGDP)

Assumed Optimal Inflation	Explanatory Variables	Coefficients	Probability of Significance	Explanatory Power/ RSS
5%	C	-0.098282	0.0006	R^2: 0.881295
	DUM1	-0.003779	0.9391	RSS: 0.020649
	DRGDP(-1)*DUM1	-0.440198	0.0789	
	DCPI(-4)	0.085984	0.0290	
	DCPI*DUM1	-0.134429	0.2269	
	D5*(DCPI-OPINF5)	-0.017021	0.6254	
	DAPOPN	12.61468	0.0004	
	DAPOPN(-1)	-14.34937	0.0008	
	DAPOPN(-3)	7.059281	0.0002	
	DREX(-4)	0.090835	0.0789	
	DRINV	0.095688	0.0085	
	DRINV(-1)	0.106283	0.0043	
	DRINV(-2)	0.083180	0.0334	
	AR(1)	-0.608337	0.0366	
9%	C	-0.098414	0.0005	R^2: 0.881450
	DUM1	-0.005299	0.9167	RSS: 0.020622
	DRGDP(-1)*DUM1	-0.440480	0.0783	
	DCPI(-4)	0.086509	0.0288	
	DCPI*DUM1	-0.131333	0.2464	
	D9*(DCPI-OPINF9)	-0.018637	0.6120	
	DAPOPN	12.68245	0.0004	
	DAPOPN(-1)	-14.43042	0.0008	
	DAPOPN(-3)	7.073308	0.0002	
	DREX(-4)	0.091373	0.0781	
	DRINV	0.095405	0.0086	
	DRINV(-1)	0.106145	0.0042	
	DRINV(-2)	0.083033	0.0336	
	AR(1)	-0.607670	0.0367	
10%	C	-0.098519	0.0005	R^2: 0.881457
	DUM1	-0.005470	0.9143	RSS: 0.020620
	DRGDP(-1)*DUM1	-0.440471	0.0782	
	DCPI(-4)	0.086515	0.0288	
	DCPI*DUM1	-0.130957	0.2493	
	D10*(DCPI-OPINF10)	-0.018932	0.6114	
	DAPOPN	12.69490	0.0004	
	DAPOPN(-1)	-14.44596	0.0008	
	DAPOPN(-3)	7.079424	0.0002	
	DREX(-4)	0.091387	0.0780	
	DRINV	0.095448	0.0085	
	DRINV(-1)	0.106148	0.0042	
	DRINV(-2)	0.082969	0.0338	
	AR(1)	-0.607746	0.0366	
11%	C	-0.098638	0.0005	R^2: 0.881455
	DUM1	-0.005597	0.9126	RSS: 0.020621
	DRGDP(-1)*DUM1	-0.440487	0.0782	
	DCPI(-4)	0.086494	0.0288	
	DCPI*DUM1	-0.130678	0.2518	
	D11*(DCPI-OPINF11)	-0.019192	0.6116	
	DAPOPN	12.70634	0.0005	
	DAPOPN(-1)	-14.46064	0.0008	

Assumed Optimal Inflation	Explanatory Variables	Coefficients	Probability of Significance	Explanatory Power/ RSS
	DAPOPN(-3)	7.086072	0.0002	
	DREX(-4)	0.091383	0.0780	
	DRINV	0.095512	0.0084	
	DRINV(-1)	0.106165	0.0042	
	DRINV(-2)	0.082906	0.0340	
	AR(1)	-0.607809	0.0366	

Source: WAMI Staff Computations

not at variant with that obtained by Seleteng (2005) for Lesotho. Beyond this level, the explanatory power of the model began to fall. Thus, for Sierra Leone, the optimal inflation rate is 10 percent.

Further, the empirical results indicate that, apart from domestic inflation rate, the principal determinants of real GDP growth in Sierra Leone over the period 1970-2006 were active population growth rate, real investment growth rate and real exchange rate. Active population growth had static positive and dynamic negative impacts on economic growth. The combined growth impact of active population growth was positive as expected *a priori*. The real investment growth had positive impact on real GDP growth in static and dynamic terms. Thus, supply-side factors contributed a great deal to real GDP growth in Sierra Leone over the study period. The fourth lag of the real exchange rate positive impact on real GDP growth, implying that real exchange rate depreciation had dynamic positive influence on economic growth. However, the poor performance of openness index and terms of trade suggest the external sector contributed very little to economic growth in Sierra Leone over the period under study. The coefficient of the war dummy variable was not statistically significant but shows a tendency of depressing real GDP growth.

Optimal Inflation for the WAMZ

There is the need to determine the optimal inflation rate for the WAMZ as a whole. Two different methodologies were used in this regard. The first approach uses the estimates of inflation thresholds in the member countries as established in the previous section to arrive at an optimal level of inflation for the Zone, while the second methodology employs panel data model estimation techniques.

Optimal Inflation for the WAMZ: Country-Specific Model Estimations

The optimal inflation for the Zone was obtained from the country-specific inflation threshold estimations. This is done by first working out the ranges within which inflation in the individual countries is pro-growth. The intersection of these ranges gives the optimal inflation rate for the Zone.

This approach, which is the most common in the literature (Seleteng, 2005), tries to establish the range within which the inflationary effect is significant. Under this approach, a trend line is constructed for the explanatory powers of a given model. The points of intersection of the trend line and the explanatory power plot give the pro-growth inflation range in each member country. From Figures 7 - 12, the ranges are as follows: The Gambia, 7-11%; Ghana, 6-12%; Guinea, 3-9%; Liberia, 3-9%; Nigeria, 9-14%; and Sierra Leone, 7-12%. The intersections of these ranges are depicted in Figure 7.13. The optimal inflation rate for the WAMZ, according to Figure 7.13 is 9%. A deviation of ±2 % could be maintained, giving a pro-growth inflation range for the Zone as 7-11%.

Figure 7.7: The Gambia - Explanatory Power Plots

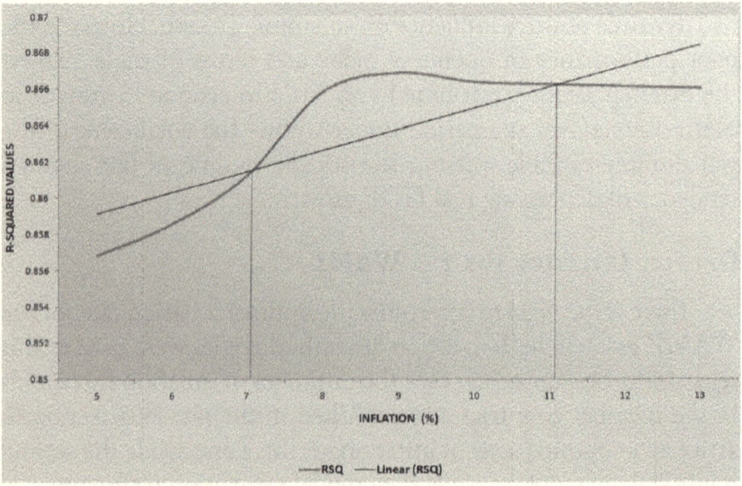

Figure 7.8: Ghana - Explanatory Power Plots

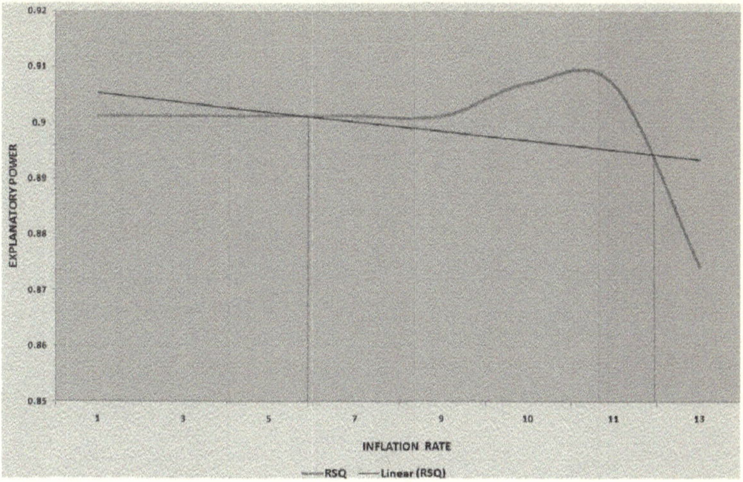

Figure 7.9: Guinea - Explanatory Power Plots

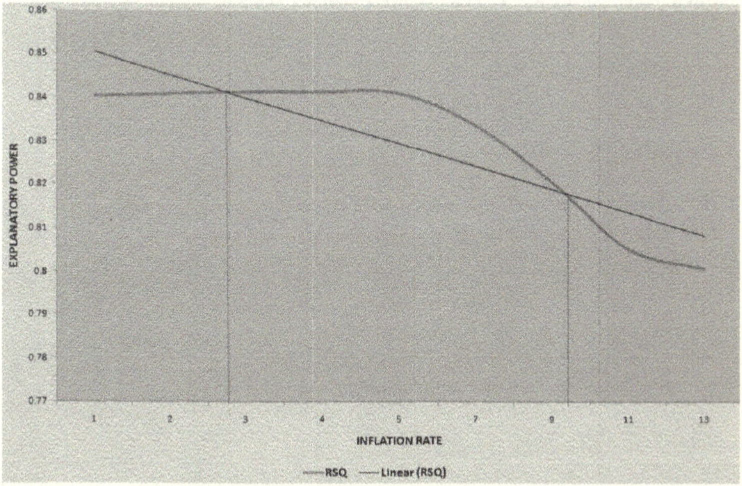

Figure 7.10: Liberia - Explanatory Power Plots

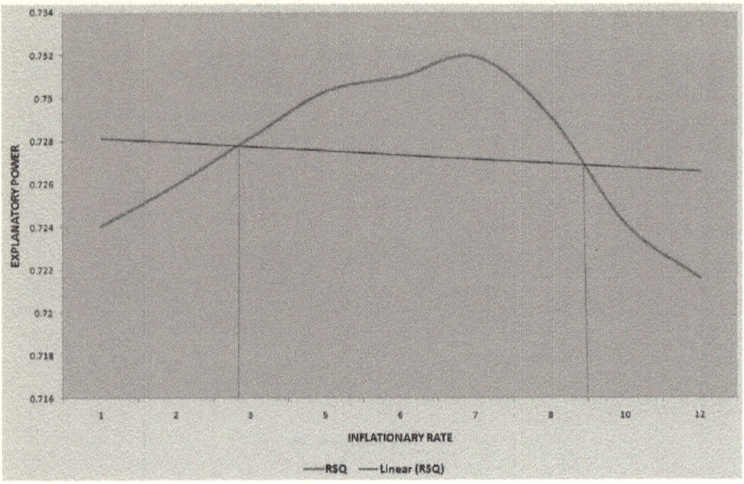

Figure 7.11: Nigeria - Explanatory Power Plots

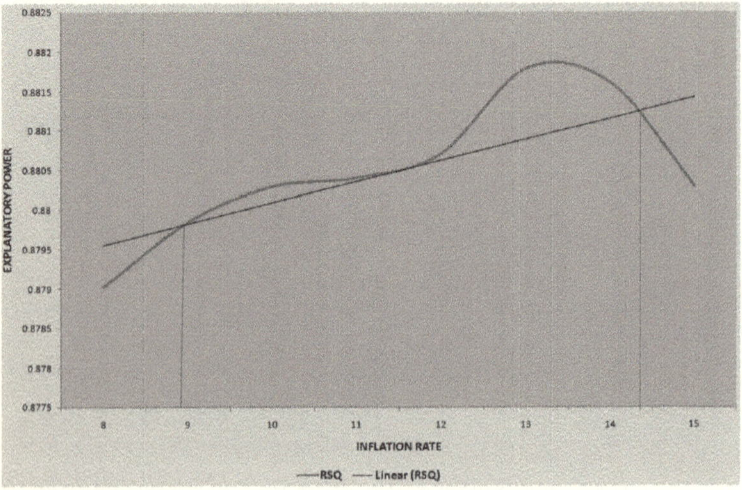

Figure 7.12: Sierra Leone - Explanatory Power Plots

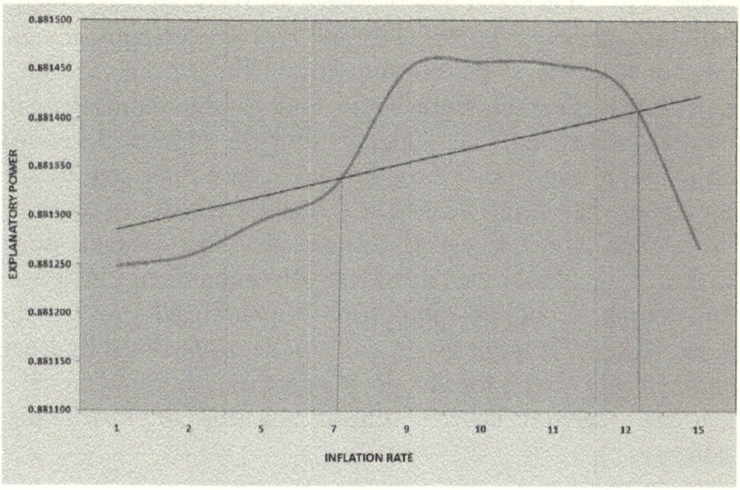

Figure 7.13: A Chart Showing the Ranges of Pro-Growth Inflation Rates in WAMZ Countries

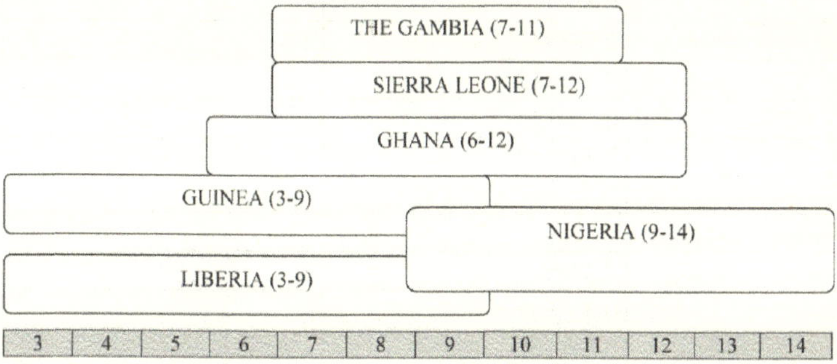

Optimal Inflation for the WAMZ: Panel-Data Model Estimations

A panel data model was also estimated to determine the optimal inflation model for the WAMZ. Cross-section fixed effects estimation technique was applied. The results are reported in Table 7.8 and graphically depicted in Figure 7.14. The detailed estimation results are presented in Appendix IV.

From the results the values of the R-squared have been oscillating. The following ranges of values for the R-squared emerge with turning points: 3-7%, 8-11% and 12-15% with optimal inflations of 4, 10 and 13 percent respectively. The panel data estimation results reflect substantially the results of the country-specific model estimations. Thus, judging from the individual country estimates, Range I may be too low for at least three countries in the Zone, while Range 3 may be too high for at least two countries in the Zone. Thus, Range II becomes the most desirable range with an optimal inflation rate of 10%. The entire Range II (8-11% inflation rate) could be appropriate for policymaking within the Zone. This result is consistent with the result obtained by Khan and Senhadji (2005) for Developing countries. Both methodologies have, therefore, delivered similar ranges of pro-growth inflation rates.

Table 7.9: Optimal Inflation Results for the WAMZ — Panel Data Estimates

Range	R-Squared	Optimal Inflation
Range I (3-7%)		
3	0.335419	
4	0.335942	4%
5	0.335412	
6	0.334744	
7	0.334547	
Range II (8-11%)		
8	0.336595	
9	0.337639	
10	0.342185	10%
11	0.342121	
Range III (12-15%)		
12	0.343780	
13	0.343925	13%
14	0.341943	
15	0.341600	

CONCLUSION

The preoccupation of this paper was to empirically estimate the threshold levels of inflation in the WAMZ. An assessment of the empirical results had been acquired through the conditional least square technique. The study also identified the determinants of growth in the WAMZ. The results showed that there exists a statistically negative relationship between inflation and economic growth for the WAMZ countries. These results are consistent with the findings of Barro (1997), Khan and Senhadji (2001), Faria and Carneiro (2001), among others. Furthermore, the empirical results strongly suggest the existence of threshold levels for all the countries, beyond which inflation exert a negative effect on growth. The results revealed the following ranges for the threshold inflation rates of the WAMZ countries; Gambia (7-11 percent), Ghana (6-12 percent), Guinea (3-9 percent), Liberia (3-9 percent), Nigeria (9-14 percent) and Sierra Leone (7-12 percent).

The results showed that except for Nigeria, WAMZ countries threshold inflation rates lie within the convergence criteria of maintaining an inflation rate not exceeding 10 percent. The results are useful for policy makers in providing some clue in setting an optimal inflation target. Policy makers should implement policies aimed at achieving the threshold inflation rate that is consistent with higher economic growth. Thus, it is desirable to keep inflation rate at least within the threshold level in member countries, as it may help maintain sustainable growth. A sustainable increase in growth can be achieved by directing monetary policy towards maintaining price stability.

REFERENCES

Ahmed, S. and M.G. Mortaza, (2005). "Inflation and Economic Growth in Bangladesh: 1981-2005".Policy Analysis Unit, *Bangladesh Bank Working paper Series* WP 0604

Andres, J. and I. Hernando (1997) "Does Inflation Harm Economic Growth? Evidence from the OECD," *NBER Paper* No. 6062.

Barro, Robert, 1991, "Economic Growth in a Cross-Section of Countries" *Quarterly Journal of Economics*, 106 (2), 407-43.

Barro R. J. (1997). Determinants of Economic Growth – A Cross-Country Empirical Study, the *MIT Press*, Massachusetts Institute of Technology.

Bruno, M. and W. Easterly. (1995). Inflation Crises and Long-Run Growth, *World Bank Policy Research Working Paper No.1517*

Burdekin, R. C. K., A.T. Denzau, M.W. Keil, T. Sitthiyot and D. Willett. (2000). When

Does Inflation Hurt Economic Growth? Different Nonlinearities for Different Economies. *Working Papers in Economics. Claremont Colleges.*

De Gregorio, J. (1991). The Effects of Inflation on Economic Growth: Lessons from Latin America, *IMF Working Paper WP/91.*

Faria, J. R. and F. G. Carneiro. (2001). Does High Inflation Affect Growth in the Long and Short-run?, *Journal of Applied Economics, IV (1)*

Fischer, S. (1993). "Inflation and Growth", *NBER Working Paper No.1235.*

Fischer, S. and F. Modigliani. (1978) "Towards and Understanding of the Real Effects and Costs of Inflation," *Weltwirtschaftliches Archiv*, 114, 810-833

Ghosh, A. and S. Phillips. (1998). Warning: Inflation may be Harmful to your Growth, *IMF Staff Papers, 45 (4)*

Gillman, M., M. Harris and M Laszlo. (2002). Inflation and Growth: Some Theory and Evidence, *Central European University Working Paper*, Department of Economics, Central European University.

Gregorio, J. (1996) "Inflation, Growth, and Central Banks: Theory and Evidence," *World Bank Policy Research Working Paper* 1575, Policy Research Department, Macroeconomics and Growth Division.

Judson, R., and A. Orphanides (1996): "Inflation, Volatility and Growth," Board of Governors of the Federal Reserve System, Finance and Economics Discussion Series, 96(19).

Khan, M. S. and A. S. Senhadji. (2001). Threshold Effects in the Relationship between Inflation and Growth, *IMF Staff Papers, 48(1)*

Lee C., S.Y Wong, (2005). Inflationary threshold effects in the relationship between financial development and economic growth: evidence from Taiwan and Japan. *Journal of Economic Development*, 30(1), 49-68.

Lucas, R. (1973). Some International evidence on Output-Inflation Tradeoffs, *American Economic Review*, 63, 326-334.

Malla, S. "Inflation and Economic Growth: Evidence from a Growth Equation," *mimeo*, Department of Economics, University of Hawai'I at Monoa, Honolulu (1997). Available at www.hawaii.edu/~malla (access date: 25, February, 2010)

Mallik, G. and A. Chowdhury. (2001). Inflation and Economic Growth: Evidence from Four South American Countries, *Asia-Pacific Development Journal*, 8(1), 123-133.

Mubarik, Yasir Ali (2005), ""Inflation and Growth: An Estimate of the Threshold Level of Inflation in Pakistan", State Bank of Pakistan Research Bulletin, 1 (1).

Mundell, R. (1965) "Growth, Stability and Inflationary Finance," *Journal of Political Economy*, 73, 97-109.

Sarel, M. (1995). Non-Linear Effects of Inflation on Economic Growth, *IMF Working Paper No. WP/95/56.*

Seleteng, M (2005). Inflation and Gortwh: An estimate of an optimal level of inflation in Lesotho. Avaliable at www.centralbank.org.ls/.../Inflation%20&%20Econo%20Growth.pdf (access date: 25, February, 2010)

Solow, R. (1956). "A Contribution to the Theory of Economic Growth." *Quarterly Journal of Economics*, 70, 65-94.

Stockman, Alan C., 1981, "Anticipated Inflation and the Capital Stock in a Cash-in-Advance Economy", *Journal of Monetary Economics,* November, 8(3),387-93.

Swan, T. (1956). Economic Growth and Capital Accumulation." *Economic Record,* 32, 344-361.

Sweidan, O. D. (2004), "Does Inflation Harm Economic Growth in Jordan? An Econometric Analysis for the Period 1970-2000," *International Journal of Applied Econometrics and Quantitative Studies,* 1(2), 41-66.

Thirlwall, A.P. and C.A. Barton (1971). "Inflation and Growth: The International Evidence." *Banca Nazionale del lavoro Quarterly Review*, 98, 263-275.

Tobin, J. (1965). "Money and Economic Growth", *Econometrica,* 33, 671-684.

Section IV

Fiscal and Financial Issues

Chapter 8

FISCAL OPERATIONS IN THE WEST AFRICAN SUB-REGION: IMPLICATIONS FOR REGIONAL ECONOMIC INTEGRATION

Akpan Ekpo and Udoma Afangideh

INTRODUCTION

Although it is generally accepted that public spending can have a direct impact on economic growth, spending in excess of revenues is not all together a good thing. Since it must be financed, it opens up an indirect channel of influence on stability and growth that operates via the macro policy mix. This involves the interaction between fiscal and monetary policy in terms of which one is "dominant" over the other. Some have seen this as a question of politicians versus technocrats, or the relative influence of ministers of finance and apex bank governors.

Ultimately, fiscal policy determines whether there is a deficit to be financed, and of what size. On the other hand, monetary policy is aimed at price stability, in the understanding that it is conducive to long-term growth. It was not uncommon in the past for monetary policy to be co-opted into financing the fiscal deficit at the expense of its primary objective of low inflation. However, experience has shown this to be an inefficient framework for macroeconomic management. Over the years monetary authorities have responded by seeking to acquire greater autonomy which charter excludes lending to government. Despite this, fiscal and monetary policies do not operate at cross-purposes.

In developed economies where fiscal deficits are for the most part financed in domestic capital markets in which the monetary authorities are also active, conflicts may arise in the area of interest rate levels. However, the situation is more complex in emerging economies where the chances of conflicting policies are far greater. This is because domestic capital markets are imperfect, which usually implies that they are incapable of financing the entire fiscal deficit and policy harmonization remains a challenge. Also, in some countries, ensuring central bank independence is still in the formative stage, despite legislation to the contrary.

Thus, institutional weakness still persists with central banks acting as financial agents for the government including its external financial operations. In a situation where there is a fiscal decision to overspend significantly, fiscal policy automatically becomes dominant over monetary policy. This dominance can adopt various forms, depending on how the deficit is financed. If external borrowing is a fiscal option, it will affect the way in which dominance plays out. The short-run consequences of fiscal dominance which are excessive inflation, exchange rate instability or high interest rates, are in themselves inimical to economic integration and development. This is because they pose serious challenges towards the realization of both the primary and secondary convergence criteria and by extension lead to further detrimental impact on trade, investment and growth operating primarily through volatility in the real exchange rate.

This paper examines fiscal operations in the West African sub-region and its implication for achieving regional economic integration. An important observation however is that a stable, coordinated, harmonized and sustained macroeconomic environment to deepen regional economic integration process remains a challenge. The paper therefore looks at the trends of fiscal operations (revenue, expenditure, debts) in the sub-region and their implications for sustaining monetary and economic integration.

Following this introduction, the paper is organized as follows: Section two discusses theoretical framework anchored on fiscal sustainability, fiscal deficits and government budget constraint, economic integration as well as reviews related literature. Section three overviews the macroeconomic environment of the sub-region. Implications of fiscal operations on convergence criteria is handled in section four. Section five highlights the implications of fiscal operations for sustaining regional integration. The paper is concluded in section six.

THEORETICAL FRAMEWORK AND LITERATURE REVIEW

The economic literature is not short of theory and opinion on the role of fiscal operations on the workings of an economy. The core argument however rested on Keynes proposition that fiscal deficit can be used to stimulate the economy out of a recession. Many have argued to the contrary claiming that fiscal deficit exacerbate economic aggregates such as interest rates, inflation and exchange rate which ultimately worsen growth and development.

Fiscal Sustainability

Fiscal expansion may be needed to provide substantial support for aggregate demand and for financial and other key sectors of the economy especially in time of crisis. The resultant deterioration of fiscal balances, expansion of government liabilities and increased risk of future losses require an articulation of a strategy to ensure sustainability of public finance.

The literature distinguishes three strands of sustainability which are derived from the broader concept of budget sustainability (Bevan, 2001). They are fiscal sustainability, absorptive sustainability and target sustainability. Fiscal sustainability concerns itself with whether a planned expenditure path can be sustained without implying infeasible or unacceptable financing consequences. It asks the question whether a spending programme is financeable without enquiring whether it is well designed or partially desirable. Absorptive sustainability is concerned with whether a planned expenditure path can be implemented given available finance; it raises the issue of absorptive capacity as a potential independent constraint on spending. Target sustainability deals with the congruence between planned expenditures and the government underlying objectives. It is more concerned with the sustainability of the objectives, given the level and composition of the budget. What is paramount is that full sustainability requires that all three component types hold simultaneously. If findings show that government spending is unsustainable in any of the three, then this would have different implications for policy.

This strategic response of fiscal sustainability falls within the purview of fiscal consolidation which is a policy aimed at reducing government deficits and debt accumulation. It involves the ability to mobilize revenue and pursue prudent expenditure progranmmes in order to maintain primary surplus or avoid deficit. It is tied up to fiscal sustainability which is a medium term concept that implies measures that relate debt stocks and flows with a proxy of the payment capacity e.g. revenue, export and GDP. Due to external financing dependency, there may not be primary surplus in the foreseeable future. Thus, fiscal policy is sustainable if the present value of future primary surpluses is equal to the current level of debt.

As economic and financial crisis abate with sharp deterioration in public finances of countries, fiscal recovery plan is needed to reduce debt burdens before long-term pressures such as education and human capacity building accumulate. Thus, adopting fiscal sustainability plan is important and necessary to ensure the achievement of the overall broader concept of fiscal consolidation.

Fiscal Deficits and Government Budget Constraint

Government budget constraint (GBC) can be represented as:

$$\int_{t=0}^{\infty} e^{-R(t)} G(t)dt \leq -D(0) + \int_{t=0}^{\infty} e^{-R(t)} T(t)dt \text{............} (1)$$

Where $G(t)$ = Government real purchases
$T(t)$ = Taxes
$D(0)$ = Initial Real Debt Outstanding

Government is confronted with the situation where the present rate of its purchases of goods and services is less than or equal to the initial wealth plus the present value of its tax receipts (net of transfer payments).

Note that $R(t)$ denotes $\int_{T=o}^{t} r(T)dT$, where $r(T)$ is the real interest rate at time T.

Therefore, the value of a unit of output at time t discounted back to time 0 is $e^{-R(t)}$. The budget constraint is thus represented as in equation (1).

It should be noted that $D(0)$ is debt rather than wealth; it enters the budget constraint negatively. The government budget constraint does not prevent it from being permanently in debt. The restriction the constraint places on the government is that the limit of the present value of its debt cannot be positive. That is:

$$\lim_{s-\infty} e^{-R(s)} D(s) \leq 0 ....(2)$$

If the real interest rate is always positive implying a positive but constant value of D indicating that the government never pays off its debt, the constraint is satisfied. Also, a policy where D is always growing meets the budget constraint if the growth of D is less than the real interest rate.

The simplest definition of the budget deficit is that it is the rate of change of the stock of debt:

$$D(t)=[G(t)-T(t)]+r(t)Dt) ....(3)$$

The rate of change in the stock of real debt equals the difference between the government's purchases and revenue, plus the real interest on its debt (equation 3). From equation 3, $[G(t)-T(t)]$ is known as primary deficit. Examining the primary rather than the total deficit is more illuminating in trying to analyse how fiscal policy contributes to the government budget constraint, that is:

$$\int_{t=0}^{\infty} e^{-R(t)}[T(t)-G(t)]dt \geq D(0) ....(4)$$

Based on equation 4, government must run large enough primary surpluses in present value to offset its initial debt.

Monetary Integration

A major prerequisite for economic and monetary integration is the achievement and sustenance of macroeconomic convergence. The achievement of a high degree of economic convergence requires institutional and legal frameworks. This is predicated on effective macroeconomic surveillance framework that focuses on convergence targets based on country specific convergence trajectory.

Thus, the notion of economic integration in the case of West African Monetary Zone (WAMZ) is hinged on certain convergence criteria which must be met before integration can be achieved. It is divided into primary and secondary criteria. There are four primary criteria which are inflation rate of equal to or less than 5%, budget deficit/GDP ratio of less than or equal to 4%, limiting apex bank financing of government budget deficit to equal to or less than 10% of previous year's tax revenue and gross external reserves of at least 6 months of imports cover. The secondary criteria consist of prohibition of accumulation of new domestic debt arrears and liquidation of existing ones, tax revenue to GDP ratio of equal to or greater than 20%, wage bill/tax revenue of equal to or less than 35%, public investment/tax revenue of equal to or greater than 20%, maintaining real exchange rate stability of not more than 5% band; and positive real interest rate.

It is expected that the principle of fiscal sustainability should drive the monetary integration process by complementing monetary policy rather than worsening it. Unsustainable fiscal policy results in fiscal dominance which is likely to undermine the primary and secondary convergence criteria. If monetary cooperation is the policy goal, convergence criteria must become an integral part of budgetary and policy formation in members states. Various policies on financial services, capital market integration and development, investment, corporate tax, fiscal management, double taxation agreement and movement of community nationals will have to be harmonized. The organizational difficulties at the national levels in harmonizing these policies continue to pose serious challenge to both the convergence programmes and economic and monetary integration at large.

Literature Review

The literature shows that the interaction between fiscal and monetary policy has been studied along different lines. The various strands identified by the literature are: (1) coordination of monetary and fiscal policy, (2) optimal monetary and fiscal policy and (3) the channels through which fiscal actions affect monetary variables and the constraints imposed by fiscal policy on the monetary authority. It is the third strand that is the most relevant to this paper. Fiscal policy can affect monetary policy in different ways: first through the impact of government inter-temporal budget constraint on monetary policy; secondly through the effect of fiscal policy on a number of monetary variables, such as interest rates, interest spreads and exchange rates.

A number of papers have tried to assess from an empirical perspective how monetary and fiscal policies interact and the evidence of fiscal dominance. Studies from industrialized countries find that monetary policy typically has not accommodated fiscal policy in the past decade, and some even suggest that monetary policy has tended to tighten in response to loose fiscal policy. Melitz (1997, 2002) finds that monetary and fiscal policy have tended to move in opposite directions. Wyplosz (1999) obtains a similar result for the EMU countries after the introduction of the 1992 Maastricht Treaty.

Favero (2002), investigating the joint behaviour of monetary and fiscal authorities in the euro area, also concludes that stabilisation of inflation has been achieved independently from the lack of fiscal discipline. This supports the idea that the monetary authorities in the euro area have been able to affect inflation rates. Von Hagen et al (2002) find that the monetary condition index reacted negatively to an increase in fiscal deficits in EMU and OECD countries over the period 1972–89, but that during the1990s the same variable was not significantly affected by fiscal deficits. A study by Favero and Monacelli (2003) also detects some evidence of fiscal dominance in the United States for limited periods of time, showing that, during the period 1960–87, it is possible to identify time windows where an empirical model based on both monetary and fiscal regime is able to track the dynamics of inflation better than a regime based on a monetary rule only.

Tanner and Ramos (2002) on EM countries, evaluate whether the policy regime in Brazil during the 1990s can be better characterised as fiscal or monetary dominant. Primary surpluses respond much more strongly to public debt (IMF, 2003). The results of these studies seem to suggest that fiscal dominance might be an issue for EMs more than for industrialised countries.

Observing fiscal operations during a period of banking crisis, Reinhart and Rogoff (2008a, 2008b, 2009) show that banking crises lead to sharp declines in tax revenues, as well as to significant increases in government spending. Their findings show that government debt rises by 86 percent during the three years following a banking crisis, and at the end of this period, growth resumes slowly to reach an average annual rate of 2½ percent in the third year after the crisis. Introducing new database on banking crisis with information on the type of policy responses implemented to resolve these crises in different countries, Laeven and Valencia (2008) opine that in a systemic banking crisis, a country's corporate and financial sectors experience a large number of defaults and financial institutions and corporations face difficulties repaying loans on time.

Thus, many researchers have concentrated on the origins of banking crisis. Their findings show that crises tend to erupt under weak macroeconomic environment especially under high inflation and interest rates as well as low growth (see Demirgüc-Kunt and Detragiache, 1998; Collyns and Kincaid, 2003). The consequences of these crises are the preoccupation of other studies (researchers) such as Reinhart and Rogoff (2009) as stated above. But Claessens, Kose, and Terrones (2008) stepped up the analysis and studied recessions caused by credit contractions, those associated with house price declines, and episodes of equity price declines. The severity and duration of recessions according to their results can be majorly determined by the interactions of macroeconomic and financial variables. In particular, they find evidence that recessions associated with credit crunches and house price busts tend to be deeper and longer than other recessions.

Another area of interest to researchers has been the analysis of policy responses to these crises. Laeven and Valencia (2008) focused on the type of containment and resolution policies aimed at stabilizing the banking sector during financial crises. Others assessed the macroeconomic response to the crises. In fact, both monetary and fiscal policy tends to be countercyclical during recessions, credit contractions, and asset price declines (Claessens, Kose, and Terrones, 2008 and IMF, 2009b). During these periods, fiscal policy appears to be more accommodative, suggesting a more aggressive countercyclical fiscal stance. Their findings also show that expansionary fiscal policy (proxied by discretionary government consumption) tends to shorten the duration of recessions.

On their part, Wachtel and Young (1987) discovered that a 1 percentage increase in the projected deficit-GDP ratio raises interest rates on the order of 6 to 16 basis points. Also, Cohen and Garnier (1991) observed a significant positive effect of deficit-GDP ratio on interest rates. Fiscal deficit has a significant effect on interest rate (Laubach, 2003). Indeed, several studies have associated budgets deficits with rising interest rates in the economy (see Miller and Russek, 1990; Elmendorf, 1993; Canzoneri et al, 2002 and Shapiro, 2004). Other studies by Gale and Orszag (2003), Dai and Phillipon (2004), Kimberly (2008), Patnaik (2000 and 2001) indicated that expected future fiscal deficits increases current long term interest rates.. In his study of India, Lal et al (2001) observed that the financing of large fiscal deficits (sales of bonds) has resulted in higher real interest rates and crowding out of private investment. According to Bhalla (1995), the floor on interest rate surprisingly does not allow causation to run from high fiscal deficits to high interest rates in India but from high interest rates to high fiscal deficits and that to reduce deficits, interest rates should be reduced.

Other studies exist which do not support the view that large deficits and debt raise interest rates as they find no link between budget deficits and interest rates. They include Elmendorf and Mankiw (1999), Evans (1987), Plosser (1987), and Chakraborty (2002). Bebi (2000) discovered a statistically insignificant effect of domestic debt-GDP ratio on lending rate, and significant fiscal deficits effect on interest rate. Anyanwu (1998) used pooled cross-section and time series data for Nigeria, Ghana and the Gambia but his result did not reveal a significant positive association between overall fiscal deficits (and its foreign financing)

Table 1: WAMZ (Zone-Wide): Selected Macroeconomic Indicators

	2001	2002	2003	2004	2005	2006	2007	2008 first half	2008	2009 first half
Output and prices										
Real GDP growth (%)*	4.9	4.8	9.1	6.4	6.4	5.6	6.1	6.4	6.4	5.5
Nominal GDP ($ billions)	71.5	75.5	89.4	100.2	112.4	159.4	214.6	105.0	209.2	90.9
Inflation Rate (end of Period)	15.2	11.6	22.1	11.5	13.4	11.5	8.2	14.4	15.2	11.2
Money and credit										
Money Supply (M2+) growth (% change)	15.7	4.1	30.2	17.8	17.7	52.0	51.7	35.8	37.0	-8.5
Velocity (Nom. GDP/M2+)	5.5	5.5	5.0	4.8	4.6	4.3	3.8	2.8	2.7	2.6
External sector										
Gross International Reserves ($ billions)	11.1	8.5	9.1	19.0	30.5	44.6	54.5	62.8	55.5	45.6
Gross International Reserves (in months of imports c.i.f.)	7.3	5.3	4.7	9.6	10.0	12.3	11.6	11.9	11.2	12.1
Governments Fiscal operations										
Tax Revenue (% of GDP)	14.6	10.7	12.1	15.3	19.7	15.3	11.1	17.0	13.6	8.6
Salary mass/Total tax revenue	30.8	48.2	30.8	25.6	21.1	22.7	34.5	41.7	33.2	58.7
Public Investments from domestic receipts	31.0	34.9	23.8	13.5	18.4	19.7	14.5	10.1	13.5	21.8
Captital Expenditures / Total Expenditures	30.0	31.2	23.8	14.7	19.4	58.7	15.4	10.0	14.2	21.3
Expenditure (% of GDP)	34.1	25.7	27.5	34.0	42.9	32.9	25.3	33.8	32.5	21.1
Fiscal Balance includ. Grants (% of GDP)	-3.5	-4.0	-2.2	-1.3	-1.1	-0.8	-0.9	-0.8	-1.1	-2.7
Fiscal Balance excl.Grants (% of GDP)	-4.2	-4.5	-2.9	-2.0	-1.8	-1.3	-1.3	-1.1	-1.5	-3.2

Source: WAMZ Authorities and WAMI Staff

(*) The real GDP Growth is on annual basis

and domestic nominal deposit interest rates. Rather, a significant positive relation was reported between domestic financing of the fiscal deficits and domestic nominal deposit rates. He concluded that focus should shift from the deficits itself to the manner of financing it.

OVERVIEW OF MACROECONOMIC ENVIRONMENT IN THE SUB-REGION

The overall macroeconomic performance of the sub-region for the period of this analysis remains mixed. After a very long time the sub-region had started to lay solid macroeconomic environment that was growth-inducing. As shown in Table 8.1, real GDP growth on average was above 5%. Gross international reserve in months of imports was on the increase. Tax revenue/ GDP was increasing. Although inflation rate was still double digit, there was some element of stability in prices of goods and services. However, these indicators of a stable macroeconomic environment were threatened by the advent of the global financial crisis which had serious negative implications for the sub-region as a whole in terms of the achievement of economic integration. Thus, macroeconomic performance of the sub- region based on the realisation of convergence criteria remains a major challenge as individual countries and different sub-groupings continue to display different outcomes.

Trend Analysis of Fiscal Operations in selected Countries of ECOWAS

Nigeria

Fiscal operations in Nigeria in the last decade show some adherence to fiscal prudence as sustained effort was made to maintain low fiscal deficit. Although fiscal deficit was still a recurrent issue in Nigeria's fiscal process as shown in Table 8.2 and Figure 8.1 of the appendix, the gap between total expenditure and revenue was low, sustainable and narrowing over time. This is not unconnected with some of the policy initiatives undertaken during the period under study such as oil price-based fiscal rule and fiscal responsibility act which were part of the overall fiscal consolida-

Table 8.2: Fiscal Balance for Nigeria (=N=Million) 2000-2008

Year	Current GDP	Revenue	Expenditure	Deficit	Deficit/GDP
2000	151877.0	153864.8	4582127.3	-103.5	0.0023
2001	171523.1	171374.5	4725086.0	-221.0	0.0047
2002	172151.1	169820.2	6012381.3	-301.4	0.0050
2003	370170.9	361713.2	8487031.6	-174.7	0.0021
2004	468295.2	461050.6	11411066.9	-172.6	0.0015
2005	597219.1	587977.8	14572239.1	-161.4	0.0011
2006	674255.7	665838.0	18564594.7	-100.8	0.0005
2007	832300.0	827400.0	20657317.7	-117.2	0.0006
2008	1387871.3	1387900.0	23842170.7	-155.5	0.0007

Source: CBN Statistical Bulletin, Golden Jubilee Edition

tion process to institute fiscal prudence in financial management of government resources. The special focus of fiscal policy has been on diversifying the economy in order to reduce overdependence on oil. This is done by broadening the non-oil tax revenue base through efficient tax administration measures as well as on expenditures that are growth enhancing.

Figure 8.1: Revenue and Expenditure for Nigeria (2000-2008)

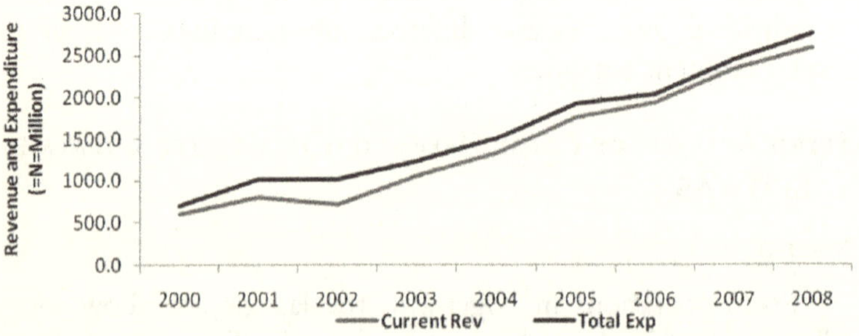

Figure 8.2a indicates the trend of deficit to GDP ratio which was rising and above the 4% target between 2001 and 2002 before falling to maintain a sustainable level within the set target.

Figure 8.2a: Deficit/GDP Ratio for Nigeria (2000-2008)

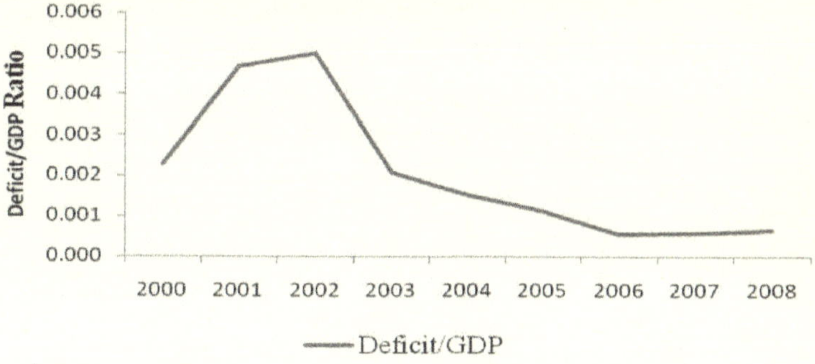

Figure 8.2b shows the trend of total debt which was on the increase until 2005 when it fell sharply due to the debt payment agreement which Nigeria entered into with the Paris club of creditors. Thereafter, Nigeria's total debt remains low and sustainable

Figure 8.2b: Total Debt for Nigeria (2000-2008)

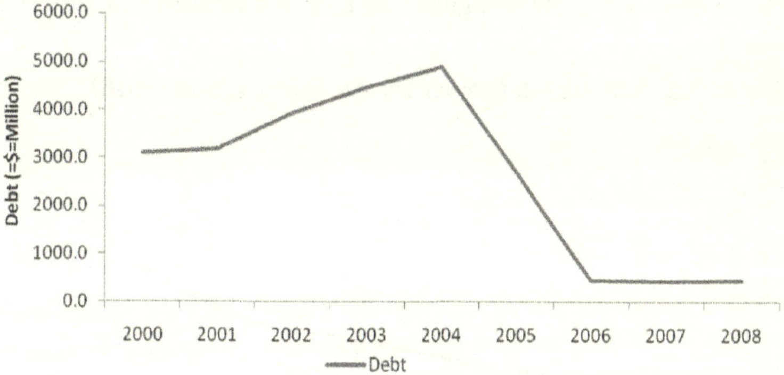

This was further reflected in Nigeria's total debt to gross domestic product as demonstrated in figure 8.3 which sharply dropped from 67.6% in 2000 to about 2% in 2008, thereby ensuring a sustainable debt management. Again, this was the outcome of the payment to the Paris club of creditors.

Figure 3: Total Debt/GDP Ratio for Nigeria (2000-2008)

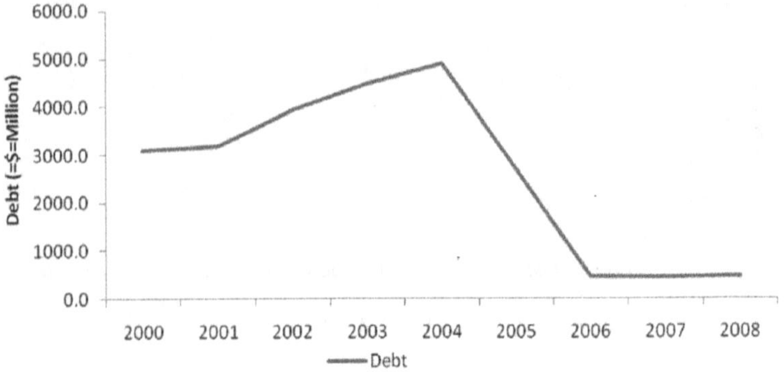

Ghana

In the case of Ghana (figure 8.4), available data also shows an efficient fiscal management as fiscal deficit was low while in some years such as 2003-2005 and 2007, fiscal surplus was actually achieved. After maintaining a sustainable level, total debt started to fall from 2003-2006 (figure 8.5) before it began to slightly rise again.

Figure 8.4: Revenue and Expenditure for Ghana (2000-2008)

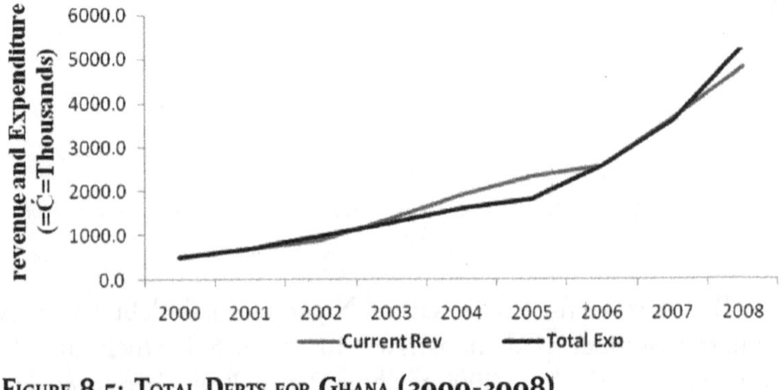

Figure 8.5: Total Debts for Ghana (2000-2008)

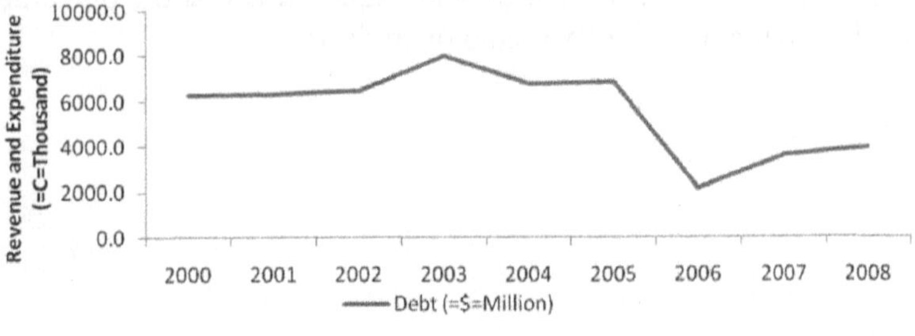

The Gambia

Available data also shows fiscal prudence in the management of The Gambian economy. Apart from 2001, fiscal surplus was observed for all the period of this analysis (figure 8.6). This good fiscal performance is attributed to improved revenue collection mechanism and fiscal discipline relating to budget execution.

Figure 8.6: Revenue and Expenditure for The Gambia (2001-2008)

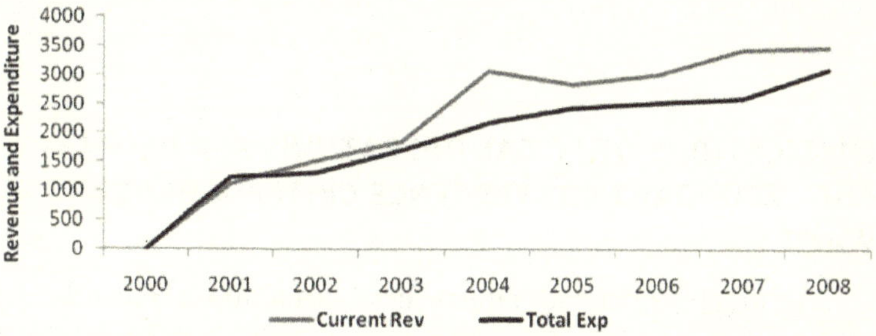

Sierra Leone

As shown in figure 8.7, fiscal deficit was part and parcel of fiscal operations in Sierra Leone for the period of this analysis. This is not unconnected with the urgent need to improve economic infrastructure to enhance rapid economic growth, job creation and poverty reduction and the vital social expenditure that is needed in critical sectors like health and education etc. As a result of efficient fiscal and macroeconomic management, total debt of Sierra Leone which was on the increase, stated to fall from 2006 (figure 8.8).

Figure 8.7: Revenue and Expenditure for Sierra Leone (2000-2008)

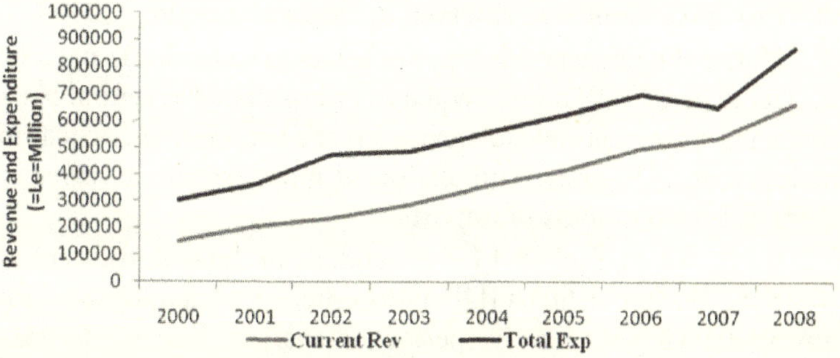

Figure 8.8: Total Debts for Sierra Leone (2000-2008)

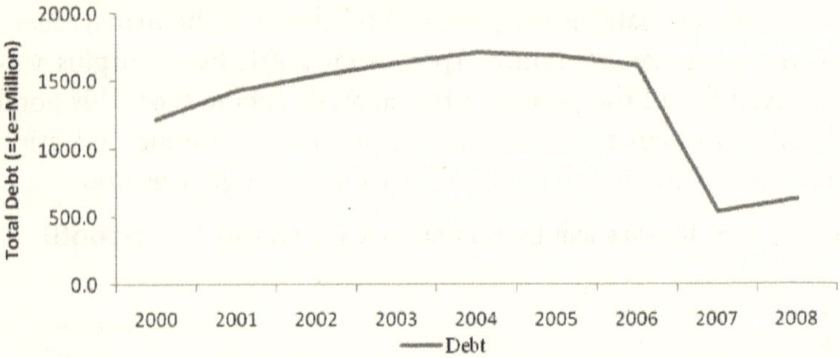

IMPLICATIONS OF FISCAL OPERATIONS FOR PRIMARY AND SECONDARY CONVERGENCE CRITERIA UNDER WAMZ

Although concerted efforts have been made towards the achievement of macroeconomic convergence in the sub-region over the years, the result (Table 8.2 in appendix) continues to vary. Sustenance of progress made by some countries in realizing targets made in preceding years continues to pose a challenge. An overview of the number of countries out of the fifteen ECOWAS member states that complied with the convergence criteria is presented in Table 8.2 in the appendix. The table indicates that only apex bank financing of budget deficit per previous year's tax revenue criterion was met by all the countries in 2005, 2007 and 2009 (projected) while projection shows that real exchange rate would be met by all countries in 2009. None of the other criteria could be met by all the countries in any single year. In fact, tax revenue per gross domestic product ratio was not met by any of the countries from 2001 to 2003. Same was observed for real interest rate in 2008.

Under the primary criteria, we isolated three criteria namely: budget deficit/GDP ratio at equal to or less than 4%, central bank financing of budget deficit/previous year's tax revenue at equal to or less than 10% and accumulation of gross external reserves to cover at least 6 months of imports.

As shown in Table 8.4 (in appendix), all the countries fail to meet the budget deficit/GDP ratio criterion simultaneously for any particular year for the period of analysis. Some countries, such as Cote d'Ivoire, Liberia except 2004 and Nigeria from 2003, met the criteria. UEMOA sub-group failed to meet the criterion but WAMZ and ECOWAS met the target from 2003. However, when Nigeria was isolated from the analysis, both WAMZ and ECOWAS failed to meet the target for the whole period.

Most of the countries performed well in the primary criterion of central bank financing of budget deficit/previous year's tax revenue. Table 8.5 (see appendix) shows that more than ten countries on average met the criteria. The UEMOA countries all met the criteria. Apart from 2001 and 2003, WAMZ and ECOWAS met the criterion as well.

Accumulation of gross external reserves to cover six months of import performed well generally as nine countries except in 2005 consistently met the criteria. UEMOA, WAMZ and ECOWAS all met the criteria. However, when Nigeria was isolated, both WAMZ and ECOWAS failed to meet the criteria.

For the secondary criteria, we discussed three of them namely: tax revenue/GDP ratio at equal or greater than 20%, wage bill/tax revenue at equal or greater than 35% and public investment/tax revenue at equal or greater than 20%.

As indicated in Table 8.7 of the appendix, the criterion of tax revenue/GDP ratio was very difficult to achieve from the point of view of individual countries, sub-regional groupings and the region as a whole. From 2001-2003, no country was able to achieve it while only two countries succeeded from 2004-2008. Projection for 2009 shows that three countries (Senegal, Ghana and Cape Verde) would achieve it. In fact, UEMOA, WAMZ and ECOWAS failed to achieve the criterion.

The wage bill/tax revenue criterion also recorded mixed fortune. Table 8.8 (see appendix) shows clearly that most of the countries could not meet this criterion. UEMOA group of countries could not achieve it in any particular year but WAMZ apart from 2002, met this criterion in all the years although the story was different when Nigeria was isolated.

The next criterion we considered is public investment/tax revenue. The result for the period of this analysis as shown in Table 8.9(see appendix) indicates that for UEMOA countries the criterion was met from 2003 while the WAMZ countries met the criteria for the period of this analysis except 2004. Interestingly, ECOWAS group met the criteria for the whole period as well but when Nigeria was isolated, they missed the target from 2000-2002.

POLICY IMPLICATION FOR SUSTAINING REGIONAL INTEGRATION

Although fiscal policy has the potential to smooth the impact of a crisis, maintain critical government services and investment programmes as well as provide countercyclical support to domestic demand, the appropriate fiscal policy framework is predicated on a country's macroeconomic stability and fiscal space to finance at sustainable rates without undermining monetary policy. A country that is constrained by lack of financing and high levels of debt distress may face limited scope for expanding fiscal policy. Thus, the appropriate speed of adjustment depends on debt levels and the availability of financing on sustainable terms. Accordingly, the following will have to be carried out to sustain the sub-regional economic integration:

Fiscal consolidation and sustainability will have to be maintained to stabilize fiscal variables. This will ultimately ensure the achievement of convergence criteria rather than acting to undermine the various convergence efforts made over the years.

Demand management policies will have to be pursued with harmonisation of monetary and fiscal policies to strengthen programme implementation.

A regional strategy must be developed and strengthened with legal framework to minimize risk on the economy of the sub-region. For instance, adopting multi-year deficit reduction programme allows citizens and creditors to adjust gradually and provides a disciplinary framework to achieve more sensible government finances. Thus, annual budgets should emanate from a medium-term framework that is linked to a broader policy initiative such as poverty reduction. Also, member countries could continue to strengthen the management and structural reforms of their economies.

In order to safeguard both national and sub-regional interests, continuous capacity building in the sub-region to provide the people the opportunities to participate in the running of their economies should be embarked upon.

Sub-regional development and integration could be enhanced by adopting new initiatives to reduce the infrastructure gap in the sub-region through massive investment in energy, roads, air transport, maritime transport and railways based on private and public partnership.

CONCLUSION

Nothing is inherently wrong with budget deficits provided they are kept at sustainable levels, financed in a non-inflationary manner and productively used. Government borrowing should bridge the resource gaps in order to promote economic growth and development and by extension, alleviate poverty. Thus, mobilization of borrowed funds from both the domestic and external markets is a legitimate public function.

However, the gradual return to fiscal dominance of most of the economies of the sub-region even before the advent of the recent global financial crisis couple with various fiscal measures adopted to cushion the effects of the crisis portends great danger for the effectiveness of monetary policy in the region. Unless adequate measures are put in place, this could jeopardize the various efforts made over the years towards monetary integration especially efforts at operating a single regional apex bank and adopting a single currency.

A return to fiscal dominance, with chronic budget deficits financed largely by high-powered money, will seriously exacerbate monetary policy in the sub-region with excessive inflationary pressures, exchange rate instability or high interest rates, which are in themselves inimical to economic development.

References

Anyanwu, J. C. (1998), "Do Fiscal Deficits Produce High Interest Rates?: The Case of Nigeria, Ghana and the Gambia, " *CBN Economic and Financial Review*, Vol. 36, No. 1, 1998

Bebi, H. (2000), "The Impact of Fiscal Deficits and Public Debt on Real Interest Rate and Investment in Namibia," *NEPRU Research Report* No. 74,

Bevan, D. L. (2001), The fiscal Deficit and Sustainability of Fiscal Policy. Tanzania Public Expenditure Review: 2000/2001. A Working Group paper prepared for the Government of Tanzania.

Bhalla, S. (1995), "This Time, It Is Already Different: A Personal Perspective", Deutsche Bank, December 7, 1995

Canzoneri, M. B., R. E.Cumby, and B. Diba, (2002), "Should the European Central Bank and the Federal Reserve be Concerned About Fiscal Policy?" Paper Presented at a Symposium held on "Re-Thinking Stabilization Policy", Federal Reserve Bank of Kansas City, August

Chakraborty L. S. (2002), "Fiscal Deficits and Real Interest Rates: An Econometric Analysis of the Deregulated Financial Regime, " *Economic and Political Weekly*, 37(19), May.

Claessens, S., A. Kose, and M., Terrones (2008), "What Happens DuringRecessions, Crunches and Busts?, " IMF Working Paper 08/274.

Collyns, C., and G.R. Kincaid (2003), "Managing Financial Crises: Recent Experience and Lessons for Latin America," *IMF Occasional Paper*, No. 217.

Cohen, D. and O. Garnier (1991), "The Impact of Forecasts of Budget Deficits on Interest Rates in the United States and other G-7 Countries, Federal Reserve Board"

Dai, Q. and T. Philippon, (2004), "Government Deficits and Interest Rates: A No-Arbitrage Structural VAR Approach", New York University First Draft, March 14, 2004

Demirgüc-Kunt, A., and E. Detragiache (1998), "The Determinants of Banking Crises in

Developed and Developing Countries," *IMF Staff Papers*, 45 (1): 81–109.

Ekpo, A. H. and J. E. Ndebbio (1993), "Fiscal Operations in a Depressed Economy: Nigeria", AERC, Nairobi, Kenya.

Elmendorf, D. W and G. Markiw, (1999), "Government Debt", in Taylor, J. and M. Woodford, (eds.) *Handbook of Macroeconomics,* Elsevier Science.

Elmendorf, D. W. (1993), "Actual Budget Deficit Expectations and Interest Rates", Harvard Institute of Economic Research, May.

Evans, P. (1987), "Interest Rates and Expected Future Budget Deficits in the U. S.", Journal of Political Economy, 95(1), 1987, pp. 34-58.

Favero, C (2002): "How do European monetary and fiscal authorities behave?" *IGIER Working Paper Series* no 214.

Favero, C and T Monacelli (2003): "Monetary-Fiscal mix and inflation performance: Evidence from the U.S.", *IGIER Working Paper Series, N*o 234.

Gale, W. G. and P. Orszag (2003), "Economic Effects of Sustained Budget Deficits", *National Tax Journal* Vol. 56 No. 3, pp. 463-485.

IMF (2009b), "From Recession to Recovery: How Soon and How Strong?" World Economic Outlook 2009, Chapter 3 (Washington, DC: IMF).

Laeven, L., and F. Valencia, (2008), "Systemic Banking Crises: a New Database, " *IMFWorking Paper* 08/224.

Lal, D., S. Bhide, and D. Vasudevan (2002), "Financial Exuberance: Savings Deposits, Fiscal Deficits and Interest Rates in India", *Working Paper* No. 821, Department of Economics, University of California, Los Angeles, December.

Melitz J. (1997): "Some Cross-Country Evidence about Debt, Deficits and the behavior of Monetary and Fiscal Authorities", *CEPR Discussion paper* no 1653.

—— (2002): "Debt, deficits and the behavior of monetary and fiscal authorities", in Marco Buti, Jürgen von Hagen and Carlos Martinez-Mongay(eds), "*The behavior of fiscal authorities – Stabilization, growth and institutions*", Palgrave, pp 215–40.Paper, 14587.

Miller, S. M. and F.S.Russek, (1990), "The Temporal Causality between Fiscal Deficits and Interest Rates", Paper Presented at the Western Economic Association, International 65th Annual Conference, San Diego, June 1990

Obi, B. and A. Nurudeen (2009), "Do Fiscal Deficits Raise Interest Rates in Nigeria? A Vector Autoregression Approach", *Journal of applied Quantitative Methods*, Vol 4, No. 3

Patnaik, P. (2000), On Some Common Macroeconomic Fallacies", *Economic and Political Weekly*, Vol. 35 No. 15, pp. 1220-1222

Patnaik, P. (2001), "On Fiscal Deficits and Interest Rates", *Economic and Political Weekly*, Vol. 36 No. 14, pp. 1160-1163

Plosser, C. I. (1987), "Fiscal Policy and the Term Structure", *Journal of Monetary Economics*, 20(2), pp. 343-367

Rogoff, K. and C. Reinhart, (2008a), "This Time is Different: A Panoramic View of Eight Centuries of Financial Crises, " *NBER Working* Paper, 13882, March.

Rogoff, K. and C. Reinhart, (2008b), "Banking Crises: An Equal Opportunity Menace, " Paper presented at the Meetings of the American Economic Association in San Francisco, December.

Rogoff, K, and C. Reinhart (2009), "The Aftermath of Financial Crises, " *NBER Working Paper*.

Sargent, T. and N. Wallace (1981): "Some unpleasant monetarist arithmetic", *Federal Reserve Bank of Minneapolis Quarterly Review*, Fall, pp 1–17.

Shapiro, D. M. (2004), "Federal Government Debt and Interest Rates", in "Discussion of Engen and Hubbard", NBER Macroeconomics Annual Conference, June.

Tanner, E. and A. Ramos (2002): "Fiscal Sustainability and Monetary versus Fiscal Dominance: Evidence from Brazil, 1991–2000", *IMF Working Paper* No 02/5. Published in *Applied Economics* 2003, 35, pp 859–73.

Von Hagen, J., A.H. Hallett and R. Strauch (2002), "Quality and Success of Budgetary Consolidations" in Marco Buti, Jürgen von Hagen and Carlos Martinez-Mongay(eds) "*The behavior of fiscal authorities Stabilization, growth and institutions*", Palgrave, pp 17–38.

Wachtel, P. and J.Young (1987), "Deficit Announcements and Interest Rates, American Economic Review 77, pp. 1007-1012.

Appendices

Table 8.2: Number of Countries that Met the Convergence Criteria in ECOWAS

Criteria/Year	2000	01	02	03	04	05	06	07	08	09*
Budget Deficit	6	6	5	5	3	5	6	8	6	5
Inflation	11	9	10	10	9	9	8	7	1	9
Reserves	10	10	9	9	9	1	9	9	9	9
Apex Bank Financing	12	13	12	11	14	15	13	15	14	15
Domestic Arrears	4	4	3	4	4	3	8	4	5	8
Tax Revenues	1	0	0	0	2	2	2	2	2	3
Salary Mass/Total Rev	6	6	5	8	5	7	8	9	7	7
Domestic Investments	6	6	5	5	7	6	7	7	7	7
Real Interest Rate	12	6	8	9	7	7	6	6	0	4
Real Exchange Rate	-	11	12	7	12	12	12	12	5	15

Source: WAMA, 2009
*Projections

Table 8.3: Total Number of Convergence Criteria Met by Each Country

Criteria/Year	2000	01	02	03	04	05	06	07	08	09*
Benin	6	7	8	7	7	5	5	9	6	8
Burkino Faso	6	6	6	7	7	6	7	7	5	7
Cape Verde	3	3	3	4	4	4	4	4	3	4
Cote d'Ivoire	5	5	5	5	6	5	7	6	4	7
Gambia	7	2	0	1	4	4	6	4	4	5
Ghana	2	1	0	2	3	3	3	4	2	4
Guinea	1	5	3	1	1	3	2	4	4	5
Guinea-Bissau	3	5	5	4	6	4	6	3	2	5
Liberia	7	4	4	3	2	3	3	3	3	3
Mali	7	5	7	8	8	7	7	8	5	7
Niger	5	6	5	7	6	5	8	7	5	8
Nigeria	5	4	4	4	5	5	5	6	5	6
Senegal	7	9	9	9	8	8	7	5	7	8
Sierra Leone	3	3	3	0	1	1	0	2	1	1
Togo	4	5	6	7	6	5	7	7	3	5

Source: WAMA, 2009.
*Projections

Table 8.4: Budget Deficit/GDP Ratio of ECOWAS Countries

Criteria/Year	2001	02	03	04	05	06	07	08	09*
Benin	2.6	3.1	4.4	5.5	4.6	2.6	1.5	3.4	5.2
Burkino Faso	6.7	9.1	8.2	8.7	9.7	11.2	12.2	8.5	11.3
Cape Verde	11.4	10.5	9.1	8.4	11.0	9.7	3.4	5.8	11.5
Cote d'Ivoire	0.4	2.0	3.2	2.6	2.8	1.6	1.4	2.3	1.1
Gambia	9.8	9.1	5.2	9.9	8.4	2.7	1.0	3.7	3.3
Ghana	13.2	8.3	7.5	8.1	6.9	12.3	14.7	18.6	12.4
Guinea	3.4	6.2	8.8	5.9	1.6	2.0	0.9	1.5	3.7
Guinea-Bissau	24.7	13.6	23.0	30.1	23.8	19.7	24.9	20.8	22.9
Liberia	1.9	1.0	3.7	4.4	0.9	3.0	3.4	2.0	2.0
Mali	9.6	6.9	5.3	6.5	7.1	7.0	8.0	8.5	9.6
Niger	8.0	8.5	7.8	9.5	9.5	6.8	8.2	6.2	13.8
Nigeria	5.8	5.9	2.8	1.7	1.3	0.6	1.2	0.2	0.8
Senegal	3.8	1.8	3.2	4.7	4.7	7.5	6.2	6.6	5.5
Sierra Leone	16.7	16.5	19.4	14.3	9.5	8.5	5.6	7.1	7.5
Togo	2.3	1.0	1.8	0.9	4.0	4.2	1.4	4.6	6.2
No. of countries that met criterion	6	5	5	3	5	6	8	6	5
UEMOA	4.3	3.8	4.4	4.9	5.4	5.2	5.2	5.2	6.0
WAMZ	6.4	6.2	3.4	2.4	1.8	1.6	2.3	1.7	1.8
WAMZ less Nigeria	10.3	8.3	8.7	8.0	5.5	8.5	9.2	11.9	9.0
ECOWAS	5.7	5.4	3.8	3.3	3.1	2.8	3.2	2.9	3.2
ECOWAS less Nigeria	5.9	5.0	5.6	5.7	5.5	6.1	6.2	6.9	6.8

Source: WAMA, 2009.
*Projections

Table 8.5: Budget Deficit Financing by the Apex Banks of ECOWAS Countries

Criteria/Year	2001	02	03	04	05	06	07	08	09*
Benin	0.0	4.6	0.0	0.0	0.0	0.0	0.0	0.0	0.0
Burkino Faso	0.0	0.0	0.0	0.0	0.0	0.0	0.0	0.0	0.0
Cape Verde	0.1	20.7	6.3	0.2	0.0	0.0	0.0	0.0	0.0
Cote d'Ivoire	0.0	0.3	0.0	0.0	0.0	0.0	0.0	0.0	0.0
Gambia	80.7	22.0	63.1	0.0	0.0	0.0	0.0	0.0	0.0
Ghana	0.0	12.1	0.0	1.6	0.0	0.0	0.0	17.3	0.0
Guinea	-0.7	24.5	14.6	26.2	-8.8	54.0	0.0	5.8	0.0
Guinea-Bissau	0.0	0.0	0.0	0.0	0.0	0.0	0.0	0.0	0.0
Liberia	0.0	0.0	0.0	0.0	0.0	0.0	0.0	0.0	0.0

Criteria/Year	2001	02	03	04	05	06	07	08	09*
Mali	0.0	0.0	0.0	0.0	0.0	0.0	0.0	0.0	0.0
Niger	0.0	0.0	0.0	0.0	0.0	0.0	0.0	0.0	0.0
Nigeria	29.3	0.0	19.7	0.0	0.0	0.0	0.0	0.0	0.0
Senegal	0.0	0.0	0.0	0.0	0.0	0.0	0.0	0.0	0.0
Sierra Leone	8.9	0.0	26.4	0.0	0.0	13.3	0.8		
Togo	0.0	0.0	0.0	0.0	0.0	0.0	0.0	0.0	0.0
No. of countries that met criterion	13	12	11	14	15	13	15	14	15
UEMOA	0.0	0.0	0.0	0.0	0.0	0.0	0.0	0.0	0.0
WAMZ	26.4	1.5	18.3	0.6	-0.2	1.1	0.0	1.4	0.0
WAMZ less Nigeria	3.3	15.3	8.8	9.0	-2.7	17.8	0.1	11.8	0.0
ECOWAS	17.5	1.1	12.1	0.4	-0.1	0.8	0.0	1.0	0.0
ECOWAS less Nigeria	0.8	4.3	2.4	2.3	-0.7	4.5	0.0	3.0	0.0

Source: WAMA, 2009.
*Projections

Table 8.6: Gross External Reserves 6 Months of Imports

Criteria/Year	2001	02	03	04	05	06	07	08	09*
Cape Verde	1.5	2.0	1.8	2.4	3.4	4.1	4.1	4.1	4.0
Gambia	7.2	2.9	3.1	4.7	5.2	4.9	4.4	4.3	4.7
Ghana	1.2	2.3	4.1	3.7	4.0	3.7	3.9	2.2	3.4
Guinea	2.8	2.3	1.6	1.2	1.1	0.8	0.4	0.5	1.1
Liberia	2.6	0.0	-0.2	0.2	0.1	0.1	0.7	0.7	0.7
Nigeria	11.3	9.9	8.5	16.1	11.8	15.1	17.4	14.7	14.6
Sierra Leone	2.3	3.1	1.7	3.3	4.8	4.9	5.1	4.3	4.8
UEMOA	6.7	7.6	6.0	6.8	5.7	6.0	6.3	6.0	6.0
No. of countries that met criterion	10	9	9	9	1	9	9	9	9
WAMZ	10.3	9.1	8.0	14.7	10.9	13.8	15.9	13.3	13.4
WAMZ less Nigeria	2.0	2.4	3.1	2.9	3.2	2.9	2.9	1.9	2.8
ECOWAS	9.0	8.5	7.2	12.0	9.1	11.1	12.6	10.8	10.8
ECOWAS less Nigeria	5.4	6.1	5.1	5.7	5.0	5.1	5.3	4.9	5.1

Source: WAMA, 2009.
*Projections

TABLE 8.7: TAX REVENUE/GDP RATIO

CRITERIA/YEAR	2001	02	03	04	05	06	07	08	09*
Burkino Faso	9.4	9.7	10.3	12.1	12.4	11.3	11.9	12.3	12.3
Cape Verde	18.7	19.7	18.6	19.6	21.0	23.0	22.8	23.9	23.9
Cote d'Ivoire	14.6	15.8	14.5	15.2	14.5	14.9	15.5	15.6	16.5
The Gambia	19.2	14.1	13.8	22.4	17.2	18.8	19.3	17.7	18.2
Ghana	17.2	17.5	19.3	22.4	21.9	21.1	23.7	23.1	22.4
Guinea	11.4	12.0	10.5	9.5	12.2	14.8	13.5	14.7	14.0
Guinea-Bissau	10.4	8.6	9.2	8.3	11.2	11.1	10.3	10.2	8.8
Liberia	11.4	10.7	6.4	9.2	14.7	13.2	12.6	12.5	12.5
Mali	12.7	12.5	14.2	15.3	15.4	14.7	14.2	13.1	14.5
Niger	8.9	10.5	10.5	11.6	10.2	10.7	11.5	10.7	11.4
Nigeria	19.5	14.0	15.7	14.8	17.2	14.9	11.7	16.2	13.5
Senegal	16.6	16.9	16.8	18.4	18.6	18.8	19.3	19.5	20.4
Sierra Leone	13.4	11.4	16.7	13.7	8.1	8.5	8.9	9.3	8.7
Togo	10.5	11.5	13.9	13.6	14.6	15.4	16.3	15.4	16.1
No. of countries that met criterion	0	0	0	2	2	2	2	2	3
UEMOA	13.7	14.6	14.4	14.8	14.7	15.1	15.6	15.4	16.4
WAMZ	19.1	14.2	15.9	15.3	17.4	15.3	12.7	16.6	14.2
WAMZ less Nigeria	15.2	15.2	16.2	17.7	17.7	18.1	19.2	19.2	18.6
ECOWAS	17.3	14.3	15.4	15.1	16.5	15.3	13.7	16.3	14.9
ECOWAS less Nigeria	14.1	14.8	14.8	15.6	15.6	16.0	16.6	16.5	17.0

Source: WAMA, 2009.
*Projections

Table 8.8: Wage Bill/Tax Revenue 35%

Criteria/Year	2001	02	03	04	05	06	07	08	09*
Benin	32.0	31.9	33.5	38.0	39.1	35.6	32.1	35.6	31.9
Burkino Faso	45.7	42.8	41.7	38.8	40.4	44.1	46.5	44.7	45.4
Cape Verde	50.3	46.3	63.2	47.9	47.1	46.0	41.6	38.1	42.7
Cote d'Ivoire	41.4	41.6	45.3	44.0	45.0	43.2	43.6	43.4	41.1
The Gambia	40.1	38.0	33.3	23.1	24.3	24.2	22.4	28.6	24.8
Ghana	52.9	57.2	49.6	46.1	44.8	44.9	46.0	45.5	45.3
Guinea	32.0	31.0	34.3	32.5	23.2	18.4	25.9	29.0	29.2
Guinea-Bissau	74.3	88.2	111.9	155	116.2	111	116.5	106.7	116.4
Liberia	29.0	19.1	26.4	48.0	59.2	34.5	32.9	28.7	35.2
Mali	29.1	30.6	27.7	31.2	30.9	31.5	33.4	38.5	36.0
Niger	40.2	38.2	37.5	35.2	34.8	33.4	31.0	33.7	32.4
Nigeria	26.4	47.2	32.6	33.8	17.9	19.5	31.6	31.2	24.3
Senegal	30.7	31.7	30.1	29.5	30.0	31.0	31.6	30.8	29.9
Sierra Leone	55.0	63.9	59.7	56.0	65.5	61.6	60.9	55.2	60.7
Togo	51.0	44.7	34.7	36.6	30.4	33.1	32.8	37.4	36.7
No. of countries that met criterion	6	5	8	5	7	8	9	7	7
UEMOA	37.7	37.2	38.3	37.5	38.1	37.6	37.7	38.4	36.7
WAMZ	28.8	47.8	34.2	34.9	20.5	21.8	32.8	32.5	26.3
WAMZ less Nigeria	46.1	48.9	45.1	41.9	39.0	37.3	40.1	40.6	40.8
ECOWAS	31.9	44.1	35.6	35.9	26.6	27.2	34.5	34.4	29.9
ECOWAS less Nigeria	40.0	40.2	40.4	38.9	38.7	37.6	38.3	38.9	37.8

Source: WAMA, 2009.

*Projections

Table 8.9: Public Investment/Tax Revenue 20%

Criteria/Year	2001	02	03	04	05	06	07	08	09*
Benin	18.9	19.3	23.2	21.5	22.8	12.8	21.0	23.7	27.3
Burkino Faso	24.6	36.0	32.7	41.9	36.3	42.7	35.6	43.7	37.9
Capc Verde	4.2	4.8	3.4	3.3	2.9	2.9	2.0	1.9	2.4
Cote d'Ivoire	7.5	11.6	10.5	9.9	10.7	15.5	12.8	14.8	13.3
The Gambia	6.1	7.5	11.0	14.2	4.8	3.1	5.6	14.7	6.0
Ghana	16.4	13.2	18.8	18.4	18.8	26.5	27.3	34.3	26.2
Guinea	5.5	10.2	12.1	16.1	12.6	12.0	11.9	12.8	12.1
Guinea-Bissau	16.9	5.9	4.2	16.9	9.3	2.2	12.2	12.4	16.9
Liberia	46.1	47.3	0.0	25.6	18.3	14.9	13.8	12.5	14.7
Mali	22.0	20.5	24.5	22.8	22.0	21.4	34.5	26.7	26.3
Niger	20.0	18.7	26.6	30.4	40.4	32.9	37.5	47.3	41.6
Nigeria	40.3	30.7	21.4	20.3	20.6	20.0	31.2	24.6	26.4
Senegal	20.5	23.5	24.1	30.0	33.7	36.6	34.8	27.9	27.1
Sierra Leone	6.6	9.4	11.3	8.2	7.9	10.6	9.1	11.3	9.6
Togo	2.5	2.6	1.7	2.3	8.4	3.7	7.1	13.8	14.2
No. of countries that met criterion	6	5	5	7	6	7	7	7	7
UEMOA	14.7	15.3	19.5	21.7	23.2	24.4	24.6	24.6	23.7
WAMZ	37.4	28.7	20.9	19.9	20.1	20.2	30.3	25.0	25.9
WAMZ less Nigeria	11.9	11.8	15.9	16.7	15.5	20.0	20.4	25.2	19.8
ECOWAS	29.8	24.3	20.2	20.5	21.1	21.5	28.2	24.7	25.0
ECOWAS less Nigeria	14.1	14.5	18.1	20.2	20.9	22.8	23.0	24.3	22.3

Chapter 9

AFRICA'S FINANCIAL AND TRADE POLICY CHALLENGES UNDER REGIONAL INTEGRATION

William A. Amponsah

INTRODUCTION

The recent global financial crisis and subsequent economic recession in industrialized nations have unraveled the inherent risks in Africa's slow movement toward achieving broad structural reforms and deep continental economic integration. Arguably, by not being well-integrated into the global financial architecture, many African countries have only borne collateral damages from globalization manifested in the rapid reductions in trade flows and lower commodity prices, deceleration in recent GDP growth, fiscal erosion, sliding FDI flows and external remittances, and reduced foreign development assistance. The crisis has also revealed the critical importance of accelerating progress in structural economic reforms to catalyze private sector development, diversifying the economic base, integrating monetary and financial institutions, and consolidating recent gains in economic growth through regional trade.

As the push for freer trade at the multilateral level, led by the World Trade Organization (WTO), has become more and more contentious, governments within geographical proximity with shared political and economic interests have increasingly focused on negotiating regional pacts as the means to enhancing policy credibility and accelerating trade and financial investments in the hopes of spurring intra-regional growth. Several factors have contributed to the current imperative for African countries to embark on regional economic integration. First, progress in negotiating global trade liberalization at the WTO has served as the main driver of the agenda to achieve Africa's regional trade integration so as to consolidate gains from globalization in the way of income growth, poverty alleviation and economic development. Second, African countries' concern about gaining market access for their products has attracted much attention during the currently stalled Doha Development Round (DDR) of multilateral negotiations. There is mounting concern in Africa about the potential deleterious impacts of trade protectionism in rich countries, especially the effects of domestic farm support and export subsidies on African agricultural trade. Third, virtually all African countries have entered into preference arrangements with the European Union (EU)[1]. African countries also enjoy preferential treatment for certain export products to major markets, such as the U.S.[2] under the General System of Preference (GSP).

Fourth, and most important, prior to the recent global financial downturn, Africa had experienced the best decade of economic growth in recent memory, led by gains in international trade by individual countries but with little effective coordination in trade, monetary and financial integration. However, the recent global financial crisis appears to threaten the recent gains in Africa's economic growth. The real sector effects emerging largely from the trade and investment channels of the crisis are proving to be

1 Because of historical colonial ties, the EU accounts for greater than two-thirds of total African trade.

2 The U.S. has established the African Growth and Opportunity Act (AGOA) through which preferential market access is granted for certain products originating from African countries can freely enter the U.S. market.

more damaging to African countries than previously anticipated (African Development Bank, 2009).

BACKGROUND AND EVOLUTION OF THE AFRICAN RECS

Africa has a multiplicity of Regional Economic Communities (RECs) with overlapping members. Therefore, to coordinate and harmonize policies among the existing RECs, the African Union (AU) was created to provide a model for continental integration. Patterned after the European Union (EU), it is envisioned to provide the institutional anchor in developing the framework and providing policy direction to achieve complete and deep African continental integration. The guidelines for the AU are provided by the Abuja Treaty of 1991. Its main goals include the integration of African productive capacity and infrastructure facilities; the eradication of poverty and ignorance; the building of genuine African-centered institutions; and the establishment of new relationships between Africa and the rest of the world (African Development Report, 2000).

The Abuja Treaty mainly focuses on establishing the African Economic Community (AEC) over 34 years (from 1994-2027) in six stages that would culminate in an economic union with a common currency, mobility of factors of production, and free trade among the 53 countries of Africa via a process of progressive integration of the RECs. A continental common market is envisioned by 2015. Article 3 of the Constitutive Act of the African Union stresses the importance of coordinating and harmonizing policies between the existing and any future RECs. Along with the New Partnership for Africa's Development (NEPAD)[3], the Abuja model of integration is conceived as a long-term development strategy aimed at integrating the sub-region's economic and non-economic sectors to achieve international competitiveness. Furthermore, it seeks to build a new institutional architecture consistent with a self-reliant development process, purports to uphold democratic principles, and foster African social and cultural values. The AU wishes to accelerate the continental integration process by creating major institutions such as the African Parliament, the African Court of Justice, the African Central Bank, and

---

3 One key principle of NEPAD is to accelerate and deepen regional and continental economic integration.

the African Investment Bank in short order, without necessarily adhering to the 34-year timeline for creating the AEC. Beyond the goal of achieving trade and market integration, the AU aims to ensure free movement of people and factor mobility, achieve macroeconomic (including financial and monetary) policy convergence, enhance savings and investments in productive sectors, provide transport and communication linkages, ensure energy sharing, and attain peace through a common regional security system.

The option of promoting trade and financial market integration at the regional level has been implemented by many neighboring countries in all regions of the world. Characterized as regional trade agreements (RTAs)[4], they typically involve discriminatory trade liberalization by member countries against the rest of the world. Over 200 RTAs have been notified to the GATT/WTO with over 150 agreements actively in force. In particular, since the inception of the WTO in 1995 over 100 agreements covering trade in goods, services, or both, have been notified to the WTO. Therefore, currently, almost all WTO member countries are members of at least one RTA and more than one third of world trade is supported by RTAs. Existing RTAs include the North American Free Trade Agreement (NAFTA), the EU, the Central American Common Market (CACM), Association of South East Asian Nations (ASEAN), Southern Cone Common Market of Latin America (MERCOSUR), etc. In Africa alone, there are at present nearly 30 different sub-regional trade agreements. In Central Africa, they include the Central African Monetary and Economic Community (CEMAC - formerly known as the Central African Customs and Economic Union - UDEAC), the Economic Community of the Countries of the Great Lakes (CEPGL), and the Economic Community of Central African States (ECCAS). In North Africa is the Arab Maghreb Union (AMU). In Southern and Eastern Africa are the Southern African Customs Union (SACU), the rand Common Monetary Area (CMA), the Southern African Development Community (SADC), the Common Market for Eastern and Southern Africa (COMESA), and the East African Community (EAC), the Indian Ocean Commission

4 The RTAs are typically free trade agreements (FTAs) and custom unions (CUs).

(IOC), and the Inter-Governmental Authority on Development (IGAD). In West Africa are the Economic Community of West African States (ECOWAS), the West African Economic and Monetary Union (WAEMU), and the Mano River Union (MRU).

This paper sets out to analyze how African countries have been impacted by the recent global financial crisis, especially given faltering efforts to attain regional integration. The next section discusses the process of global financial stress transmission. It is followed by analysis of the recent African economic performance in the aftermath of the recent global economic crisis. That is followed by the discussion of macroeconomic policy challenges facing the region in implementing regional integration. It also provides insights on the financial and monetary institutional architecture challenges necessary in mainstreaming African macroeconomic integration, given existing RECs, rather weak national currencies (and exchange rate mechanisms), and chronic budget problems. The penultimate section provides conclusions and discusses implications from lessons learnt for enhancing Africa's regional integration beyond the recent financial crisis.

THE PROCESS OF GLOBAL FINANCIAL STRESS TRANSMISSION

African countries appear to have only been dealt a glancing blow to date from the deleterious impacts from the current global financial crisis. How has this happened, and how are the stress from financial crises transmitted from advanced economies to other markets? Financial stress transmission occurs through global and country-specific factors (see Figure 9.1). It results from common global shocks. For example, global shifts in market sentiment or risk aversion may manifest themselves through herd behavior in markets, cross-country contagion, and common lender effects (such as from the blanket withdrawal of funds by highly exposed financial institutions). Mainly because of financial globalization, many emerging markets have achieved financial integration from portfolio equity and direct investment. Financial integration has, however, increased unevenly across regions. Whereas 70 percent of countries have increased their gross external positions, those in Africa have seen declines[5] (IMF, 2009).

The country-specific factors can be grouped into two categories: (i) financial and economic linkages between emerging and advanced economies; and (ii) domestic vulnerabilities stemming from economic policies or from structural characteristics. The two channels of stress transmission emphasized by the literature occur through trade and financial channels[6]. Financial stress can rise in response to actual or incipient capital outflows initiated by investors in advanced economies following a financial shock. It may also increase through losses incurred on emerging economy assets invested in advanced economies that are realizing a crisis. Financial stress can also occur through trade linkages in response to actual or incipient declines in exports to advanced economies in crisis, reflecting current or expected slowdowns in demand. This source of financial stress transmission mechanism is increasingly important to most African countries, especially during the ongoing global financial crisis.

Country-specific sources of vulnerability to external shocks include solvency and liquidity problems, weaknesses in domestic balance sheets, and factors related to openness (see for example Kamisky and Reinhart, 1999; Calvo, 2005; Edwards, 2005). These factors heighten the susceptibility to capital account and currency crises, and potentially increase the rate of transmission of financial stress originating in investor economies. They may also cause investors to pull out from a country and create self-fulfilling investor expectations. A second country-specific measure of vulnerability is the level of foreign exchange reserves. Following the Asian crisis, for example, many countries strengthened their reserve positions in months of import coverage (IMF, 2009). In part because of the commodity price boom through mid-2008, many commodity-exporting countries in Africa, the Middle East, etc., realized positive fiscal balances and, therefore, increased their reserve buffers. Consequently, those frontier and emerging African countries that are

---

5 Recent declines in the external positions of African countries often were the result of debt relief.

6 Eichengreen and Rose (1999); Glick and Rose (1999); and Forbes (2001) stress trade linkages while Kamisky and Reinhart (2003) and others stress financial channels.

also commodity exporters (such as Nigeria) were expected to have reduced their vulnerability to external financial shocks by having strengthened their foreign exchange reserves during the commodity price boom immediately prior to the current financial crisis.

The current global financial crisis originated from the collapse of the market for sub-prime mortgages in the U.S. in 2007. Many analysts predicted indirect or delayed impacts of the financial crisis on Africa, mainly because the financial sector in Africa remained quite shallow, uncompetitive, and weakly integrated into global markets. Therefore, it was believed that African economies would be shielded from the "toxic assets" that set off the global financial crisis. In reality, the continent has avoided the recession that has plagued other regions of the world. However, aggregate figures appear to mask differences across countries. The crisis has hit harder at African frontier and emerging markets (such as South Africa, Nigeria, Ghana, Kenya, and Tunisia) that were relatively more integrated into global financial markets, and resource-rich countries (such as Angola, Cameroon, Equatorial Guinea, Gabon, Nigeria, and Sudan). Coupled with the commodity price declines since mid-2008, revised projections from the crisis have indicated a downturn in African GDP along with those of all industrialized economies (see Figure 9.2). The main shock buffeting African economies to date is the severe deterioration in external growth through Africa's real economy that has resulted in (i) declining terms of trade, (ii) reduced demand for exports, (iii) falling foreign direct investment (FDI), remittances from overseas workers, tourism, and aid flows, (iv) reduced access to global financial markets, and (v) access to trade credit (Kasekende *et al.*, 2010; IMF, 2009).

AFRICAN ECONOMIC PERFORMANCE FOLLOWING THE RECENT GLOBAL RECESSION

Africa recorded its best economic growth in recent memory during the period between 2000 and the first half of 2008. After achieving 4.8 percent growth from 2000 through 2004, African economies recorded the overall real GDP growth rate of 6.1 percent in 2007 having grown from 6.0 percent in 2006 and 5.7 percent in 2005 (see Table 9.1) fueled largely by robust global demand and high commodity prices, consolidation of macroeconomic stability and prudential macroeconomic management, increased oil production in certain countries, increased capital inflows, debt relief, and China's recent economic growth. All sub-regions, including Sub-Saharan Africa (see Table 9.1 and Figure 9.2) experienced robust positive growth, although oil-exporting countries grew at a higher rate than oil-importing countries. Global economic growth, on the other hand, slowed from about 3.9 percent in 2006 to 3.6 percent in 2007, although growth in advanced economies fell slightly lower (see Figure 9.2) in large part because of high oil prices and turbulence in financial markets.

Despite the upturn in economic growth, SSA remained the lagging region with respect to achieving the Millennium Development Goals (MDGs)[7]. This is because compared to other regions of the world, for decades prior to the 2000s Africa had generally been characterized by low economic growth. Therefore, the region is still far from reaching the targeted goal of an annual growth rate above 7 percent a year projected for attaining similar quality of life with other developing countries. However, there have been significant regional differences in SSA performance. Economic growth has largely been led by the Southern Africa region (see Figure 9.2). Therefore, the recent downturn in per capita GDP and real GDP growth, following the global financial crisis, also represents a threat in reversing recent progress made in achieving MDG targets, especially in halving poverty by 2015.

Impacts of the Crisis on African Trade

Many African economies have relied heavily on export markets to grow. World trade was projected to shrink by 11 percent in 2009, its first decline since 1982 and reportedly the biggest drop since the mid-1940s. Exports from advanced economies were expected

7 In September 2000, 189 member countries of the United Nations adopted eight MDGs, committing to making substantial progress by 2015 toward the eradication of poverty and achieving other human development goals such as universal primary education, gender equality and empowerment, reduce child mortality, improve maternal health, combat HIV/AIDS and other diseases, ensure environmental sustainability, and develop a global partnership for development.

to drop by over 13 percent, while exports for poorer countries were expected to fall by over 6 percent (IMF, 2009). For African countries, early indicators were that the recent declining global demand for merchandise exports and terms of trade began during the second half of 2008 (Figure 9.3). African exports were, therefore, projected to continue facing a contracting global market in 2009 and 2010. Therefore, since global commodity (especially oil) prices[8] have declined, African countries exported less quantities on average, and received relatively less revenues from their exports than in 2008.

The African Development Bank (2009) estimated that trade revenues in Africa would decline by $251.2 billion in 2009 from an expected level of $634.6 billion, and also by an additional $277.3 billion in 2010 from an expected level of $692 billion (see Figure 9.4). Early signals also showed that African imports from the U.S., EU, and China[9] fell rapidly more than from any other developing regions as well as the rest of the world during the last quarter of 2008 and first quarter of 2009. For example, Figure 9.5 shows substantial decline in U.S. imports (by about 57 percent) from Africa during the time period, and Figure 9.6 shows that these trends were for primary as well as manufactured goods. The total value of U.S. trade with Africa rose by 29 percent between 2007 and 2008. However, total exports to the U.S. from all 41 countries eligible for trade benefits under the African Growth and Opportunity Act (AGOA)[10] declined by nearly 63 percent through the first half of 2009, compared to the same period in 2008.

As Figures 7 and 8 also reveal, EU and China imports from Africa also fell very rapidly (and by similar percentages) during the early period of the crisis compared to other developing countries and the world. In particular, recent growth in Africa has relied on commodity exports to China, making the region vulnerable to fluctuations in China's economic growth. We must note that prior to

8 Oil and mineral fuels account for 80 percent of all U.S. imports from Africa, and 92 percent of all U.S. imports under AGOA.

9 The U.S., EU and China account for nearly 70 percent of African trade.

10 Data is available at http://www.agoa.info. AGOA is a U.S. trade preference program to eligible SSA countries that are pursuing market reform measures and was begun in 2000 (P.L. 106-200, as amended). It provides certain goods from SSA duty-free access to the U.S. market.

the recent crisis, Africa had been the beneficiary of increased South-South trade and capital inflows. In particular, African exports to China alone were reported to have quadrupled between 2000 and 2005 to $19.5 billion, while African countries continued to be flooded with imports of manufactured goods from Asia. Additionally, FDI was recorded to have increased from 5 percent in 1990 to 17 percent in 2005, originating mainly from Asia[11] (*Economic Report on Africa*, 2008). In 2007, 13 percent of African exports were destined for China, and 10 percent of African imports originated from there (U.S. Department of Commerce, 2009). China's trade with Africa grew by 62 percent during the first eight months of 2008 to $74 billion (Oxford Analytica, 2009). Despite the impact of the financial crisis, Sino-African trade for 2008 was reported at $106.8 billion (Reuters, 2009). In large part, recent Sino-African trade growth has catalyzed Chinese investment in major infrastructure projects in Africa; a major incentive in enhancing economic competitiveness of the region. China's domestic stimulus package has relied on infrastructure construction, which has kept the demand for primary resources such as oil, copper, tin, and lumber quite steady (Standard Bank, 2009).

Statistics also show that African countries' exposure to advanced economies – the degree to which economic shifts in developed countries may impact African economies through decreased demand for African exports – has increased. On average, a 1 percent decline in (trade-weighted) world growth is associated with roughly 0.5 percent decline in GDP growth in Africa (IMF, 2009). Compounding the trade shortfall, many African countries that depend on international tourist arrivals (trade in services) were faced with a global decline of about 8 percent during the first four months of 2009 compared to 2008 (U.N. World Tourism Organization, 2009).

Impacts of the Crisis on Macroeconomic Activity

The current external shocks resulted in severe slowdown in macroeconomic activity in African countries. As commodity-based revenues dwindled, the overall fiscal position of the African region also deteriorated. Real GDP growth (Table 9.1) was projected to deteriorate from about 5.7 percent in 2008 to 2.8 percent

11 Asian FDI flows are mainly from China, India and the Gulf States.

in 2009, led in large part by the Southern Africa region and oil-exporting countries. Africa's current account balance was also expected to deteriorate from the overall surplus of 3.5 percent of GDP in 2008 to projected deficits of 3.8 and 3.6 percent, respectively, in 2009 and 2010 (Table 9.2) stemming from the financial crisis. This external account erosion is expected to be higher in West, East and Southern Africa. On average, the downturn was also most pronounced in oil-exporting countries. Africa's budget surplus has also been revised from 2.3 percent of GDP in 2008 to deficits of 5.4 and 5.1 percent, respectively, of GDP in 2009 and 2010; led by the budget deficit of oil exporters that is forecasted to reach 7.7 and 7.4 percent of GDP, respectively, in 2009 and 2010 (Table 9.3). Many African countries have experienced depreciation of their currencies relative to the U.S. dollar, putting pressure on their accumulated reserves. According to the IMF (2010), South Africa's economy, for example, contracted by about 1.75 percent in 2009 to its lowest growth rate in a decade, as capital outflows forced sharp adjustment in asset prices (mainly in equity, bond, and currency markets) and in real activity. Although South Africa's growth is projected at 2.5 percent in 2010 and 3.5 percent in 2011, that growth will be tempered by high unemployment, tight credit, and the recent strength of the rand.

Inflation pressures were also expected to be tempered in 2009 and 2010, stemming from the deep downturn in economic activities and depressing oil and other commodity prices (see Table 9.4). For the African region as a whole, inflation was projected to decrease gradually from 11 percent in 2008 to 8.5 percent in 2009, mainly because the pass-through of commodity price changes is usually more limited in Africa than in more advanced economies.

Nevertheless, SSA appears to have weathered the global crisis relatively well, and is expected to soon rebound. SSA's growth is projected to accelerate to 4.7 percent in 2010 and 6 percent in 2011. The region's relatively quick recovery would stem from the relatively limited integration of most economies into the global economy and the limited impacts of their terms of trade, the rapid normalization of global trade and commodity prices, and the use of countercyclical fiscal policies. Banking sectors have also proved resilient, and private capital inflows have resumed into the region's more integrated economies (IMF, 2010). The IMF (2010) projects that the recovery of oil prices and stronger global demand would raise growth for the region's oil exporters to 6.7 percent in 2010 and 7 percent in 2011.

According to the IMF (2010), although there are various risks to the outlook in the region, the following are noteworthy. First, compounding the hesitant recovery in advanced economies is the impacts in different SSA countries of a recovery pattern that gives rise to wide swings in commodity prices. For example, higher-than-expected energy prices would benefit oil exporters while dampening growth and raising inflation in oil importers. Second, the outlook for official aid flows to the region is subject to downside risks, given the large output declines in major donor countries, their protracted recoveries, and heightened fiscal pressures.

LESSONS STEMMING FROM THE GLOBAL RECESSION

The following are the derived lessons from the economic literature[12] about past recessions: (i) Recessions associated with financial crises have been more severe and longer lasting than those associated with other shocks. Recoveries from such recessions have been typically slower, associated with weak domestic demand and tight credit conditions; (ii) monetary policy seems to have played an important role in ending such recessions and strengthening recoveries. Its effectiveness, however, is weakened in the aftermath of a financial crisis; and (iii) fiscal stimulus appears to be particularly helpful during recessions associated with financial crises. Stimulus is also associated with stronger recoveries; however, the impact of fiscal policy on the strength of the recovery is found to be smaller for economies that have higher levels of debt.

At the onset of the crisis, African policymakers were sensitized about the importance of undertaking fiscal stimulus packages and other countercyclical actions to mitigate the effects of the financial crisis. For example, South Africa introduced a mix of fiscal stimulus package worth R 787 billion (about $100 billion) for public investment during 2010-12, accompanied by the reduction in interest rate by cumulative 500 basis points between December 2008 and October 2009. Other frontier countries such as Mau-

12 See IMF (2009, p.98).

ritius, Botswana, Nigeria, and Kenya have also adopted countercyclical fiscal stimulus, financial sector injections or monetary and fiscal policy packages to mitigate the effects of the financial crisis. However, many African countries do not have the capacity to respond on their own, absent any form of assistance from advanced economies. For example, in Ghana the combination of limited reserves and unsustainable fiscal balances raised barriers for the government in implementing a stimulus package. In addition, African countries must be aware of the deleterious impacts of high public debt and continuous borrowing during the crisis.

Although SSA appears to be rebounding from the financial crisis, it is uncertain how quickly African countries would fully recover from the potential human and social costs of the global recession[13]. The downside risks stem from a deeper and more prolonged slump in global growth that could continue to lower export demand, decrease tourism revenues, and further dampen workers' remittances. From our foregoing analysis, the crisis appears to have affected the fiscal space through two channels: (i) directly through revenue losses and (ii) indirectly through automatic stabilizers associated with slower economic activity (Kasekende *et al.*, 2010). As was also anticipated, commodity-related revenues appeared to have been lost, especially to leading commodity exporters like Angola, Botswana, Gabon, and Nigeria where export revenues account for a substantial share of total government revenues. In part because of the linkages of the export sector with the rest of the economy, job losses in the export sector would also be transmitted to the general economy via losses in incomes. Another potential outcome stemming from the losses in current account and fiscal space is that the financial crisis would likely reduce the capacity of many African countries from mounting countercyclical measures to stimulate their economies[14], especially in providing trade

13 A major cost is in the potential increase in unemployment and/or underemployment in many countries.

14 For example, in 2009 Ghana experienced falling reserves that led to fiscal deficit of about 10 percent of its GDP and associated current account deficit following grants, high inflation and low reserves that made it impossible for the Government of Ghana to implement a stimulus package (IMF, 2009).

financing for exporters[15]. In previous financial crises, a drop in the availability of trade financing negatively impacted the operations of private firms in many developing countries and, consequently, their ability to recover. Nonetheless, it is unclear whether the current crisis will elicit a similar impact (Humphrey, 2009).

Another area in which the crisis is expected to affect African trade is that mainly because of underdeveloped domestic financial systems and the scarcity of self-financing, most African firms may rely on letters of credit from destination countries to facilitate exporting. These providers of letters of credit, in a business climate characterized by tight credit and high uncertainty (and potential lack of trust), would likely want to reduce their risk exposure and credit. Thus, credit rationing would increase trading costs and contribute to further dampening African exports.

Furthermore, Berman and Martin (2009)[16] make the case that in past recessions and financial crises affecting its trade partners, SSA economies, in particular, were hit with greater intensity and it took them longer than other regions to recover. They explain that this may not be simply due to the composition of primary products in the exports basket of SSA countries, nor the movement of primary products prices to the business cycle in industrial countries. Rather, the longer recovery time by SSA countries to crises stemming from partner countries may be explained by the time it takes for African firms to develop product niches with high quality products, and the ability to move higher up on the value chain. These processes require skilled managers and workers. As Figure 9.10 shows, when the trade partner is an industrial country, recovery to pre-crisis levels is much longer for SSA countries (about 7 years) than for the rest of the world (about 5 years). If current expectations hold, then Africa would emerge out of the current crisis faster than in the past.

Moreover, although world trade has increased by about 25 percent since the inception of the WTO in 1995, stemming from the greater integration of global markets, Africa's share of world

15 Trade finance refers to the role of banks, institutions, and private corporations in facilitating the movement of merchandise in global trade.

16 The authors apply the gravity model in computing impulse responses.

trade is only about 2.8 percent, having fallen from 10 percent in the early 1960s (African Development Bank, 2009). Additionally, intra-regional trade is quite modest, and it is estimated at just 8.3 percent of Africa's exports and 9.3 percent of imports[17]. Low intra-African trade results from the lack of diversity in production and infrastructure that constrain movements of goods and services in Africa. It is also widely acknowledged that individual African country markets are small and low intra-African trade constrain the ability of African firms from "learning-by-doing" and gaining the necessary experiences to sustain inherent risks, and to enable them to effectively compete in more sophisticated global markets. Therefore, despite the recent improvements in the enabling environment in conducting business on the continent, there is sufficient fear that the recent global financial crisis may stymie inflows of foreign FDI and foreign assistance from advanced economies sorely needed to catalyze productive investments.

It should be noted that capital flows[18] helped to fuel Africa's recent economic growth. However, the tightening of global credit conditions has started reducing FDI and reversing portfolio flows, especially to emerging and frontier African markets. Indeed, with global credit conditions remaining tight, the financing of external deficits must be expected to continue remaining strained, even for emerging and frontier African markets; although frontier markets (such as Ghana and Kenya) will benefit from improved access to international bond markets. At the onset of the crisis, there was a sudden increase in protectionist measures taken by some countries that also heightened the fear that despite existing trade arrangements, African countries will begin to face barriers in gaining access to international markets; especially given the stalemate in WTO talks. The region must also take advantage of rapid developments

17 Intra-regional trade as measured here includes only formal or documented trade between African countries. However, it is important to note that informal cross-border trade occurs in Africa, especially where people of similar tribes are found across border areas or where goods of common interest have historically been traded among people.

18 Capital flows include foreign direct investment (FDI), portfolio investment flows, worker remittances, and foreign aid.

in information and communication technology, the liberalization of financial markets, and the global factor movements necessary to spur production and trade, at least at the regional level.

There are also lessons for African nations to learn from the recent chaotic response by the EU stemming from Greece's debt and financial debacle, and the potential contagion effects on the Euro-zone's financial stability. The Greek crisis has turned into Europe's sovereign-debt crisis. Greece holds only 2.6 percent of the Euro-zone GDP, is struggling with a 13.6 percent budget deficit and a stock of government debt equal to 115 percent of its GDP. Unfortunately, Greece has not been able to rebound from its economic woes because of fiscal retrenchment, and it lacks a strong export base. It cannot devalue its currency because it is in the Euro zone. And worse of all, its population is in turmoil because it is unwilling to endure the cuts in wages and services necessary in making the economy competitive. After a period of dithering, the European Union and the IMF have put together a bailout package worth $957 billion to rescue Greece and other nations[19] to provide short-term protection against debt default. However, investors are fearful that it would drag out the economic pain and eventually hurt the European financial system in the process. As of the time of writing, European stock markets had responded with fallen stock values, and the Euro had fallen to its lowest value against the dollar at $1.2385 (equivalent to 13 percent depreciation since the beginning of 2010). Financial markets in the U.S. have also responded negatively to the news, with markets worrying about a whole cascading of weakness stemming from Europe being transmitted through the Euro to the U.S.

For the first time in its history, the European Central Bank agreed to calm the financial turmoil by buying government bonds; a clear departure from its mandate of focusing solely on price stability and adding to the pressures undermining the Euro. The worry in the U.S. is that the dollar's appreciation might push up prices of U.S. exportable goods in a reversal of fortune and harm U.S. trade with Europe, with huge implications in dragging down U.S. economic growth.

---

19 The other countries in wait are Spain and Portugal. For the moment, the debts of the three countries have been downgraded, and Italy has come perilously close to a failed debt auction.

For Africa, potential impacts from the Greek debt crisis could include (i) higher capital cost for emerging economies arising from the public debt issue and potential sovereign risk; (ii) delayed recovery in the European zone stemming from huge spending cuts; and (iii) relative decline in export price competitiveness from euro currency depreciation. However, it is not clear if political instability stemming from budget consolidation measures undertaken in Greece (such as increased taxes and reduced government spending) would result in spillovers to Africa. Of course, Africa must learn to build credence with the rest of the world by undertaking transparent and effective policies.

AFRICA'S KEY POLICY CHALLENGES UNDER MARKET INTEGRATION

Prior reforms in macroeconomic policies and debt relief initiatives that were undertaken in the 2000s by many African countries are believed to have contributed to the reduced impacts of the global financial crisis on the region (African Development Bank, 2010). The lessons from the recent global recession provide support for the accelerated implementation of protocols by the African RECs to ensure fully functioning integrated markets. However, the region faces broad challenges in achieving regional integration. In the following sections, we review two key challenges in ensuring macroeconomic policy convergence and financial and monetary integration, major bottlenecks stemming from the recent financial crisis.

CHALLENGES IN ACHIEVING MACROECONOMIC POLICY CONVERGENCE

The global monetary system in the wake of the Bretton Woods conference of 1944 served to reduce the sense of global economic insecurity that occurred in the 1930s, and ushered most developed and some developing countries into the period of the "Golden Age, " characterized by low inflation, low unemployment, and highly improved living standards. However, during the second half of the 1960s through the 1970s, the confluence of shocks led by the OPEC oil crisis created instability in the international monetary arrangement leading to the adoption of a system of flexible exchange rates. For the most part, major industrialized nations have geared their monetary policy goals toward eliminating domestic inflation while ignoring the misalignment of exchange rates and debt problems of many developing countries. Although in the 1990s the volatility of exchange rates in developing countries declined from their peaks of the 1980s, much of the decline was limited to the middle income countries. Therefore, through the 1990s, most developing countries (including African countries) experienced volatility in their real exchange rates than in advanced industrialized economies (World Bank, 2005). Attempts at minimizing exchange rate volatility with currency pegs[20] resulted in various currency crises, including the Asian financial crisis of 1997-1998, and the collapse of Argentina's currency board and subsequent recession. For the developing countries, the past three decades have been characterized by chronic inflation, exchange rate instability, and low economic growth. Mundell[21] (2002) places the blame squarely with the deterioration of the global international architecture and especially the lapse in discipline due to the absence of an international monetary system.

Admittedly, Africa's share of global trade is low, and the region is not well-integrated with the global financial system. Yet, Africa is more open to trade with the rest of the world than most other developing countries (Mold, 2006). As already discussed, one of the strident sources from which the recent financial crisis impacts Africa is through its trade with the major industrialized nations. Therefore, African countries (especially the leading commodity exporters) are very vulnerable to any volatile changes in their terms of trade and trade revenues. And despite recent debt forgiveness, many African countries are also vulnerable to any

---

20 Many developing countries linked their currencies to the dollar.

21 In fact, Mundell bemoans the political choice in anchoring any future African regional currency to either the U.S. Dollar or Euro for political expediency. In the same paper, he raises the critical importance of establishing a well-disciplined African Central Bank (ACB) whose behavior may not necessarily lead to regional inflation and instability as the existing national central banks. The ACB must define the price or exchange index for stability, lock in the exchange rate, make effective monetary policy for the region and fulfill stabilization targets, and deal with issues of seigniorage (perhaps per the equity position of each nation as done by the European Central Bank).

shifts in exchange rates since they finance their trade and repay their debts in foreign currency. This is why the efforts at achieving African regional integration must succeed. African countries must take the necessary steps to reduce their vulnerability to external shocks so as to motivate economic development. This message is quite clear. And the imperatives for engendering success must rest on the RECs.

Macroeconomic policy coordination among African countries is very important. Currently, the African Union, African Development Bank, and the United Nations Economic Commission for Africa (UNECA) coordinate annual conferences of Ministers of Finance, Planning and Economic development to discuss monetary and fiscal policy issues that are impacting African economies. The process affords opportunity to strategize macroeconomic policy coordination. The African Union has also instituted an African Peer Review Mechanism (APRM) as a self-monitoring process to encourage conformity to political, economic and governance values, codes and standards among its members so as to achieve sustained economic development. However, the APRM is voluntary and no self-enforcing mechanism has been put in place.

Poor macroeconomic policy coordination creates opportunities for spillovers across national borders in the form of arbitrage and smuggling activities. Inadequate fiscal discipline and poor monetary instruments tend to contribute to macroeconomic uncertainty. The absence of macroeconomic policy harmonization also creates barriers against controlling inflation, inducing savings and investment, and rationalizing government fiscal policies. However, there are mounting challenges in ensuring macroeconomic policy responses in a region with such diverse economies. For example, monetary policy would have to be eased by the regional central bank during periods of inflationary declines for some countries, while on the other hand, other countries facing demand pressures and excessive inflation may require tightening monetary policy. Furthermore, inflationary pressures can mount from budget deficits and excessive monetary expansion to undermine trade liberalization and this can lead to nations increasing tariffs or tightening non-tariff barriers. Most importantly, slow progress in achieving regional monetary unions would create bottlenecks against effective trade implementation in the form of diverse and competing local currencies with poor convertibility across the region and diverse exchange rate systems. So, what process must African RECs follow?

To be successful in creating a monetary union and a common market in which goods, services, capital and persons would move freely, African RECs have been called upon to (i) liberalize the exchange rates of the member states to facilitate trade and capital movements within the region; (ii) harmonize the economic, fiscal, and monetary policies of the member states so as to reduce currency misalignment, and establish a consultative and coordinating machinery; (iii) strive to achieve convertibility within the region of member states' national currencies; (iv) mobilize financial resources for trade expansion and development projects and programs; (v) reduce the cost of exchanging currencies in intra-REC trade and improve the transparency of prices, so as to promote intra-REC trade and investment flows; (vi) improve price stability and allocation of resources within the region; and (vii) develop a coordinated management strategy that will promote national actions towards monetary and fiscal policy harmonization (U.N. Economic Commission for Africa and Africa Union, 2008, p. 11).

Major implementation challenges involve instituting guidelines for macroeconomic surveillance of key macroeconomic variables to be respected by member states. One action step recommended is for the RECs to put in place a multilateral surveillance mechanism to ensure coherence and convergence of macroeconomic policies through compliance by member states. Accordingly, agreed targets have been set for budgetary balance, inflation, and public debt. The idea is to succeed in enhancing monetary cooperation, promoting discipline and setting up regional payment systems and clearing houses within the RECs. However, key challenges would include capacity-building efforts aimed at providing technical assistance to member states, harmonization of statistics, conducting seminars and workshops to sensitize member states, and putting in place effective legal enforcement mechanisms to ensure that the objectives of macroeconomic convergence are met.

For example, the ECOWAS is leading the way in formulating plans to establish the West African Monetary Zone[22] that will use a common currency. However, it is facing challenges in implementing the common currency. Following the "Accra Declaration" by the Gambia, Ghana, Guinea, Liberia, Nigeria and Sierra Leone, the idea of the West African Monetary Zone (WAMZ) was motivated. The WAMZ has given birth to, among others, the West African Monetary Institute (WAMI) whose operational functionality is not unlike the European Monetary Institute (EMI), and which is supposed to serve as a forerunner of the idea of a common central bank. The signatories have, to date, struggled with the inception of a common currency (that could be merged with the CFA Franc zone), but which has been postponed to the year 2015. The Monetary Zone will be supported by institutions such as the West African Monetary Agency (WAMA) and the West African Monetary Institute (WAMI).

Although the ECOWAS has implemented a number of measures in line with its objective of achieving a comprehensive Monetary Cooperation Program (MCP), it has faced challenges that have delayed its implementation. Among the list of factors causing such delays include lack of political will, and the fact that the required monetary harmonization has not been achieved. Therefore, the date for the single monetary zone has been postponed at various times. Prior to the financial crisis, the economic performance of countries in the ECOWAS zone was modest, averaging about 4 percent between 2001 and 2005; clearly below the 7 percent needed to achieve the millennium development goal of halving poverty by 2015. All the countries recorded various levels of growth, with Cote d'Ivoire, Guinea, Guinea Bissau, Niger, Senegal, and Togo averaging about 4 percent, and Burkina Faso, Cape Verde, The Gambia, Ghana, Liberia, Nigeria, and Sierra Leone registering above 5 percent. For example, whereas prudent fiscal and monetary management of the Ghanaian economy has led to more than average growth, Cote d'Ivoire's GDP growth was negative from 2001 through 2003. The

22 This will comprise Gambia, Ghana, Guinea and Nigeria. The UEMOA and CEMAC present other monetary unions. The Common Monetary Area uses the South African rand alongside other currencies in southern Africa.

inflation rates in ECOWAS have been relatively good, averaging less than 9 percent from 2001 through 2005. Most notably, members of the WAEMU's CFA zone registered very low rates of inflation due to the peg of the CFA to the Euro. However, the central banks of the Gambia, Ghana, Guinea, and Nigeria have been working hard to reduce their double-digit inflation to the required single digit and up to 5 percent from 2003. Although the ECOWAS region attracts substantial levels of FDI, most of it goes to Nigeria's oil-producing sector. The fact that WAEMU members have achieved greater macroeconomic stability, despite relying largely on primary commodity exports, is noteworthy.

Financial Sector Challenges

A key challenge in Africa's long-term development strategy is financial sector development; a sector in which Africa lags behind all regions of the world. Levine (1997) reviews the literature on the evolution of financial markets in economic development. The author shows that the development of financial markets and associated institutions plays a crucial role in the rates of future economic growth, capital accumulation, technological change and economic development. Economic theory indicates that financial markets and associated institutions minimize information and transaction costs. Therefore, investment decisions, savings rates, technological innovation, and long-run growth rates of a country or region crucially depend on its level of financial development. Merton and Bodie (1995) also show that financial markets and institutions facilitate the allocation of resources across space and time, especially when faced with uncertainty and risks.

The economic literature delineates five functional roles of financial markets and institutions namely, (i) the management of liquidity risks[23]; (ii) information acquisition and resource allocation; (iii) monitoring of investment projects; (iv) mobilization of savings; and (v) the facilitation of the exchange of goods and

---

23 Financial markets and institutions mitigate the frictions associated with liquidity risk by converting assets into purchasing power (or currency) at agreed prices. Therefore, liquid capital markets are where financial instruments are traded relatively easily, and they limit uncertainty about the timing and settlements of trades.

services (Levine, 1997). Diamond and Dybvig (1983) illustrate a model that links liquidity with economic growth during periods of external shocks. According to the authors, in the absence of financial markets in a risky environment, capital funds are usually committed to liquid and low return projects. However, the stock markets enable equity holders to freely sell their shares and investors to have access to capital. Therefore, financial markets and institutions also reduce liquidity risk by trading equities and assisting in banking intermediation. Typically, stock markets also play a very useful role in acquiring, disseminating, and managing information about investment opportunities by publishing prices of financial instruments and monitoring projects. This enables consumers of investment information to be efficient economic agents as they direct their resources to other gainful economic activities.

Despite the economic development functions of financial markets and institutions, there are few functioning financial markets in Africa[24]. Generally, in the formal market banks play a limited role in African economies, while cash remains the dominant financial instrument. Unlike in developed economies, there has been no systemic banking crisis in Africa following the global financial crisis. Commercial banks and other financial institutions so far remain largely sound. However, cross-border banking system linkages are minimal. There is less exposure to complex financial products, and with the exception of the frontier and emerging markets, financial systems are not well integrated with other global financial markets (IMF, 2009). Therefore, the effects of the recent financial crisis were not expected to directly impact many African countries with less-developed financial systems. How would domestic African banking systems be affected in the long-run? The expectation is that in the long-run financial risks could mount in all countries, and we should anticipate that domestic banking systems would be weakened over time from the deterioration in credit quality associated with the slowdown in the growth of African economies, losses on financial assets, and capital repatriations by foreign-owned parent banks.

24 Frontier and emerging financial markets in Africa are found in South Africa, Nigeria, Ghana, and Kenya.

In the late 1980s and early 1990s, however, many African countries experienced systemic banking crises, preceded mainly by significant deterioration in asset quality either linked to worsening macroeconomic environments or inadequate lending procedures and insufficient application of good regulations. In part because the fiscal costs involved in recapitalizing and injecting liquidity back into banks[25] were very large, many loss-generating public banks were privatized. Therefore, it is important to note that African banking systems are currently dominated by large shares of foreign ownership, especially following recent financial market liberalizations supported by the IMF between 1996-99 and 2000-03. These have rendered state banks as less important in many African countries than in other developing countries. However, several countries, such as Ethiopia, still have a significant presence of state banks, with limited access by foreign banks.

Because of the dominance of foreign banks, African countries are increasingly at risk from parent (foreign) banks that may choose to withdraw funds from local bank subsidiaries in African countries. To be sure, risks of contagion from distressed foreign parent banks can be transmitted to local subsidiaries within SSA if: (i) they withdraw capital from African subsidiaries; (ii) if they call in loans to their African subsidiaries; (iii) if they no longer invest local profits in local subsidiaries; or (iv) if they adopt any combination of the listed policies. Therefore, it is important that the financial sector, especially banks, be monitored vigilantly in order to minimize vulnerabilities and mitigate risks.

Gulde *et al* (2006) indicate that financial sectors in SSA, especially in the low-income countries, are small and are dominated by banks (by up to 80 percent of the assets). The size of about half of the SSA countries' financial systems, measured in terms of M2, is less than $1 billion[26]. However, financial sectors in non-oil middle-income SSA countries tend to be significantly deeper and sounder, and provide greater access to funds.

Empirical studies (Allen and Ndikumana, 2002; Gelbard and Leite, 1999) reveal that countries with good-functioning finan-

25 In some countries these reached between 11 and 16 percent of GDP.

26 This is not much larger than a small bank in a rich country.

cial systems in SSA grow faster. Additionally, the IMF's financial indicators for SSA show that among SSA countries other than oil producers, those economies that grew the fastest between 1960 and 2004 were those that were also the most financially developed (see also Gulde *et al*, 2006; Appendix 3).

Real interest rates for lending in SSA are among the highest in the world, and are a major impediment to lending activities (Gulde *et al,* 2006). Nevertheless, SSA banks are profitable (even with high overhead costs), based mainly on interest-related incomes. Additionally, interbank activity tends to be limited in most SSA countries. Indeed, tracking data from interbank money markets in WAEMU and CEMAC illustrates the minimal interbank activities of the markets[27]. Non-bank financial institutions (NBFI), such as insurance, microfinance and pension funds tend to be small relative to the population base of most countries[28]. Banking sectors in SSA tend to also have higher concentration ratios than in other low-income countries, based mainly on the relatively small size of their financial markets (Bossone *et al*, 2002), and they also tend to be inefficient. Additionally, banking market efficiency is negatively correlated with inflation, corruption, and concentration (Detragiache *et al*, 2005).

Banks in most African countries also suffer from weak legal systems and unclear property rights. According to Gulde *et al* (2006), banks face a regulatory framework that is largely consistent with international norms, but implementation of supervision is hampered by chronic forbearance. Many African countries, especially those outside the CFA zone and the rand CMA, have since 2004 moved from an exchange rate to a monetary anchor[29]. South Africa and Ghana are among countries that maintain the

---

27 Despite a common currency, shared central banks in each subregion, and similar rules, because of limited interaction among markets, prices for financial services (interest rates) may not necessarily converge. Therefore, there is little progress toward the "law of one price" with respect to lending rates of WAEMU and/or CEMAC.

28 Based on IMF survey, NBFIs account for less than 10 percent of the total financial system assets.

29 Only 6 small countries still maintain the exchange rate anchor.

inflation-targeting regime. With limited capital mobility and incomplete regional financial integration, the central banks in the CFA franc zone have been able to pursue monetary targets along with the exchange rate anchor. All told, although many African countries have a range of monetary policy instruments, in the presence of high and persistent unremunerated excess liquidity they have not been efficient. For example, according to IMF calculations, on average, excess reserves were more than 13 percent of total deposits, though they exceeded 30 percent in Equatorial Guinea, Ethiopia, Guinea-Bissau, the Comoros, and Chad.

Financial integration would offer the opportunity for each African country's financial market to be closely associated with those in its region and then to the rest of the world. To achieve regional financial integration would require formal partnerships to eliminate restrictions on cross-border financial services and adopt flexible rules to encourage foreign financial institutions to operate in the region. It would also require harmonizing policies, rules and standards governing regulations, accounting and auditing[30], and even taxes among the member countries. Given the small size of African countries and their markets, regional financial integration offers many advantages in attracting participation from financial institutions from within the region and rest of the world. Among the potential advantages are economies of scale, the removal of certain credit constraints faced by potential investors in the region, and the reduction of market risks to firms and financial institutions. Greater opportunities would be offered for risk sharing and risk diversification, improved capital allocation among investment opportunities, and the potential for higher economic growth. This arrangement should lead to deeper integration of African financial markets with global financial markets and strengthen financial ties in providing services linked to trade and investment deals. It must be noted that the WTO has encouraged the inclusion of trade in financial services into its trading protocol, and this ought to ensure enhanced access to markets of and national treatment by signatories in the areas of banking, securities and insurance. However, African RECs must strike the proper balance on allow-

30 This must include harmonizing the criteria for valuating bank asset risks to protect against shocks and regulatory arbitrage.

ing foreign financial institutions to operate unchecked in regional markets; especially in moving from the region in search of better opportunities when shocks occur.

CONCLUDING COMMENTS AND SUGGESTIONS ON THE WAY FORWARD

African countries have been victims of a global financial crisis that has disrupted and set back the region's progress in its unprecedented millennial match toward achieving its highest economic growth, and potentially set the region back from progress in reducing poverty. A major lesson for Africa stemming from the financial crisis is the need for gradual implementation of capital account liberalization so as to prevent sudden cessation of capital flows. Under regional integration, this would require managing capital accounts of members through a regional central bank that would institute a flexible exchange rate system, impose sterilized interventions, and maintain control over capital inflows and outflows.

Whereas good macroeconomic policies, debt relief initiatives, and structural reforms undertaken during the early 2000s, and poor linkages to global financial markets may have helped the region in avoiding severe damages to some economies, many more vulnerable countries have been incapable of mounting the necessary counter-cyclical measures to rebound from the effects of the crisis. Only few African countries have been able to implement stimulus packages, expansionary monetary policies, trade assistance, reforms and emerging regulations of the financial sector, and other social measures to induce greater demand for goods and services.

The most significant impacts on African countries appear to be on their revenues from commodity exports, in large part because of declining prices for global commodities and the resulting negative effects on terms of trade. This has affected the balance of trade and external reserves, as well as the fiscal balances of many African countries. Whereas inflationary pressures have been reduced, the consequences of declining FDI, foreign remittances, and foreign aid are leaving damaging effects on Africa's economic recovery. Although the recent global recovery from the recession points to a revision of the Africa's real GDP growth of about 4.5 percent in 2010, it is still below the average of about 6 percent attained before the crisis hit. Moreover, it is not clear what the long-term implications of the global recovery from the crisis would mean for the African region. What is amply clear is that with many analysts predicting the usual slower recovery by African countries, policy actions must be undertaken to forestall any underlying supply-side constraints, and to make African countries more resilient to additional external shocks. This paper concludes that Africa is still open to the downside risks from any potential increase in sovereign debt constraints that would choke off the demand for African exports and that would continue to exacerbate FDI flows to the region.

This has placed the question of accelerating Africa's efforts at achieving regional integration back into focus. Indeed, given the global impacts of the financial crisis, it provides a unique opportunity for African countries to speak with a collective voice on the debate about its role in constructing any future global monetary and financial architecture. It is imperative for African RECs and governments to seize the moment literally in seeking to deepen regional integration efforts by continuing to harmonize macroeconomic and financial policies that would pool resources for regional investment, enhance greater regional and global participation in trade in goods and services, build the regional infrastructure, promote efficient growth of the industrial manufacturing sector, and improve education and health services. It is also important for regional institutions to unite in seeking new business opportunities, and undertake pro-business policies that will offer incentives to increase jobs creation and improved living standards by creating more robust, competitive and diversified businesses. Since most national markets in Africa are simply too small and/or inadequate to sustain large-scale economic operations, economic integration must be viewed as important for utilizing Africa's human and physical potential, instituting credible policies, and for realizing its prime objectives of accelerating economic growth and reducing poverty. The multiplicity of RECs in all African sub-regions raises challenges on consolidating them so as to develop coherent policies and to streamline all sub-regional agendas, harmonize protocols to strengthen cross-border initiatives, and remove duplication so as to unite regional markets.

The capacities of RECs would be further weakened by worsening financial constraints if as a result of the financial crisis they face difficulties in accessing funds from their member states. This would widen the gap between national aspirations for achieving integration that are expressed in treaties and protocols on the one hand, and the ability to actually implement them on the other hand. In addition, needed regional infrastructure and trade facilitation projects would be jeopardized. This will be unfortunate, since it will definitely further weaken the African continent's ability to absorb the impacts from the crisis and would further increase its marginalization in the global economy. These summary concerns will definitely pose major challenges for African governments but also existing African institutions such as the African Union, the African Development Bank, the United Nations Economic Commission for Africa, and all the RECs in finding solutions to offset the nebulous challenges in accelerating economic development and poverty alleviation facing the continent. Likewise, African governments would need the support of their development partners to build the region's infrastructure (road, rail, air) to link all African nations and sub-regions more closely so as to reduce transaction costs in conducting business and socio-cultural interactions. In addition, transit facilitation, documentation and procedures along major transport corridors in the region must be improved. These must also be complemented with effective ICTs that link the nations and region to the rest of the world for the purpose of conducting business.

The combined effects of interim protectionist measures and subsidies to industries undertaken by some rich countries while some developing countries are increasing tariffs and restricting imports will have long-run deleterious impacts on African trade flows. Furthermore, African trade will be squeezed by the lack of trade credit, especially for small-to-medium size enterprises, that are the typical sources of diversification of African products and jobs creation. Based on the financial market characteristics in Africa, the financial crisis will reinforce existing market failures by worsening allocation of credit to businesses.

Additionally, deeper integration will require strengthening financial systems integration. This will require a comprehensive program to strengthen and streamline financial sector policies and financial infrastructure such as the regulatory framework and payments systems. This will help in the development of strong financial markets and institutions, including banks and non-bank institutions, and enhance the financial system's ability to mobilize and allocate resources for development financing. Certainly, this will be critical for supporting private sector development, regional and international trade, economic growth, and poverty reduction. Since financial policies are important for the efficient functioning of firms, regional bodies such as the Intergovernmental Authority on Development (IGAD), the African Development Bank, the African Union, etc., must adopt policies that encourage investment and industrial cooperation. Although ambitious, perhaps incentives could be given to firms to promote intra-African trade. Furthermore, labor laws, and patent and property rights laws would have to be rationalized.

To modernize African production processes would require investment in regional energy sources. But energy policy must span agriculture to industrial manufacturing. Regional energy policies must take into consideration the need to exploit economies of scale to supply cheap energy. Africa's vast water resources must be channeled toward expanding agricultural irrigation and hydroelectric projects. This would also require excellent management of water resources.

The completion of regional agreements represents processes rather than discrete events. The implementation schedules for most reforms must be viewed as ongoing over time, but they must have definite completion points. Fortunately, Africa has set a long schedule for processes leading to the formation of the AEC in 2027. Therefore, the AU, African RECs and all associated institutions can build on lessons learned from existing sub-regional and bilateral arrangements. An African regional trade agreement can help African countries to build on their comparative advantages, sharpen their industrial efficiency, and act as a springboard to integrate into the world economy. It can also help strengthen the political commitment to an open economy, improve technical, management and competency skills, educate civil society and more actively engage the business community. More importantly,

African negotiators can use the opportunities in strengthening their negotiations skills. The combination of reforms and skills development will build credibility for Africa in the eyes of the world and, hopefully, reward the region with greater access to markets.

To that end, a framework for monitoring African countries' progress in achieving macroeconomic policy convergence and monetary integration would be necessary and ought to be vested in an autonomous monitoring institution such as a regional central bank or court of justice or a regional parliament, etc. Of course, it is important that African countries develop credible national institutions to reinforce regional institutions. Furthermore, governments ought to be willing to give up some of their sovereignty to achieve effective integration.

Whereas it is generally agreed that African countries must be held accountable for accomplishing their reforms and development, international organizations and donor groups can complement their efforts. First, it would help if the DDR can reach agreement on all matters in regards to trade policies before it to provide free access to African products and services. Removal of trade barriers could contribute to gains in incomes that could make up for declining levels of potential external assistance to Africa and dwindling fiscal space in African countries, especially in the more fragile ones. The present drive towards market openness, though successful to a great extent, has not led to full access to markets. Significant impediments to free trade in goods and services still exist that prevent nations from reaping the full benefits from international trade. Many developed countries also impose non-tariff barriers in the form of price supports, subsidies, and special marketing arrangements that tend to keep out agricultural products from developing countries. Other restrictive policies include product standards and health regulations. Although Africa may be accorded preferential treatment, these preferences have not increased African trade. Therefore, it may be in African countries' interests to support broad-based multilateral liberalization in agriculture during future rounds of global trade negotiations.

Additionally establishing institutions that can intermediate with global financial and extralegal institutions will be critical.

For example, lessons from the 1990s global financial meltdown (in Southeast Asia and Latin America) and the recent global financial crisis seem to suggest that the potential risks from financial globalization may be very high. Although Africa has avoided the direct risks by not being active players in global finance to date, regional institutions must carefully review the relevant lessons learned in the way forward. The relevant question is how to achieve sustainable economic growth through regional and global integration without being exposed to major external shocks that would exacerbate current poverty levels in Africa?

References

African Development Bank, 2000, *African Development Report*. New York: Oxford University Press.

African Development Bank, 2009, "Panel 2: The Financial Crisis, Trade and Regional Integration in Africa." Concept Note. African Development Bank Annual Meetings, High Level Seminar. Tunis, Tunisia.

African Development Bank, 2010, "Containing the Impact of the Global Crisis and Paving the Way to Strong Recovery in Africa." *Policy Briefs of the Financial Crisis*, No. 2/February.

Allen, D.S. and Leonce Ndikumana, 2002, "Financial Intermediation and Economic Growth in Southern Africa, " *Journal of African Economies*, Vol. 9, No. 2 (June), pp. 132-60.

Berman, N. and P. Martin, 2009, "The Vulnerability of Sub-Sahara Africa to the Financial Crisis: The Case of Trade." Background paper for the *2009 European Report on Development*.

Bossone, Biagio, P. Honoha, and M. F. Long, 2002, "Policy for Small Financial Systems." In Financial Sector Policy for Developing Countries: a Reader, G. Caprio, P. Honohan, and D. Vittas (eds). New York: Oxford University Press, for the World Bank.

Calvo, Guillermo A., 2005, *Emerging Capital Markets in Turmoil: Bad Luck or Bad Policy?* Cambridge, Massachusetts: MIT Press.

Detragiache, Enrica, P. Gupta, and Thierry Tressel, 2005, "Finance in Lower-Income Countries: An Empirical Exploration, " IMF Working Paper 05/167, Washington, DC: International Monetary Fund.

Diamond, D. and P. Dybvig, 1983, "Bank Runs, Deposit Insurance, and Liquidity." *Journal of Political Economy*, 91(3):401-19.

Economic Report on Africa 2008, Africa and the Monterrey Consensus: Tracking Performance and Progress, Addis Ababa, Ethiopia: United Nations Economic Commission for Africa (March).

Edwards, Sebastian, 2005, "Capital Controls, Sudden Stops, and Current Account Reversals."

NBER Working Paper No. 11170, Cambridge, Massachusetts: National Bureau of Economic Research.

Eichengreen, Barry and Andrew Rose, 1999, "Contagious Currency Crises: Channels of Conveyance." In *Changes in Exchange Rates in Rapidly Developing Economies*, Takatoshi Ito and Anne Kruger (eds.), Chicago: University of Chicago Press.

Forbes, Kristin, 2001, "Are Trade Linkages Important Determinants of Country Vulnerability to Crises?" NBER Working Paper N. 8194, Cambridge, Massachusetts: National Bureau of Economic Research.

Gelbard, Enrique, and Sergio Pereira Leite, 1999, "Measuring Financial Development in Sub-Saharan Africa," IMF Working Paper 99/105, Washington, DC: International Monetary Fund.

Glick, Reuven and Andre K. Rose, 1999, "Contagion and Trade: Why Are Currency Crises Regional?" *Journal of International Money and Finance*, Vol. 18 (August), pp. 603-17.

Gulde, Anne-Marie, Catherine Pattilo, and Jakob Christensen, with Kevin Carey and Smita Wagh, 2006, *Sub-Saharan Africa: Financial Sector Challenges*. Washington, DC: International Monetary Fund.

Humphrey, John, 2009, "Trade Financing: Is It a Barrier to Africa's Exports?" *Vox* (April).

International Monetary Fund (IMF), 2009, "Crisis and Recovery". *World Economic Outlook* (April).

______, 2010, "Rebalancing Growth." *World Economic Outlook* (April).

Kaminsky, Graciela L. and Carmen M. Reinhart, 1999, "The Twin Crises: The Causes of Banking and Balance-of-Payments Problems." *American Economic Review*, Vol. 89 (June), pp. 473-500.

______, 2003, "The Center and the Periphery: The Globalization of Financial Turmoil, " NBER Working Paper No. 9479, Cambridge, Massachusetts: National Bureau of Economic Research.

Kasekende, Louis, Zuzana Brixova, and Leonce Ndikumana, 2010, "Africa: Africa's Counter-Cyclical Policy Responses to the Crisis." *Journal of Globalization and Development*, Vol. 1, Issue 1, Article 16.

Levine, R., 1997, "Financial Development and Economic Growth: Views and Agenda," *Journal of Economic Literature*, 35, pp. 688-726.

Merton, R. and Z. Bodie, 1995, "A Conceptual Framework for Analyzing the Financial Environment." In *The Global Financial System: A Functional Perspective*, D. B. Crane, K. A. Froot, S. P. Mason, A. Perold, R. Merton, Z. Bodie, E. R. Sirri, and P. Tufano, Boston: Harvard University Press.

Masson, Paul and Catherine Patillo, 2004, "A Single Currency for Africa?" Finance and Development (December), pp. 9-15.

Mold, Andrew, 2006, "Tackling the Commodity Price Problem – New Proposals and Revisiting Old Solutions." In *African Development Yearbook 2006*, Mareike Meyn (ed.) Institute for World Economics and International Management (IWIM), University of Bremen.

Mundell, Robert, 2002, Views on "Defining Priorities for Regional Integration in Africa." U.N. Economic Commission for Africa (UNECA), Addis Ababa.

Oxford Analytica, 2008, "Africa: Growth to Suffer Despite Insulated Banks." (October 15).

Reuters, 2009, "Factbox – China's Growing Business in Africa." (February 12).

Standard Bank, 2009, *Implications of the Financial Crisis in Sino-African Relations.* (June 30).

UNECA and African Union, 2008, *Assessing Regional Integration in Africa III: Towards Monetary and Financial Integration in Africa.*

U.N. World Tourism Organization, 2009, "World Tourism in the Face of the Global Economic Crisis." (May 12).

U.S. Department of Commerce, International Trade Administration, 2009, U.S. – African Trade Profile. (July).

World Bank, 2005, "Economic Growth in the 1990s – Learning from a Decade of Reform." Washington, D.C., Chapter 4.

Figure 9.1: The Transmission of Financial Stress: Schematic Depiction of Effects

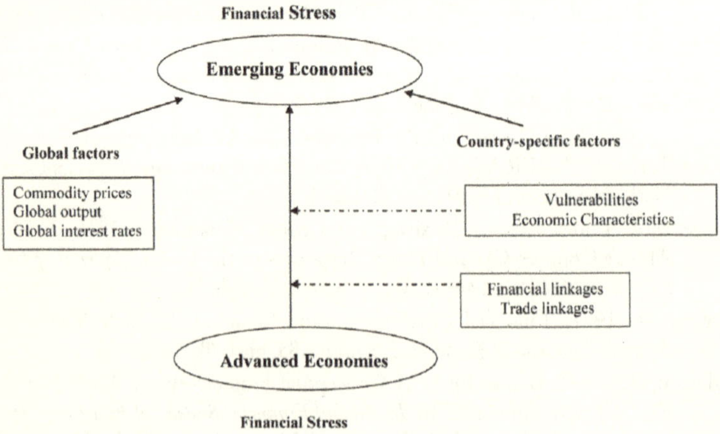

Source: IMF (2009).

Figure 9.2: Real GDP Growth in SSA and Advanced Economies: Different Forecasts

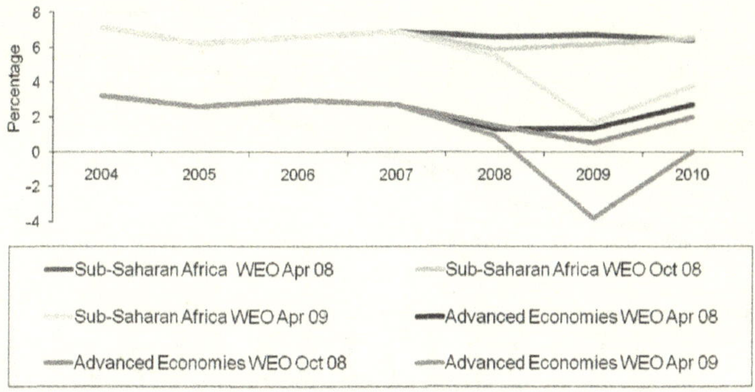

Source: IMF, World Economic Outlook, various sources.

Figure 9.3: Africa's GDP per Capita

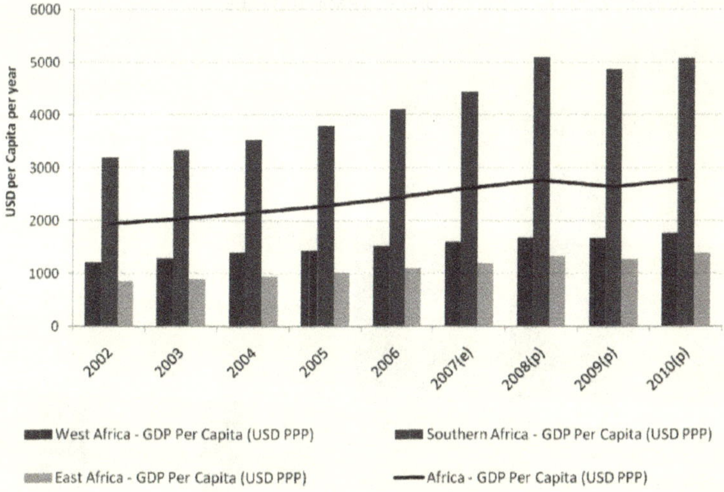

Figure 9.4: World Merchandise Imports

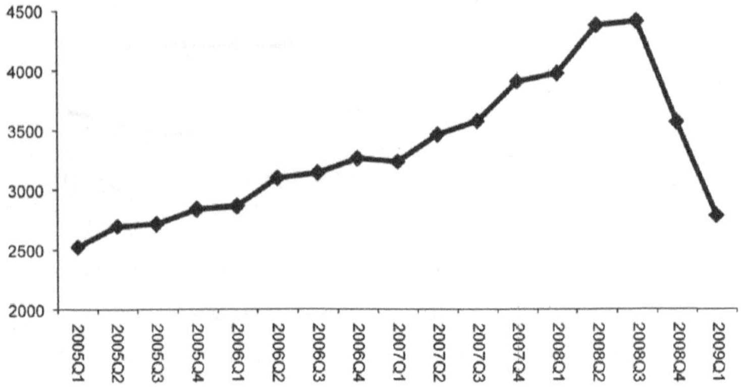

Source: WTO Secretariat, 2009

Figure 9.5: Effect of Recession on Trade Revenue

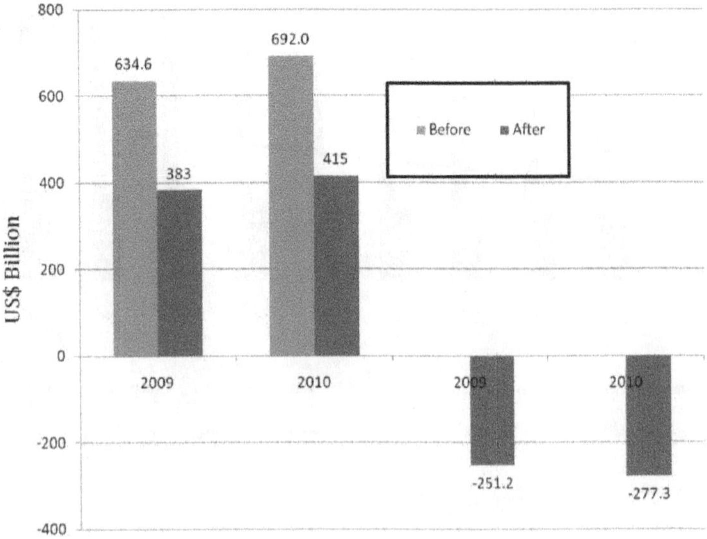

Source: African Development Bank (AfDB), March 2009

Figure 9.6: Trends in U.S. Imports Following Recession

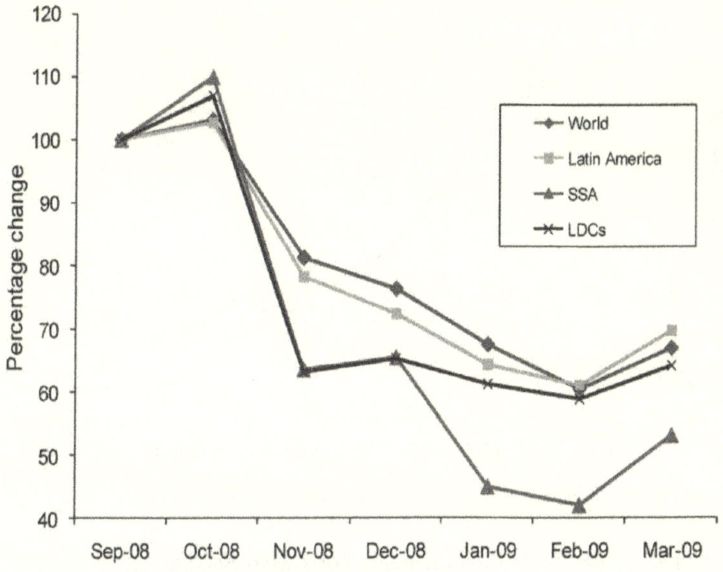

Source: US Trade Commission, Online Dataset

Figure 9.7: Trends in U.S. Imports: Primary versus Manufacturing

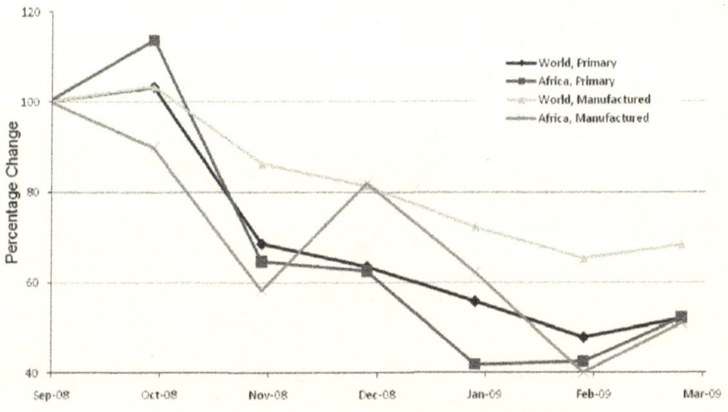

Source: US Trade Commission, Online Dataset

Figure 9.8: Trends in EU Imports Following Recession

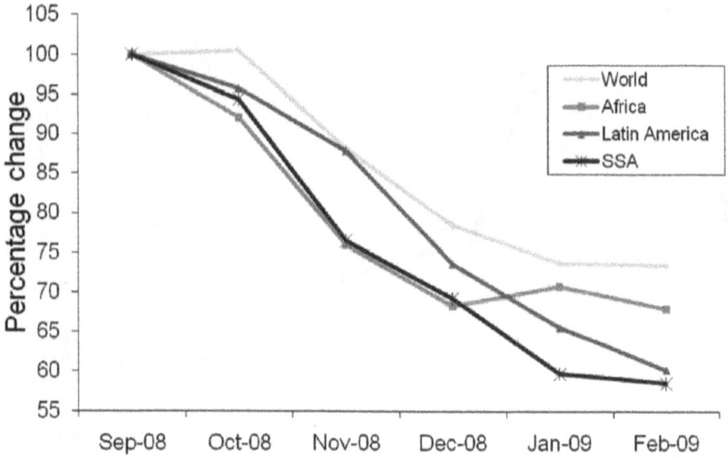

Source: Global Trade Atlas

Figure 9.9: Trends in China Imports Following Recession

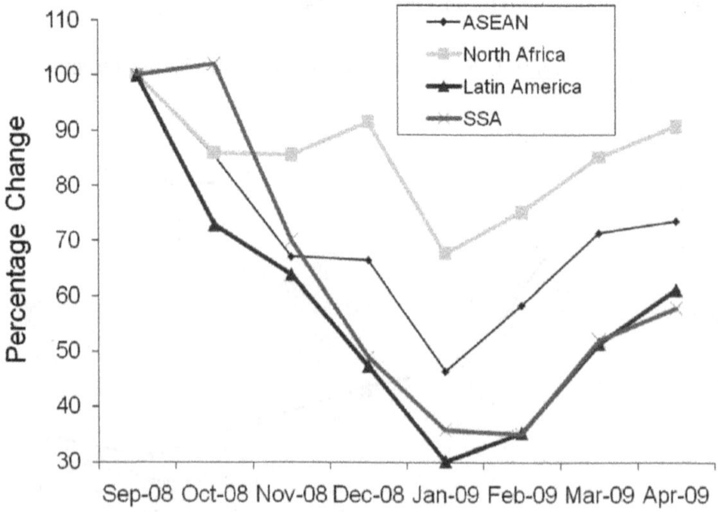

Source: Global Trade Atlas

Figure 9.10: Impulse Response to Shocks Affecting Trade Partners

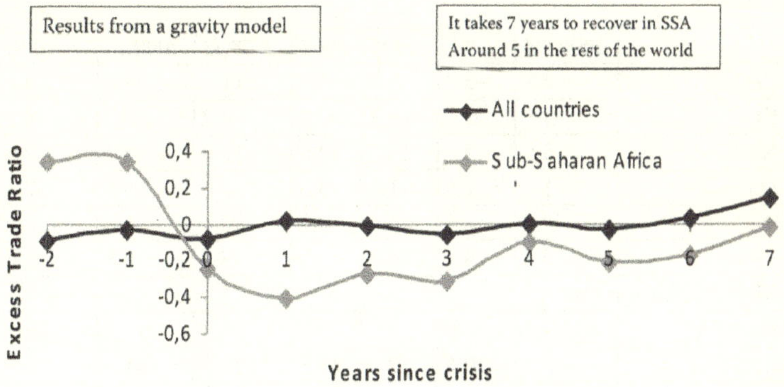

Source: Berman and Martin, 2009

Table 9.1: Africa's Real GDP Growth (in %)

	2000-04	2005	2006	2007	2008(e)	2009(p)	2010(p)
Central	5.7	5.3	3.4	4.0	5.0	2.8	3.6
East	4.9	7.1	7.6	8.8	7.3	5.5	5.7
North	4.1	4.9	5.6	5.3	5.8	3.3	4.1
South	4.1	6.3	6.8	7.0	5.2	0.2	4.6
West	7.1	5.7	5.1	5.4	5.4	4.2	4.6
Africa	4.8	5.7	6.0	6.1	5.7	2.8	4.5
Memorandum items							
North Africa (incl. Sudan)	4.2	5.0	6.1	5.7	6.0	3.5	4.2
Sub-Saharan Africa	5.2	6.2	5.9	6.4	5.5	2.4	4.7
Oil-exporting countries	5.4	6.3	6.1	6.8	6.6	2.4	4.5
Oil-importing countries	4.1	5.0	5.8	5.4	4.6	3.3	4.5

Source: African Economic Outlook 2009 (preliminary estimates), AfDB, 2009.
Note: (e) denotes an estimate and (p) a projection

Table 9.2: Africa's External Current Account, including grants (in % of GDP)

	2000-04	2005	2006	2007	2008(e)	2009(p)	2010(p)
Central	-4.1	-0.8	1.9	-0.5	11.2	-4.6	-2.4
East	-5.5	-6.7	-9.3	-9.3	-6.2	-7.5	-8.1
North	5.6	12.6	15.2	12.9	12.0	2.9	2.8
South	-1.1	-1.8	-1.1	-3.3	-2.0	-6.8	-7.4
West	-2.4	2.6	4.4	-0.2	0.4	-8.3	-6.8
Africa	0.6	3.5	4.8	2.4	3.5	-3.8	-3.6
Memorandum items							
North Africa (incl. Sudan)	4.5	10.6	12.4	10.3	10.5	1.3	0.9
Sub-Saharan Africa	-2.0	-0.7	0.4	-2.3	-0.4	-6.8	-6.4
Oil-exporting countries	3.0	10.6	13.1	8.9	9.8	-3.9	-2.9
Oil-importing countries	-1.6	-3.4	-4.0	-4.9	-5.3	-3.5	-4.7

Source: African Economic Outlook 2009 (preliminary estimates), AfDB, 2009.
Note: (e) denotes an estimate and (p) a projection.

Table 9.3: Africa's Overall Fiscal Balance, including grants (in % of GDP)

	2000-04	2005	2006	2007	2008(e)	2009(p)	2010(p)
Central	2.0	6.9	17.5	7.4	13.3	4.0	4.8
East	-2.2	-2.0	-3.9	-3.6	-2.3	-4.8	-5.2
North	-1.1	4.5	6.4	3.5	2.9	-6.1	-5.8
South	-2.5	0.4	3.2	2.3	1.9	-4.6	-3.6
West	-0.5	5.2	6.4	-0.4	-0.2	-8.8	-9.4
Africa	-1.4	2.8	5.0	1.9	2.3	-5.4	-5.1
Memorandum items							
North Africa (incl. Sudan)	-1.0	3.9	5.5	2.7	2.7	-6.6	-6.3
Sub-Saharan Africa	-1.7	2.1	4.7	1.4	1.8	-4.9	-4.7
Oil-exporting countries	0.3	7.3	8.6	4.0	5.1	-7.7	-7.4
Oil-importing countries	-2.9	-1.7	1.1	-0.5	-2.0	-2.8	-2.5

Source: African Economic Outlook 2009 (preliminary estimates), AfDB, 2009.
Note: (e) denotes an estimate and (p) a projection

Table 9.4: Africa's Consumer Prices (Inflation in %)

	2000-04	2005	2006	2007	2008(e)	2009(p)	2010(p)
Central	15.8	5.4	6.3	2.9	8.8	7.2	6.5
East	5.9	7.3	12.0	10.1	17.8	10.2	8.0
North	2.6	4.7	3.6	6.8	8.1	7.6	5.2
South	13.8	6.6	7.4	9.8	13.2	9.0	7.9
West	10.3	14.0	7.4	5.4	10.6	8.6	8.2
Africa	7.9	7.1	6.4	7.5	11.1	8.5	6.9
Memorandum items							
North Africa (incl. Sudan)	2.9	4.8	4.5	7.0	8.6	7.7	5.4
Sub-Saharan Africa	11.6	8.8	7.7	7.9	12.9	9.0	7.9
Oil-exporting countries	9.8	8.5	5.9	7.2	10.0	9.1	7.1
Oil-importing countries	6.0	5.6	7.0	8.0	12.3	7.7	6.6

Source: African Economic Outlook 2009 (preliminary estimates), AfDB, 2009.
Note: (e) denotes an estimate and (p) a projection

Chapter 10

BANK CONCENTRATION AND MONETARY POLICY TRANSMISSION: AN EVALUATION IN WEST AFRICAN ECONOMIC AND MONETARY UNION (WAEMU) AND LESSONS FOR WEST AFRICAN MONETARY UNION (WAMZ)

R. Seydou Ouédraogo[1]

INTRODUCTION

This paper examines the impact of bank concentration on monetary transmission in West African Economic and Monetary Union (WAEMU) and draws implications particularly for the

1 I'm grateful to Michel Normandin, Jean-Marin Serre, Diery Seck, Lansané Condé and thus has many participants of conferences, BCEAO May 2010, WAMI CREPOL June 2010 and colleagues of CERDI for helpful comments. I thank Ferdinand Mito-Yobo for rereading the paper.

West African Monetary Zone (WAMZ). It is in the middle way of two literatures: the monetary transmission, *credit view* theories, and the economics of banking industry.

While the money view considers the banking system as neutral *vis-à-vis* the transmission of monetary policy, the modern view assigns it a prominent role (Bernanke et Gertler, 1995). In fact, introduction of information asymmetries in modern theories has entailed the need to reassess the transmission mechanisms and to attribute a prominent role to financial intermediaries. Banks in particular react to monetary shocks not only through their liabilities but also and especially through their assets adjustment by a specific response in their credit supply function. An extensive program of empirical research was drawn from credit channel theories. If banks play a specific role in the monetary channels, then one can expect differences in the transmission of the monetary policy according to bank net worth.

Authors have widened their interest for the characteristics of banks and banking industries. They focused their attention on the impact of balance sheet variables such as liquidity, size and capitalization (Kashap and Stein, 1995, 1997, 2000, Peek and Rosengren, 1995; Farinha and Marques, 2002; Kakes and Sturm, 2002 ; Ouédraogo, 2008, etc.), the structure of loans portfolios (Cechetti, 1999; Kashap and Stein, 1997), as well as the resilience and banking concentration (Adams and Amel, 2005, Berger and al. 2004; Kashap and Stein, 2007; Cechetti, 1999; Corvoisier and Gropp, 2002, etc..), etc. Empirical researches assessing the impact of banking structures made, implicitly or explicitly, assumptions due to the industrial economy banking. In particular the search for an impact of bank concentration is based on the intuition that the industrial organization of banking markets affects the behavior of banks and thus their response to monetary shocks.

Bank concentration is referred as an inhibition factor of the effectiveness of monetary policy in WAEMU. Nubukpo (2007) points out that this concentration is an important cause of inefficiency of BCEAO policy. But there is no empirical investigation of this effect[2]. This study provides a test of this hypothesis.

2 A part from Ouédraogo (2010b).

Moreover, many of the above mentioned works were undertaken to examine differences in transmission with respect to asymmetries in banking and financial sectors in monetary unions. Several empirical results show asymmetrical patterns of monetary shocks propagation conditioned by differences between the structural factors in a monetary union. These asymmetries are one of the main potential challenges monetary unions have to face; and eventually WAEMU and the project of WANZ are not an exception.

How to evaluate the likely constraints of the effectiveness of monetary policy in a union which is not yet effective? From the experience of WAEMU countries, I could forecast the implications for WANZ. This approach has been that taken by several researches based on the evidence for the U.S. to derive some implications for the European Union before the implementation of the euro (Kashap and Stein, 1999, Cecchetti, 1999, for example). I focus my interest on bank concentration. I estimate the concentration levels in the WAEMU banking sectors, and show that these levels entail serious constraint to the effectiveness of the policy of the BCEAO, as their difference between countries are very high. From this result, I infer implications for WANZ. Particularly, I emphasize on the need to harmonize bank regulation policies and / or a definition and an adjustment of institutional framework of the union in order to mitigate these constraints.

The study has several contributions. The empirical literature on monetary transmission in the WAEMU and WANZ countries remained largely rooted in traditional theories of money view. Works that recognized the relevance of the credit view are often constrained themselves to add only one variable of bank credit in the arguments that explain growth and inflation. If the factors that determine the sensitivity of the supply of bank loans to monetary shocks have been highlighted in theoretical terms, they have not been evaluated empirically. Based on credit view theories and by trying to study a factor capable of blocking the transmission, this research provides an explanation of the weak relationship revealed by previous studies between the monetary instruments and the outcome variables.

The VAR model is the most used technique by studies of monetary policy in the WAEMU countries. The techniques of cointegration in panel that have very interesting statistical properties, is a second contribution of the article.

The bank concentration in the WAEMU is assessed by the Herfindhal-Hirschman Index (*HHI*) using an original database that I compiled from publications of the Commission bancaire of the WAEMU on individual balance sheets of banks. This database is another contribution of the study.

The examination of the implications for WANZ countries is the fourth contribution of the paper because it can recommend additional points on the agenda of the construction of the monetary union.

The article is structured as follows. In Section 2, I present a discussion of the literature on both theoretical and empirical effects of banking industries structure on the monetary transmission. The review of theoretical work is structured around two main models of economics of banking: the *Structure-Conduct-Performance* (SCP) model and the *Efficient Structure* (ES) hypothesis. Each of these two competing hypotheses can allow us to foresee an inhibiting effect of bank concentration on the effectiveness of monetary policy. The empirical results of previous studies have hardly considered explicitly the impact of concentration along with the bank credit supply as variable of interest. In any case this issue has not been empirically addresses, to my knowledge, in African economies.

Using *HHI* Index, section 3 seeks to assess the concentration of national banking industries in the WAEMU. It appears that, although this index is still significant, it has globally decreased over the period 1991-2006 except in Togo. Section 4 provides a description of the variables, data, strategy and econometric techniques. The empirical analysis is based on panel series, previously subject to unit root tests of Im, Pesaran and Shin (1997, 2002 and 2003) and Hadri (2000). These tests conclude that the data are nonstationary. Panel cointegration analysis is then made using Pedroni (2004) and Kao (1999) tests which reveal the existence of co-integrating vectors that are estimated by the *Fully Modified Ordinary Least Squares technique (FMOLS)* of Pedroni (1996). Section 5 discusses the results of the study. It appears that bank concentration hampers the BCEAO monetary transmission. The effect of inefficiency resulting from this market structure is at least equivalent to six times the effect of monetary policy as measured actually. On the basis of these econometric results, section 6 draws the implications for the WAMZ. Concluding remarks are made in Section 7.

BANK CONCENTRATION AND MONETARY POLICY TRANSMISSION

Theoretical argumentations can be used to explain the effects of bank concentration on the effectiveness of monetary policy (2.1). Empirical works are focused on the evaluation of these theoretical assumptions (2.2).

Theoretical approach

A substantial literature is devoted to the study of concentration and competition in the banking sector because of the prominent economic role played by banks and policy implications which can be inferred from these works (Berger et al. 2003). Authors have examined the effects of concentration and competition on the performance of the sector, and their impacts on the monetary transmission. The credit view literature explored industrial organization of banking systems, because this, like asymmetric information, is decisive in the transmission of the monetary shocks (Lensink and Sterken, 2002). As the organization of the banking industry determines the behavior of banks, it may affect their responses to changes in policy as it. Two competing models from researches on industrial economics, try to explain the effects of market structure on the performance of banking sector and the policy transmission.

Structure-Conduct-Performance (SCP) model

The conventional model of industrial economics predicts that banks behaviors are determined by the structure of the banking industry which key factors are the number, the size and the concentration of suppliers (Dietsch 1992). According to this model originally formalized by Bain (1951), the quantities and prices of banks' products are determined by the degree of competition and concentration. Concentration reflects a situation of no competition (or very low competition) which induces the same behaviors and outcomes of monopoly or oligopoly markets. In situation of market concentration, some banks are able to extract monopoly rents. They determine production levels and prices which are socially suboptimal, but consistent with maximum levels of profitability. These big banks have market power, and then can absorb changes in monetary policy to protect their profitability. Therefore they are less sensitive to policy impulses. In other words a monetary shock will have less impact on interest rates and credit levels in concentrated markets relative to a situation of competition. Particularly larger banks have less incentive to automatically and immediately transmit the impulses that could undermine their profitability, while small banks are more constrained to these impulses.

Khemraj (2008) proposed a transmission model for a developing economy whose banking sector is oligopolistic and characterized by excess liquidity. He designed his research on previous theoretical frameworks such as the pioneering work of Klein (1971) on monopolistic bank industrial organization. Khemraj model is based on a central assumption: the credit markets and government securities are oligopolistic. In these markets the buyers (mostly banks) are in very small number so that they have market power. They have a pricing policy that consists of an increase in their marginal cost and the risk-free interest rate. They require a minimum interest rate before any loan and below this rate they prefer to accumulate liquidity surpluses. This is reflected by a horizontal line of their preference for liquidity's curve[3] at a high interest rate. Using stimulations, the author shows that a liquidity shock from the Central Bank lead to no shift, or very small, in bank loans in the flat part of the curve.

Ouédraogo (2010) proposed an adaptation of Khemraj's model to WAEMU economies and drew several theoretical propositions such as an inhibition effect of concentration on the sensitivity of bank loans to BCEAO monetary impulses.

---

3 Khemraj (2008) verifies this hypothesis on data from several African countries whose economies including Zambia, Namibia, Uganda, and Tanzania. In my thesis pending defense (CERDI, 2010), I show that data from Ivory Coast are consistent with this hypothesis.

The "Efficient Structure" hypothesis

In contrast to the SCP model, the hypothesis of the *"Efficient Structure"* attributed to Demsetz (1973) and others associates market concentration to greater efficiency of large banks rather than the use of market power. The efficient management of some banks gives them more important market share and profitability and leads to greater concentration. The difference in efficiency explains the differences in response to monetary policy.

Large banks are more efficient and then more able to absorb monetary shocks so that a more concentrated banking industry will result, all things being equal, in a lower credit channel. In any case, the expected effect of concentration on the credit channel is the same in the two competing hypothesis with only one difference. In fact, the predictions of the two models differ according to the direction of monetary policy (Lensink and Sterken, 2002). According to the hypothesis of efficiency, the policy transmission is symmetrical in situation of expansion or contraction. However, an asymmetry exists between the two situations according to the SCP model. Banks with market power will be quicker to send a tightening of monetary policy on loans conditions and deposits.

Empirical literature

Empirically, the impact of banking industry structure on the policy transmission has often been examined through the effects on interest rates and the amount of loans. Several studies have shown interest rate viscosity or asymmetry of transmission following the direction of policy in a context of low concentration or banking competition. According to the pioneering models of imperfect competition of Klein (1971) and Monti (1972), banks use their market power to set appropriate interest rates. Changes in interest rates also depend on the conditions of competition in the sector. Leuvensteijn and al. (2008) analyze the impact of competition on deposit rates and bank loans over the period of 1994-2004 in European countries. They find that the high the competition, the low the gap between interest rates. Using error-correction model (ECM), they show that bank interest rates are more sensitive to changes in market rates in a competitive situation.

Maudos and Fernández de Guevara (2004) show that an increase in the market power of banks leads to higher net interest margins in the European Union. This finding is similar to those of Corvoisier and Gropp (2002). Both authors show that in concentrated markets, the interest rates charged to borrowers are higher, while those of deposits are lower. Cottarelli and Kourelis (1994) and Borio and Fritz (1995) find that the transmission of monetary policy is constrained by the stickiness of interest rates in an uncompetitive environment. On an international sample, Cottarelli and Kourelis (1994) find no effect of different levels of concentration on the transmission of monetary policy. On the other hand, is the perspective of contestable markets (Baumol, Panzar and Willig, 1982), they find that the barriers to entry in the banking industry limit the effects of monetary shocks. For Adams and Amel (2005), this result could be due to the hypothesis of the study that assigns a nationwide level to banks. Hannan and Berger (1991) test with success the price rigidity in the U.S. banking industry. For both authors, concentrated markets are experiencing viscosity of interest rate. However, they show an asymmetry of transmission following the cycle of monetary policy. In a period of policy tightening, the adjustment of bank rates is quicker, tending to show collusion between banks. Cottarelli and al. (1995) confirm this result for Italy. The rigidity of interest rates is asymmetric depending on the cycle of monetary policy. The results of Graeve and al. (2004) indicate that Belgian banks which have a market power have also a less competitive pricing policy. Using an indicator of deregulation designed by Gual (1999), Mojon (2001) shows that bank competition allows rapid adjustment of bank deposit rates consecutively with lower money market rates in the Euro zone. By contrast, it tends to reduce incentives for upward adjustments in a very tight market conditions. Gropp and al. (2007), De Bondt (2005), Sander and Kleimeier (2002, 2004); Scholnick (1996) and Heinemann and Schüler (2002) give proof to asymmetries in policy transmission. The bank competition is associated with more favorable pricing practices to customers. As a prelude to the common European currency Kashyap and Stein (1997) review a range of factors that could potentially affect the credit channel in European countries. They emphasize the role of bank concentration. From various indicators of concentration, they distinguish groups of countries according to the potential impact on policy transmission. Cecchetti (1999) takes the same perspective and assesses the concentration of banking in the European Union countries, in other European countries, in Japan and in the United States. The concentration levels of different banking systems explain in part differences in transmission patterns between these countries. The results of these initial studies on transmission asymmetries between European countries are confirmed by Sørensen and Werner (2006). They show that differences in country-transmission profiles of the monetary policy interest rates are to a certain extent, explained by the disparate levels of competition in national banking sectors. Beside the impact of concentration and price competition in the banking industry, several studies have considered their effects on the quantity of credit and thus on investment and growth.

Using a growth model Pagano (1993) shows that the concentration of banking markets can reduce the volume of loanable funds and thereby weaken the growth. With their market power, banks may administer high loan rates and offer low rates for deposits. In a general equilibrium model Guzman (2000) shows that in case of credit rationing, monopoly banking markets require greater levels of rationing compared to a competitive banking industry.

Adams and Amel (2005) in a study on data from the Community Reinvestment Act over 1996 to 2002 assess the impact of concentration on the transmission of monetary shocks to loans for small businesses in the United States. They introduced in an equation of credit determination, a multiplicative variable between monetary policy and the Herfindahl-Hirschman Index. Using estimation in difference, they get results that tend to show that bank concentration weakens the credit channel.

Recent empirical works based on the EP hypothesis suggest that the structure of banking markets may have multiple effects yet different from those expected from the intuition of the SCP model. For Cetorelli (2001), the effects of banking market structure on the real economy can be considered in terms of trade-off between induced social losses and beneficial consequences; for example on banks investment in the selection of projects (Cetorelli and Peretto, 2000 for example). However this literature is not explicitly linked to the transmission channels.

In sum, it is generally expected that a concentrated banking sector or with little competition has a greater resilience to monetary policy. Countries with high levels of concentration of bank industry will have, all things being equal, a less effective monetary policy, particularly in its ability to influence in a desirable way prices and quantity of loans. One might say in other words that concentration weakens the bank lending channel. It is precisely this assumption that we want to test for the economies of the WAEMU. Though this assumption is often pointed out in the literature (Nubukpo, 2007, for example) it is not however tested empirically. In brief, how the influence of monetary policy on credit supply is affected by the concentration structure of the banking industry?

BANK CONCENTRATION IN WAEMU

The industrial economics provides concentration indexes used as traditional instruments to measure the structure of a market (Bajo and Salas, 1999). These indexes take into account two essential aspects of industry structure: the number of firms and the unequal distribution of their size. Generally, they are defined by the following formula:

$$CI = \sum_{i=1}^{n} S_i W_i$$

Where CI is the concentration index, S_i the market share of bank i, W_i the weight given to bank i and n the number of banks in the market. Two types of concentration indices can be obtained from this general formula. The first is given by the following formula:

$$CR_k = \sum_{i=1}^{k} S_i$$

Where CR_k is the concentration ratio which is the market share of the *k* largest firms.

The CR_k indicator varies between 0 and 1. If the industry is characterized by a great number of firms which have comparable sizes, the indicator is close to 0. In contrast, the oligopolistic nature of the industry leads to an index close to 1. However, the

FIGURE 10.1: BANK CONCENTRATION IN WAEMU

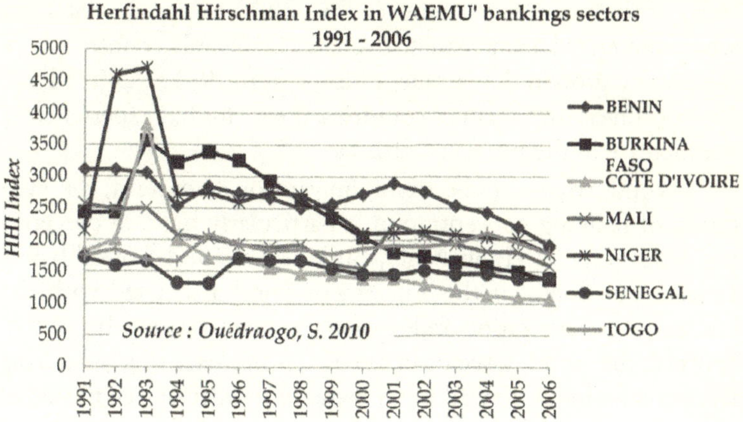

HHI indexes are multiplied by 10000.

index does not differentiate a pure monopoly, where n = 1, from an oligopoly, where n = k, and n> 1 (Bikker and Haaf, 2000). In both cases, $CR_k = 1$. Moreover small firms whose sizes are less than the kth largest bank are not included in the computation of the concentration index, and this is the main limitation of this index.

A second indicator, the Herfindahl-Hirschman Index (HHI), takes into account all the firms in the market. It is obtained by the following formula:

$$HHI = \sum_{i=1}^{n} S_i^2$$

The *HHI* is often used in the SCP model. It gives more weight to major banks and avoids the problem of arbitrary choice of *k* in the ratios CR_k. Though the HHI is more appropriate to measure the industry concentration, it requires however the comprehensive information on market shares of all banks in the sector.

Following Adams and Amel (2005), Berger and al. (2004) and Bos (2004), this study measures the concentration by the *HHI* relative to bank credit market.

Figure 10.1 shows the *HHI* trend over the period 1991-2006 for domestic industries of WAEMU. One can make at least three general observations. First, we observe a fairly clear trend for each country. All banking industries are experiencing a weakening trend of their concentration over the period, except that of Togo where the *HHI* has increased. This later is the only country where there was a drop in the number of firms from 1991 to 2005 (Table 10.1 in annex). In the other countries, the sector has experienced a net increase in the number of banks.

Second, whatever the trend, upward or downward, the evolution of banking concentration is particularly high, in descending order respectively in Niger, Burkina Faso and Cote d'Ivoire. Indeed, the slopes of the adjustment lines[4] associated with the scatter of concentration index of these countries are higher. In contrast, the banking sector in Senegal is the least affected during the same period; followed in an increasing order of magnitude of changes respectively by the banking markets of Togo, Benin and Mali. Changes in the number of banks remains a relative cause of concentration of the sector even if it may affect it. In fact, the banking sector in Benin for instance has experienced the largest increase in operating firms. However, the magnitude of changes in the *HHI* in this country is among the smallest.

Thirdly, Côte d'Ivoire and Senegal have the lowest *HHI*. After 1996, the market of Côte d'Ivoire was less concentrated, but prior to that year it was the Senegalese market. The *HHI* in Burkina Faso since 1995 has shown a downward trend toward the concentration level of the two largest economies of the WAEMU. Scores of the country are very close to those of Senegal during the latest years of the period under review.

Assessment of the concentration throughout the last years 2000-2006, revealed that the market was more concentrated in Togo than in Mali and moreover reached the same concentration level as Niger's industry. In recent years, the banking sector in Benin is by far the most concentrated of the WAEMU.

In sum the restructuration of banking industry has led to the sale of some institutions, helped to restore areas previously in crisis and attracted new firms. Due to the combined effect of these different factors and the dynamic sharing of markets, the bank concentration has shown some improvements. There is a decreasing trend

4 The adjustment lines are not reported here to avoid overloading the graphs.

of the concentration in all the countries except Togo, with different rates of progression: decline most pronounced in Niger, Burkina Faso and Côte d'Ivoire, smoother in Senegal, Benin and Mali. The Togolese market place is contrary has been more concentrated.

Anyway all levels of concentration in the banking industries of the WAEMU remain relatively high. In 2005, the two largest banks controlled 34% of the Ivorian market, against 52% in Niger and nearly two-thirds (63%) in Benin. In the same year, the figures for the three largest banks were 47% for Côte d'Ivoire, 70% and 75% respectively for Niger and Benin. In 2005 again, all "national leader" bank controlled at least one-fifth of the total market in their respective country. In Benin, the first bank represented alone nearly half (43%) of the market, against only 34% in Mali. Moreover, asymmetries between countries are important: markets in Ivory Coast, Senegal, Burkina Faso and Mali are, in descending order, the most concentrated. The gap between the *HHI* of countries at both ends of the rankings, Côte d'Ivoire and Benin, is considerable: about one for two.

This configuration of the banking industries may pose a double constraint on the monetary policy. On one hand the concentrated nature of the industry can be a source of inefficiency of monetary impulses, with a decrease in ineffective in almost all countries over the period as the concentration curves were downward sloping. On the other hand the asymmetric effects of the policy of the BCEAO can be reinforced by the disparities between the *HHI* indexes. If this second constraint is related to asymmetries in banking sectors, the first however is due to their resilience against the policy.

Given the limited effectiveness of the policy of the BCEAO, the relevance of an empirical evaluation of the effects of banking structure on the monetary transmission is to identify and measure additional causes; and to work out appropriate strengthening policy in a context where it remains subject to several constraints (Nubukpo, 2002 and 2007; Saxegaard, 2006; Diagne and Doucouré, 2000; etc.).

DATA AND METHODS

Variables and data

The endogenous variable

The objective of the study is to assess the impact of bank concentration on the transmission of BCEAO policy. Like the empirical literature assessing the credit view (Bernanke, 1983; Kashyap, Stein and Wilcox, 1993; Bernanke and Blinder, 1992, Kashyap and Stein, 1994, 1995, 1997, 2000, Kishan and Opiela, 2000 and Adams and Amel, 2005), the endogenous variable chosen is the supply of bank credit to the economy. In credit rationing context, credit supply is the critical factor (Greendwald and Stiglitz, 2003). Demand exceeds supply but lenders have no incentive to increase interest rates because, through adverse selection, it would deteriorate the quality of their portfolios by increasing their risk (Stiglitz and Weiss, 1981). Ultimately the profitability of banks would be affected. In such circumstances, it is likely that movements in interest rates charged by banks are not a perfect informative indicator of market equilibrium. Jaffee and Stiglitz (1990) conclude that where there is credit rationing, the supply of credit is the key variable and is related to monetary shocks than its cost (interest rate).

Monetary policy

BCEAO has two main leading rates: the discount rate is the rate of last resort, and the repo rate. This is an intermediate rate between the discount rate and money market rate. Since liberalization reforms, market mechanisms are the first choice tools in the indirect management of bank liquidity. The handling of the repo rate allows the central bank to influence money market rates. Therefore monetary policy is captured by this indicator, the repo rate, as shown in previous empirical researches (Nubukpo, 2002 and 2007). Based on historical data provided in the central bank website, I arranged the repo rate in annual time series (see variables description in appendix).

The effect of concentration on the transmission of monetary policy to bank

Several empirical studies capture the impact of a bank characteristic (balance sheet variables, market power, concentration, etc.) on the policy transmission through crossed variables (e.g. Kashap and Stein, 1995.1997, 2000 or Farinha and Marques, 2002). Particularly, in their study on the impact of concentration on bank loans in USA, Adams and Amel (2005) used a multiplicative variable. Following their work, I enter into the determining equation of bank loan, a multiplicative variable between monetary policy and bank concentration, to capture the effect of the later on the former.

Others determinants of bank lending

According to the literature a set of determinants of bank loans is used in the credit equation as control variable. These determinants are related to bank characteristics (Bank) and the macroeconomic conditions (Macro). The bank variables included in the equation are: deposits, capitalization, assets and bank liquidity. Deposits, capitalization and assets are expected to be positively related to credit. In contrast a negative coefficient is expected for bank liquidity. The macroeconomic variables are production and prices. Economic activity rises with bank loans while rising prices does the opposite. These variables can also take into account the heterogeneity between different economies of WAEMU.

All variables are in logarithm form except bank concentration and monetary policy.

HHI index were constructed using a database of individual bank balance sheets that I compiled from WAEMU banking commission reports. The macroeconomic variables are from the *World Development Indicator 2008* database and covered the period 1991 to 2006, during which occurred the banking sector liberalization. The construction of variables are reported in the appendix. By choosing *Cred* for bank loan supply, *Pol* for monetary policy, *Concent* for bank concentration, *Bank* and *Macro* for vector of variables, respectively related to the banking sector and to the macroeconomic conditions, i and t indices respectively identifying countries and time, one can write the equation of the credit as follows:

$$logCredit_{it} = \beta_1 Pol_t + \beta_2 Concent_{it} + \beta_3 (Pol \times Concent)_{it} + \gamma logBank_{it} + \delta logMacro_{it} + \alpha_i + \varepsilon_{it} \quad (1)$$

Where α_i are fixed effects for countries and ε_{it} are random error terms. *Logx* indicates the natural logarithm of variable *x*. Under these conditions, coefficients β_1 and β_2 respectively capture the effects of monetary policy and banking concentration; and β_3 reflects the cross effect of these two variables on the bank loan. According to monetary policy theories, a positive monetary shock affects negatively banks' reserves and thus their ability to lend. Therefore, the theoretical prediction gives a negative coefficient to monetary policy: $\beta_1 < 0$. In the SCP model, banking concentration is supposed to lead to non-competitive behaviors which may consist of a downward adjustment of amounts of credit in order to maximize profitability. In these situations, credit rationing may be more pronounced (Guzman, 2000). In this case the effect of concentration on the supply of credit will appear negative: $\beta_2 < 0$. But the sign of the coefficient β_2 may be statistically insignificant or even different from the perspective of the expected multiple effects of the concentration predicted by works supporting the *Efficiency hypothesis* (Ceterolli, 2001). In this case, bank concentration is the result of gains in market shares by more competitive banks as they have more efficient structure. In the context of the WAEMU economies, the hypothesis of efficiency seems highly unlikely given the history of banking industries, low innovation and the gap between the needs of the economy and the supply of bank products. Therefore, I favor the hypothesis of $\beta_2 < 0$. β_3 captures the cross effect of the concentration and monetary shocks on loans. If $\beta_3 > 0$ and significant, one can conclude that bank concentration reduces the impact of monetary policy on credit supply, then the main hypothesis will be verified.

Methods

Unit root tests

To avoid spurious regressions, stationarity analysis is a prerequisite in the econometric treatment of time series. I use two tests of panel unit root: Im, Pesaran and Shin (1997, 2002 and

2003) test, and Hadri (2000) test. The test of Im, Pesaran and Shin (IPS) is based on the null hypothesis of unit root. It allows the alternative hypothesis in a double heterogeneity: heterogeneity in the autoregressive root and the present of a unit root in the panel. Hence it addresses the critics regarding the test of Levin, Lin and Chu (2002) which considers a homogeneous unit root (Hurlin and Mignon, 2005). The IPS test is based on the average individual statistics of Dickey-Fuller and Augmented Dickey-Fuller. It specifies the normally distributed errors. Unlike this test, Hadri (2000) test uses the Lagrange multiplier method and is based on the null hypothesis of stationarity. It also provides a flexible alternative hypothesis to include the simultaneous presence of nonstationary heterogeneous or homogeneous, and stationarity in the panel.

Cointegration tests

Cointegration analysis is done through Pedroni (2004) and Kao (1999) tests. Pedroni (1999, 2004) offers tests of cointegration in multivariate relations while taking into account the heterogeneity of co-integrating vectors. Precisely, it is about seven tests of which fourare based on within dimension (within panel cointegration statistics) and three on the between statistics (panel mean group cointegration statistics). All these tests are based on the null hypothesis of no cointegration. However they differ in their alternative hypothesis. The mean group tests are more general because they allow heterogeneity among individuals. Pedroni tests have however a practical limit. In fact, their implementation with usual software does not allow more than seven variables (six explanatory variables in RATS and seven in Eviews). In these circumstances, only the Kao (1999) test will be done.

The Kao (1999) ADF test is applied on residuals of regressions and can be implemented in the presence of multivariate models under the null hypothesis of no cointegration. Unlike Pedroni (2004) tests, Kao (1999) considers co-integrating vectors homogeneous for all variables. With Monte Carlo simulations, Gutierrez (2003) shows that the smaller the sample size, the more Kao test dominate those of Pedroni. In particular, for low and fixed time dimension (T = 10), when N increases, Kao test is more powerful. Given the small time dimension of the study sample (T = 16), priority is given to the Kao test.

Strategy for estimating cointegration relations

Biases we face, while assuming an asymptotic distribution of OLS estimators, are more accurate in dynamic panel data context than in time series. To avoid this problem, Adams and Amel (2005) estimate their credit equation in difference. However, this strategy has the disadvantage of losing information and this would be very harmful for the data of the study. For nonstationary panel configurations, appropriate techniques can give efficient estimators. These methods include the dynamic ordinary least squares (DOLS) of Kao and Chiang (2000), and Mark and Sul (2003) which are parametric estimators; and a semi-parametric estimator *Fully Modified Ordinary Least Squares (FMOLS)* of Pedroni (2000). I use the latter method. FMOLS estimator takes into account nuisance parameters and possible phenomena of autocorrelation and heteroscedasticity of residuals. It is asymptotically unbiased and normally distributed. It also deals with the endogeneity of explicative variables (Pedroni, 1996 and 2000).

FMOLS estimator offers both individual coefficients as well as group means. The mean group panel estimator allows testing the alternative hypothesis of a cointegrating vector, and remains consistent otherwise. Moreover, in small samples it also has better properties than the pooled panel estimator. For these reasons, the *mean group panel* is preferred (Pedroni, 2000).

Relation (1) can be rewritten as an equation to be estimated by *FMOLS*. Writing down in detail the control variables, we obtain the following equation:

$$logCred_{it} = \beta_{1i}Pol_{t} + \beta_{2i}Concent_{it} + \beta_{3i}(Pol \times Concent)_{it} + \beta_{4i}logCap_{it} + \beta_{5i}LogDep_{it} + \beta_{6i}logLiq_{it} + \beta_{7i}logAss_{it} + \beta_{8i}logProd_{it} + \beta_{9i}logIPC_{it} + \alpha_{i} + \varepsilon_{it} \quad (2)$$

Where log *Cred*= logarithm *Cred* credit to the economy; *Pol* = monetary policy; Concent = bank concentration; *logCap* = log of bank equity capital; *logDep* = logarithm of bank deposits; *logLiquid* = logarithm of bank liquidity; *logAss* = log banking assets; *logProd*

= log of GDP; *logCPI* = logarithm of consumer price index; *i* and *t* correspond respectively to country and time indices.

Only the estimated of average coefficients (panel mean group) will be presented and discussed. In this case, the coefficients of equation (2) lose their index *i* and stand for the group average.

Before presenting the econometric results, let us keep in mind that the central hypothesis of the study is validated when $\beta_3 > 0$. The coefficients β_1, β_2, β_6 and β_9 are expected to be negative while the positive sign is expected for β_4, β_5, β_7 and β_7.

RESULTS

Results of the analysis of the stationarity of the series are presented in Table 10.2 in appendix. The IPS statistics allow accepting the null hypothesis of nonstationarity for all variables. These results are confirmed by the Hadri test which rejects the hypothesis of stationarity for all variables. The research of unit root in first difference is unsuccessful. Indeed, the IPS tests in difference indicate the rejection of the hypothesis of nonstationarity. The Hadri test accepts the stationarity in difference of all variables except credit. For the latter, I consider the results of the IPS test[5]. Therefore, it is established that all variables are integrated of order one (I (1)).

Table 10.3 in appendix, reports the cointegration tests. Of all Pedroni tests, at least two tests reject the null hypothesis of no cointegration for all equations. The two rho tests (panel and group) reject for all equations the null hypothesis of no cointegration. For equation 3 in particular, four tests support the existence of cointegration relationship. Nonetheless, for all equations, the Kao test accepts the alternative hypothesis of cointegration at 1% level (5% for equations 1 and 2). In conclusion, the tests overall support the existence of co-integrating vectors between the variables. The equations under estimation are in cointegration relations. Results of estimations using *FMOLS* method are presented in Table 10.4.

---

5 The Levin, Li and Chu (2002) test (not reported here) supports this result.

Control variables

Overall, the coefficients associated with variables in the seven (7) estimated relations have their expected signs. Bank deposits emerge with a positive and significant coefficient at 1% level. This positive relation between deposits and credit is required in all estimations, the introduction of the multiplicative variable and other variables related to banking sector will not affect the significance of the coefficient. A larger collection of deposits increases loanable resources and encourages banks, other things being equal, to increase the supply of credit. The ratio of deposits keeps a relatively high economic significance in all estimations. Other things held constant, when collection of deposits rises by 10%, the banking sector expands its loans by 6.3% (according to results of Equation 7).

Bank asset is positively associated with a significant coefficient; three out of four at 1% level and only one case 5% level. However, the holding of cash is made at the expense of loans. The coefficient of liquidity is negative and significant at 1% level. The adjustment of credit is 3.2% for an increase of 10% in total balance sheet of the sector, all things being equal (equation 7) against a decline of 1.6% for an increase of 10% in liquidity. The equity capital strengthens the supply of credit in case at 1% level. But this influence is very small in economic terms, like that of liquidity.

The effect of production appears positive and significant in all estimations, at the 1% five times, and two times at 5% level, and this is consistent with the theoretical prediction. Bank loan rises by 2.27% for a 5% increase economic growth. Again, as expected, the influence of prices appears negative. The coefficient of price is significant at 1% level in all our estimations. Inflation hampers bank activities. A 5.5% reduction in credit supply is associated with an increase 5% in the general level price (equation 7).

Monetary Policy, bank concentration and the crossed effect

The impact of monetary policy is consistent with the theoretical prediction and remains significant in all equations. Monetary shocks appeared in fact with a negative and significant coefficient at 1% level. Monetary shocks appeared in fact with a negative and significant coefficient at 1% level. This result is robust to all control variables. A positive monetary shock reduces, other things being equal, the supply of credit. However the coefficients of the monetary variable are very small like in previous empirical results (Nubukpo, 2002; Ouédraogo, 2008, 2010a).

HHI index is negatively related to the supply of credit in all cases. Statistically, the effect of concentration is significant at the 1% level, five (5) times out of six (6). The only estimation for which the coefficient is not significant, excludes several control variables. Whatever the case, the introduction of all control variables and the multiplicative does not alter the significance of HHI coefficient. This reveals the consistency of the results with the theoretical arguments of SCP model. Bank concentration, in this case, characterizes a situation of weak competition which allows banks to provide a level of credit close to the monopoly equilibrium credit supply. Competition in the sector is so similar to a Cournot model (Cetorelli, 1999).

A first indication of the impact of bank concentration on monetary transmission can be drawn from comparing the coefficients of the monetary policy within the first three (3) estimated equations (Table 10.4). Indeed, one can observe that by introducing the *HHI* index in equation 2, the coefficient of monetary policy rises in absolute terms as compared to equation 1. The same coefficient rises (in absolute value) when we pass from equation 2 to equation 3; that means we have the policy and concentration factors along with their multiplicative factor in the equation. In other words, after controlling for concentration, the influence of monetary policy appears more important, and the transmission is further enhanced as we introduce the cross effect between policy and concentration. Since the effect of monetary policy is weaker when the influence of concentration is not isolated, one can infer that concentration decreases monetary policy transmission. This is an initial proof for the central hypothesis of the study. Still the investigation strategy is mainly based on the consideration of the multiplicative factor between monetary policy and concentration.

The variable of interest is associated with a positive coefficient and significant at 1% level. This is a very interesting result, as in all regressions monetary policy and concentration have their expected

Table 10.4: FMOLS estimations of the impact of bank concentration on BCEAO monetary policy transmission to bank lending

Dependant variable: Log bank loans							
Explanatory variables	(1)	(2)	(3)	(4)	(5)	(6)	(7)
Log GDP	0.99*** (5.47)	0.95*** (4.16)	0.86*** (4.40)	0.71*** (3.02)	0.26** (2.28)	1.31*** (4.67)	0.54** (2.18)
Log Prices	-1.35*** (-8.04)	-1.17*** (-7.88)	-1.01*** (-4.42)	-0.76*** (-3.11)	-1.25*** (-9.41)	-0.80*** (-4.03)	-1.11*** (-10.03)
Log Deposits	0.67*** (7.75)	0.57*** (7.68)	0.62*** (7.37)	0.43*** (4.03)	0.62*** (7.71)	0.07*** (2.92)	0.63*** (9.34)
Monetary policy	-0.03*** (-2.92)	-0.05*** (-4.27)	-0.20*** (-7.03)	-0.19*** (-8.15)	-0.17*** (-7.46)	-0.15*** (-6.61)	-0.10*** (-4.52)
HHI		-0.56 (-1.16)	-6.02*** (-5.85)	-5.99*** (-6.82)	-5.92*** (-7.21)	-4.42*** (-5.64)	-2.82*** (-4.44)
HHI × Monetary Policy			**0.79*** (5.96)**	**0.78*** (7.10)**	**0.76*** (7.37)**	**0.54*** (5.82)**	**0.31*** (4.57)**
Log Asset				0.46*** (4.45)	0.92*** (7.10)	0.37** (2.20)	0.32* (1.82)
Log Liquidity					-0.14*** (-9.02)		-0.16*** (-9.72)
Log Equity Capital						-0.16 (-1.38)	0.14*** (2.65)
Observations		112	112	112	112	112	112

t statistics are in brackets. ***, ** and * indicate the significance respectively at 1%, 5% and 10% levels.

Table 10.6: FMOLS estimations of the impact of bank concentration on the monetary policy transmission in order to determine the economical size of the concentration effect

Dependant variable: Log bank loans						
Explanatory variables	(1)	(2)	(3)	(4)	(5)	(6)
Log GDP	0.99*** (5.47)	0.86*** (4.40)	0.86* (1.89)	0.71*** (3.02)	0.69** (2.13)	1.31*** (4.67)
Log Prices	-1.35*** (-8.04)	-1.01*** (-4.42)	-0.98*** (-4.15)	-0.76*** (-3.11)	-0.87*** (-3.79)	-0.80*** (-4.03)
Log Deposits	0.67*** (7.75)	0.62*** (7.37)	0.40*** (3.20)	0.43*** (4.03)	0.51*** (4.32)	0.07*** (2.92)
Monetary policy	**-0.03*** (-2.92)**	**-0.20*** (-7.03)**	**-0.03*** (-3.81)**	**-0.19*** (-8.15)**	**-0.02** (-2.40)**	**-0.15*** (-6.61)**
HHI		-6.02*** (-5.85)		-5.99*** (-6.82)		-4.42*** (-5.64)
HHI × Monetary Policy		**0.79*** (5.96)**		**0.78*** (7.10)**		**0.54*** (5.82)**
Log Asset			0.43*** (3.76)	0.46*** (4.45)	0.27 (1.55)	0.37** (2.20)
Log Equity Capital					0.03 (-0.26)	-0.16 (-1.38)
Observations	112	112	112	112	112	112
t statistics are in brackets. ***, ** and * indicate the significance respectively at 1%, 5% and 10% levels.						

signs and always emerge with significant coefficients. According to the assumptions we made on the coefficients of the variables, we deduce that the negative impact of a tightening of the monetary policy on credit supply is affected by bank concentration. In other words, bank concentration reduces the effectiveness of monetary policy by weakening the credit channel.

How important is this inhibition effect of bank concentration on the effectiveness of the BCEAO policy? One might think *a priori* to compare the size of the multiplicative variable coefficients on one hand, and on the other, the coefficient the monetary policy. However, since these factors have different measurement unit, every comparison would lead to spurious results. An alternative would be to compare the size of the coefficients of the single variable of monetary policy, size obtained in the estimations where the effect of concentration on policy is isolated to the size obtained without controlling the effect of concentration. The results reported in Table 10.6 aim at this goal. First, the cointegration relations are highlighted, as illustrated in Table 10.5 in Appendix.

Two major observations can be made. First, it appears that every time the concentration effect is isolated, mainly by including the HHI and HHI x Monetary Policy, the coefficient of the monetary policy is always higher in absolute value. In fact, according to estimations (1) and (2) of Table 10.6, the coefficient of monetary shocks pass from - 0.03 to - 0.20 (while in it pass from - 0.03 to - 0.19 for results (3) and (4); and from - 0.02 to - 0.15 for results (5) for (6)). As mentioned above, this supports the results of a negative impact of the concentrated structure of the banking industry on the sensitivity of bank loans to monetary shocks.

Secondly, comparison of the monetary policy coefficients of between the estimates with and without controlling the effects of the concentration gives almost similar proportions. From estimation (1) to (2), the effect of the policy appears 6.7 fold stronger. This proportion is 6.3 and 7.5 respectively from estimation (3) to (4) and from (5) to (6).

The same estimations, as well as those in Tables 1 and 2, replicated by using alternative indicators of concentration (CR_1, CR_2 and CR_3) lead to similar results, although less robust[6].

These results validate the main hypothesis of the study. Clearly, the impact of concentration on the monetary transmission is at least six (6) times the measured effect of the policy. In other words, the channel of policy transmission - the offered channel - is blocked at 6/7th by the concentrated structure of banking sector. Or, in more optimistic terms, one could say that there are opportunities for a significant strengthening of BCEAO policy *via* a reduction of the oligopolistic nature of banking industries.

The concentration of the banking industry is a source of inefficiency for the transmission of monetary policy in the WAEMU. The resulting inefficiency is equivalent to more than six times the transmission actually measured.

---

6 These results are not reported here and are available on request.

IMPLICATIONS

A corollary can be drawn from the main econometric results: the dispersion of the concentration profiles between the different banking industries of the WAEMU (in 2004 Benin *HHI* was the double of the *HHI* of Cote d'Ivoire) induces asymmetric effects to monetary policy. In other words, the common policy is transmitted asymmetrically in the banking sectors conditional to their level of concentration. This is consistent with results obtained in the European Union and the United States with respect to various financial structures (Kashap and Stein, 1995.1997; Cechetti, 1999; Mojon, 2000; Corvoisier and Gropp, 2002, Farinha and Marques, 2002; Kakes and Sturm, 2002, etc.). It shows that monetary unions must consider the differential impact of their common policy, differences arising from differences in their financial structures.

Asymmetric profiles of the banking industries concentration will not be automatically disappear with the achievement of the ECOWAS common currency. Conversely, banking structures are already very different. Bank concentration is relatively lower in Ghana than in Cote d'Ivoire, yet the former has the least concentrated banking industry in the WAEMU. In 2000 the HHI was 1070 for Ghana for 1360 for Côte d'Ivoire. In 2006, this index was 870[7] in Ghana against 1060 in Côte d'Ivoire. Relative to WAEMU countries, and compared with the banking sector of Ghana, the Nigerian industry seems even more concentrated (2100 and 1790 for Nigeria; and 1070 and 870 for Ghana respectively in 2000 and 2006; a ratio of one for two). Comparison of Ghana and Guinea-Bissau in 2000 provides an extreme case because the banking industry of the latter country was a pure monopoly. Although we were unable to compute the concentration indicators for other economies in the WAMZ, the differences are probably more pronounced than within the WAEMU countries alone. In all cases, these different levels of concentration, if they remain unchanged the advent of WANZ; will alter the transmission of the common monetary shocks. Several other important differences between the financial structures of the WAMZ countries are able to deepen these asymmetries transmission. The financial sectors have very

7 HHI indexes are multiplied by 10000.

different size and their performances are not identical. Moreover, legislation and bank regulation policies are singular.

A double implication can be drawn for the WAMZ. First, a successful monetary policy needs to take into account the structure of banking sector. Secondly, the construction of the monetary union should expand the criteria of convergence to harmonization of policies, and banking and financial structures. The persistent disparities in the WAEMU after several decades of union show that asymmetries do not cancel out by themselves. It seems appropriate to include in the agenda of the monetary union construction some chapters of harmonization of regulation policies, and of bank and financial sectors in general.

All the same, it is unlikely that a program of convergence of financial structures leads to a complete reduction of differences, hence the necessity to cope with the remaining asymmetries. The institutional architecture of the common monetary policy can be frame out with flexibility in order to take into account these residual differences between financial sectors.

CONCLUSION

Based on the modern theories of monetary transmission that assign a prominent role for banks, this study has assessed the impact of bank concentration on patterns of transmission of monetary shocks in the countries of WAEMU. Using panel cointegration techniques, including tests of Pedroni (2004) and Kao (1999), cointegration relations have been highlighted and subsequently estimated by the *FMOLS* estimator proposed by Pedroni (1996). The study shows that bank concentration affects negatively the supply of credit. This result seems to be consistent with theoretical arguments of the SCP model. The concentration is characteristic in this case by a Cournot competition model (Cetorelli, 1999). The effect of concentration on the transmission of monetary policy is captured by a multiplicative variable.

The results indicate that bank concentration affects the transmission of BCEAO policy. The relative ineffectiveness of monetary policy is itself conditioned by the disparity between the country banking markets. In fact, differences in level of bank concentration are sources of asymmetries in the transmission of policy within economies. Regulatory policies must consider concentration and competition. At least, these policies could be calibrated so as to take into account, not only their effects on the effectiveness of monetary policy, but also on the financing of the economy by banks.

Moreover, the contrasting profiles of concentration in banking sectors of the WAWMU and WAMZ are not without impact on the monetary transmission. Therefore the construction of the West African Monetary Zone should expand the convergence criteria for the harmonization of policies and banking and financial structures.

BIBLIOGRAPHY

Adams, R. M. et Amel, D. F. (2005). "The Effects of Local Banking Market Structure on the Bank-Lending Channel of Monetary Policy", Finance and Economics Discussion Series 2005-16. Washington: Board of Governors of the Federal Reserve System, 2005.

Altunbas, Yener, Fazylov, Otabek, et Molyneux, Philip (2002). "Evidence on the Bank Lending Channel in Europe," Journal of Banking and Finance, 26(11), pp. 2093-2110.

Bain J. (1951). "Relation of the profit rate to industry concentration: American manufacturing", Quarterly Journal of Economics, vol. 65.

Bajo, O. et Salas, R. (1999). "Inequality foundations of concentration measures: an application to the Hannah-Kay indices", ftp://ftp.econ.unavarra.es/pub/DocumentosTrab/DT9901.PDF.

Berger, A.N., Herring, R.J. et Szegö, G.P. (1995). "The role of capital in financial institutions", Journal of Banking and Finance, Vol. 19, N° 3-4, June, pp. 393-430.

Bernanke, Ben S., et Alan S. Blinder (1988): "Credit, Money, and Aggregate Demand," American Economic Review, 78(2), pp. 435-39.

Bernanke, Ben S., et Alan S. Blinder (1992). "The Federal Funds Rate and the Channels of Monetary Transmission," American Economic Review, 82(4), pp. 901-21.

Bernanke, Ben et Gertler, Mark (1995). "Inside the Black Box: The Credit Channel of Monetary Policy Transmission," Journal of Economic Perspectives, 9(4), pp.27-48.

Bernanke, B., M. Gertler et S. Gilchrist (1999). "The Financial Accelerator in a Quantitative Business Cycle Framework," in J. Taylor et M. Woodford, eds., Handbook of Macroeconomics, Volume 1c (North Holland: New York).

Bikker, Jacob A., et Haaf, Katharina (2002). "Competition, Concentration, and Their Relationship: An Empirical Analysis of the Banking Industry, " Journal of Banking and Finance, 26(11), pp. 2191-2214.

Bikker, Jacob A., Finnie, Paul. et Spierdijk, Laura (2007). "The Impact of Market Structure, Contestability and Institutional Environment on Banking Competition", Utrecht School of Economics Tjalling C. Koopmans Research Institute Discussion Paper Series 07-29, http://www.koopmansinstitute.uu.nl.

Bresnahan, Timothy F. 1989. "Empirical Studies of Industries with Market Power." In *Handbook of Industrial Organization*, Volume II, edited by Richard Schmalensee and Robert D. Willig. Amsterdam, Elsevier Science: 1011-57.

Carlino G. A. et Robert H. DeFina: (1996). "Does Monetary Policy Have Differential Regional Effects?" Federal Reserve Bank of Philadelphia Business Review, March/April 1996.

Carlino, G. A. et DeFina, R. (1998). "The Differential Regional Effects of Monetary Policy, "The Review of Economics and Statistics, 34: 572-87.

Carlino, Gerald A. and Robert DeFina. 1999. "The Differential Effects of Monetary Policy: Evidence from the U.S. States, " *Journal of Regional Science*, 39: 339-58.

Cecchetti, Stephen G. (1995). "Distinguishing Theories of the Monetary Transmission Mechanism." Federal Reserve Bank of St. Louis Review, 77(3), pp. 83-97

Cecchetti, Stephen G. (1999). "Legal Structure, Financial Structure, and the Monetary Policy Transmission Mechanism, " Federal Reserve Bank of New York Economic Policy Review, 5(2), pp. 9-28.22

Cetorelli, N. (1999). "Competitive analysis in banking: Appraisail of the methodologies", Federal Reserve Bank of Chicago, Economic Perspectives, 1er Trimestre, 23 (1).

Corvoisier, Sandrine, et Gropp, Reint (2002). "Bank Concentration and Retail Interest Rates, "Journal of Banking and Finance, 26(11), pp. 2155-2189.

Cottarelli, Carlo, et Angeliki Kourelis (1994). "Financial Structure, Lending Rates, and the Transmission Mechanism of Monetary Policy, " International Monetary Fund Staff Papers, 41(4), pp. 587-623.

Diagne, A. et Doucouré, F. B. (2000). « Les Canaux de Transmission de la Politique Monétaire dans les Pays de l'UEMOA », Mineo, C.R.E.A, FASEG, Université Check Anta Diop, Dakar, juillet 2000, 33p.

Doe L. et S. Diarrisso (1998). «De l'origine monétaire de l'inflation dans les pays de l'UEMOA», (480/481/482), avril/mai/juin.

Diop P. L. (1998). «L'impact des taux directeurs de la BCEAO sur les taux débiteurs des banques», (483/484), juillet/août/septembre.

Freixas, Xavier, et Jean-Charles Rochet (1998). MicroEconomics of Banking. The MIT Press, Cambridge, Massachusetts.

Gutierrez, L. (2003). "On the power of panel cointegration tests : a Monte Carlo comparison", Economics Letters, 80, pp. 105-111.

Hadri, K. (2000) : "Testing for Unit Roots in Heterogeneous Panel Data", Econometrics Journal, 3, 148-161.

Hannan, Timothy H., et Allen N. Berger (1991). "The Rigidity of Prices: Evidence from the Banking Industry," American Economic Review, 81(4), pp. 938-945.

Honohan, P. (1993): «Financial sector failures in Western Africa», *The Journal of Modern Africa Studies*, 31, 1, 1993, 49-65.

Hurlin, C. et Mignon, V. (2005). "Une synthèse des tests de racine unitaire sur données de panel", Economie et Prévision, 169-170-171, pp. 253-294

Hurlin, C. et Mignon, V. (2006). "Une Synthèse des Tests de Cointégration sur Données dePanel", .

Im, K.S., Pesaran, M.H. et Shin, Y. (1997). "Testing for Unit Roots in Heterogenous Panels", DAE, Working Paper 9526, University of Cambridge.

Im, K.S., Pesaran, M.H. et Shin, Y. (2002). "Testing for Unit Roots in Heterogenous Panels", revised version of the DAE, Working Paper 9526, University of Cambridge.

Im, K.S., Pesaran, M.H. et Shin, Y. (2003). "Testing for unit roots in heterogeneous panels", Journal of Econometrics, 115, pp. 53-74.

Kao, C. (1999). "Spurious regression and residual-based tests for cointegration in panel data", Journal of Econometrics, 90, pp. 1-44.

Kao, C. et Chiang, M.H. (2000). "On the estimation and inference of a cointegrated regression in panel data", Advances in Econometrics, 15, edited by B. Baltagi et C. Kao, pp. 179-222, Elsevier Science.

Kakes, J., et Sturm, J.E., (2002). "Monetary policy and bank lending: Evidence from German banking groups". Journal of Banking and Finance 26, this issue.

Kashyap, A.K., et Stein, J.C., (1995a). "Monetary policy and bank lending". In: Mankiw, N.G. (Ed.), Monetary Policy. Chicago University Press, Chicago, IL, pp. 221–256.

Kashyap, A.K., et Stein, J.C., (1995b). "The impact of monetary policy on bank balance sheets". Carnegie-Rochester Series on Public Policy 42, 142–196.

Kashyap, A.K., et Stein, J.C. (1997). "The role of banks in monetary policy: A survey with implications for the European Monetary Union". Federal Reserve Bank of Chicago Economic Perspectives September–October, 2–18.

Kashyap, A.K., et Stein, J.C., (2000). "What do a million observations on banks say about the transmission of monetary policy? The American Economic Review 90 (3), 407–428.

La Porta, Rafael, Florencio Lopez-de-Silanes, Andrei Shleifer, and Robert W. Vishny. (1997). "Legal Determinants of External Finance." *Journal of Finance* 52: 1131-1150.

La Porta, Rafael, Florencio Lopez-de-Silanes, Andrei Shleifer, and Robert W. Vishny (1998). "Law and Finance." *Journal of Political Economy* 106: 1113-1155.

Lensink, R et Sterken, E. (2002). "Monetary transmission and bank competition in the EMU", Journal of Banking & Finance 26 (2002) 2065–2075.

Leuvensteijn, M. , Sørensen, C. K., Bikker, J.A. et Rixtel, A.A.R.J.M., (2008). "Impact of bank competition on the interest rate pass-through in the euro area", Tjalling C. Koopmans Research Institute Discussion Paper Series nr: 08-08

Mojon, B. (2000). «Structures financières et transmission de la politique monétaire en Europe, analyses comparatives de l'Allemagne, la France, l'Italie et le Royaume-Uni, » Working Papers 1998-12, CEPII research center.

Nachane, D M, Ray, P et Ghosh, S. (2001). "Does monetary policy have differential state-level effects? An empirical evaluation" Economic and Political Weekly November 23, 2002.

Nubukpo, K. K. (2002). « L'impact de la variation des taux d'intérêt directeurs de la BCEAO sur l'inflation et la croissance dans l'UMOA », Notes d'Information et Statistiques de la BCEAO, 2002, juin, N°526.

Nubukpo, K. K. (2007a). « Politique monétaire et servitude volontaire : la gestion du Franc CFA par la BCEAO », Politique africaine N°105, Khartala, Paris, mars 2007.

Nubukpo, K. K. (2007b). « L'efficacité de la Politique Monétaire en Situation d'Incertitude et d'Extraversion: Le Cas de l'Union Economique et Monétaire Ouest Africaine (UEMOA) », The European Journal of Development Research, Volume 19, Issue 3 September 2007 , pages 480 – 495.

Ouédraogo, Seydou, (2007). «Banque et transmission de la politique monétaire dans l'UEMOA : une analyse théorique », working paper.

Ouédraogo, Seydou, (2008). «Canal du prêt bancaire dans l'UEMOA : une approche en panel non stationnaire », working paper.

Ouédraogo, Seydou, (2010 a). «Libéralisation financière, concentration bancaire, excès de liquidité bancaire et transmission de la politique monétaire dans l'UEMOA », article proposé pour le prix du Gouverneur Fadiga, BCEAO.

Ouédraogo, Seydou, (2010 b). « Concentration bancaire et efficacité de la politique monétaire dans l'UEMOA », communication 5eme colloque BCEAO/Universités Centres de recherches, Dakar 24 et 25 mai 2010.

Pedroni, P. (1996). "Fully modified OLS for heterogeneous cointegrated panels and the case of purchasing power parity", Working Paper in Economics, Indiana University.

Pedroni, P. (1999). "Critical values for cointegration tests in heterogenous panels with multiple regressors", Oxford Bulletin of Economics and Statistics, S1, 61, pp. 653-670.

Pedroni, P. (2004). "Panel cointegration. Asymptotic and finite sample properties of pooled time series tests with an application to the PPP hypothesis", Econometric Theory, 20(3), pp. 597-625.

Rajan, Raghuram G., et Luigi Zingales. (1998). "Financial Dependence and Growth." American Economic Review 88, 559-586.

Appendix

Table 10.1: Number of banks by country in WAEMU

	Benin	Burkina Faso	Côte d'Ivoire	Mali	Niger	Senegal	Togo
1991	4	8	16	7	7	10	9
1992	4	8	15	7	6	10	9
1993	4	8	14	7	5	9	9
1994	5	7	15	7	5	9	8
1995	5	5	15	7	5	9	7
1996	5	5	15	7	6	9	7
1997	5	6	15	7	6	9	7
1998	5	7	15	7	6	9	7
1999	5	7	15	9	7	10	7
2000	5	7	15	9	7	10	7
2001	6	7	15	10	7	11	7
2002	6	7	16	9	7	11	7
2003	7	7	16	9	7	12	7
2004	9	8	16	10	8	12	6
2005	11	9	19	11	9	13	7
2006	12	11	18	12	10	18	10
2007	12	12	18	13	10	16	11
2008	12	12	18	13	10	16	11

Source: synthesis of the author from various annual reports of the banking commission of the WAEMU.

Table 10.2: Unit root tests

	Tests in level		Tests in difference	
Variables	*IPS*	*Hadri*	*IPS*	*Hadri*
Log Bank loans	0.33152	5.23897	-2.63777	1.84699
Log Deposits	1.56538	6.87373	-3.38008	0.48502
Log GDP	0.25190	7.18898	-3.25414	0.27496
Log total Asset	0.03627	6.61693	-3.65838	1.39080
Log bank Liquidity	-0.94195	5.04885	-3.56605	1.58547
Log Prices	-0.77125	6.55859	-3.72602	0.01206
Monetary Policy	-1.01616	10.6558	-9.38219	-0.22926
Log Equity capital	-0.65421	3.76140	-5.72352	0.42748
HHI	-1.26774	12.0367	-4.87565	1.06875
HHI x Monetary Policy	-0.40959	3.67166	-4.47307	0.75146

All statistics are N(0, 1). Tests include intercept and trend.

Table 10.3: Cointegration Tests

Equations	KAO ADF	Pedroni tests						
		Pedroni Panel				Pedroni Group		
		v-Stat	rho-Stat	PP-Stat	ADF-Stat	rho-Stat	PP-Stat	ADF-Stat
1	-2.250803	-1.859512	3.325370	-1.008134	-1.376448	4.371365	-9.064395	-1.329875
2	-2.351122	-2.654155	3.817553	0.174265	-2.095211	4.772324	-7.943524	-2.057793
3	-2.146675	-3.511588	4.548665	0.317726	0.328521	5.219760	-7.721049	-0.948292
4	-3.118636							
5	-3.199827							
6	-3.161921							
7	-3.138855							
All statistics are N(0, 1). Pedroni tests include intercept and trend.								

Table 10.5: Cointegration tests for regressions assessing the economic importance of the effect of concentration on the monetary transmission (Table 10.6).

Equations	KAO ADF	Pedroni tests						
		Pedroni Panel				Pedroni Group		
		v-Stat	rho-Stat	PP-Stat	ADF-Stat	rho-Stat	PP-Stat	ADF-Stat
1	-2.250803	-1.859512	3.325370	-1.008134	-1.376448	4.371365	-9.064395	-1.329875
2	-2.146675	-3.511588	4.548665	0.317726	0.328521	5.219760	-7.721049	-0.948292
3	-3.495064	-2.938938	4.084634	-1.979311	2.272216	4.937681	-8.546119	2.905723
4	-3.118636							
5	-3.700118	-2.673750	4.316282	-2.089951	3.457670	5.258091	-9.638635	4.489689
6	-3.161921							
All statistics are N(0, 1). Pedroni tests include intercept and trend.								

Table 10.7: Variables description

Variables	Descriptions	Sources
Bank loans	Credit to the economy	Annual balance sheets of bank WAEMU banking commission
Bank deposits	Private deposits	
Equity capital		
Bank asset	Bank total assets	
Bank liquidity	Cash + Interbank (Claims – Depts) including central bank	Calculated from the individual balance sheets of banks of the WAEMU banking commission.
Bank concentration	Herfindahl-Hirschman index according to bank lending	
Monetary policy	BCEAO repo rate. Based on historical data I arranged the repo rate in annual time series	www.bceao.int
Consumer Price Index	Base 100 in 2000. For Benin the 1991 observation is an average value of 1992 and 1993 because series for this country is not available in the WDI 2006 for 1992.	
Production	Current GDP local price	WDI 2008

Chapter 11

STOCK MARKET INTEGRATION IN THE WAMZ: IMPLICATIONS FOR MONETARY UNION

Williams Abraham

INTRODUCTION

The Economic Community of West African States (ECOWAS) aims to establish an economic union among its members by creating a monetary union and adopting common economic, financial, social, and cultural policies. ECOWAS members that are not members of The West African Economic and Monetary Union (UEMOA) agreed to harmonize their monetary and fiscal policies with those of UEMOA, with a view to establishing a monetary union in ECOWAS and preparing the ground for a possible merger with UEMOA. To accelerate the pace of integration, Ghana and Nigeria introduced a Fast-Track Initiative in 2000 to establish a second monetary zone in the region called the West African Monetary Zone (WAMZ), among The Gambia, Ghana, Guinea, Liberia, Nigeria, and Sierra Leone. WAMZ is meant to harmonize the macroeconomic policies of the countries so as to have a common currency in circulation, while ECOWAS expects to achieve monetary integration through the merger of UEMOA and WAMZ once WAMZ becomes a single monetary zone.

This study examines the integration of stock markets in the West African Monetary Zone and the implication for its monetary union objective. The study builds on the works of Twu (2005) and Oshikoya (2009). Twu (2005) argued for the unification of stock markets in the WAMZ, but the study did not employ specific econometric framework to examine the linkages of the Nigerian and Ghanaian stock exchanges in the WAMZ. On the other hand, Oshikoya (2009) noted that financial and economic integration in the WAMZ would play a supportive role to the success of monetary union in the WAMZ. The study however did not pay particular attention to stock market integration. The present study fills these gaps by providing empirical evidence concerning the integration of stock markets in the WAMZ.

The study is arranged into five sections. Section one presents the introduction and objective of the study, while section two reviews related literature. In section three, the research methodology is presented, while section four presents and discusses the result from the finding of the study. Lastly, section five presents the summary of findings and conclusion.

REVIEW OF LITERATURE

Integration refers to a process of unifying markets and enabling convergence of risk adjusted returns on the assets of similar maturity across the markets. On the other hand equity market (also known as stock market) is an aspect of capital market (market for long term funds) where the shares of quoted companies are bought or sold. Advancement in technology has facilitated rapid integration of this market across the globe in recent times.

Ogun and Adenikinju (1992) proposed the need for African Economic Research in the process of integrating African Regions. The economic wisdom for this they argued was from available statistics which suggested that of all the groups in the world, Africans trade least with each other. Though their study related more to integration of trade unions such as the Economic Community of West African States (ECOWAS), East African Community (EAC) and so on, they concluded that African economy stands to gain if markets are integrated.

Rousseau and Wachtel (1999) examined the relationship between equity markets and economic growth using panel data by employing vector autoregressions that apply the generalized method of moment's techniques. The panel data covered 47 countries including Cote d'Ivoire, Kenya, Morocco, Nigeria and Zimbabwe from 1980 to 1995. The study found that Stock markets can promote economic performance by 1) providing an exit mechanism to venture capitalists, 2) offering liquidity to investors that encourages international diversification and portfolio flows, 3) providing firms with access to permanent capital which can then be placed in large, indivisible projects, and 4) generating information about the quality of potential investments.

Kim and Singal (2000) investigated the effect of market opening on stock market returns, volatility, and market efficiency using selected emerging markets. The study covered 27 countries (including Nigeria and Zimbabwe). Employing nonparametric test and ARCH/GARCH models to the data collected, the study found that stock returns increase immediately after market opening but fall subsequently.

Mundell (2002) made a strong case for a single common currency in Africa, pointing out the benefits to include increased macroeconomic stability. The study however argued that the success of monetary integration would also depend on the interplay of various political and institutional factors. Sighting the experience of the European Monetary Union among others, the study suggested that the balance between the costs and benefits of integration and its long term sustainability are heavily affected by the ability to design institutions that take political economy constraints into account.

Zafar and Kibota (2003) argued that regional integration provides a framework that would remove restrictive trade practices, streamline customs procedures, increase macroeconomic policy surveillance, and guarantee great fiscal discipline. Benefits from Integration should however not be limited to the tangible and intangible outcomes from trade, but also through the provision of necessary technical and infrastructural improvements that will enhance the realization of the benefits. Other gains from integration was stated to include improvements on roads, transportation and marketing infrastructure, information and communication technology support systems, enhancement of trans-boundary and inter-regional knowledge and information sharing.

Twu (2005) argued that integration of stock markets in the WAMZ would attract some benefits to the region. These benefits were listed to include: attracting foreign investors, enhancement of corporate orientation, introduction of new financial products, reduction of interest's rates, promotion of trade and investment, providing a platform for the privatization of public corporations, promotion of mergers and acquisition, and enabling the integration of stock market in the WAMZ into the global market. The study further provided steps that are necessary for the unification of stock markets in the WAMZ to include: harmonization of accounting, legal and financial reporting system, merger of the Nigerian stock exchange and the Ghanaian stock markets, incorporating merged stock markets in Nigeria, opening of stock exchange branches in other member countries, and training of financial analyst/journalist.

Agathee (2008) tested for interdependence between the Mauritian stock market and six African equity markets, namely Botswana, Malawi, Namibia, South Africa, Zambia and Zimbabwe using weekly stock indexes from January 2000 to September 2007. Applying Granger causality test, it was found that there was almost no lead-lag relationship except that Zimbabwe led Mauritius. The Engle-Granger and Johansen tests of cointegration further showed a strong cointegrating relationship involving the Stock exchange of Mauritius and the other African markets.

Oshikoya (2009) in his paper monetary unions and among developing and emerging markets noted that financial integration is an important element of any regional integration process, especially for a monetary union. He further argued that the financial sector must be adequately prepared to promote financial inclusion and sustain a changeover to a new currency. On stock markets, the paper noted that some countries in the WAMZ have established stock exchanges but that, these stock markets operate within the confines of their national boundaries with few linkages to other member countries.

The Benefits and Costs of Stock Market Integration

Integrating the stock markets within a sub-region, a region or in the globe is generally seen as beneficial for a variety of reasons, including their ability to attract inward portfolio investment, boost domestic savings, and improves the pricing and availability of capital for domestic investment. More importantly, stock markets are seen as enhancing the operations of the domestic financial system in general (Kenny and Moss, 1998).

In recent years, and coupled with the wave of globalization, there has been a shift from bank–based capital market development to a more holistic approach that aims at globalizing securities' market and other financial institutions. Popiel (1990) emphasized that some of the strengths that make the stock markets focal point of the shifting emphasis are their ability to mobilize long–term savings for financing entrepreneurs, encourage broader ownership of firms, and improve the efficiency of resource allocation through competitive pricing mechanism. Demirguc-kunt and Levine (1996) argued that apart from these primary benefits, globalizing stock markets will accordingly ensure efficient financial intermediation and would bring further gains to the various economies. Integrating of stock market would also bring about a shift from debt to equity financing across countries (Tella and Adesoye, 2008).

Integration of stock markets also bring about increased exposure of countries to increased vulnerability and external shocks, through contagion, which raises a number of critical problems. The problems associated with this include exchange and interest rates volatility and strong capital outflows which have adverse effect on sustainable growth and macroeconomic management (Kibuthu, 2005).

One other challenge for stock market integration within the WAMZ would be the respective national policies on the limit of investing social security funds in equities.

Stock Market in the WAMZ

The WAMZ member countries include: The Gambia, Ghana, Guinea, Liberia, Nigeria, and Sierra Leone. Of these countries, only Nigeria and Ghana have well established and functional stock markets. Those of other countries are still at their infancy or newly established.

The Nigerian stock exchange was established in 1960, while that of Ghana was established in 1989 but started trading in 1990. The settlement cycle for the NSE is T + 3 and the securities traded are ordinary and preference stocks and government bonds. On the other hand, the trading cycle for GSE is T + 5and the securities traded are ordinary stocks and corporate bonds. The NSE trades from Monday to Friday between the hours of 11.00am and 1.00pm each while the GSE trades on Mondays, Wednesday and Friday, between the hours of 10.00am 12.00pm.

RESEARCH METHODLOGY

The data collected for the study were time series data of daily closing equity prices for Nigeria and Ghana from 5th November 2007 to 3rd July 2009. The data (which is available for download from www.africanfinancialmarkets.com) were collected on a five day (Monday to Friday) basis in the context of the global financial crisis. Though the Ghanaian stock exchange operates three times in a week, day-to-day averages were used to cover for non-trading days (i.e. Tuesdays and Thursdays). The basic idea behind cointegration is that if, in the long-run, two or more series move closely together, even though the series themselves are trended, the difference between them is constant (Chimobi, 2010). A lack of cointegration suggests that such variables have no long-run relationship.

Various methods for measuring market integration such as: Bounds testing approach of the autoregressive distributed lag model, the Johansen cointegration using Vector autoregressive model, the Augmented Engle Granger (AEG) cointegration test, and so on, are properly documented in the literature (e.g. Fosu and Magnus, 2006; and Chimobi, 2010). Of these methods, the AEG cointegration test is the oldest and relies so much on the nonstationarity of the variables with the hope of obtaining a residual that would be stationary at levels and on nothing else (Yamamoto and Kurozumi, 2006). The Bounds testing approach on the other hand, do not bother about unit root in the variables except when the variables are I(2) i.e. stationary at second difference (Fosu and

Magnus, 2006). The Johansen cointegration technique involves testing the order of integration of the individual series under consideration using any of the procedures such as the Augmented Dickey-Fuller (ADF) or the Phillip-Perron (PP). The general form of ADF test is estimated by the following regression

$$\Delta y_t = \alpha_0 + \alpha_1 y_{t-1} + \sum_{i=1}^{n} \alpha_2 \Delta y_i + e_t \text{ without deterministic trend} \quad (1)$$

$$\Delta y_t = \alpha_0 + \alpha_1 y_{tt-1} + \sum_{i=1}^{n} \alpha_2 \Delta y_i + \delta_t + e_t \text{ with deterministic trend} \quad (2)$$

Where:

Y is a time series (i.e. for NSE or GSE), t is a linear time trend, Δ is the first difference operator, α_0 is a constant, n is the optimum number of lags in the dependent variable, e is the error term and δ is used to represent the deterministic in the Augmented Dickey Fuller test.

The Phillip Peron equation is presented below:

$$\Delta y_t = \alpha_0 + \alpha_1 y_{t-1} + e_t \quad (3)$$

Johansen's methodology takes its starting point in the vector auto regression (VAR) of order P given by

$$y_t = A_1 y_{t-1} + \ldots + A_p y_{t-p} + Bx_t + \varepsilon_t \quad (4)$$

where y_t is a k vector of endogenous variables, x_t is a d vector of exogenous variables, $A_1, \ldots, A_p$ and B are matrices of coefficients to be estimated, and ε_t is a vector of innovations that may be contemporaneously correlated with their own lagged values and uncorrelated with all of the right hand side variables. There are two approaches to the estimation of the vector autoregressive (VAR) model. One is the estimation of a direct model stated below:

$$y_t = m + A_1 y_{t-1} + A_2 y_{t-2} + \ldots + A_p y_{t-p} + \varepsilon_t \quad (5)$$

i.e a VAR(p) process, where m is the intercept

Or

$$y_t = m + \alpha_1 y_{t-1} + \alpha_2 y_{t-2} + \ldots + \alpha_p y_{t-p} + \varepsilon_t \quad (6)$$

i.e a AR(p) process.

The other approach requires reparametizating the equation in the form:

$$\Delta yt = m + ß_1 \Delta y_{t-1} + \ldots + ß_{p-1} \Delta y_{t-p+1} - \Pi y_{t-1} + \varepsilon_t \quad (7)$$

Where:

$$\Pi = \sum_{i=1}^{p} A_i - I \quad (8)$$

Direct estimation of equation (7) however is appropriate if all the eigen values of Π are numerically less than one. The second approach is appropriate when the y variables are not stationary. The number of r possible cointegrating vectors, are determined and the equation (7) is estimated with the Π matrix (Johnston and DiNardo, 1997). Johansen's method includes the Eigen value and one can see if they are numerically less than one. The cointegrating relationship is then obtained and the decision on cointegration deduced using the t-statistic.

RESULTS AND DISCUSSIONS

This section is discussed in two parts: the trend discussion of the data collected and discussion on Johansen's cointegration.

Trend Analysis

The stock market indices for Nigeria (NSE) and Ghana (GSE) over the sample period (2007 to 2009)[1] are presented in their level and difference form's below:

1 The data were collected daily on a 5-day weekly basis (Monday to Friday). Tuesday and Thursday values for the GSE were inter-day averages.

FIGURE II.I: STOCK MARKET TREND FOR NIGERIA AND GHANA IN LEVELS AND FIRST DIFFERENCE: 2007-2009

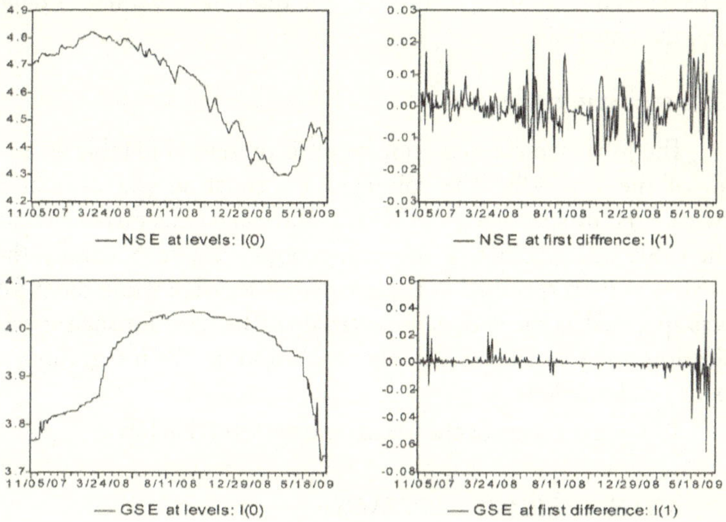

Source: Researchers presentation.

The level form of the stock market indices are presented in the left hand part of figure 1 above, while the right hand part show the trends in their first difference form. It can be seen that, for the NSE, the level form trend showed a slow rising in the early part, while the GSE showed a steady upward movement. At the point were the NSE peaked, the GSE continued to rise slowly and maintained a sustained peak period as the NSE experienced rapid decline. When the NSE, bottomed out however, the GSE declined rapidly. Clearly, the illustration using the level trend showed that the NSE and the GSE might be moving in different direction.

Looking at the differenced trend on the left part of the graph, it can be seen that while the NSE tend to be volatile all through the sample period, the GSE was stable for most of the period except in its early and late tail end.

The test for stationarity using the Augmented Dickey Fuller and Phillip Peron tests are presented in the appendix. The results show that both variables are I(1) i.e. stationary at first difference. The results are presented in tables 1 and 2 of the appendix.

The eigen values obtained from the Eviews output were also numerically less than one: providing further evidence to use the Johansen cointegrating technique. The result is presented in table 3 of the appendix.

Cointegration Analysis

The Johansen cointegration result is presented in table 4a and 4b of the appendix. The cointegration equation was estimated twice. First by specifying the NSE as the exogenous variable while the GSE was specified as the endogenous variable. Secondly, the GSE was then specified as the exogenous variable while the NSE was specified as the endogenous variable. The need for such specification was to arrive at a stable conclusion on the integration of both stock markets.

The linear forms of the results are presented below:

$$\Delta NSE_t = -0.00071 - 17.78\Delta GSE_{t-1} \qquad (9)$$

S.e (14.29)

t-stat (1.244)

$$\Delta GSE_t = -0.00000399 - 0.0562\Delta NSE_{t-1} \qquad (10)$$

S.e (0.0452)

t-stat (1.243)

(s.e: = standard error)

T-values at 0.10, 0.05 and 0.01 critical values are 1.645, 1.96 and 2.32 respectively

The results show that both stock markets are not integrated. The cointegrating coefficient is negative and the tabulated t-values at 10%, 5% and 1% are greater than the computed t-value implying that the null hypothesis of *no cointegration* between the Nigerian and the Ghanaian stock exchanges is accepted.

SUMMARY OF FINDINGS AND CONCLUSION

The study suggests that stock markets within the WAMZ are not integrated. Contrary to the works of Twu (2005) and Oshikoya (2009) who argued that unification of stock markets within the

WAMZ play a supportive role in monetary union objective, this study showed that stock markets in the WAMZ are not integrated and thus do not support the monetary union objective of the WAMZ. This finding however focused on the financial crisis period and therefore calls on further studies to include samples within and outside the periods associated with the financial crisis.

References

Agathee, U.S (2008). *"Interdependence of the Stock Exchange of Mauritius with Selected African Stock Markets: An Empirical Study"*. A paper presented at the EABR & TLC Conferences Proceedings Rothenburg, Germany.

Chimobi, O.P. (2010) "The Estimation of Longrun Relationship between Economic Growth, Investment and Export in Nigeria" *International Journal of Business and Management* 5(4): 215 - 222

Demirguc-Kunt, Asli and Ross. Levine (1996) "Stock Market Development and Financial Intermediaries: Stylized Facts," *The World Bank Economic Review* 10(2): 291- 232.

Fosu, O.E and Magnus, F.J (2006) "Bounds Testing Approach to Cointegration: An Examination of Foreign Direct Investment Trade and Growth Relationships. *American Journal of Applied Sciences* 3 (11): 2079-2085

Johnston, J. and DiNARDO J. (1997). *Econometric Methods*. NewYork: McGraw Hill.

Kenny, Charles, and Todd D. Moss, 1998, "Stock Markets in Africa: Emerging Lions or White Elephants?" *World Development, Vol. 26*, pp. 829-43.

Kibuthu, G.W (2005) "Capital Markets in Emerging Economies: A Case study of the Nairobi Stock Exchange". A thesis submitted for the award of Master of Arts in Law and Diplomacy http://fletcher.tufts.edu.

Kim, E.H and V. Singal (2000). "Stock Market Openings Experience of Emerging Economies". *Journal of business 7(3)*: 25-66.

Mundell, Robert A. (2002). "Does Africa Need a Common Currency?" in *The Third African Development Forum: Defining Priorities for Regional Integratio*n, Addis Ababa: Economic Commission for Africa.

Ogun, Oluremi and Adeola, Adenikinju (1992). *"Integrating the African Region: Lessons from Historical Experiences"*. A paper presented at the Nigerian Economic Society (NES) 1992 Annual Conference.

Oshikoya, Temitope W. (2009) *"Monetary Unions among Developing and Emerging Markets"* A paper presented at the Central Bank of Nigeria (CBN) 50th Year Anniversary at the Congress Hall of the Transcorp Hilton, Abuja, (Nigeria).

Popiel, P.A.(1990) "Developing Financial Markets in Sub-Saharan Africa" EDI working papers. Washington D.C.; The World Bank.

Rousseau, P.L and P. Wachtel (1999) *"Equity Markets and Growth: Cross-Country Evidence on Timing and Outcomes, 1980-1995".* A paper presented at the1998 meetings of American Economic Association and Society.

Tella, S.A and B. Adesoye (2008). *"Internationalisation of Africa's stock markets: prospects and Challenges".* A paper presented at the Department of Economics Olabisi Onabanjo University, Ogun state.

Twu, Mia (2005) Unified Stock Market for the Promotion of Business Activities in West African Monetary Zone (WAMZ). http://nccuir.lib.nccu.edu.tw/handle/140.119/33947

Yamamoto, T. and Kurozumi E. (2006). "Test for long-run granger non-causality in co integration systems". *Journal of Time Series Analysis 27(5): 703-724*

Zafar, Ali and Keiko Kubota (2003) "Regional Integration in Central Africa: Key Issues". *African Regional Working Paper Series No. 52: pp 32 (June).*

Appendix

Table 11.1: Unit Root test for Stationarity at Levels

Variables	ADF (Intercept)	ADF (Intercept and Trend)	PP (Intercept)	PP (Intercept and Trend)
GSE	-0.166 (-3.447)*	-2.027 (-3.983)*	-0.187 (-3.447)*	-2.993 (-3.983)*
NSE	0.081 (-3.447)*	-1.853 (-3.983)*	-0.294 (-3.447)*	-1.953 (-3.983)*

Note: Figures in parenthesis indicate critical Mackinnon 1% critical value for rejection of hypothesis of unit root.

Source: Author's Estimation using Eviews.

Table 11.2: Unit Root test for Stationarity at First Difference

Variables	ADF (Intercept)	ADF (Intercept and Trend)	PP (Intercept)	PP (Intercept and Trend)
GSE	-24.656 (-3.447)*	-26.746(-3.983)*	-24.304 (-3.447)*	-26.548 (-3.983)*
NSE	-12.738 (-3.447)*	-12.742 (-3.983)*	-13.000 (-3.447)*	-13.004 (-3.983)*

Note: Figures in parenthesis indicate critical Mackinnon 1% critical value for rejection of hypothesis of unit root.

Source: Author's Estimation using Eviews.

Table 11.3: Eigen Values

Sample: 11/05/2007 7/03/2009

Included observations: 432

Test assumption: Linear deterministic trend in the data

Series: D(GSE) D(NSE)

Lags interval: 1 to 1

Eigen value	Likelihood Ratio	5 Percent Critical Value	1 Percent Critical Value	Hypothesized No. of CE(s)
0.368432	276.2503	15.41	20.04	None **
0.164662	77.72508	3.76	6.65	At most 1 **
*(**) denotes rejection of the hypothesis at 5%(1%) significance level				
L.R. test indicates 2 cointegrating equation(s) at 5% significance level				

Table 11.4a: Johansen Cointegration Test for NSE, GSE

Sample: 11/05/2007 7/03/2009

Included observations: 432

Test assumption: Linear deterministic trend in the data

Series: D(NSE) D(GSE)

Lags interval: 1 to 1

Normalized Cointegrating Coefficients: 1 Cointegrating Equation(s)

D(NSE)	D(GSE)	C
1.000000	-17.77793	-0.000710
	(14.2975)	
Log likelihood	3174.626	

Table 11.4b: Johansen Cointegration Test for GSE, NSE

Sample: 11/05/2007 7/03/2009

Included observations: 432

Test assumption: Linear deterministic trend in the data

Series: D(GSE) D(NSE)

Lags interval: 1 to 1

Normalized Cointegrating Coefficients: 1 Cointegrating Equation(s)

D(GSE)	D(NSE)	C
1.000000	-0.056250	3.99E-05
	(0.04524)	
Log likelihood	3174.626	

Section V

Human Development

Chapter 12

DOES REGIONAL EURO-CURRENCY INTEGRATION PROMOTE HUMAN DEVELOPMENT IN SUB-SAHARAN AFRICA?

Juliet U. Elu and Gregory N. Price

INTRODUCTION

Since 1990, when the United Nations Development Programme (UNDP) introduced the Human Development Index (HDI), the majority of Sub-Saharan African countries have been classified as being low in human development. The HDI, motivated to measure the capabilities of individuals to enjoy a high quality of life (Sen, 1985), is a summary index of the incomes, education and life expectancy of the average individual in a country. The persistent low HDI for the majority of Sub-Saharan African countries underscores the importance of economic growth, which presumably raises living standards. However, the economic growth and human development nexus is far from straightforward. The causal pathway between growth and human development appears to be two-way. In general it appears that on the one hand economic growth is important for human development, yet it also appears to be the case that persistent and sustainable economic growth requires human development (Ranis and Stewart, 2007).

In this paper, we consider whether a particular institutional arrangement matters for human development in Sub-Saharan Africa—regional euro-currency integration. As there is evidence that regional euro-currency integration enhances economic growth in Sub-Saharan Africa (Elu and Price, 2010), it is plausible that such institutional arrangements can also improve human development, as it is a function of economic growth. In particular, we consider whether membership in the CFA Franc Zone has a beneficial impact or not, on human development in Sub-Saharan Africa.

Our inquiry is related to a broad literature that considers the extent to which economic growth is pro-poor (Ravallion and Chen, 2003) and raises the functional capabilities of individuals, as measured by the HDI. The idea that economic growth can reduce poverty has been supported empirically in the analyses of Tendulkar and Jain (1995), Kakwani and Pernia (2000), and Dollar and Kraay (2002). With respect to economic growth enhancing the broader functional capabilities that engender human development, Dreze and Sen (1990), are skeptical, whereas Ranis and Stewart (2007), Elu (2000), and Anand and Ravillion (1993) find that economic growth does engender improvements in human capabilities as measured by several components of the HDI that measure those functional capabilities important for economic well-being. Our inquiry is also related to the literature on the effects of monetary/currency unions in Sub-Saharan Africa. To the extent that currency unions in Africa are capable of engendering higher levels of trade and economic growth between members (Anyanwu, 2003; Tsangarides, Ewenczyk and Holej; 2006; Masson, 2008), our analysis will inform the extent to which currency unions can improve living standards from a broad welfarist perspective—human development. In this context, our analysis provides empirical insight on the extent to which regional currency regions in Sub-Saharan Africa are welfare optimal with respect to favorably affecting overall social well-being.[1]

1 Debrun, Masson and Pattillo (2003) evaluated the experience of WAEMU countries, and conclude that it appears to be consistent with an optimal currency union (McKinnon 1963, Alesina and Barro, 2002).

Last but not least, our inquiry contributes to the literature that attempts to explain the causes and consequences of economic growth in Sub-Saharan Africa.[2] To the extent that regional currency integration provides an institutional framework that is pro-growth in Sub-Saharan Africa (Elu and Price, 2010), it may constitute a source of reducing poverty and increasing human development. As such, regional currency integration could be an important policy intervention for raising living standards in Sub-Saharan Africa beyond merely raising per capita incomes. We report results below that indeed support this idea. Parameter estimates across various specifications of a parsimonious relationship between the growth in human development, economic growth and currency union membership in Sub-Saharan Africa between 1999 - 2006 reveal that membership in the CFA Franc Zone causes higher growth in human development as measured by the HDI.

The remainder of this paper is organized as follows. In the second section, we motivate a particular theoretical relationship between long-run human development and economic growth. While the connection between human development and economic growth has been viewed as being bi-causal (Ranis and Stewart, 2007), when one considers longevity as a manifestation of human development, the long-run relationship between economic growth, nutrition and life expectancy suggests that at least in the long-run, economic growth is decisive for living standards and human development. We report parameter estimates across several specifications of the relationship between human development, economic growth, and regional currency union membership in the third section. The last section concludes the paper.

THEORY AND EMPIRICAL METHODOLOGY

Theoretically, the relationship between human development and economic growth has been viewed as one characterizing simultaneity. This is particularly the case if human development is broadly viewed as the development of human capabilities that

---

2 See for example Easterly and Levine (1997); Sachs and Warner (1997); Elu (1998); Temple (1998); Azam, Fosu, and Ndung'u (2002); Price (2003); Papp, Franses, and van Dijk (2005); Gyimah-Brempong and Corley (2005), Fosu (2008) and Muhammad (2009).

engender the capacity of high living standards. In the absence of human capabilities, no production—the rate of increase of which economic growth measures—could not take place. Conversely, economic growth can engender higher human capabilities. Such simultaneity has been recognized (Ranis and Stewart, 2007; Anand and Ravaillion, 1994; and Boozer et al. 2003) and empirical strategies to estimate the parameters of this relationship have been based on which causal pathway is relevant—from human development to economic growth, or vice versa.

In our analysis, we commit to a specification in which economic growth causes human development. We take seriously and as compelling the evidence of Fogel (2004a, 2004b) that improvements in human stature over the past 300 years have been caused by increases in food productivity which enabled better nutrition. Fogel concludes that the increase in agricultural productivity since 1700 permitted the population of the world to increase tenfold, removed at least half of humankind from chronic malnutrition, reduced the incidence of nutrition- related disabilities, and at least doubled life expectancy at birth. As these outcomes are all associated with enhanced human capabilities, they inform a compelling case that at least in the long-run, economic growth causes enhanced human capabilities/development.

Given our hypothesized causal pathway between human development and economic growth, let h_{oit} and h_{it}^* be actual/initial and steady-state human development for country i at time t respectively. Our hypothesized causal pathway suggests that in the long-run, human development in a particular country is determined by the growth of output and regional currency union membership as it can potentially affect economic growth. As such we posit that $h_{it}^* = \beta_0 + \beta_1 RCU_{it} + \beta_2 dlnq/dt + \beta_3 RCU_{it} \times dlnq/dt$ where β_0 is a constant, RCU_{it} is an indicator of whether or not a country i holds currency union membership at time t, and q_{it} is the total output of country i at time t. The interaction term captures the growth effects specific to regional currency union membership, as found in Elu and Price (2010).

Approximating around the long-run steady-state, where $dln\, h_{it} /\text{dt} = \lambda\, [ln(h_{it}^*) - ln(h_{oit})]$, an explicit regression specification for human development for country i at time t is:

$$ln(h^*_{it}) - ln(h_{oit}) = \theta lnh_{oit} + \theta\beta_0 + \theta\beta_1 RCU_{it} + \theta\beta_2 dlnq_{it}/dt + \theta\beta_3 x\, dlnq_{it}/dt + \varepsilon_{it} \quad (1)$$

where $\theta = 1 - exp(-\lambda t)$, λ = is the rate at which a country converges to its long-run steady- state human development, and ε_{it} is a stochastic error term.

DATA AND RESULTS

Our data consists of a panel of 48 Sub-Saharan African countries over the period 1999 - 2006. We choose this time period as it allows us to capture the effects of the establishment of the CFA Euro Franc Zone for a subset of the countries in our sample.[3] The data are from two sources. Our measures of output growth for each country--Gross Domestic Product in U.S Dollars in particular—are from *World Development Indicators 2007* compiled by the International Bank for Reconstruction and Development (World Bank). Our measure of belonging to a regional euro-currency zone is dichotomous, and based on a country's membership in the Central African Franc Zone as identified by Elu and Price (2010). We create dummy variables for a country's membership in the: (1) Central Africa Franc Zone (CFAZ), (2) West African Economic and Monetary Union (WAEMU), and (3) Economic and Monetary Union of Central Africa (CEMAC). As a human development measure, we use the human development index (HDI) reported in the United Nations Development Programme *Human Development Report* for the years 1999 - 2006. For each country, the HDI consists of three components: 1.) Life expectancy at birth as a measure of health and longevity for a country's

---

3 On January 1, 1999 the euro, by becoming the common currency for 11 countries in Europe, 14 countries in Sub-Saharan Africa that constitute the CFA Franc Zone (CFAZ) are economies with currencies pegged to the euro. CFAZ consists of two separate regional currency and economic unions in Sub-Saharan Africa: 1. A subset of countries in the West African Economic and Monetary Union (WAEMU) and 2. The Central African Economic and Monetary Community (CEMAC). The subset of WAEMU countries include Benin, Burkina Faso, Cote d' Ivoire, Guinea-Bissau, Mali, Niger, Senegal and Togo. The CEMAC countries are Cameron, Central African Republic, Chad, Congo Republic of, Equatorial Guinea, and Gabon.

population, 2.) The adult literacy rate and the combined primary, secondary, and tertiary gross enrollment ratio, as a measure of the knowledge and educational capacity of a country's population, and 3.) The natural logarithm of gross domestic product per capita at purchasing power parity as a measure of the standard of living for a country's population.

To the extent that ε_i represents country-specific differences in levels of human development, it is potentially correlated with output and institutional arrangements such as membership in a currency union.[4] Neglecting this correlation if it exists leads to biased parameter estimates. For panel data, it is standard to account for heterogeneity with a dynamic panel estimator—based on Instrumental Variables (Arellano and Bond, 1991), or Generalized Methods of Moments (GMM) (Arellanno and Bover, 1995). To check for robustness across identifying assumption we estimate the parameters of (1) with both the Instrumental Variables random effect panel data estimator of Hausman and Taylor (1981), and a System GMM estimator. As our specification of the human development growth nexus is parsimonious, any omitted variables could be a source of bias, particularly if variables that are important for economic growth are omitted—which introduces an endogeneity bias to parameter estimates. As such, system GMM parameter estimates of our parsimonious human development growth specification, which are designed to accommodate endogeneity bias, will provide a robustness check relative to simple pooled Ordinary Least Squares, and Hausman-Taylor IV estimates.

Table 12.1 reports the mean and standard deviation of the covariates over the 1996 - 2006 time period across the relevant subsample of Sub-Saharan African countries in our panel data. The average growth rate in human development is approximately similar for all countries. In contrast, the average growth rate of output varies, and higher on average for those Sub-Saharan African countries that were members of CFAZ, and particularly higher on average for CEMAC members. The variations in aver-

---

4 For additional evidence of heterogeneity among countries and its econometric implications, see the analyses of Islam (1995), Phillips and Sul (2007), Okada (2006), Durlauf, Kourtellos, and Minkin (2001), and Lee, Pesaran, and Smith (1998).

ages across the subsamples are suggestive of currency union membership having a causal effect on the growth rate of output, but not on human development. However, for the countries with CFAZ membership, the counterfactual is what would their growth rates in human development and output have been had they not been CFAZ members, and a simple comparison of averages based on currency union membership or not cannot determine this.

Table 12.2 reports pooled Ordinary Least Squares (OLS) parameter estimates for the specification in (1). We report on three specifications of the regional currency membership dummy and its interaction with output growth for: 1) Being a member of the CFA Franc Zone—CFAZ, 2) Being a member of WAEMU only, and 3) Being a member of CEMAC only. As diagnostic measures we also report the adjusted R^2, and a chi-square test for the coefficients being jointly insignificant. The pooled OLS parameter estimates in Table 12.2 suggest that being a member of a euro-currency union enhances human development. The dummy for euro-currency union membership and its interaction with economic growth is positive for membership in general (CFAZ), but the pro-human development impact seems to be associated mainly with being in CEMAC. This suggests that all regional currency unions in Sub-Saharan Africa are not similar with respect to their effects on human development. As diagnostics measures we report a chi-square test for the joint insignificance of the estimated parameters, and the adjusted R^2.

The pooled OLS parameter estimates in Tables 2 ignore any unobserved heterogeneity in the error term—or unobserved country-specific differences which can lead to biased estimates on the effects of the regressors on the growth of human development. Given the possibility of unobserved country-specific differences , Table 12.3 reports Hausman-Taylor random effect parameter estimates. Our motivation for considering this estimator, relative to the dynamic panel estimators based on first differenced IV (Arellano and Bond, 1991), or GMM (Arellano and Bower, 1995), is based on how we measure membership in a regional euro-currency union. In our data, membership in a euro-currency union does not vary over the sample time period. As such, their impact in dynamic fixed effect first-differenced panel data estimators based on first differences equal zero, and their impact on the dependent variable cannot be estimated.[5] The Hausman-Taylor parameter estimates reported in Table 12.3 also assume that unobserved country-specific heterogeneity is random, and correlated with the regressors.[6] As diagnostics measures we report a chi-square test

---

5 Greene (2003) provides a useful overview of the analytics of dynamic panel data estimators. To see the virtue of the Hausman-Taylor estimator, consider a dynamic panel formulation of our human development specification:

$$h_{it} - h_{it-1} = \mathbf{\ddot{a}}' w_{it} + \mu_i + \varepsilon_{it}$$

$$w_{it} = [h_{it-1}, \mathbf{x}_{1it}', \mathbf{x}_{2it}', \mathbf{z}_{1i}', \mathbf{z}_{2i}']'$$

where $\delta`$ is a vector of coefficients, μ_i is an unobserved country-specific error term—the random effect, ε_{it} is an idiosyncratic error term, x^{1it} is a vector of time varying variables uncorrelated with μ_i, x^{2it} is a vector of time varying variables correlated with μ_i, z^{1i} is a vector of time invariant variables uncorrelated with μ_i, and z^{2i} is a vector of time varying variables correlated with μ_i. To identify $\delta`$ given unobserved heterogeneity (μ_i), the key assumptions are $E[\mu_i \mid x^{1it}, z^{1i}] = 0$ and $E[\mu_i \mid x^{2it}, z^{2i}] \neq 0$. Hausman and Taylor (1981) show that the group mean deviations of the vectors x and z can be used as instruments to obtain a random effect estimate of $\delta`$, and some of the regressors are allowed to be correlated with the unobserved random effect. This estimator allows the inclusion of time invariant dichotomous variables, and they are not dropped if used as instruments since the IVs are transformations based on deviations from group means. This in contrast to the dynamic panel first difference estimators proposed by Arellano and Bond (1991) and Arellano and Bower (1995). These estimators use as instruments first differences of the regressors, which drop dichotomous variables included in the regression specification.

6 In particular, our Hausman-Taylor parameter estimates assume the following: 1) $h\,(h_{oit-1})$ is time varying, exogenous and uncorrelated with the random effect, 2) $dlnq_{it}/dt$ and $RCU_{it} \times dlnq_{it}/dt$ are time varying, endogenous and correlated with the random effect, and 3) RCU_i is time invariant, exogenous, and uncorrelated with the random effect. The first assumption characterizes the unobservable factors that condition $dlnq_{it}/dt$ and $RCU_{it} \times dlnq_{it}/dt$.

for the joint insignificance of the estimated parameters, and ρ, the correlation between the regressand and its predicted value.

Similar to the pooled OLS parameter estimates, the Hausman-Taylor parameter estimates in Table 12.3 suggest that with the exception of WAEMU, regional euro-currency union membership has a positive impact on human development in Sub-Saharan Africa—at least with respect to the overall effect. Nonetheless, the interaction of the growth of output with currency union membership remains positive in patterns similar to the OLS parameter estimates. In general, judging by the value of ρ, the Hausman-Taylor parameter estimates explain at least 71 percent of the variation in human development growth rates for Sub-Saharan Africa. This suggests that the OLS parameter estimates are perhaps poorly identified, and allowing for endogeneity for at least some of the regressors improves the explanatory power of the specification. To the extent that the endogeneity results from unobserved and omitted variables that are important for human development, it also suggests that the Hausman-Taylor parameter estimates reported in Table 12.3 are robust estimates of the effects of economic growth and regional euro-currency members on human development in Sub-Saharan Africa.

Our econometric specification of human development is dynamic, and the number of countries in the sample is large relative to the number of time periods. Moreover, the appearance of a lagged dependent variable introduces a correlation between any individual country fixed effect and the lagged variable—and possibly other dependent variables, undermining the consistency of both OLS and the Hausman-Taylor estimators where fixed effects are assumed. (Anderson and Hsiao, 1982; Nickell, 1981; Hsiao, 2003). Consistent estimation of a dynamic relationship when there is correlation between individual fixed effects and dependent variables can proceed from Generalized Method of Moments (GMM) estimators (Holtz-Eakin, Newey ,and Rosen, 1998; Arellano and Bond, 1991), which we provide and report on in Table 12.4.

We estimate two-step system GMM parameter estimates with collapsed instruments, as the difference GMM specifications always dropped the currency union membership variable, and system

GMM is theoretically compatible with the implied dynamics of our human development growth specification.[7] We use forward orthogonalized instruments so as to maximize the sample size (Roodman, 2009). In each instance, identification was enabled by using as instruments for each country: 1.) Health expenditures as a fraction of GDP, 2.) Public spending on education as a fraction of GDP, 3.) Primary education expenditure per student, 4.) Secondary education expenditure per student, 5) Employment to population ratio (age 15 - 24), 6.) Total population, and 7.) Crude death rate per 1,000 population. Each instrument is based on data reported for each country in *World Development Indicators* for each year during 1999 - 2006. All reported standard errors are robust. As diagnostics measures, each specification reports the Hansen test of overidentifying restrictions, the number of instruments, and a chi-square test for the joint significance of all parameters except the constant.[8]

In general, the system GMM parameter estimates conform in sign, significance, and pattern with the OLS and Hausman-Taylor parameter estimates, particularly with respect to the effects of euro-currency union membership on the growth of human development. As the system GMM estimates are robust with respect to possible endogeneity of all the regressors, that euro-currency union membership has a positive effect on the growth of human development suggests that our hypothesized causal pathway is indeed relevant for Sub-Saharan African countries. The GMM parameter estimates suggest that long-run steady-state improvements in human develop-

7 As Roodman (2009) notes, the number of instruments with difference and system GMM estimators is quadratic in the time dimension T. This can result in the overfit of endogenous variables, and render unreliable tests for overidentifying restrictions. Collapsing instruments minimizes these complications. System GMM is also compatible with our dynamic specification of human development that assumes Sub-Saharan African countries are not too far from their steady-state level of human development. In this context, the coefficient on the lag of human development captures whether or not there is convergence to the steady-state, implying its coefficient is less than unity. This restriction also implies stationarity (Blundell and Blond, 1998).

8 As two-step system GMM is robust with respect to autocorrelation, we do not report autocorrelation tests as diagnostics.

ment are determined by economic growth. Moreover, it appears that currency unions catalyze higher growth which translates into higher growth in human development in the long-run. In the case of the euro-currency unions in our analysis, this results seems to hold for those Sub-Saharan African countries that belong to CEMAC. The system GMM parameter estimates in table 4 suggest that membership in WAEMU appears to have no effect on economic growth, and a negative effect on the growth of human development.

CONCLUSION

This paper examined the effects of membershipe in the CFA Franc Zone on human development in Sub-Saharan Africa. Viewing regional currency integration as an institutional arrangement that can potentially catalyze economic growth, this paper hypothesized a long-run steady-state relationship between human development, economic growth, and membership in a regional currency union. Parameter estimates from a parsimonious dynamic econometric specification of this relationship suggest that regional euro-currency integration in Sub-Saharan Africa has a beneficial impact on human development.

As in Elu and Price (2010), we suspect that the negative results for WEAMU are a result of these countries also being linked through a regional trade union—ECOWAS. Relative to CEMAC countries, ECOWAS members appear to have different economic fundamentals that may alter the effects of economic growth and regional currency union membership has on. human development. Hammouda et al. (2009) for example find that relative to CEMAC countries, output growth among ECOWAS member countries depends more on labor-intensity, and relative to CEMAC, labor mobility has been restricted as a matter of policy among ECOWAS member countries. To the extent that this reduces total factor productivity growth in WAEMU countries relative to CEMAC countries, the WAEMU countries in our sample may not be as close to their steady-state growth relative to CEMAC countries, which is perhaps reflected in our parameter estimates.

Our results also have several policy implications. First, our findings suggest that economic growth is an engine for human development in Sub-Saharan Africa. As such, the poverty reduction targets of the Millennium Development Goals can also be satisfied within a policy framework that prioritizes economic growth. Second, our results also suggest that some institutional arrangements such as the formation of regional currency unions can also foster human development. In this context, policies that implement pro-growth regional currency integration arrangements are a potential source of enhancing the capabilities of individuals to enjoy higher living standards in Sub-Saharan Africa.

TABLE 12.1: MEAN AND STANDARD DEVIATION OF COVARIATES

	COUNTRY SUBSAMPLE			
VARIABLE	NON-CFAZ	CFAZ	WAEMU	CEMAC
Human Dev. Growth Rate	.015	.015	.014	.015
1999 - 2006:	(.048)	(.048)	(.046)	(.049)
$h(h_t) - h(h_{it-1})$				
GDP Growth Rate	.075	.113	.085	.146
1999 - 2006:	(.111)	(.126)	(.093)	(.150)
$dlnq_{it}/dt = ln(q_{it}) - ln(q_{it})$				
Number of Observations	215	90	49	41

Notes: Standard deviation reported in parentheses. For both the Human development and GDP/output variables, the growth rates are the average in the natural log differences of the current over the previous periods value, which are the values used to estimate parameters. CFAZ = Central African Franc Zone, WAEMU = West African Economic and Monetary Union, CEMAC = Economic and Monetary Union of Central Africa.

TABLE 12.2: POOLED ORDINARY LEAST SQUARES (OLS) PARAMETER ESTIMATES

	RCU_{it} = CFAZ MEMBERSHIP	RCU_{it} = WAEMU MEMBERSHIP	RCU_{it} = CEMAC MEMBERSHIP
Regressand: $ln(h_{it}) - ln(h_{it-1})$ (1999 - 2006)			
Regressors:			
$\theta\beta_o$	-.020	-.021	-.020
	(.009)[b]	(.009)[b]	(.009)[b]
$\theta \times ln(h_{oit})$	-.041	-.039	-.037
	(.011)[a]	(.011)	(.010)[a]
$\theta\beta_1 \times RCU_{it}$	-.018	-.016	-.014
	(.007)[b]	(.009)[c]	(.010)
$\theta\beta_2 \times dlnq_{it}/dt$	.068	.091	.084
	(.028)[b]	(.024)[a]	(.026)[a]

$\theta\beta_3 \times RCU_{it} \times dlnq_{it}/dt$	.104	.095	.082
	(.047)[b]	(.075)	(.054)
# of Observations	305	305	305
Diagnostics:			
$x^2:(\Sigma\beta_i X_i = 0)$	9.05[a]	8.09[a]	7.97[a]
ρ	.096	.085	.084

Notes:

a - Significant at the .01 level.
b - Significant at the .05 level.
c - Significant at the .10 level.

Table 12.3: Hausman-Taylor Parameter Estimates

	RCU_{it} = CFAZ Membership	RCU_{it} = WAEMU Membership	RCU_{it} = CEMAC Membership
Regressand: $ln(h_{it}) - ln(h_{it-1})$ (1999 - 2006)			
Regressors:			
$\theta\beta_o$	-.081	-.089	-.089
	(.023)[a]	(.023)[a]	(.025)[a]
$\theta \times ln(h_{oit})$	-.121	-.129	-.124
	(.028)[a]	(.029)[a]	(.029)[a]
$\theta\beta_1 \times RCU_{it}$	-.029	-.035	-.014
	(.019)	(.025)	(.028)
$\theta\beta_2 \times dlnq_{it}/dt$	.073	.102	.093
	(.029)[b]	(.027)[a]	(.027)[a]
$\theta\beta_3 \times RCU_{it} \times dlnq_{it}/dt$	.139	.097	.124
	(.053)[b]	(.073)	(.065)[b]
# of Observations	305	305	305
Diagnostics:			
$x^2:(\Sigma\beta_i X_i = 0)$	45.58[a]	40.85[a]	41.93[a]
ρ	.617	.621	.637

Notes:

ρ - is the correlation between $ln(h_{it}) - ln(h_{it-1})$ and its predicted value.
a - Significant at the .01 level.
b - Significant at the .05 level.
c - Significant at the .10 level.

Table 12.4: System GMM Parameter Estimates

	RCU_{it} = CFAZ Membership	RCU_{it} = WAEMU Membership	RCU_{it} = CEMAC Membership
Regressand: $ln(h_{it}) - ln(h_{it-1})$ (1999 - 2006)			
Regressors:			
$\theta\beta_o$	-.027	-.027	-.029
	(.010)[a]	(.012)[a]	(.009)[a]
$\theta \times ln(h_{oit})$	-.054	-.048	-.050
	(.014)[a]	(.011)[a]	(.011)[a]
$\theta\beta_1 \times RCU_{it}$	-.030	-.023	-.031
	(.011)[b]	(.013)[c]	(.013)[b]
$\theta\beta_2 \times dlnq_{it}/dt$	.046	.078	.073
	(.034)[a]	(..042)[c]	(.030)[b]
$\theta\beta_3 \times RCU_{it} \times dlnq_{it}/dt$	.204	.144	.211
	(.085)[a]	(.132)	(.071)[b]
# of Observations	305	305	305
Diagnostics:			
Number of Instruments:	65	65	65
Hansen Test of overidentifying restrictions:	42.75	47.76	40.87
χ^2_{R-K}			
$H_0: \Sigma\beta_i = 0$	20.58[a]	35.61[a]	29.09[a]
χ^2_{K-1}			

Notes:

a - Significant at the .01 level.

b - Significant at the .05 level.

c - Significant at the .10 level.

References

Alesina, Alberto and Robert J. Barro. 2002. "Currency Unions", *Quarterly Journal of Economics*, 117: pp. 409 - 436.

Anand, Sudhir and Martin Ravallion. 1993. "Human Development in Poor Countries: On the Role of Private Incomes and Public Services". *Journal of Economic Perspectives*, 7: pp. 133 - 150.

Anderson, Theodore W. and Cheng Hsiao. 1982. "Formulation and Estimation of Dynamic Models Using Panel Data", *Journal of Econometrics*, 18: pp. 47 - 82.

Anyanwu, John C. 2005. "Estimating the Macroeconomic Effects of Monetary Unions: The Case of Trade and Output", *African Development Review*, 15: pp. 126 - 145.

Arellano, Manuel and Stephen Bond. 1991. "Some Tests of Specification for Panel Data: Monte Carlo Evidence and an Application to Employment Equations", *Review of Economic Studies*, 58: pp. 277 - 297.

Arellano, Manuel and Olympia Bover. 1995. "Another Look at the Instrumental Variables Estimation of Error Component Models", *Journal of Econometrics*, 68: pp. 29 – 52.

Azam, Jean-Paul., Augustin Fosu, and Njugana S. Ndung'u. 2002. "Explaining Slow Growth in Africa", *African Development Review*, 14: pp. 177 - 220.

Blundell, Richard, and Stephen Bond. 1998. "Initial Conditions and Moment Restrictions In Dynamic Panel Data Model", *Journal of Econometrics*, 87: pp. 115 - 143.

Boozer, Michael; Gustav Ranis, Frances Stewart, and Tavneet Suri. 2003. "Paths To Success: The Relationship Between Human Development and Economic Growth", Center Discussion Paper #874, Economic Growth Center, Yale University, New Haven, CT.

Debron, Xavier, Masson, Paul., and Catherine Pattillo. 2003. "West African Currency Union Rationale and Sustainability", *CESifo Economic Studies*, 49: pp. 381 - 413.

Dollar, David and Aart Kraay. 2002. "Growth is Good for the Poor", *Journal of Economic Growth*, 7: pp. 195 - 225.

Dreze, Jean, and Amartya Sen. 1990. *Hunger and Public Action*. Clarendon Press. Oxford, UK.

Durlauf, Steven N., Andros Kourtellos and Artur Minkin. 2001. "The Local Solow Growth Model", *European Economic Review*, 45: pp. 928 - 940.

Easterly, Willliam and Richard Levine. 1997. "Africa's Growth Tragedy: Policies and Ethnic Divisions", *Quarterly Journal of Economics*, 113: pp. 1203 - 1250.

Elu, Juliet and Gregory N. Price. 2010. "The Impact of the Euro-CFA Franc Zone on Economic Growth in Sub-Saharan Africa", in African Development Bank and United Nations Economic Commission for Africa (Eds.) *Globalisation, Institutions and African Economic Development û Proceedings of the African Economic conference 2008*, Economica, Paris, FR.

Elu, Juliet. 2000. "Human Development in Sub-Saharan Africa: Analysis and Prospects for the Future", *Journal of Third World Studies*, 17: pp. 53 - 71.

Elu, Juliet. 1998. "ECOWAS and Economic Integration in West Africa", *Journal of African Finance and Economic Development*, 3: pp. 149 - 169.

Fogel, Robert W. 2004a. *The Escape from Hunger and Premature Death, 1700-2100: Europe, America, and the Third World*, Cambridge University Press, New York, NY.

Fogel, Robert W. 2004b. "Health, Nutrition, and Economic Growth", *Economic Development and Cultural Change*, 52: pp. 643 - 658.

Fosu, Augustin K. 2008. "Democracy and Growth in Africa: Implications of Increasing Electoral Competitiveness", *Economics Letters*, 100: pp. 442 - 444.

Greene, William H. 2003. *Econometric Analysis*, 5th Edition, Prentice Hall, Upper Saddle River, NJ.

Gyimah-Brempong, Kwabena and Marva E. Corley. 2005. "Civil Wars and Economic Growth In Sub-Saharan Africa", *Journal of African Economies*, 14: pp. 270 - 311.

Hammouda, Ben Hakim, Stephen N. Karingi, Angelica E. Njuguna, and Mustapha Sadri Jallab. 2009. "Why Doesn't Regional Integration Improve Income Convergence In Africa?", *African Development Review*, 21: pp. 291 - 330.

Hausman, Jerry A., and William E. Taylor. 1981. "Panel Data and Unobservable Individual Effects", *Econometrica*, 49: pp. 1377 - 1398.

Holtz-Eakin, Douglas, Whitney Newey, and Harvey S. Rosen. 1988. "Estimating Vector Autoregressions with Panel Data", *Econometrica*, 56: pp. 1371 - 1395.

Hsiao, Cheng. 2003. *Analysis of Panel Data*, 2nd Edition, Cambridge University Press, Cambridge, UK.

Islam, Nazrul. 1995. "Growth Empirics: A Panel Data Approach", *Quarterly Journal of Economics*, 110: pp. 1127 - 1170.

Lee, Kevin., M. Hashem Pesaran, and Ron Smith. 1998. "Growth Empirics: A Panel Data Approach—A Comment", *Quarterly Journal of Economics*, 113: pp. 319 - 323.

Kakwani, Nanak, and Ernesto M. Pernai. 2000. "What is Pro-Poor Growth?", *Asian Development Review*, 18: pp. 1 - 16.

Masson, Paul R. 2008. "Currency Unions in West Africa: Is the Trade Effect Substantial Enough to Justify Their Formation?", *World Economy*, 31: pp. 533 - 547.

McKinnon, Ronald. 1963. "Optimum Currency Areas", *American Economic Review*, 52: pp. 717 - 725.

Muhammad, Andrew. 2009. "Would African Countries Benefit From The Termination of Kenya's Economic Partnership Agreement (EPA) with the EU? An Analysis of EU Demand for Imported Roses", *Journal of Agricultural Economics*, 60: pp. 220 - 238.

Nickell, Stephen. 1981. "Biases in Dynamic Panel Models with Fixed Effects", *Econometrica*, 49: pp. 1417 - 1426.

Okada, Toshiro. 2006. "What Does The Solow Model Tell Us About Economic Growth?", *Contributions to Macroeconomics*, 6: pp. 1 - 30.

Papp, Richard., Philip Hans Franses, and Dick Van Dijk. 2005. "Does Africa Grow Slower than Asia, Latin America,and the Middle East?: Evidence from a New Data-based Classification Method", *Journal of Development Economics*, 77: pp. 553 - 570.

Phillips, Peter C.B. and Donggyu Sul. 2007. "Some Empirics On Economic Growth Under Heterogeneous Technology", *Journal of Macroeconomics*, 29: pp. 455 - 469.

Price, Gregory N. 2003. "Economic Growth in a Cross-section of Nonindusrial Countries: Doe Colonial Heritage Matter for Africa?", *Review of Development Economics*, 7: pp. 478 - 495.

Ranis, Gustav and Frances Stewart. 2007. "Dynamic Links Between Economcy and Human Development", in Jose Antonio Campo, K.S Jomo, and Sarbuland Khan, (Eds.) *Policy Matters: Economic and Social Policies to Sustain Equitable Development*, Zed Books LTD, London, UK.

Ravallion, Martin and Shaohua Chen. 2003. "Measuring Pro-Poor Growth", *Economics Letters*, 78: pp. 93 - 99.

Roodman, David. 2009. "How to do Xtabond2: An Introduction to Difference and System GMM in Stata", *Stata Journal*, 9: pp. 86 - 136.

Sachs, Jeffrey D. and Andrew Warner. 1998. "Sources of Slow Growth in African Economies", *Journal of African Economies*, 6: pp. 335 - 376.

Sen, Amartya. 1985. *Commodities and Capabilities*. Oxford University Press. Oxford, UK.

Temple Jonathan. 1998. "Initial Conditions, Social Capital, and Growth in Africa", *Journal of African Economies*, 7: pp. 309 - 347.

Tendulkar, Suresh D. and L.R. Jain. 1995. "Economic Growth, Relative Inequality, and Equity: The Case of India'", *Asian Development Review*, 13: pp. 138 - 168.

Tangararides, Charalambos G., Pierre Ewencyk, and Michael Holej. 2006. "Stylized Facts On Bilateral Trade And Currency Unions: Implications for Africa", *International Monetary Fund Working Paper No. 06/31*, Washington DC.

World Development Indicators.. 2007. The International Bank for Reconstruction and Development. Washington DC. USA.

Human Development Report. Various years: 1997 - 2007. United Nations Development Programme. New York, NY.

Chapter 13

EDUCATION, REGIONAL INTEGRATION, AND DEVELOPMENT IN WEST AFRICA

Kwabena Gyimah-Brempong

INTRODUCTION

The relationship between education and economic development has long been recognized in the development literature. On the one hand, education is seen as a product of the development process that is worthy of pursuit by itself (note that education is the MDG # 3). On the other hand, education is considered a crucial input into the development process. It is considered an input to economic growth, health outcomes, institutional development, and possibly trade integration, among others. At the policy level, especially in the West African sub-region, there have been, and continue to be serious attempts at achieving regional integration in order to reap the benefits of such integration. However, the literature on education production itself suggests that investment in education is influenced by the growth rate of income and integration (Gyimah-Brempong and Wilson: 2004, among others). Despite this possible connection (although indirect) there is very little theoretical or empirical work that investigates the relationship between regional integration and education development.

Although education is considered important in the development literature, there have been few empirical studies to measure its importance in the integration process in African countries. The few empirical studies on the relationship between education and development have focused almost exclusively on the income growth effects of education. Second, it is not clear which level of education is appropriate for development in the context of low income countries and whether all development outcomes are equally affected by all levels of education. While the World Bank and other international development organizations argue for a focus on primary education, some researchers suggest that it is higher education that is relevant for long term development. For West African countries, this debate has hardly begun.

This paper uses panel data from West African countries over the 1960-2008 period to investigate the effects of education on economic development. Specifically, I investigate the relationships among regional integration, investment in education and the growth rate of per capita income. I also investigate the level of education—primary, secondary, tertiary—that integration mostly affect, if it indeed does affect investment in education. I must mention at the outset that I do not investigate any causal relationship; rather what I investigate is the correlation between integration and educational investment. My approach is to estimate an aggregate education production function in which integration is an added regressor. I disaggregate education into primary, secondary, and tertiary education, thus allowing me to investigate the effects of integration on different levels of education investment.

I have chosen to focus on West Africa for a number of reasons. First, the region has one of the lowest rates of education attainment, especially higher education, in the developing world. Second, the region is also one of the least developed as defined by several indicators—income, human development, health, gender equity, integration, political stability, among others. The combination of low levels of education and development suggests that the marginal effect of a change in education is likely to be high. Third, although the region is less developed, it is going through rapid change and it may be interesting to investigate what role education plays in this process. Finally, West African policy makers are pursuing polices of regional integration as a means of accelerating development. To the extent that education increases outward orientation, education can help in this process of integration. In addition to knowing the general effects of education on development, it may be nec-essary for policy makers to know which levels of education are relevant for a particular development outcome, especially regional integration. It may be helpful for policy makers to quantify or analyze this effect of education on regional integration in West Africa.

This paper makes some contributions to the literature on the relationship between education and integration. As far as I know, this is the only paper that investigates the relationship between regional integration and investment in education in West Africa. In addition, I also look at investment at different levels of education to allow for possible differential effects of integration on different levels of education rather than treat education as one unit thus assuming that the integration effect is uniform at all levels. Third, I use three different panel data estimation methods to ensure that my results do not depend on the method of estimation. Finally, I investigate the relationship among integration, education investment and the growth rate of per capita income.

The results of this paper can be briefly summarizes as follows: I find that conditional on other variables, integration has positive and significant impact on investment in education at all levels. The integration elasticities of investment in education are 0.25 for primary education, 0.80 for secondary education and 0.60 for tertiary education. I also find that integration has a direct and significant effect on the growth rate of per capita income after adjusting for its effect through investment in education. The results of this paper suggest that integration has two important benefits—increased human capital formation through education and increased growth rate of per capita income—for the West African region.

The rest of the paper is organized as follows: Section 2 briefly reviews the literature on the relationship between education and development, especially as it relates to African countries, section 3 introduces the equation(s) to be estimated, section 4 discusses the data and estimation methods, while section 5 presents and discusses the statistical results. Section 6 concludes the paper.

PREVIOUS STUDIES

Most studies on the effects of education on income growth have used cross-country data and focused on the effects of education on economic growth (Barro: 1999, Romer: 1990, Atardi and Sala-i-Martin: 2003, Nelson and Phelps: 2006, Gyimah-Brempong et al: 2006, Ciccone and Papaionnou: 2009, among others). Others use time series data (e.g. de la Croix et al: 2008) or cross-state data within a country (Baldwin and Borrelli: 2008) to investigate the effects of education on income growth. These authors generally find education to have positive and significant effect on income growth rate. The growth effect comes through several channels; among them are the ability to create and absorb new technologies, improved health, increased savings and investments (especially in human capital), and the externalities effects of education. With the exception of Gyimah-Brempong et al (2006) and Self and Grabowsky (2004), all these studies assume that the growth impact of education is uniform across all levels of education. There is preliminary evidence that the growth impact of education varies with the level of education. Moreover, none of these studies investigate the effects of regional integration and education on growth in the same equation. I try to address these issues in this paper.

There is almost no literature on the effects of integration on investment in education. Studies that look at investment in education have focused on the effects of income, institutions, or some policy change at the macro level or in input efficiency, input demand, and incentives to invest in education at the micro level. The empirical literature on regional integration (trade) has generally employed gravity models to investigate the determinants of integration or the effects of integration on trade and although some of these studies have included education as a control variable in estimation, there have been no attempts to investigate the effects of regional integration on investment in education in either the developing world generally, or West Africa in particular.

For regional integration in Africa, UNECA (2004) finds that the major determinant is lack of infrastructure while Bah and Tapsoba (2010) find that civil conflict increases regional integration in the short run in West Africa but the effect tapers off over time. Jones (2002) tests for beta and sigma convergence in Economic Community of West African States (ECOWAS) and conclude that there is convergence of per capita income among ECOWAS countries. Aryeetey (2001) investigates how the smaller countries in West Africa can provide a stimulus to support Nigeria's leadership for deeper integration in ECOWAS countries. None of these studies investigates the effects of integration on investment in education.

Research that investigate the determinants of investment in education and that income, institutions, demographic factors, and government policies are important determinants of investment in education. Very few studies investigate the effects of regional integration on investment in education; neither do these studies combine a study of the effect or regional integration on investment in different levels of education and the effects of integration and education on income growth rate. I try to fill the gaps in the literature in this study.

MODEL

There are several reasons to have a significant relationship between regional integration and human capital formation, especially in West Africa. Among these is the income effect: integration, where successful, increases income growth rate, hence the income of the integrated region. The literature on education production suggests that increased income leads to higher investment rate in education, all things equal. The second possible mechanism is the incentive effect. Integration leads to a wider labor market for participants to operate in hence increases the returns to education at all levels, especially higher education. This is not unlike the increased emigration of labor from Africa to the developed world. To participate in the increased migration opportunity, one has to increase one's human capital endowment hence investment in education increases.

On the supply side, there is the scale and scope effects in the supply of education that comes with integration. Integration leads to a wider supply of educational opportunities (quantity, quality, and different mix of courses) for students from different countries in the region. For example Nigerian students can study in Ghanaian universities, Ghanaian students study in Senegalese universities while Senegalese students study in Nigerian universities. The availability of a larger number of students suggest the possibilities of educational institutions reaping the benefits of economies of scale and of scope in the provision of education, hence reducing the cost of provision. Competition among larger number of suppliers will also increase quantity, improve quality, and provide choice for students. All these could lead to increased investment in education as integration expands.

The above discussion leads me to begin with a simple model of investment in education (E) in a country at time t as a function of the strength of regional integration in the country's regional grouping (RINT) and all other factors, including institutions, that influence investment in education (**X**). Formally, I specify the general education production function as:

$$E_{ijt} = f(RINT_{it}; \mathbf{X}); \quad f'_{RINT} > 0 \qquad (1)$$

where E_{ijt} is country i's investment in education level j at time t, $RINT_{it}$ is country i's level of integration into the region in period t and **X** is a vector of other variables that affect investment in education at the aggregate level. It is possible that different levels of education may be impacted differently by integration as well as other variables, hence my reason for looking at the relationship between different levels of education rather than treating education as one continuous variable. I note that not all variables in the **X** vector may enter every level of education investment in this study, and some elements of the **X** vector may be endogenous.

In addition to investigating the effects of integration on education investment, I also investigate the joint effects of integration and education investment on the growth rate of per capita income. My concern is whether integration has a significant growth impact besides its impact through increased investment in education. I do so by estimating a growth equation that has the degree of integration and investment in different levels of education as additional regressors. This is similar to the traditional specification of growth equations in the literature (Atardi and Sala-i-Martin: 2003, Barro: 1997, Romer: 1989, Solow: 2003, and Gyimah-Brempong et al: 2006, among others) but different in that I specify education as a discontinuous variable as well as the inclusion of RINT. The growth equation I estimate is:

$$y_{it} = y(RINT_{it}; E_{jit}; X) \tag{2}$$

where y_{it} is the growth rate of income in country i in period t and all other variables as de ned above.

Equations (1) and (2) are written at general levels. To estimate the equations, I must provide specific functional forms as well as define the variables contained in the **X** vector. Because economic theory does not provide guidance as to specific functional forms for these equations, I specify linear (in coefficients) functional forms for the equations. It is possible that RINT affects different levels of education investment differently, similar to the findings by some researchers that education affects income growth in a discontinuous way (Gyimah-Brempong et al: 2006, Self and Grabowsky: 2004). The education investment and income growth equations I estimate are written as:

$$E_{ijt} = \alpha_0 + \alpha_1 RINT_{it} + X'\beta + \varepsilon \tag{3}$$

$$y_{it} = \gamma_0 + \gamma_1 RINT_{it} + \gamma_2 primary_{it} + \gamma_3 secondary_{it} + \gamma_4 tertiary_{it} + X'\delta + \varepsilon \tag{4}$$

where α, β, δ, γ, and ε, and all variables are as defined in the text above. I note that not all elements of the **X** vector enters both equations in the estimation. I will de ne the variables in **X** in the data section.

DATA AND ESTIMATION METHOD

DATA

The dependent variables in this paper are investment in education and the growth rate of per capita income. Following Barro (1997), Barro and Lee (2000), Jamison et al: (2007) and Gyimah-Brempong and Wilson (2004), I measure investment in education as net enrollment rate of the relevant population. As argued above, I disaggregate education investment into various levels of education so I measure investment as net primary school enrollment rate (primary), net secondary school enrollment ratio (secondary) and net tertiary enrollment ratio (tertiary). I measure the growth rate of per capita income (y_{it}) as the annual growth rate of per capita real GDP expressed in PPP_{2000}.

There are several possible ways to measure RINT. Since regional integration is multi-dimensional and more involved, it is unlikely that any measure will reffect total regional integration. I therefore use trade integration as my measure of RINT. I proxy RINT by the relative volume of intra-regional trade in a country relative the country's total trade. Following De Lombaerde and Van Langenhove (2006), I measure RINT as:

$$RINT^{it} = (M^{jit}+E^{jit}) \, / \, (M_{it}+E_{it})$$

where M^{jit} and E^{jit} are imports and exports of country i from region j at time t, M_{it} and E_{it} are total imports and exports of country i at time t.[1]

Independent variables contained in the **X** vector in the study are per capita income (income), investment/GDP ratio (invest), government consumption (govcon), population growth rate (popgro), foreign aid (aid), two measures of governance, rule of law (rulelaw) and the quality of bureaucracy (bureau), and a dummy variable measuring whether a country is landlocked (landlock). Income is the real per capita GDP with 2000 purchasing power parity (PPP) as the base, govcon is the ratio of government consumption expenditures to GDP, annual growth rate of population (popgro), while aid is measured as the net aid disbursement/GDP ratio. I follow earlier researchers and measure invest as the gross domestic fixed investment/GDP ratio in a country. landlock is a dummy variable that takes the value of unity if a country is landlocked and zero otherwise.

Data for this study comes from several sources. Data on education was obtained from Barro and Lee (2010). This data set is a revised and updated version of the Barro-Lee data (2000), is from 1960 to 2010 and covers more countries than the 2000 data set. Income, its growth rate, investment, and other socioeconomic variables were obtained from the World Bank's World Development

Indicators, 2009 (on-line version), data for calculating RINT were obtained from International Monetary Fund's Direction of Trade Statistics, various years, while the data for landlock was calculated by the author using the political map of Africa.

I obtained the aidgni data from OECD Development Assistance Committee (DAC), 2009 on line version at http://www.oecd.org/dac/stats/dcrannex, 2009 while data for rulelaw and bureau were obtained from International Country Risk Guide (ICRG), Political Risk Points by Components, ICRG, 2009. The data are from 1960 to 2008. Because of lack of observations for some years for some variables, the sample has 378 observations for the education and y_{it} equations. The data covers 20 countries[2] in West Africa over the sample period. Because observations are not available for every year, the samples are unbalanced panel.

Summary Statistics of the sample data are presented in table 1. Generally, the data reveals that the degree of regional integration in West African countries is relatively low and highly variable while income growth rate is low. The general impression one gets from the data is that the general level of development in West Africa is very low and highly variable. The rate of investment in education, especially tertiary education, in West African countries during the sample period is relatively low. In addition to low rate, education investment in the region was also highly variable both across countries and through time. Although educational investment in the region is relatively low, it grew relatively fast during the sample period.

ESTIMATION METHODS

I estimate equations 3 and 4 with panel data from 1960 to 2008. In both the education investment and income growth equations, I include lagged dependent variables as regressors on account that enrollment rate at any level of education in a country is partly dependent on enrollment rates in the previous period. In the income growth equation, the level of income at the beginning of the period is included as a regressor, as is traditionally the case. Some of the regressors in **X** can be considered endogenous (e.g. education and RINT in the growth equation, and income in the education equation). It is well known that in the presence of dynamics and endogenous regressors, neither the fixed effects (FE) nor the random effects (RE) estimator produces consistent estimates. I therefore use Arellano and Bond's two step dynamic panel data estimator (Arellano and Bond: 1991) to estimate the two equations. The DPD estimator is a GMM estimator that produces consistent estimates in the presence of dynamics and endogenous regressors.

The DPD estimator consistently estimates dynamic panel data equations and has been used in several recent empirical growth research that uses panel data. However when the series are persistent, as these variables are likely to be, lagged levels of endogenous and predetermined regressors tend to be weakly correlated to their subsequent first differences, thus leading to biased estimates on account of weak instruments. Blundell and Bond (1998) have introduced the systems DPD estimator to correct this problem. The systems estimator adds a levels equation that uses lagged values of first differences of endogenous and predetermined regressors as instruments to the difference equation and jointly estimate the two equations as a system. I use external aid/GDP ratio (aid), infant mortality rate (infantmort), and the rule of law (lawandorder) as additional instruments for income in the education equation while I use government consumption/GDP ratio (govcon) and the growth rate of population (popgro) as additional instruments for EDU in the income growth equation. I test for the exogeneity of all regressors as well as the appropriateness of the instrument vector.

Although the DPD estimator produces consistent estimates, I also present coefficient estimates from other estimators. I also estimated the education equation using instrumental variable (IV) panel regressions for the education and a Hausman-Taylor estimator for the income growth equation. I present FE estimates for both equations for comparison. Both IV and DPD estimators estimate the education and growth equations as individual equations. Given the possible correlation among the two variables, the DPD and the IV estimators could lead to loss of efficiency in estimation. I therefore use the Seemingly Unrelated Regressions (SUR) to estimate the two equations as a system of equations and present the estimates for comparison.

RESULTS

The estimates of the equations are presented in tables 13.2-13.3. Table 13.2 presents the estimates for the education investment equation while coefficients for the income growth equation is presented in table 13.3. To conserve space, I do not present the full sets of estimates or regression and diagnostic statistics in this paper.

Regional Integration and Education Investment

Table 13.2 presents the estimates for the education investment equation. To focus on the basic results of interest, I present only the coefficients of RINT for the three levels of education for each of the estimators I use. Column 3 present the DPD estimates, column 4 presents the IV panel estimates, while column 5 presents the SUR estimates. For the purposes of comparison, I present FE estimates in column 2. Although not presented, the regression statistics indicate that the equation fits the data reasonable well. I reject the null hypothesis that all regression coefficients are jointly equal to zero at α= .01, Hansen's J as well as C statistics suggest that the instrument vector is appropriate. The Hausman statistics also indicate that not all regressors are exogenous hence the estimators I use rather than the FE estimator is appropriate. The coefficients of all other variables are as expected and most are significantly different from zero at α= .05 or better.

The DPD estimates presented in column 3 show that the coefficient of RINT in the primary, secondary and tertiary equations are positive, relatively large and significantly different from zero at α= .05 or better. The coefficients range from 0.25 for primary to about 0.8 for secondary. Since the equations are estimated in double log form, the coefficients are elasticities and they indicate a very strong relationship between the degree of regional integration and investment in education at all levels in West African countries.[3] The relationship is strongest for investment in secondary education with an estimated elasticity of 0.8, followed by investment in tertiary education with and estimated elasticity of .6, while investment in primary education is the weakest with an estimated elasticity of about 0.25.

Since the equations are estimated in double log form, the coefficients are elasticities and they indicate a very strong relationship between the degree of regional integration and investment in education at all levels in West African countries. The estimates, however indicate that the relationship between regional integration and investment in education in West African countries is not uniform across all levels of education. The relationship is strongest for investment in secondary education with an estimated elasticity of 0.8, followed by investment in tertiary education with an estimated elasticity of .6, while investment in primary education is the weakest with an estimated elasticity of about 0.25. Test of equality of the coefficient estimates of the different levels of education produced a χ^2 statistic of 28.98. This is far into the rejection region so I reject the null hypothesis of equality of the coefficients. I am not able to offer an explanation as to why the relationship between education investment vary by the level of education. This is left for another research project.

The relationship between regional integration and investment in education in West Africa is similar to the results of studies that find that emigration leads to increased investment in education in particular and human capital generally as summarized by Nyarko (Nyarko: 2009). The results are also consistent with the theoretical and empirical literature on education production functions that suggest a strong positive relationship between income growth, scale economies and investment in education (de la Croix et al: 2008, Gyimah-Brempong and Wilson: 1994, among others). I note that while I find a positive and significant relationship, I cannot claim that the relationship is causal; I do not investigate the mechanisms through which the two variables are related either. All my results imply is that one of the unintended benefits of regional integration in West Africa is increased investment in education at all levels of education.

Education and Income Growth

Table 13.3 presents the estimates of the effects of different levels of education and regional integration on the growth rate of per capita income in West Africa. Column 3 presents the estimates from the Arellano and Bond two-step estimator, column 4 presents the estimates from a Hausman-Taylor (HT) estimator that uses being landlocked as the constant variable, while column

5 presents the estimates from a Fixed Effects estimator. I present OLS estimates in column 2 for the purposes of comparison.

Regression statistics (not presented) suggest that the growth equation fits the data reasonably well and the coefficient estimates have the expected signs. I reject the null hypothesis that all coefficient estimates are jointly equal to zero, that there is second-order serially correlated error terms, and the Hansen J and C tests results suggest an appropriate instrument vector. The Hausman statistics lead me to reject the null hypothesis that all regressors are exogenous, hence the OLS estimator is not an appropriate estimator for the growth equations. I also note that because of the inclusion of lagged endogenous regressor, the FE estimates may be inconsistent. Further discussion of the results will therefore not include the OLS and FE estimates.

The coefficients of the education variables (primary, secondary, and tertiary) are positive and significantly different from zero at = :05 or better in the DPD. This suggests that all levels of education have significantly positive impacts on income growth rate in West Africa, all things equal. A likelihood ratio test to test the null hypothesis that primary, secondary, and tertiary are jointly equal to zero produce χ^2 statistics of 12.86 and 11.21 for the DPD and HT estimates. With 3 degrees of freedom, I reject the null that education has no significant effects on income growth. The coefficient of RINT in column 3 is positive and significant at $\alpha = .01$ suggesting that aside from its effects on different levels of investment in education, regional integration is positively correlated with the growth rate per capita income in West Africa, all things equal.

The magnitude of the coefficients on primary, secondary and tertiary may suggest that different levels of education have different effects on income growth with tertiary having the most effect. Elasticities of growth with respect to primary, secondary and tertiary, calculated at the means of the variables, are 0.1, 0.13, and 1.22 for the HT estimates and 0.0, 0.125, and 9.55 respectively for the DPD estimates.[4] In general, I can conclude that education has a positive and significant impact on the growth rate of real GDP in West Africa. Moreover, my estimates indicate that the growth impact of tertiary education is much higher than secondary and primary levels of education, all things equal.

If the coefficients of primary, secondary, and tertiary are the same, then there is a loss of efficiency in breaking education into various levels. I therefore test to see if the coefficient estimates of the three levels of education are equal. The likelihood ratio test to test the equality of the coefficients of all levels of education produced a χ^2 statistic of 28.59. This is well into the rejection region so I reject the null hypothesis of equality of the coefficients of different levels of education. The test result suggests that not disaggregating education into various levels will lead to biased estimates of the coefficient of education.

My result that primary, secondary and tertiary education have significant growth impact in West Africa is consistent with research that finds that education positively affects economic growth (Jamison et al: 2007, Gyimah-Brempong et al: 2006, Atardi and Sala-i-Martin: 2003, Baldwin and Borrelli: 2008, among others). My results that integration has a significantly positive effect on the growth rate of per capita income is consistent with the literature on regional integration; after all the reason for integration is to reap the benefits that comes with such integration with faster economic growth being one of the most obvious benefits.

ROBUSTNESS TESTS

The results presented above are from the DPD estimates. It is possible that my results depend crucially on this estimator. To test for this possibility, I used different estimators to estimate the equations. Columns 4 and 5 in table 13.2 presents estimates from an instrumental variable panel regression (which is part of Baum's IVREG2 routine for STATA) and Seemingly Unrelated Regressions (combining the education equations and growth equation) respectively. In both columns, the coefficient RINT is positive and statistically significant at $\alpha = .05$ or better. Moreover, the magnitudes of the coefficients are similar to their counterparts in column 3. Finally, the rank ordering of the coefficient estimates do not change with the estimator I use. Similarly, the Hausman-Taylor and FE estimates I present in columns 4 and 5 in table 3 for the growth equations indicate that regional integration and all levels of education have positive and statistically significant impact on the growth rate of per capita income. I conclude from this exercise that my result is not determined by the estimator I use.

The second set of robustness test I conduct is to change the specifications of the equation I estimate. In the growth equation for example, I alternatively entered *aidgni* in a quadratic form, added government consumption (govcon), and replaced bureau by laworder. These specifications did not qualitatively change the coefficients of primary, secondary, and tertiary in that equation. Moreover, these specifications did not change the order of the rankings of the growth effects of the various levels of education. I conclude from these exercises that my results are robust to the measure of education and model specification.

CONCLUSION

This paper uses panel data and a variety of estimators to investigate the effects of regional integration on investment in education as well as the joint impact of regional integration and investment in education on the growth rate of per capita income in West Africa. Controlling for a number of covariates, I find that regional integration is positively correlated with investment in education at all levels in West Africa. Furthermore, I find that the impact of integration on education investment differ according to the level of education. I estimate integration elasticities of 0.25. 0.80, and 0.60 for primary, secondary and tertiary education investment respectively. I also find that education and regional integration individually and jointly have significant positive effects on the growth rate of per capita income, all things equal. In addition, the growth impact of education I find varies according to the level of education; in general, the effect increases with the level of education. My results are robust to model specification and estimation methods. The results are consistent with the results of research that finds that education has significant impacts on several development outcomes.

The results, however, should be viewed with caution. First, my study does not establish causality; it only established correlation. Second, I do not investigate the mechanisms through which this correlation is established; mechanisms that may be important in themselves for policy or theoretical purposes. Third, my measure of integration may be too narrow and may have missed important aspects of integration. Finally, integration itself may be influenced by education thus making it an endogenous regressor that I do not seriously investigate in this paper. This could have important consequences for my estimates.

Notwithstanding the caveats above, my results have policy and research implications. My results suggest that a positive side benefit of regional integration may be increased investment in education in particular and human capital generally. The strengths of these benefits may differ according to the level of education involved. Secondly, integration leads to faster growth rate of per capita income both directly and indirectly through increased investment in education. My results should therefore give further encouragement to policy makers pursuing regional integration in West Africa.

Notes

1. Technically, both the numerator and the denominator are weighted by the GDP of each country. However, because GDP is both the denominator and denominator, it gets eliminated from the expression.
2. The countries in the sample are Benin, Burkina Faso, Cameroon, Cape Verde, Chad, Cote d'Ivoire, Gabon, Gambia, Ghana, Guinea, Guinea-Bissau, Equatorial Guinea, Liberia, Mali, Mauritania, Niger, Nigeria, Senegal, Sierra Leone, and Togo. While some of the countries in the sample do not t into the WAMI criteria, I had to make some compromises in order to get a reasonable sample for the analysis.
3. To prevent taking the logs of negative values (where it is necessary), I transformed the variables by adding the absolute value + 1 to all values to the variables before taking logs.
4. I do not calculate the elasticities for insignificant coefficients. I do not report the elasticities for the FE and OLS since I have argued that these estimates are not appropriate.
5. I do not present the results of these estimates for space considerations.

References

Appiah, E. N. and W. McMahon (2002), "The Social Outcomes of Education and Feedback on Growth in Africa", *Journal of Development Studies*, **38** 94), 27{68.

Arellano, M. and S. Bond (1991), "Some Tests of Speci cation for Panel Data: Monte Carlo Evidence and an Application to Employment Equations", *Review of Economic Studies*, **58**, 277-297.

Aryeetey, E (2001), Regional Integration in West Africa, OECD Development Center Working Paper No. 170.

Atardi, E. V. and X. Sala-i-Martin (2003), The Economic Tragedy of the XXth Century: Growth in Africa, NBER Working paper No. 9865, Cambridge, MA, NBER.

Bah, A. and S. J. Tapsoba (2010), Civil Conflicts and Regional Economic Integration Outcomes in Africa, CERDI Working Papers No. 201009.

Baldwin, N. and S. A. Borrelli (2008), "Education and Economic Growth in the United States: Cross-National Applications for Intra-National Path Analysis", *Policy Sciences*, **41** (2), 182-2004.

Barro, R. J. and J. Lee (2010), A New Data Set of Educational Attainment in the World, 1950-2010, NBER Working Paper No. 15902.

_____ (2001), "International Data on Educational Attainment: Updates and Implications", *Oxford Economic Papers*, 53 (3).

Barro, R. J. (1997), "Human Capital and Growth in Cross-Country regressions", *Swedish Eco-nomic Policy Review*, **6** (2), 237-277.

Ciccone, A. and E. Papaioannou (2009), "Human Capital, the Structure of Production and Growth", *Review of Economics and Statistics*, **91** (1), 68-82.

de la Croix, D., T. Lindh, and B. Malmberg (2008), "Swedish Economic Growth and Education Since 1800", *Canadian Journal of Economics*, **41** (1), 166-185.

De Lombaerde, P. and L. Van Langenhove (2006), "Indicators of Regional integration: Con-ceptual and Methodological Aspects", in P. De Lombaerde (ed.), *Assessment and Measurement of Regional Integration*, (London: Rutledge).

Gyimah-Brempong, K., O. Paddison, and W. Mitiku (2006), "Higher Education and Economic Growth in Africa", *Journal of Development Studies*, **42** (3), 509-529.

Gyimah-Brempong, K. and W. Wilson (2004), "Health Human Capital and Economic Growth in Sub-Saharan Africa and OECD Countries", *Quarterly Review of Economics and Finance*, **44**(2), 296-320.

Jamison, E. A., D. T. Jamison, and E. A. Hanushek (2007), "The Effects of Education Quality on Income Growth", *Economics of Education Review*, **26**, 727-780.

Jones, B (2002), "Economic Integration and Convergence of Per Capita income in West Africa", *African Development Review*, **14** (1), 18-47.

Nelson, R. and E. Phelps (2006), "Investment in Human, Technical Diffusion and Economic Growth", *American Economic Review*, **61**, 69-75.

Nyarko, Y. (2009), Human Capital Formation in Africa: The Role of EU Policies, ERD Policy Papers No. ERD 2010/09.

Romer, P. (1989), "Human Capital and Growth: Theory and Evidence, Carnegie-Rochester Conference Series on Public Policy, **32**, 251-286.

Self, S. and R. Grabowsky (2004), "Does Education at All Levels Cause Growth? India, A Case Study", *Economics of Education Review*, **23**, 47-55.

Solow, R. M. (2003), "Foreword" in G. McMahon and L. Squire (eds.), Explaining Growth: A Global Research Project, IEA Conference 137 (New York: Palgrave McMillan).

Table 13.1: Summary Statistics of Sample Data

Variable	Mean	Standard Dev	Minimum	Maximum
y_ (%)	1.2061	9.6803	-10.4801	12.0671
income (PPP_{2000})	2249.05	4138.39	136.52	28536.20
gini (%)	49.5066	10.6549	32.7041	76.2000
xgrow	6.5267	21.5604	-50.1001	38.1248
trade (%)	3.7427	1.5599	0.6320	6.8232
popgro (%)	2.7467	1.0379	-5.737	8.5777
aidgni (%)	13.7638	12.1099	0.00	78.7069
bureau	1.221	0.9804	0.00	9
laworder	2.4441	0.9517	0.001	5.00
govcon	13.4724	5.8924	2.8607	45.2974
invest	20.4160	12.5686	-3.7625	62.5779
primary	3.8531	2.6587	0.3030	11.201
secondary	1.2892	0.9638	0.10	4.258
tertiary	0.7262	0.5548	0.0	2.300
landlock	0.020	0.060	0.00	1.00

Note: these are unweighted averages.

Table 13.2: Estimates of Education Attainment

Variable	FE	DPD	GMM	SUR
primary	0.2887	0.2462	0.2563	0.2520
	(5.32)	(2.10)	(2.09)	(2.79)
secondary	0.4699	0.8216	0.7988	0.8122
	(5.63)	(8.53)	(8.59)	(9.21)
tertiary	0.4919	0.6287	0.6361	0.6328
	(6.81)	(5.88)	(6.21)	(6.23)
N	378			

+ absolute Value of t" statistics in parentheses. 2-tail sig. at α = 10; 2-tail significance at α = 0:05; 2 tail significance at α = 0:01

TABLE 13.3: ESTIMATES OF GROWTH EQUATION

Variable	OLS	DPD	Hausman-Taylor	FE
	(2)	(3)	(4)	(5)
RINT	0.0176	0.0756	0.0776	0.0413
	(2.11)	(5.30)	(5.17)	(3.22)
xgrow	0.0934	0.2125	0.0792	0.0891
	(5.57)	(3.28)	(5.59)	(5.80)
aidgni	-0.0405	0.2525	0.0985	0.1637
	(0.93)	(1.96)	(2.35)	(2.35)
bureau	0.1128	0.2183	0.2989	0.2272
	(1.79)	(1.89)	(1.47)	(2.16)
tertiary	0.4287	9.5488	1.2220	0.3395
	(1.68)	(2.62)	(3.86)	(2.78)
secondary	0.1281	0.1248	0.1313	0.2689
	(1.28)	(1.78)	(2.38)	(1.98)
primary	0.0.0023	0.0038	0.1093	0.1014
	(0.19)	(0.55)	(3.50)	(3.46)
civwar	-0.2139	-0.6251	-0.2179	-0.4126
	(2.16)	(2.89)	(2.18)	(2.98)
landlock			0.3631	
			(0.28)	
N	378			

Dependent Variable: Growth Rate of per capita GDP.
+ absolute Value of t" statistics in parentheses. 2-tail sig. at α = 10; 2-tail significance at α = 0:05; 2 tail significance at α = 0:01

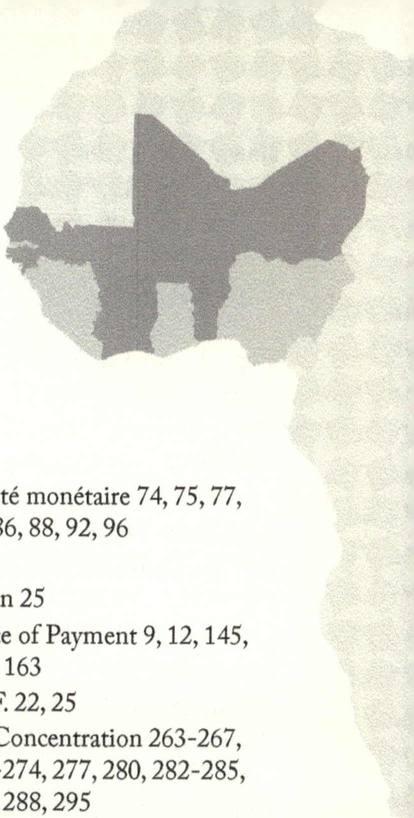

Index